Relational Methods
for Computer Science Applications

Studies in Fuzziness and Soft Computing

Editor-in-chief
Prof. Janusz Kacprzyk
Systems Research Institute
Polish Academy of Sciences
ul. Newelska 6
01-447 Warsaw, Poland
E-mail: kacprzyk@ibspan.waw.pl
http://www.springer.de/cgi-bin/search_book.pl?series=2941

Ewa Orłowska
Andrzej Szałas

Editors

Relational Methods for Computer Science Applications

With 23 Figures
and 13 Tables

Physica-Verlag

A Springer-Verlag Company

Prof. Dr. Ewa Orłowska
Institute of Telecommunications
ul. Szachowa 1
04-894 Warsaw
Poland
orlowska@itl.waw.pl

Prof. Dr. Andrzej Szałas
University of Warsaw
Institute of Informatics
ul. Banacha 2
02-097 Warsaw
Poland
szalas@mimuw.edu.pl

ISSN 1434-9922
ISBN 978-3-662-00362-6   ISBN 978-3-7908-1828-4 (eBook)
DOI 10.1007/978-3-7908-1828-4

Cataloging-in-Publication Data applied for
Die Deutsche Bibliothek – CIP-Einheitsaufnahme
Relational methods for comptuer science applications: with 13 tables / Ewa Orłowska; Andrzej Szałas ed. –
Heidelberg; New York: Physica-Verl., 2001
   (Studies in fuzziness and soft computing; Vol. 65)

Physica-Verlag Heidelberg New York
a member of BertelsmannSpringer Science+Business Media GmbH

© Physica-Verlag Heidelberg 2001
Softcover reprint of the hardcover 1st edition 2001

Hardcover Design: Erich Kirchner, Heidelberg

SPIN 10790877   88/2202-5 4 3 2 1 0 – Printed on acid-free paper

Preface

The origins of relational theories can be found in the work of three 19th century mathematicians: Augustus de Morgan (1864, *On the syllogism IV and on the logic of relations*), Charles Sanders Peirce (1882, *Brief description of the algebra of relatives*) and Ernst Schröder (1895, *Vorlesungen über die Algebra und Logik der Relative*). The modern origins of the theory of relations are due to Alfred Tarski (14 January 1902, Warsaw - 26 October 1983, Berkeley). His paper '*On the calculus of Relations*' published in 1941 gave rise to an algebraic theory of relations which is still extensively studied.

In the 1970s, the applications of relational theories to various applied sciences emerged. Nowadays relational theories are experiencing a period of extensive development, with the emergence of new theories and systems allowing better understanding and better use of such theories. Relational theories have been used, among others, in the following fields:

- Theory of programs: program specification, program verification, modelling concurrency, process calculi, semantics of programming languages;
- Databases: relational databases, tabular methods, dependency theory, rectangular and difunctional decomposition of databases;
- Computational linguistics: relational semantics of natural languages, relational grammars, Lambek calculus;
- Spatial reasoning: modelling of relationships between space regions;
- Handling uncertainty: fuzzy relations, many-valued relations, information relations.

Indeed, the concept of relation emerges again and again throughout computer science, from its theoretical foundations to very practical implementations.

The book presents representative examples of recent applications of relational theories to the above multifarious domains.

The first part presents applications of relational theories to programming. In the paper '*Towards a Uniform Relational Semantics for Tabular Expressions*' by Jules Desharnais, R. Khedri and Ali Mili, a uniform description of tabular expressions proposed by Parnas is presented, and its applications to analysis of large relations occurring in programming practice are discussed. The paper '*Translating Relational Programs into Prolog*' by Barry Dwyer deals with a relational programming language called Libra. A translation of Libra into Prolog is presented and discussed. In the paper '*A Calculus for Program Construction Based on Fork Algebras, Design Strategies and Generic Algorithms*' by Marcelo Frias, Gabriel Baum and Armando Haeberer, a methodology for program construction based on first-order theory of fork algebras is presented. Parametric algorithms are derived from generic specifications according to some known program design strategies. The paper

'*Processes as Relations*' by Michael Winter and Peter Kempf presents a part of Robin Milner's system CCS in terms of an algebra of relations. A concept of relational bisimulation is introduced and studied.

The second part is devoted to reasoning about constraints in information systems. In the paper '*A Tableaux Procedure for the Inference Problem for Association Rules*' by Wendy MacCaull, a relational proof system for reasoning about association rules derived from information systems is presented, and decidability of the implication problem for the association rules is proved. The paper '*On a Static Verification of Integrity Constraints in Relational Databases*' by Jaroslaw Kachniarz and Andrzej Szałas presents a method of constraint verification in relational databases based on elimination of second-order quantifiers.

The third part includes recent developments in the area of relational models used in spatial reasoning and linguistics. The paper '*Contact Relation Algebras*' by Ivo Düntsch develops a theory of algebras of binary relations generated by contact relations. The theory is motivated, among others, by qualitative spatial reasoning. In the paper '*Relations Old and New*' by Joachim Lambek, an ordered residuated monoid of relations is studied, and applications of relations to antrophology, linguistics, computer science, algebra and category theory are discussed. In the paper '*Relational Models for the Nonassociative Lambek Calculus*' by Marek Szczerba, a relational representation of residuated groupoids is presented. As a consequence, a complete relational semantics for the nonassociative Lambek calculus is obtained.

The fourth part presents applications of relational structures in various theories of uncertainty, in particular in many-valued logics, information logics and algebras inspired by rough sets. In the paper '*Coping with Semilattices of Relations in Logics with Relative Accessibility Relations*' by Stephane Demri, translations between various logics with relative accessibility relations and the standard modal logics are presented. It is shown that the translations preserve decidability provided that one of the operators is a semilattice operator. The paper '*A Relational Formalisation of a Generic Many-Valued Modal Logic*' by Beata Konikowska and Ewa Orłowska presents a general scheme of a complete Rasiowa-Sikorski style relational proof system for many-valued modal logics. The paper '*An Application of Standard BAO Theory to Some Abstract Information Algebras*' by Eric SanJuan and Luisa Iturrioz shows how the Jonsson and Tarski's results on canonical extensions of Boolean algebras with operators apply to information algebras, and how these results can be used for developing representational mechanisms of algebras related to uncertainty.

The fifth part presents recent developments in the proof theory of relation algebras, in the decidability theory of relation and cylindric algebras and in Dedekind categories. The paper '*Proof Systems in Relation Algebra*' by Lev Gordeev deals with a proof theory of relational theories. A comparison of various deduction systems for relation algebras is presented. In the paper *'Connections Between Cylindric Algebras and Relation Algebras'* by Robin Hirsch and Ian Hodkinson, a technique of obtaining relation algebras from cylindric algebras of a finite dimension is discussed and several decidability/undecidability results are presented. The paper *'Lattices in Dedekind Categories'* by Yasua Kawahara presents an element-free description of partially ordered sets with joins and meets. The description is given in terms of Dedekind categories.

The sixth part presents generalisations of the theory of Boolean algebras with operators and of the theory of cylindric algebras. Both generalisations are motivated by problems related to representation of incomplete information. In the paper *'Beyond Modalities: Sufficiency and Mixed Algebras'* by Ivo Düntsch and Ewa Orłowska, the class of Boolean algebras with sufficiency operators and the class of Boolean algebras with mixed (modal and sufficiency) operators are introduced and investigated. The motivation for introducing those classes stems from the theory of information systems with incomplete information. A representation theory and duality theory for these new classes of algebras is outlined. In the paper *'Cylindric Algebras for Partial Relational Systems. Quasicylindric Algebras'* by Artur Woliński, a new class of algebras conceived as an algebraic counterpart to partial first-order logic is introduced and investigated. In analogy to the relational semantics of the classical first order logic provided by cylindric algebras, the class of quasicylindric algebras provides a relational semantics for partial first-order logic, where a complete information about meanings of predicates might not be available.

The idea of this book originated during the International Seminar on Relational Methods in Logic, Algebra and Computer Science, RelMiCS'4, held in Warsaw, Poland, in September, 1998. The Seminar was organised by Stefan Banach International Mathematical Centre, Institute of Informatics of the University of Warsaw and the National Institute of Telecommunications, Warsaw.

The Seminar was the fourth in the series of meetings of the members of the RelMiCS group. The group has as its major aim to serve as a research and information clearing house for applications of relational methods, and to help coordinate the efforts of researchers from the whole world working in this field. The group was established in 1992 by the researchers who participated in a Banach Centre semester on foundations of computer science.

Warszawa,   *Ewa Orłowska*
August 2000   *Andrzej Szałas*

Contents

Part II
Relational Constraints

Chapter 5
A Tableaux Procedure for the Implication Problem for Association Rules

Chapter 6
On a Static Verification of Integrity Constraints in Relational Databases

Part III
Relations in Linguistics and Spatial Reasoning

Chapter 11
A Relational Formalisation of a Generic Many–Valued Modal Logic 183
Beata Konikowska, Ewa Orłowska

Chapter 12
An Application of Standard BAO Theory to Some Abstract Information Algebras 203
Eric SanJuan and Luisa Iturrioz

Part V
Theories of Relations

Chapter 13
Proof Systems in Relation Algebra 219
Lev Gordeev

Chapter 14
Connections Between Cylindric Algebras and Relation Algebras 239
Robin Hirsch and Ian Hodkinson

Chapter 15
Lattices in Dedekind Categories 247
Yasuo Kawahara

Part VI
Generalizations of Theories of Relations

Chapter 16
Beyond Modalities: Sufficiency and Mixed Algebras 263
Ivo Düntsch and Ewa Orłowska

Chapter 17
Cylindric Algebras for Partial Relational Systems. Quasicylindric Algebras 287
Artur Woliński

Part I

Relations
in Programming

Chapter 1
Interpretation of Tabular Expressions Using Arrays of Relations*

Jules Desharnais[1], Ridha Khédri[2], and Ali Mili[3]

[1] Département d'informatique
Université Laval
Québec, QC, G1K 7P4 Canada
Jules.Desharnais@ift.ulaval.ca
[2] Department of Computing and Software
Faculty of Engineering
McMaster University
1280 Main Street West
Hamilton, ON, L8S 4K1 Canada
khedri@mcserg.cas.mcmaster.ca
[3] Institute for Software Research
1000 Technology Drive
Fairmont, WV, 26554 USA
amili@cs.wvu.edu

Abstract. Tabular expressions are a means to represent the complex relations that are used to specify or document software systems. We show how a simple and powerful algebra of arrays of relations can be used to give a semantics to tabular expressions. This opens up the door to new types of tabular expressions and, more importantly, brings a set of algebraic laws for the manipulation of tables. The algebra we present is based on the fact that matrices of relations are themselves relations to which the usual relational operators can be applied, in addition to array operators.
Keywords: tabular expressions, arrays of relations, semantics, algebra, software specification

1 Introduction

Parnas *et al.* [10,11,13] have proposed *tabular expressions* as a means to represent the complex relations that are used to specify or document software systems. The idea is that a tabular expression is much easier to understand and verify than a long linear formula. Tabular expressions are intended to supplement, not replace, notations used by engineers. They were found to be useful for describing large mathematical relations in practical applications [2,6–8,14,17].

* This research was supported by NSERC (Natural Sciences and Engineering Research Council of Canada) and by FCAR (Fonds pour la Formation de Chercheurs et l'Aide à la Recherche, Québec).

A semantics of tabular expressions, generalizing previous work and introducing new types of tables, is given in [10]. We show here how a simple and powerful algebra of arrays of relations can be used to further generalize this semantics, at least as far as the types of tables presented in [10] are concerned. This opens up the door to new types of tabular expressions and, more importantly, brings a set of algebraic laws for the manipulation of tables. The algebra we present is based on the known but little used fact that matrices of relations are themselves relations to which the usual relational operators can be applied [15,16]. In addition, other array operators can be applied to them [5,9]. For simplicity, in this short text, we restrict ourselves to zero-, one- and two-dimensional arrays.

2   An algebra of arrays of relations

Our notation for relations and relational operators is that of [1]. The notation for arrays and array operators is inspired by that of the programming language APL [5,9]. Let $\mathfrak{R}$ be a (homogeneous or heterogeneous) relation algebra. An array over $\mathfrak{R}$ is simply an array whose entries are elements of (the carrier set of) $\mathfrak{R}$; more precisely, it is a function

$$A : I_0 \times \ldots \times I_{n-1} \to \mathfrak{R} \ ,$$

where $n \geq 0$ and each I_i is an index set of the form $\{0, \ldots, k_i - 1\}$, for some $k_i \geq 0$ (empty arrays are allowed). The number n is the *dimension* of A. In this paper we consider

- 0-dimensional arrays: these are called *scalars*. In our context, a scalar is a relation.
- 1-dimensional arrays: these are called *vectors* (of relations) or *tuples*. For instance, the one-dimensional array $(P \quad Q \quad R)$ is a vector.
- 2-dimensional arrays: these are called *matrices*.

The *shape* of an array is a vector of natural numbers giving the number of components along each coordinate. For instance, assuming that P, Q and R are relations,

$$\mathsf{shape}(R) = (\ ) \ ,$$
$$\mathsf{shape}((P \quad Q \quad R)) = (3) \ ,$$
$$\mathsf{shape}\left(\begin{pmatrix} P & Q & R \\ S & T & U \end{pmatrix}\right) = (2 \quad 3) \ .$$

An array with shape (0) has dimension 1 and is empty; an array with shape (1) has dimension 1 and has one entry; an array with shape $(2 \quad 0)$ has two rows and no column (it has dimension 2 and is empty, since it has no column).

If A is a vector and M is a matrix, then $A[i]$ denotes the i-th element of A and $M[i,j]$ denotes the element in row i and column j of M (that is, $A[i]$

is the application of function A to i and $M[i,j]$ is the application of function M to i and j).

We now define relational operations on arrays. Complementation, join, meet, composition and converse are defined as follows. Let A, B, L, M and N be arrays over $\mathfrak{R}$ such that $\mathsf{shape}(A) = \mathsf{shape}(B) = (\,l\,)$, $\mathsf{shape}(L) = \mathsf{shape}(M) = (\,l \quad m\,)$ and $\mathsf{shape}(N) = (\,m \quad n\,)$. For all i, j, k such that $0 \leq i < l$, $0 \leq j < m$, $0 \leq k < n$,

$$\overline{A}[i] = \overline{A[i]} \qquad\qquad \overline{M}[i,j] = \overline{M[i,j]}$$
$$(A \cup B)[i] = A[i] \cup B[i] \qquad (L \cup M)[i,j] = L[i,j] \cup M[i,j]$$
$$(A \cap B)[i] = A[i] \cap B[i] \qquad (L \cap M)[i,j] = L[i,j] \cap M[i,j]$$
$$M^{\smile}[j,i] = (M[i,j])^{\smile}$$
$$(M\,;N)[i,k] = \textstyle\bigcup_{j=1}^{m} M[i,j]\,;N[j,k]$$

Note that if $\mathfrak{R}$ is a heterogeneous algebra, the operations on relations must be correctly typed for the operations on arrays to be defined.

In addition to these standard operations [16], we define the following ones. Let A, B, M and N be arrays such that $\mathsf{shape}(A) = l$, $\mathsf{shape}(B) = m$, $\mathsf{shape}(M) = (\,l \quad m\,)$, $\mathsf{shape}(N) = (\,m \quad n\,)$, and let R be a relation (note that R is a scalar, A and B are vectors, and M and N are matrices). Also, let $\oplus$ and $\otimes$ denote any of the binary relational operators $(\cup, \cap, ;)$. For all i, j, k such that $0 \leq i < l$, $0 \leq j < m$, $0 \leq k < n$,

$$(A \circ . \oplus B)[i,j] = A[i] \oplus B[j] \qquad\qquad \text{outer product of vectors}$$
$$(M \oplus . \otimes N)[i,k] = \textstyle\bigoplus_{j=1}^{m} M[i,j] \otimes N[j,k] \quad \text{inner product of matrices}$$
$$\oplus/A = \textstyle\bigoplus_{i=1}^{l} A[i] \qquad\qquad \text{reduction of a vector}$$
$$(\oplus/M)[i] = \textstyle\bigoplus_{j=1}^{m} M[i,j] \qquad\qquad \text{column-reduction of a matrix}$$
$$(\oplus\!\!\not/M)[j] = \textstyle\bigoplus_{i=1}^{l} M[i,j] \qquad\qquad \text{row-reduction of a matrix}$$
$$(R \oplus M)[i,j] = R \oplus M[i,j] \qquad\qquad \text{relation-matrix binary operation}$$
$$(M \oplus R)[i,j] = M[i,j] \oplus R \qquad\qquad \text{matrix-relation binary operation}$$
$$(A \oplus_{[1]} M)[i,j] = A[i] \oplus M[i,j] \qquad\quad \text{vector-matrix binary operation}$$
$$(M \oplus_{[1]} A)[i,j] = M[i,j] \oplus A[i] \qquad\quad \text{matrix-vector binary operation}$$
$$(B \oplus_{[2]} M)[i,j] = B[j] \oplus M[i,j] \qquad\quad \text{vector-matrix binary operation}$$
$$(M \oplus_{[2]} B)[i,j] = M[i,j] \oplus B[j] \qquad\quad \text{matrix-vector binary operation}$$

The notation for the inner and outer products is that of **APL**. One can see that the relational composition of matrices is only a special case of an inner product, since $M\,;N = M \cup . ;N$. We give two examples of these operations:

$$(P \quad Q)\circ.\cap(R \quad S \quad T) = \begin{pmatrix} P \cap R & P \cap S & P \cap T \\ Q \cap R & Q \cap S & Q \cap T \end{pmatrix}$$

$$(P \;\; Q) \cap_{[1]} \begin{pmatrix} R & S & T \\ U & V & W \end{pmatrix} = \begin{pmatrix} P \cap R & P \cap S & P \cap T \\ Q \cap U & Q \cap V & Q \cap W \end{pmatrix}$$

For a generalization of these operations to higher-dimensional arrays, see [5].

The five standard operators satisfy the usual relational laws. As for the other operators, we only mention the following laws:

$$A \cup_{[1]} M = M \cup_{[1]} A$$
$$A \cap_{[1]} M = M \cap_{[1]} A$$
$$B \cup_{[2]} M = M \cup_{[2]} B$$
$$B \cap_{[2]} M = M \cap_{[2]} B$$
$$R \cup (U/M) = U/(R \cup M)$$
$$R \cap (U/M) = U/(R \cap M)$$
$$R \,;(U/M) = U/(R\,;M)$$
$$R \,;(\cap/M) \subseteq \cap/(R\,;M)$$
$$U/(U \!\!\not\!/ M) = U \!\!\not\!/ (U/M)$$
$$\cap/(\cap \!\!\not\!/ M) = \cap \!\!\not\!/ (\cap/M)$$
$$(A \circ . \cup B) \cup M = (A \cup_{[1]} (B \cup_{[2]} M))$$
$$(A \circ . \cap B) \cap M = (A \cap_{[1]} (B \cap_{[2]} M))$$
$$(A \circ . \cap B) \cup M = (A \cup_{[1]} M) \cap (B \cup_{[2]} M)$$
$$(A \circ . \cup B) \cap M = (A \cap_{[1]} M) \cup (B \cap_{[2]} M)$$

Dual properties are obtained by switching $\cup$ and $\cap$.

3   Tabular expressions

To illustrate how the array operators introduced in the previous section can be used to give the semantics of tabular expressions, we briefly present the examples of [10]. See Figures 1 to 6.

A tabular expression consists of a set of declarations (the left table in the figures) together with a set of arrays consisting of n vectors, called *headers*, and an n-dimensional array, called a *grid* (given on the right in the figures). The cells of the arrays with a single-line border are called *guard cells*; those of the arrays with a double-line border are called *value cells*. The declaration table gives

- the types of the input variables. These variables define the input state space.
- the types of the output variables (defining the output state space) when the tabular expression describes a relation modifying the output state. This occurs in Figures 3 and 5. Output variables may not appear in guard cells.

Input variables	$x, y \in \mathbb{R}$
Result type	$\mathbb{R}$
CCG	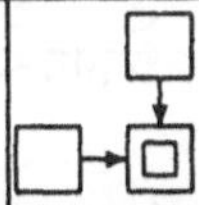 (diagram)
P_T	$H_1 \wedge H_2$
r_T	G
Function name	f
C_T	$\bigcup_{i=1}^{2} \bigcup_{j=1}^{3} f_{i,j}$

$$H_2$$

H_1	$y = 10$	$y > 10$	$y < 10$
$x \geq 0$	0	y^2	$-y^2$
$x < 0$	x	$x + y$	$x - y$

$$G$$

$$f(x,y) = \begin{cases} 0 & \text{if } x \geq 0 \wedge y = 10 \\ y^2 & \text{if } x \geq 0 \wedge y > 10 \\ -y^2 & \text{if } x \geq 0 \wedge y < 10 \\ x & \text{if } x < 0 \wedge y = 10 \\ x + y & \text{if } x < 0 \wedge y > 10 \\ x - y & \text{if } x < 0 \wedge y < 10 \end{cases}$$

Fig. 1. A function table with the value cells in the grid

Input variables	$x_1, x_2 \in \mathbb{R}$
Result type	$\mathbb{R}$
CCG	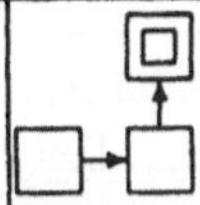 (diagram)
P_T	$G[H_1/\#]$
r_T	H_2
Function name	g
C_T	$\bigcup_{j=1}^{3} \bigotimes_{i=1}^{2} g_{i,j}$

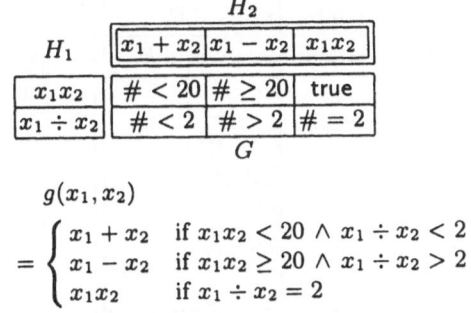

$$H_2$$

H_1	$x_1 + x_2$	$x_1 - x_2$	$x_1 x_2$
$x_1 x_2$	$\# < 20$	$\# \geq 20$	true
$x_1 \div x_2$	$\# < 2$	$\# > 2$	$\# = 2$

$$G$$

$$g(x_1, x_2)$$
$$= \begin{cases} x_1 + x_2 & \text{if } x_1 x_2 < 20 \wedge x_1 \div x_2 < 2 \\ x_1 - x_2 & \text{if } x_1 x_2 \geq 20 \wedge x_1 \div x_2 > 2 \\ x_1 x_2 & \text{if } x_1 \div x_2 = 2 \end{cases}$$

Fig. 2. A generalized decision table

Input variables	$x \in \mathbb{R}$
Output variables	$y_1, y_2 \in \mathbb{R}$
CCG	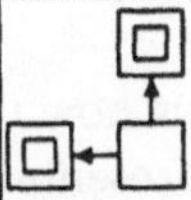 (diagram)
P_T	G
r_T	$H_1 \otimes H_2$
Relation name	Υ
C_T	$\bigcup_{i=1}^{3} \bigcup_{j=1}^{2} \Upsilon_{i,j}$

$$H_2$$

H_1	$y_2 = 0$	$y_2 = 1$
$y_1^2 + x = 1$	$x = 0$	$0 < x < 1$
$y_1^2 + x = 0$	$x < -1$	$-1 \leq x < 0$
$y_1 = x^2$	$x = 1$	$x > 1$

$$G$$

$$x \Upsilon (y_1, y_2)$$
$$\Leftrightarrow \begin{cases} (x = 0 & \wedge\ y_1^2 + x = 1 \wedge y_2 = 0) \\ \vee\ (0 < x < 1 & \wedge\ y_1^2 + x = 1 \wedge y_2 = 1) \\ \vee\ (x < -1 & \wedge\ y_1^2 + x = 0 \wedge y_2 = 0) \\ \vee\ (-1 \leq x < 0 \wedge y_1^2 + x = 0 \wedge y_2 = 1) \\ \vee\ (x = 1 & \wedge\ y_1 = x^2 \quad\ \wedge\ y_2 = 0) \\ \vee\ (x > 1 & \wedge\ y_1 = x^2 \quad\ \wedge\ y_2 = 1) \end{cases}$$

Fig. 3. A relation table with the value cells in the headers

Input variables	$x, y \in \mathbb{R}$
Result type	$\mathbb{R}$
CCG	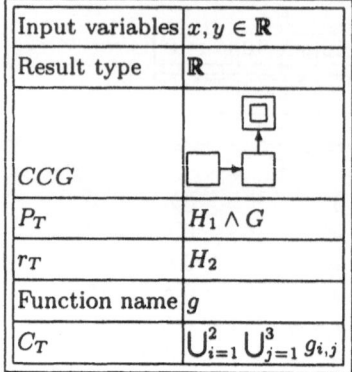
P_T	$H_1 \wedge G$
r_T	H_2
Function name	g
C_T	$\bigcup_{i=1}^{2} \bigcup_{j=1}^{3} g_{i,j}$

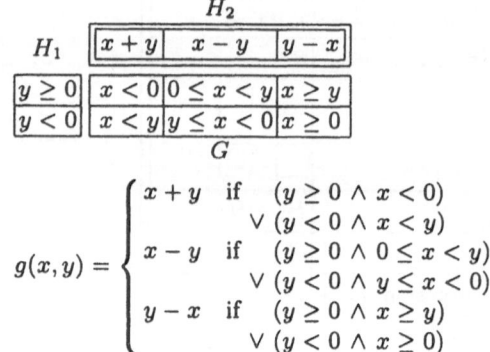

$$g(x,y) = \begin{cases} x+y & \text{if} \quad (y \geq 0 \wedge x < 0) \\ & \qquad \vee (y < 0 \wedge x < y) \\ x-y & \text{if} \quad (y \geq 0 \wedge 0 \leq x < y) \\ & \qquad \vee (y < 0 \wedge y \leq x < 0) \\ y-x & \text{if} \quad (y \geq 0 \wedge x \geq y) \\ & \qquad \vee (y < 0 \wedge x \geq 0) \end{cases}$$

Fig. 4. A function table with the value cells in a header

Input variables	$x_1, x_2 \in \mathbb{R}$
Output variables	$y_1, y_2, y_3 \in \mathbb{R}$
CCG	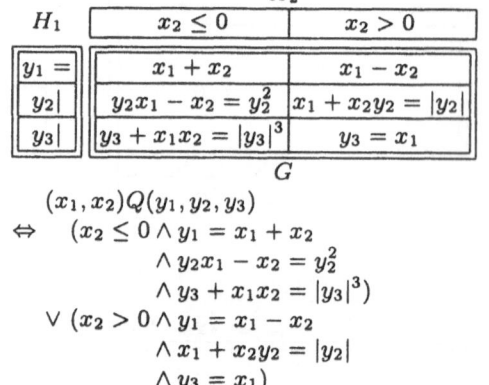
P_T	H_2
r_T	$H_1 \circ G$
Relation name	Q
C_T	$\bigcup_{j=1}^{2} \bigotimes_{i=1}^{3} Q_{i,j}$

$$\begin{aligned} (x_1, x_2) Q(y_1, y_2, y_3) \\ \Leftrightarrow \quad & (x_2 \leq 0 \wedge y_1 = x_1 + x_2 \\ & \wedge y_2 x_1 - x_2 = y_2^2 \\ & \wedge y_3 + x_1 x_2 = |y_3|^3) \\ \vee \; & (x_2 > 0 \wedge y_1 = x_1 - x_2 \\ & \wedge x_1 + x_2 y_2 = |y_2| \\ & \wedge y_3 = x_1) \end{aligned}$$

Fig. 5. A vector table

- the type of the result when the tabular expression describes a function that does not modify the output state. This occurs in Figures 1, 2, 4 and and 6 [1].
- the CCG (Cell Connection Graph), which shows how to read the tabular expression, but is redundant in the examples presented here.
- the guard predicate P_T, showing how to combine the guard cells.
- the relation predicate r_T, showing how to combine the value cells to obtain a relation.
- the name of the function or relation defined by the tabular expression.
- the expression C_T of the function or relation defined by the tabular expression. This is a combination of the *table elements*, such as $f_{i,j}$ in Fig. 1. There is one table element for each cell of the grid; the value of the table

---

[1] In these cases, Janicki [10] considers that the name of the function is also the name of an output variable; we prefer to avoid this overloading.

Input variables	$Temperature \in \{hot, cold\}$
	$Weather \in \{sunny, cloudy, rainy\}$
	$Windy \in \{true, false\}$
Result type	{go sailing, go to beach, play bridge, garden}
CCG	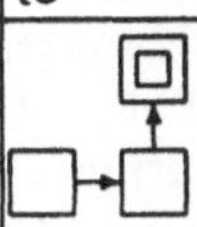
P_T	$H_1 = G$
r_T	H_2
Function name	ϕ
C_T	$\bigcup_{j=1}^{5} \bigotimes_{i=1}^{3} \phi_{i,j}$
Notation	* means "don't care"

H_2

H_1	go sailing	go to beach	go to beach	play bridge	garden
Temperature	*	*	hot	*	cool
Weather	sunny, cloudy	sunny	cloudy	rainy	cloudy
Windy	true	false	false	*	false

G

$\phi(Temperature, Weather, Windy)$

$$= \begin{cases} \text{go sailing} & \text{if } (Weather = \text{sunny} \vee Weather = \text{cloudy}) \wedge Windy = \text{true} \\ \text{go to beach} & \text{if } (Weather = \text{sunny} \wedge Windy = \text{false}) \\ & \quad \vee (Temperature = \text{hot} \wedge Weather = \text{cloudy} \wedge Windy = \text{false}) \\ \text{play bridge} & \text{if } Weather = \text{rainy} \\ \text{garden} & \text{if } Temperature = \text{cool} \wedge Weather = \text{cloudy} \wedge Windy = \text{false} \end{cases}$$

Fig. 6. A decision table

element indexed by i, j is $P_T(i, j) \wedge r_T(i, j)$. For instance, in Fig. 1,

$$f_{1,3} \Leftrightarrow H_1[1] \wedge H_2[3] \wedge G[1, 3] \Leftrightarrow x \geq 0 \wedge y < 10 \wedge f(x, y) = -y^2 ,$$

where $G[1, 3]$ is understood to be $f(x, y) = -y^2$.

Note that the goal of the whole construction is to define C_T.
    We now point out specific details of the tables.

- The set $\mathbb{R}$ is that of real numbers.
- The notation $G[H_1/\#]$, in Fig. 2, means to substitute terms of the header H_1 for the place holder # in the corresponding grid cells; for example, from $H_1[1]$ and $G[1, 2]$, one obtains $x_1 x_2 \geq 20$.

- The operator $\otimes$ [2] used in Figures 2, 3, 5 and 6 is a generalization of intersection (necessary to combine heterogeneous relations with different output variables); it may simply be thought of as the conjunction of predicates.
- The operator $\circ$ used in Fig. 5 is concatenation. Thus, the value part of the table element $Q_{1,1}$ is $y_1 = x_1 + x_2$, and that of $Q_{3,2}$ is $y_3 \mid y_3 = x_1$. This last expression is read "y_3 such that $y_3 = x_1$". This notation is used to provide a visual cue that y_3 is the only relevant output variable; no other output variable may occur in the corresponding row of the grid (this is a simple syntactic check). Note that instead of the present configuration, one could obtain the same effect by writing "$y_1 \mid$" in $H_1[1]$, with "$y_1 = x_1 + x_2$" in $G[1,1]$ and "$y_1 = x_1 - x_2$" in $G[1,2]$.

4 Semantics of tabular expressions

Before using our array operators, we have to explain how each entry of the headers or grid can be viewed as a relation. We discuss one way of doing it and consider the various cases that appear in the figures. In the definition of relations, we will use greek letters for dummy variables that are not variables of the state space.

1. Guard cells
    - Predicates defining guards, such as those of H_1 and H_2 in Fig. 1 or those of G in Fig. 3 are interpreted by *right-ideal* relations, also called *vectors* [16] (a right ideal r is a relation satisfying $r = r \,;\, V$, where V is a universal element). For instance, the predicate $x \geq 0$, in header H_1 of Fig. 1, can be assigned the semantics

$$\{((x,y),\alpha) \mid x \geq 0 \land \alpha \in \mathbb{R}\} \ .$$

    Note that the type of the relation is chosen to match that of f.
    - A relation can also be associated to predicates with place holders; for instance, the predicate $\# < 20$, in Fig. 2, defines the relation

$$\{(\alpha,\beta) \mid \alpha \in \mathbb{R} \land \beta \in \mathbb{R} \land \alpha < 20\} \ .$$

    The type of α is that of $H_1[1]$ and the type of β is that of g.
    - A constant term a in a guard cell is associated with a right ideal of the form

$$\{(a,\alpha) \mid \alpha \in \text{output or result space}\} \ .$$

    E.g., cloudy in Fig. 6 corresponds to the relation

$$\{(\text{cloudy},\alpha) \mid \alpha \in \{\text{go sailing, go to beach, play bridge, garden}\}\} \ .$$

    The relation of an enumeration such as sunny, cloudy (or *) is the union of the relations of the individual constants.

---

[2] Not to be confused with the operator $\otimes$ used in the previous section.

- A variable acts like a projection. Thus, *Weather* in Fig. 6 corresponds to the relation

$$\{((Temperature, Weather, Windy), \alpha) \mid Weather = \alpha\} \ .$$

2. Value cells

  - The semantics of a term $t(x_1, \ldots, x_n)$ is the relation

$$\{((x_1, \ldots, x_n), t(x_1, \ldots, x_n))\} \ .$$

    For example, the relation corresponding to $G[2, 3]$ in Fig. 1 is

$$\{((x, y), x - y)\} \ ,$$

    which can also be written as

$$\{((x, y), \alpha) \mid \alpha = x - y\} \ .$$

    Similarly, the semantics of **garden** in Fig. 6 is

$$\{((Temperature, Weather, Windy), \text{garden})\} \ .$$

  - The semantics of a predicate relating the input and output variables is the relation that it naturally defines; thus, the predicate $y_1^2 + x = 1$, in Fig. 3, defines the relation

$$\{(x, (y_1, y_2)) \mid y_1^2 + x = 1\} \ .$$

    The type of the relation is determined by the input and output spaces.
  - The semantics of "$y_1 =$" in Fig. 5 is

$$\{(\alpha, (y_1, y_2, y_3)) \mid \alpha = y_1\} \ .$$

  - The semantics of "$y_2|$" and "$y_3|$" in Fig. 5 is the identity on the output space, that is,

$$\{((y_1, y_2, y_3), (y_1, y_2, y_3))\} \ .$$

Once the semantics of the expressions appearing in the headers and grids is fixed, the relations corresponding to the tabular expressions can be given. For the six examples considered here, these expressions are

- Figure 1: $f = \cup/\cup{\not=}\big((H_1 \circ_\bullet \cap H_2) \cap G\big).$
- Figure 2: $g = \cup/\Big(\big(\cap{\not=}(H_1 \mathbin{;_{[1]}} G)\big) \cap H_2\Big).$
- Figure 3: $\varUpsilon = \cup/\cup{\not=}\big((H_1 \circ_\bullet \cap H_2) \cap G\big)$ (same as for Fig. 1).
- Figure 4: $g = \cup/\Big(\big(\cup{\not=}(H_1 \cap_{[1]} G)\big) \cap H_2\Big).$

- Figure 5: $Q = \cup/\left(\left(\cap f(G\,;_{[1]}H_1)\right)\cap H_2\right)$.
- Figure 6: $\phi = \cup/\left(\left(\cap f(H_1\,;_{[1]}G)\right)\cap H_2\right)$.

These expressions can be transformed using algebraic laws, for instance to yield different evaluation orders. As an example, the definitions given in Section 2 easily lead to the equality

$$\cup/\cup f\left((H_1\circ_\bullet\cap H_2)\cap G\right) = \cup/\left(\left(\cup f(H_1\cap_{[1]}G)\right)\cap H_2\right)$$

(compare the expressions of f, Υ and h above). The expression on the left constructs the matrix $H_1\circ_\bullet\cap H_2$ and thus requires more space for its evaluation than the expression on the right.

The relation algebraic approach naturally leads to the consideration of other operations on tables. To illustrate that point, we first define the pointwise application of the converse operator to a vector or a matrix. This operator is denoted by $^\wedge$ and is defined as follows:

$$A^\wedge[i] = (A[i])^\smile, \qquad\qquad M^\wedge[i,j] = (M[i,j])^\smile .$$

Now consider the left table in Fig. 7. It has two guard headers, H_1 and H_2, with $H_1 = H_2$. The pointwise converse operator is applied to H_2 in the definition of the relation of the table, R. The role of H_2 is then one of postrestriction on the value cells of G, contrary to the role of prerestriction played by H_1. With respect to the previous examples, this is a new role; the expressions "$c' = 2$" and "$c' = 3$" in Fig. 7 come from $H_2^\wedge$.

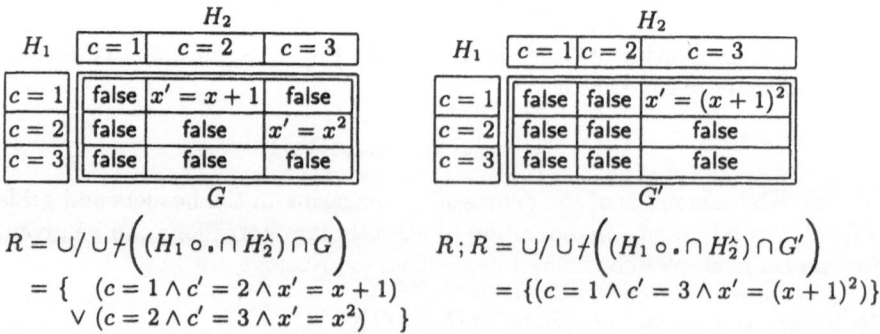

$$R = \cup/\cup f\left((H_1\circ_\bullet\cap H_2^\wedge)\cap G\right)$$
$$= \{\ \ (c = 1 \wedge c' = 2 \wedge x' = x + 1)$$
$$\vee\ (c = 2 \wedge c' = 3 \wedge x' = x^2)\ \ \}$$

$$R\,;R = \cup/\cup f\left((H_1\circ_\bullet\cap H_2^\wedge)\cap G'\right)$$
$$= \{(c = 1 \wedge c' = 3 \wedge x' = (x + 1)^2)\}$$

Fig. 7. Composing a table with itself

The table represents algorithmic information: between the control points $c = 1$ and $c = 2$, the action $x' = x + 1$ is carried out, and between $c = 2$ and $c = 3$, it is $x' = x^2$. Thus the table is an "unreduced" view of a sequence of actions. Let $H = H_1 (= H_2)$. Using the definitions of the various operators, and the fact that the entries of H are pairwise disjoint, one can show that

$$R;R = \left(\cup/\cup f\!\left((H \circ \bullet \cap H^{\wedge}) \cap G\right)\right); \left(\cup/\cup f\!\left((H \circ \bullet \cap H^{\wedge}) \cap G\right)\right)$$
$$= \cup/\cup f\!\left((H \circ \bullet \cap H^{\wedge}) \cap G;(H \cap_{[1]} G)\right) .$$

Thus, in the right table of Fig. 7, $G' = G;(H \cap_{[1]} G)$ is obtained by a simple composition of matrices. This table presents a reduced view of the sequence of actions, which have been composed into a single action going on between control points $c = 1$ and $c = 3$.

5   Conclusion

The tabular expressions that were presented above correspond to relational array expressions with n vectors and one n-dimensional array (the grid). Since there are several other possible array expressions, this may hint at other types of tabular expressions, for instance tables with more than one header for a given dimension, or tables with more than one grid, or n-dimensional headers. Of course, whether these are useful in practice is a different matter. With respect to the work presented in [10], the approach introduced here has the advantage of building over the well-known structure of relation algebras, which means that a large set of laws is immediately available, whereas in [10], the laws satisfied by the various combinators have to be proved from scratch.

Part of our future research will consist in designing/improving the notation for n-dimensional arrays and proving additional laws. Because arrays are functions from an index set to a relation algebra, the Bird-Meertens formalism [4] should prove to be useful, since it is a compact calculus dealing with functions and providing many high-level abstractions. On the application side, we intend to explore the refinement of specifications given as array expressions, the representation of so-called *scenarios*[3] by tables [3,12], and the transformation of tables from one type to another [18,19].

References

1. Brink C., Kahl W. and Schmidt G. (Eds.) (1997) Relational Methods in Computer Science. Springer
2. Clements P.C. (1981) Function specifications for the A-7E function driver module. NRL Memorandum Report 4658, United States Naval Research Laboratory, Washington D. C., 27 November
3. Desharnais J., Frappier M., Khédri R. and Mili A. (1998) Integration of sequential scenarios. IEEE Trans. on Software Engineering, 24(9):695–708, September

---

[3] A scenario is a partial description of the interactions between an environment and a system.

4. Gibbons J. (1994) An introduction to the Bird-Meertens formalism. Available at http://www.brookes.ac.uk/~p0071749/, November
5. Gilman L. and Rose A.J. (1976) APL: An Interactive Approach. John Wiley & Sons, New York, 2nd edition
6. Heninger K.L. (1980) Specifying software requirements for complex systems: New techniques and their application. IEEE Transactions on Software Engineering, SE-6(1):2–13, January
7. Heninger K.L., Kallander J., Parnas D.L. and Shore J.E. (1978) Software requirements for the A-7E aircraft. NRL Memorandum Report 3876, United States Naval Research Laboratory, Washington D. C.
8. Hester S.D., Parnas D.L. and Utter D.F. (1981) Using documentation as a software design medium. Bell System Technical Journal, 60(8):1941–1977, October
9. Iverson K.E. (1962) A Programming Language. John Wiley & Sons, New York
10. Janicki R. (1997) On a formal semantics of tabular expressions. Research Report CRL 355, Communications Research Laboratory, Faculty of Engineering, McMaster University, Hamilton, On, L8S 4K1 Canada, Oct. Available at http://www.crl.mcmaster.ca/SERG/serg.publications.html
11. Janicki R., Parnas D.L. and Zucker J. (1997) Tabular representations in relational documents. In: Brink et al. [1], Chap. 12, 184–196
12. Khédri Ridha (1999) Sequential scenarios verification and integration using tabular expressions. Research Report CRL 374, Communications Research Laboratory, Faculty of Engineering, McMaster University, Hamilton, On, L8S 4K1 Canada, June. Available at
    http://www.crl.mcmaster.ca/SERG/serg.publications.html
13. Parnas D.L. (1992) Tabular representation of relations. CRL Report 260, Communications Research Laboratory, Faculty of Engineering, Communications Research Laboratory, Faculty of Engineering, McMaster University, Hamilton, Ontario, Canada, October. Available at http://www.crl.mcmaster.ca/SERG/serg.publications.html
14. Parnas D.L., Asmis G.J.K. and Madey J. (1991) Assessment of safety-critical software in nuclear power plants. Nuclear Safety, 32(2):189–198, April-June
15. Schmidt G. (1981) Programs as partial graphs I: Flow equivalence and correctness. Theoret. Comput. Sci., 15:1–25
16. Schmidt G. and Ströhlein T. (1993) *Relations and Graphs, Discrete Mathematics for Computer Scientists.* EATCS-Monographs on Theoretical Computer Science. Springer
17. van Schouwen A.J. (1990) The A-7 requirements model: Re-examination for real-time systems and an application to monitoring systems. Technical Report 90-276, Queen's University, C&IS, Telecommunications Research Institute of Ontario (TRIO), Kingston, Ontario, Canada, May. Reprinted as Research Report CRL 242, Communications Research Laboratory, Faculty of Engineering, McMaster University, Hamilton, On, L8S 4K1 Canada
18. Shen H. (1995) Implementation of table inversion algorithms, Research Report CRL 315, Communications Research Laboratory, Faculty of Engineering, McMaster University, Hamilton, On, L8S 4K1 Canada, December. Available at http://www.crl.mcmaster.ca/SERG/serg.publications.html
19. Zucker J.I. (1996) Transformations of normal and inverted function tables. Formal Aspects of Computing, 8:679–705

Chapter 2
Translating Relational Programs into Prolog

Barry Dwyer

Department of Computer Science
University of Adelaide
Adelaide, South Australia 5005
dwyer@cs.adelaide.edu.au

Abstract. The binary relation algebra has operators that correspond to well-known programming constructs. As a result, it is to possible base useful programming languages on it. An earlier paper by the author described such a language. Since Prolog predicates define relations between variables, Prolog is often considered to be a relational language. In fact, there are several straight-forward translations from relation algebra expressions to Prolog rules. This paper explores this idea in depth, showing how relation algebra can be translated into Prolog.
Keywords: programming languages, relational programming, programming language translators, Prolog, binary relations, higher-order relations

1   Objectives

Earlier papers by the author discussed LIBRA, a Lazy Interpreter of Binary Relational Algebra [4,5]. LIBRA was an attempt to provide an efficient general-purpose programming language with clean semantics. It did not try to be a general relational expression solver. A relational language regards programs as input-output relations, which may be combined by a rich set of operators. Many of these operators are analogous to familiar programming constructs. For example, relational composition is analogous to piping the output of one program into the input of another, and transitive closure is analogous to looping or searching. It is important to distinguish this use of the word 'relational' with its use in databases or in Prolog programming: the relations involved are always binary, and their inputs are always known.

Relational programs are not reversible: results cannot be turned into data. Relational programs are a subset of expressions in binary relational algebra — except that its notation has to be adapted to use a restricted character set. Notational differences apart, a relational program and its specification should be algebraically equivalent. An advantage of relational programming is that, given an input-output specification in the binary relation algebra— or in the 'Z' specification language [9], for example—it should be possible to prove the correctness of a program by purely algebraic means.

On the other hand, an arbitrary relational expression is not necessarily a correct program because the programming system might be unable to evaluate it. For example, it might be asked to find the transitive closure of a relation. If the graph of the relation contained cycles, the program might be caught in an infinite loop, even though the closure itself was finite. It is the programmer's job to transform the specification so that this can't happen.

In many implementation details, LIBRA was based on Prolog. The original implementation of LIBRA was an interpreter, which unfortunately proved too slow except for solving trivial problems. A better alternative is to compile relational programs, and it is relatively easy to translate them into Prolog. It is desirable that their efficiency should not be greatly different from equivalent programs written directly in Prolog.

Since the LIBRA acronym is no longer appropriate, we refer to the relational language as RL. Its syntax is similar to that of LIBRA, although there are some changes, described later.

2 Design philosophy

A problem in designing any programming language based on relations is to decide how the relational specification of the program should relate to its behaviour.

One interpretation is to say that program P **satisfies** relation R if, for every input x in the domain of R, program P produces *any* output y such that xRy. For example, if R is specified as the union of relations R_1 and R_2, then P may produce an output that satisfies either R_1 or R_2. Such an 'any solution' interpretation becomes awkward to use when specifications are combined under intersection. If R is the intersection of R_1 and R_2, and P implements R, then P must satisfy *both* R_1 *and* R_2. Suppose that P is decomposed into two corresponding parts, P_1 and P_2, such that P_1 satisfies R_1 and P_2 satisfies R_2. If P_1 produces *any* output that satisfies R_1, and P_2 produces *any* output that satisfies R_2, the two outputs may disagree, so P as a whole may produce *no* output, even when the intersection of R_1 and R_2 is not empty. To find an output that satisfies R, P_1 and P_2 must produce several outputs, until a common one is found.

This consequence of the 'any solution' interpretation means that, if programs can be composed from sub-programs by intersection, the behaviour of sub-programs has to be different from the behaviour of programs. Sub-programs must produce many outputs to ensure that the program can produce one. This is not satisfactory. Intersection is too valuable to throw away. It is an abstraction of the generate-and-test strategy that programmers often use.

Consequently, RL adopts an 'all solutions' interpretation. This means that program P satisfies relation R if, for each input x in the domain of R, program P produces *all* outputs y such that xRy. If P needs to generate only one output, it may choose one arbitrarily by using RL's non-deterministic selection operator. The 'all solutions' interpretation poses the question of how to represent the several outputs of a program. One option is to collect them as a set. To be consistent, we ought then to present a program's input as a set, otherwise it would be awkward to form the composition of two programs: the first would form a set of outputs, so the second ought to accept a set of inputs.

The 'set of outputs' option is possible, but rather unexciting. It is merely functional programming with sets: the set of outputs given by a relational program becomes a function of its set of inputs. There is also a danger that the sets will be too large to store.

A second option is for a program to enumerate its outputs one by one, over a period of time, which avoids the need to store potentially infinite data structures. It seems reasonable though, that a program shouldn't promise much about the order in which it generates its outputs. It might even produce the same output more than once. For example, if a program explores paths in a directed graph, looking for certain goal vertices, it cannot be expected to find the goals in some particular order, nor can it promise not to find the same goal twice by two different paths. Otherwise the program would have to store all its results—inheriting the disadvantages of the 'set of outputs' option. Consequently, RL programs promise little about the order of their outputs. In principle, they could be produced in parallel. The 'enumeration' option is certainly the more interesting from a programmer's point of view. However, since RL offers means of constructing sets as data objects, the programmer can choose to store a set of outputs when it is useful to do so. This flexibility permits trade-offs between space and time, a feature of all practical programming languages.

Suppose it is desired to find the intersection of relations R_1 and R_2, both of which map x to many outputs. Suppose R_1 is implemented by program P_1 and R_2 is implemented by program P_2. P_1 might map x onto y_1, say, and P_2 would then test if it could also map x onto the same value. In the worst case, P_2 might need to enumerate many values of y before finding y_1—or failing to. If P_1 generates N_1 values of y and P_2 generates N_2 values, the complexity of finding the intersection in this way is $O(N_1 N_2)$. On the other hand, if the programmer arranges for the two sets of outputs to be stored, sorted, and merged, it is only $O((N_1 + N_2) \log(N_1 + N_2))$. This clearly shows that it can be useful to represent relations as data objects.

3   Avoiding interpretation

A feature of LIBRA was its ability to treat any relational data object as a program. For example, it could read an arbitrary relation from the keyboard, then execute it. Indeed, this was necessary to support LIBRA's interactive approach to program development. An unfortunate consequence of this feature is that a full interpreter of the language has to be available at run time. This is not a normal feature of compiled languages. In these, if the expression '1+2' is read in, it cannot be handed over to a general-purpose interpreter, but the program must identify the specific structure and act on it according-ly. In other words, if a program needs to evaluate arithmetic expressions entered as data, the programmer has to write the statements that do it. It was decided to follow the same course in translating RL. Although this makes some programs harder to write, knowing that there is no interpreter to fall back on is a good discipline in writing the translator.

How can it be decided when a relational object should be executed, and when it should be treated as data? The LIBRA system always attempted to reduce arguments to their simplest form, therefore '1+2' would always be converted to '3' at the first opportunity. This means duplicated work: structures are inspected to see if they can be simplified every time they are passed as arguments. It also makes it impossible to deal with '1+2' as an expression tree abstractly, as other languages can, because the interpreter converts '1+2' to '3' as soon as it can.

Most languages let a programmer control when an expression should be treated as data, and when it should be evaluated. Adding this useful feature to LIBRA's syntax means making a small revision. A relation is usually defined as a pattern followed by a predicate. The pattern is treated symbolically; only the predicate is evaluated. In RL's syntax, for example,

```
commute -> {X+Y -> Y+X : X+Y>0}.
evaluate -> {X+Y -> Z : Z=X+Y, X+Y>0}.
```

the commute relation reorders X and Y symbolically, but evaluate finds their sum. (Both examples evaluate 'X+Y>0'.) The original LIBRA interpreter chose between these two alternatives at execution time, depending on whether X and Y were already grounded. This small change to the notation means that the RL translator can always tell where an expression is used symbolically and where it is to be evaluated, eliminating execution time testing. More importantly, the RL translator may always assume that a set or relation is finite if the programmer asks for it to be evaluated.

The translator is itself written in Prolog. There are several good reasons for this choice. Prolog provides simple means of parsing text and excellent facilities for manipulating syntax trees [6]. It also interfaces beautifully with the target language, which is, of course, Prolog.

4   Modelling sets and relations in Prolog

A Prolog predicate with one argument models a test for set membership, e.g., s(X) can be said to succeed if and only if $X \in s$. A Prolog predicate with two arguments establishes a binary relation. Prolog can therefore model the expression XrY as r(X,Y). Since relations are special kinds of sets, this poses a small difficulty in compiling set operations such as union and intersection, because relations have two arguments, but sets have only one. Perhaps, rather than use a predicate that takes a pair of arguments to represent a relation, it is better to use one that takes a single argument, which is itself a pair. For uniformity, we might choose to model XrY as r((X,Y)) rather than r(X,Y). Actually, this is not wise, because most Prolog systems branch directly to rules according to the principal functors of their first arguments [8].

This means, for example, that given a relation from numbers to colours expressed in the form:

```
colour(1,red).
colour(2,green).
colour(4,blue).
```

and a particular argument, such as 4, a typical Prolog system will test only one rule. However, if the same relation were expressed in the form:

```
colour((1,red)).
colour((2,green)).
colour((4,blue)).
```

its first argument would have the principal functor ',' (comma) in each case, and Prolog would need to scan all three rules.

A second way to make sets and relations uniform would be to give sets a dummy second argument. One way to do this is by repeating their first arguments, making the sets into identity relations. Unfortunately, a set and the identity relation on it are not the same object, so this idea should be rejected. An alternative is to give the second argument a special value. This was the choice taken in Drusilla [3], but it lead to contexts where it was necessary to find the relational inverse of a set, which seems very inelegant.

5   Simple data structures

In a language based on binary relations, only pair formation and set formation make sense as data structuring primitives. These operations are sufficient to model any structure [10]. For example, tuples or records can be built up from pairs of pairs; lists of length N can be modelled by sequences, which are functions from the first N positive numbers, and functions are themselves sets of pairs. Abstractly, relations are also sets of pairs.

Prolog programmers typically use lists to represent sequences, and ordered lists to represent sets. Since sequences are special kinds of relations, and therefore kinds of sets, it is important to tag lists so that it is clear what they represent. This can be done by letting set(L) be the list representation of a set, and seq(L) be the list representation of a sequence, where L is a list. Any finite set or relation represented as a Prolog predicate can easily be converted into a data structure. For example, given a set s defined by:

```
s(a). s(b). s(c). s(d). s(e).
```

it may be desired to express it as a tagged ordered list:

```
set([a,b,c,d,e]).
```

The conversion can be done as follows:

```
s_to_set(set(L)) :- setof(X,s(X),L).
```

Using Prolog's setof predicate is a general strategy that can be applied to change any finite set or relational expression to ordered list form. From a list, the set may be converted to a more sophisticated form, such as a search tree. However, for the present, we shall assume that sets are represented by ordered lists. Actually, the implementation of sequences needs to be a little more complex than a simple list; RL sequences are double ended, and allow both head and tail operations. Fortunately, a simple implementation of such sequences exists that works well in almost all circumstances: back-to-back lists. These have the form,

```
seq(L,R)
```

where L represents the start of the sequence, and R represents the reverse of the rest of it. Back-to-back lists have constant amortised cost per operation when used as stacks or queues (from either end), except in some situations when backtracking is involved [8].

RL's built-in sequence operators may then be defined in terms of the following predicates:

```
<-(seq(L,R),seq(R,L)).
#(seq(L,R),X) :- length(L,XL),length(R,XR),X is XL+XR.
head_tail(seq([],R),H,seq(T,[])) :- reverse(R,[],[H|T]),!.
head_tail(seq([H|T],R),H,seq(T,R)).
front_last(seq(L,[]),A,seq(L,Z)) :- reverse(L,[],[Z|A]),!.
front_last(seq(L,[Z|A]),seq(L,A),Z).
&&(seq(L1,R1),seq(L2,R2),seq(L3,R3)) :-
        reverse(R1,[],R4),append(L1,R4,L3),
        reverse(L2,[],L4),append(L4,R2,R3).
reverse([],R,R).
reverse([H|T1],T2,R) :- reverse(T1,[H|T2],R).
append([],L,L).
append([H|T1],L2,[H|T3]) :- append(T1,L2,T3).
```

However, sequences are just special kinds of relations: sets of ordered pairs from natural numbers to terms. This means that the same sequence can be represented in at least two ways: as a seq structure or a set structure. This means that library predicates must be able to accept arguments in unexpected forms, e.g:

```
<-(set(X),Z) :- set_to_seq(set(X),Y), <-(Y,Z).
```

It follows that two sequences can be equal, but Prolog will fail to unify them. We therefore need a library predicate, eq, to test if two structures represent the same object. We also need additional rules in the definitions of the sequence operators to handle set structures.

6   Translating relational operators

Translating set and relational operations into Prolog then becomes beguilingly easy. Table 6.1 shows how several useful set operations can be translated. It is assumed that s, s1 and s2 are the names of constant sets. In any particular translation these names are replaced by names appearing in the program.

Table 1. Set Operators

intersection	`'s1 meet s2'(X,Y):- s1(X,Y),s2(X,Y2),`
	`                         eq(Y,Y2).`
	`'s1 meet s2'(X,Y):- !.`
	`'s1 meet s2'(X):- s1(X),s2(X2),`
	`                      eq(X,X2).`

union	`'s1 join s2'(X,Y):- s1(X,Y); s2(X,Y).` `'s1 join s2'(X):- s1(X); s2(X).`

asymmetric difference	`'s1 omit s2'(X,Y):-`
	`s1(X,Y),s2(X,Y2),eq(Y,Y2),!,fail.`
	`'s1 omit s2'(X,Y):- r1(X,Y).`
	`'s1 omit s2'(X,Y):- !.`
	`'s1 omit s2'(X):- s1(X),s2(X2),`
	`                      eq(X,X2),!,fail.`
	`'s1 omit s2'(X):- s1(X).`

Cartesian product	`'s1 x s2'(X,Y):- s1(X),s2(Y).`

all members	`'@s'(X,Y):- s(X,Y).`
	`'@s'(X,Y):- !.`
	`'@s'(X):- s(X).`

non-deterministic selection	`'i s'(X,Y):- s(X,Y),!.` `'i s'(X):- s(X),!.`

size	`'#s'(Y):- setof((X,X1),s(X,X1),L),`
	`                length(L,Y),!.`
	`'#s'(Y):- setof(X,s(X),L),length(L,Y).`

set reduction	`'s>>->op'(X):- bagof(Z,s(Z),L),`
	`                     's>>->op'(L,X).`
	`'s>>->op'([X|[]],X).`
	`'s>>->op'([H|T],X):- 's>>->op'(T,Y),`
	`                         op(((H,Y),X)).`

reduce to set	`'s>>->'(set(Y)) :- setof(X,s(X),Y).`

The **meet** operator finds the intersection of two sets or relations. The first rule deals with relations, and the second rule prevents relations being dealt with by the third rule, which deals with sets. Since Y and Y2 might have different representations, it is necessary to compare them using **eq**. A similar strategy is needed for **omit**: if s2 contains a member that is equal to a member of s1, it is not in their difference, even if it has a different representation.

The reduction operators may be less familiar. 'Set reduction' combines members of a set using a commutative associative operator, as when adding a set of numbers to form a total. 'Reduce to set' serves the useful function of storing a set of results as a data structure.

Table 2 shows how several useful relational operations can be translated. It is assumed that r, r1 and r2 are the names of constant relations, N is a constant integer, and s is a set.

Table 2. Set operators

```
composition                  | 'r1 o r2'(X,Z):- r1(X,Y),r2(Y,Z).
reflexive transitive closure | 'r^*'(X,X).
                             | 'r^*'(X,Z):- r(X,Y),'r^*'(Y,Z).
transitive closure           | 'r^+'(X,Z):- r(X,Y),'r^*'(Y,Z).
limit                        | 'r^~'(X,Y):- 'r^*'(X,Y),not(r((Y,_))).
power                        | 'r^+N'(X,Y):- 'r^+'(N,X,Y).
                             | 'r^+'(0,X,X):- !.
                             | 'r^+'(N,X,Z):- r(X,Y),N1 is N-1,
                             |                        'r^+'(N1,Y,Z).
inverse power                | 'r^-N'(X,Y):- 'r^+'(N,Y,X).
extension                    | 'r1 else r2'(X,Y):- r1(X,Y).
                             | 'r1 else r2'(X,Y):- not(r1(X,_)),r2((X,Y)).
over-ride                    | 'r1 but r2'(X,Y):- r2(X,Y).
                             | 'r1 but r2'(X,Y):- not(r2(X,_),r1(X,Y).
domain                       | 'dom r'(X)  :- r(X,_).
codomain                     | 'codom r'(Y):- r(_,Y).
apply                        | '!r'(X,Y):- r(X,Y).
apply once                   | 'r~'(X,Y):- r(X,Y),!.
parallel operator            | '(r1,r2)\\op'(X,Y):- r1(X,Y1),r2(X,Y2),
                             |                        op((Y1,Y2),Y).
sequence reduction           | 'r>>=>op'(Z):- setof((X,Y),r(X,Y),L),
                             | 'r>>=>op'(L,Z).
                             | 'r>>=>op'([(X,Y)|[]],Y).
                             | 'r>>=>op'([(X,Y)|T],Z):-'r>>=>op'(T,W),
                             |                          op(Y,W,Z).
image                        | 's image r'(set(Z)) :-
                             |            setof(Y,X^(s(X),r((X,Y)),Z),!.
                             | 's image r'(set([])).
```

The closure and power operators provide means of looping or searching. Extension and over-ride are used to combine two relations so that one takes precedence over the other. The 'parallel' operator allows operations to be applied to matching elements of structures such as vectors or matrices. Sequence reduction is similar to set reduction, but the operator doesn't need to be commutative. It might be used to flatten a list of lists into a single list.

Table 6.3 shows how restriction operations can be translated. It is assumed that r is the name of a constant relation, and s is a constant set. Restriction operators limit the domain or codomain of a relation to a particular set; anti-restriction operators limit them to its inverse.

Table 3. Restriction operators

right restriction	`'r?>s'((X,Y)):- r((X,Y)),s(Y).`
right anti-restriction	`'r\?>s'(X,Y):- r(X,Y),not(s(Y)).`
left restriction	`'s<?r'(X,Y):- s(X),r(X,Y).`
left anti-restriction	`'s<\?s'(X,Y):- r(X,Y),not(s(X)).`

7   Prolog and RL as relational languages

Given that these translations are relatively simple, why not use Prolog directly?

First, relational programming permits a variable-free style. It has been argued by the functional programming community that variables are an evil on a par with 'go to' [1], although, like Prolog, modern functional languages do allow variables in patterns [2]. In RL we may write 'r1 o r2' for the composition of two relations, but Prolog needs 3 variables to achieve the same effect. (See Table 2.)

Second, Prolog has a rather flat syntax; it has a small number of operators, which can be combined in many ways. It is therefore necessary to read a Prolog program carefully to discover its 'shape'.

Third, Prolog's cut operator (!) needs to be used with care. In RL, its use is encapsulated into safe contexts.

Fourth, although the correctness of some Prolog programs can be established mathematically, proof at the level of the predicate calculus can be tedious.

Fifth, a desire to treat program objects and data uniformly (unlike Prolog) means that translation sometimes becomes complex. This issue is discussed in Sect. 9.

Sixth, embedding recursion within the closure operators means that there is little reason to write RL programs that are explicitly recursive. Since recursion can be used to simulate 'go to', and in Prolog it frequently is, there are strong reasons for wishing to restrict its use. However, there remain problems, such as syntax analysis, where recursive definitions seem natural, so RL does not ban them.

8   An example translation

The above data representations, combined with the rules for set and relational operators, suffice for the translation of simple programs. The following example is taken from an earlier paper by the author [5]. It illustrates the use of relations both as data and as program objects.

> A farmer has with him a sack of corn, a chicken, and a rather vicious dog. He reaches a river, which he must cross in a small boat. The boat has only space enough for the farmer and one item. He must therefore ferry the corn, chicken and dog from the left bank to the right bank of the river one item at a time. The problem is that he cannot leave the dog alone with the chicken, for it will certainly eat it, nor can he trust the chicken alone with the corn. How can he ferry them all across safely?

The program is explained here one relation at a time. Each definition of the original program appears as a comment, followed by its translation. It is a line by line translation; each definition is translated independently of the rest. The translation has been 'cleaned up' to make it more readable, e.g., by giving variables meaningful names.

The required expression is a *plan*: a sequence of states that solves the problem. Plans are constructed by applying the transitive closure of the relation add_to_plan to an initial plan: a sequence containing just the initial state. If the resulting plan is in the set solved, it satisfies the whole expression:

```
% solution -> [initial_state]!add_to_plan^+ ?>solved.
solution(Sol) :-
        initial_state(IS),Plan=seq([IS],[]),
        add_to_plan(Plan,New),'add_to_plan^*'(New,Sol),
        solved(Sol).
'add_to_plan^*'(X,X).
'add_to_plan^*'(X,Z) :-
        add_to_plan(X,Y),'add_to_plan^*'(Y,Z).
```

The initial state is one where everything is on the left bank, and nothing is on the right bank:

```
% initial_state -> (everything,{}).
initial_state((set(L),set([]))) :- setof(X,everything(X),L).
```

The final state is one where nothing is on the left bank, and everything is on the right bank:

```
% final_state -> ({},everything).
final_state((set([]),set(R))) :- setof(X,everything(X),R).
```

In this context, 'everything' comprises the farmer, the dog, the corn and the chicken. We can ignore the boat, because it is always on the same side of the river as the farmer.

```
% everything -> {'Farmer'; 'Dog';'Corn';'Chicken'}.
everything('Farmer').
everything('Dog').
everything('Corn').
everything('Chicken').
```

The problem is solved if the last term of a plan sequence is the final state:

```
% solved -> {Plan:last(Plan)=final_state}.
solved(Plan) :- front_last(Plan,_,S),final_state(S).
```

Adding to a plan is the composition of two steps: suggesting a new state, and checking to see it is not already part of the plan. This avoids aimless cycles between states.

```
% add_to_plan -> suggest o verify.
add_to_plan(Plan,New) :-
        suggest(Plan,Next),verify(Next,New).
```

We suggest a new state by applying the relation `cross_river` to the last state of the plan:

```
% suggest -> {Plan -> Plan,last(Plan)!cross_river}.
suggest(Plan,(Plan,NewS)) :-
        front_last(Plan,_,S),cross_river(S,NewS).
```

Provided that the new state is not already a term of the plan, we append it to the plan. We have to be careful here; we must test if the state is a member of the codomain of the plan, not a member of the plan itself. The elements of the plan are number-state pairs:

```
% verify ->
%       {Plan,State -> Plan&&[State] : State\?codom Plan}.
verify((Plan,S),NewP) :-
        not(apply(Plan,(_,S))),&&(Plan,seq([S],[]),NewP).
```

It is possible to cross the river either from left to right or right to left:

```
% cross_river -> left_to_right join right_to_left.
cross_river(S,NewS) :- !,
        left_to_right(S,NewS); right_to_left(S,NewS).
cross_river(X) :-
        left_to_right(X); right_to_left(X). % (X is a set)
```

The boat can only cross from left to right if the existing state has the farmer on the left bank and the resulting state will not be unsafe:

```
% left_to_right ->
%          farmer_on_left <? ferry_object \?> unsafe.
left_to_right(S,NewS) :-
        farmer_on_left(S),
        ferry_object(S,NewS),
        not(unsafe(NewS)).
```

Testing if the farmer is on the left bank is a simple membership test:

```
% farmer_on_left -> {Left,Right: 'Farmer'?Left}.
farmer_on_left((Left,Right)) :- apply(Left, 'Farmer').
```

To cross the river, we choose any object on the left bank, and move it to the right bank along with the farmer. If the chosen object is the farmer, then the farmer crosses the river alone:

```
% ferry_object -> {Left,Right -> Left,Right,@Left}}
%              o {Left,Right,Choice ->
%                      Left omit{Choice}omit{'Farmer'},
%                      Right join{Choice}join{'Farmer'}}.
ferry_object((L,R),(L2,R2)) :-
        apply(L,C),
        omit(L,set([C]),L1),omit(L1,set(['Farmer']),L2),
        join(R,set([C]),R1),join(R1,set(['Farmer']),R2).
```

The proposed new state is unsafe if the chicken can eat the corn or the dog can eat the chicken:

```
% unsafe -> {Left,Right:Left includes{'Chicken'; 'Corn'}
%                     v Left includes{'Dog'; 'Chicken'}}.
unsafe((L,R)) :-
        includes(L,set(['Chicken', 'Corn']),'True');
        includes(L,set(['Chicken', 'Dog']),'True').
```

(We don't need to worry about the right bank, because the farmer will be there.)

Crossing from right to left could be programmed as a mirror image of crossing from left to right. Instead, we use a short-cut. If the existing state does not have the farmer on the left, we notionally swap the left and right banks, cross from left to right, then swap them back again:

```
% right_to_left -> farmer_on_left<\?swap
%                 o left_to_right o swap.
right_to_left(S,NewS) :-
        not(farmer_on_left(S)),
        swap(S,S1)),left_to_right(S1,S2),swap(S2,NewS)).
```

Swapping the left and right banks is trivial:

```
% swap -> {Left,Right->Right,Left}.
swap((L,R),(R,L)).
```

The translation needs the support of several library predicates. The operations on sequences were introduced earlier. The `apply` predicate is used to apply a relation or set to an argument when the relation or set is a variable. The `join`, `omit` and `include` predicates support set operations on data. They, and the `apply` predicate, are described in the next section.

9   Compiling relational arguments

Programmers distinguish programs from data. Program objects are known at compile time, and are constant at execution time; data objects are variable at execution time and unknown at compile time. The distinction is rather fuzzy. Data objects can remain constant, and in Prolog, it is possible, although usually inefficient, to create program objects at execution time.

It is only logical that a relational language should be able to manipulate relations as data objects. This means that relational operations such as union, intersection, composition and closure ought to be applicable to data structures as well as predicates.

An ability to express relations as data structures or as predicates gives the programmer a necessary flexibility. If a relation is small and frequently used, the programmer can choose to make it into a data structure; if it is large or infrequently used, it is better expressed as a program. However, it would be a syntactical blemish if an RL program had to be written differently depending on which form was chosen. For example, the arguments of a higher-order relation may be other relations. How its arguments are represented should not matter to the programmer while writing the higher-order relation. This means RL may need to interpret the same higher-order relation differently depending on the form of its arguments. For reasons discussed in Sect. 10, the translator generates a program that detects the representation of a relational or set argument at execution time. Although this is dangerously close to interpreting rather than translating, this treatment is only reserved for relations that appear as arguments. Constant relations are translated more efficiently.

Consider a relation `maplist`, whose function is to apply a given relation R to all the elements of a sequence. For simplicity, we assume the sequence is known to be represented as a back-to-back list. Provided R is bound to a predicate name, this can be translated as:

```
maplist((R,seq([],[])),seq([],[])) :- !.
maplist((R,S1),S2) :-
        head_tail(S1,X,Xs),
        head_tail(S2,Y,Ys),
```

```
G =..[R,(X,Y)],call(G),
maplist((R,Xs),Ys).
```

This translation will work correctly if R is bound to a predicate name, but it won't work if R is bound to a data structure. So we need to deal with this case separately. Assuming, for simplicity, that a set is represented as an ordered list, we can develop a general apply predicate, which is satisfied if its second argument is an element of its first argument. In the case that the set is represented by a list, it tests if its second argument is in the list. In the case that the relation is defined by a predicate, it calls it, as before.

```
apply(set(S),X) :- !,member(X,S).
apply(S,(X,Y)) :- !,G=..[S,X,Y],call(G).
apply(S,X) :- G=..[S,X],call(G).
member(X,[X|_]).
member(X,[_|T]) :- member(X,T).
```

We may then translate maplist as,

```
maplist((_,seq([],[])),seq([],[])): -.
maplist((R,S1),S2) :-
        head_tail(S1,X,Xs),
        head_tail(S2,Y,Ys),
        apply(R,(X,Y)),
        maplist((R,Xs),Ys).
```

We can obviously extend this basic approach to other representations of finite relations. One possibility is that the relation is another sequence represented as a back-to-back list:

```
apply(seq(L,R),(X,Y)) :- !,member_seq(L,R,1,X,Y).
member_seq([],[],_,_,_) :- !,fail.
member_seq([Y|_],_,N,N,Y).
member_seq([_|L],R,N,X,Y) :-
        N1 is N+1,member_seq(L,R,N1,X,Y).
member_seq([],R,N,X,Y) :-
        reverse(R,[],L),member_seq(L,[],N,X,Y).
```

It is obvious that this approach can be extended to deal with any number of data structures. It is also possible for one relation to be the result of applying another relation. For example, the higher-order relation add, which can be defined in RL as follows:

```
add -> {N->{X->X+N}}.
```

maps N onto a *relation* whose second argument is N plus its first argument.

Dealing with this case is more problematic. Given N=3, the original LIBRA interpreter would have returned the expression {X->X+3}, but this is undesirable, as it would need a run-time interpreter to apply the expression to an argument. Unfortunately, the obvious alternative:

```
add(N,(X,Y)) :- Y is X+N.
```

won't work because Prolog's is operator needs its second argument to be grounded, and X is required here to remain unbound.

A workable alternative is to return a kind of lambda function, into which the expression has been pre-compiled:

```
add(N,lambda(X,Y is X+N,Y)).
```

where the structure lambda(X,R,Y) denotes the relation that relates X and Y according to expression R. It now becomes necessary to add a further rule to apply to deal with this new case:

```
apply(lambda(X0,R0,Y0),(X,Y)) :- !,
        copy_term(lambda(X0,R0,Y0),
        lambda(X,R,Y)),
        call(R).
```

where copy_term is needed to prevent the following case from failing:

```
add(3,R),apply(R,(2,Y)),apply(R,(3,Z)).
```

The call of add binds R to lambda(X,Y is X+3,Y). Without copy_term, R would become bound to lambda((2,5 is 2+3,5) by the first call of apply, and the second call of apply would fail.

A similar problem appears when dealing with set operations. Although we expect set variables to be represented by ordered lists, we cannot rule out the possibility that they are represented by predicates. The following implementation of omit shows the general idea:

```
omit(set(S1),set(S2),set(S3)) :- !,omit_set(S1,S2,S3).
omit(S1,S2,set(S3)) :-
        setof(X,(apply(S1,X),not(apply(S2,X))),S3).
```

If the two sets to be joined are represented by ordered lists, the work is passed to omit_set, which deals with this case efficiently. Otherwise, Prolog's setof predicate is used to find all members of the first set that are not members of the second. This second alternative uses apply, so that the forms of the sets won't matter. It would possible to add further cases to deal with other data structures, such as sequences.

The point is that the special case can be evaluated more efficiently than the general one. In the general case, if one set contains N_1 elements and the other contains N_2 elements, finding their difference can take time $O(N_1 N_2)$. But finding the difference of ordered lists only takes time $O(N_1 + N_2)$, as follows:

```
omit_set([],_,[]).
omit_set([X|S1],S2,S3) :- omit_set(S2,X,S1,S3).
```

```
omit_set([],X,S,[X|S]).
omit_set([X2|S2],X1,S1,S3) :-
        compare(Rel,X1,X2),
        omit_set(Rel,X1,S1,X2,S2,S3).
omit_set(=,_,S1,_,S2,S3) :- omit_set(S1,S2,S3).
omit_set(<,X1,S1,X2,S2,[X1|S3]) :- omit_set(S1,[X2|S2],S3).
omit_set(>,X1,S1,X2,S2,S3) :- omit_set(S2,X1,S1,S3).
```

Similar techniques are used to implement join and includes.

10   Optimisation

Executing a translated program proves dramatically faster than interpreting
the original. In the case of the above planning problem, execution is some 30
times faster than interpretation. On the other hand, it is still 4 times slower
than executing one translated by hand, as follows:

```
solution([([],['Chicken', 'Corn','Dog','Farmer'])|P]) :-
      add_to_plan_plus([(['Chicken','Corn','Dog','Farmer'],
                        [])],[([],_)|P]).
add_to_plan_plus(P,[NS|P]) :-
        P=[S|_],cross_river(S,NS),not(member(NS,P)).
add_to_plan_plus(P,FP) :-
        P=[S|_],cross_river(S,NS),not(member(NS,P)),
        add_to_plan_plus([NS|P],FP).

cross_river(S,NS) :-
        ( farmer_on_left(S) -> left_to_right(S,NS)
        ; right_to_left(S,NS)
        ).
left_to_right(S,NS) :-
        ferry_object(S,NS),not(unsafe(NS)).
farmer_on_left((Left,Right)) :- member('Farmer',Left).
ferry_object((L,R),(L1,R1)) :-
        member(C,L),
        delete_set(L,C,L0),delete_set(L0,'Farmer',L1),
        insert_set(R,C,R0),insert_set(R0,'Farmer',R1).
unsafe((L,R)) :-
        member('Chicken',L),
        (member('Corn',L); member('Dog',L)).
right_to_left((L,R),(L1,R1)) :-
        left_to_right((R,L),(R1,L1)).

% Library predicates
delete_set([],_,[]).
```

```
delete_set([X|S],X,S) :- !.
delete_set([X|S],Y,[X|S1]) :- delete_set(S,Y,S1).
insert_set([],X,[X]).
insert_set([H|S],X,S1) :-
        compare(Rel,H,X),
        insert_set(Rel,H,S,X,S1).
insert_set(=,H,S,_,[H|S]).
insert_set(>,H,S,X,[X,H|S]).
insert_set(<,H,S,X,[H|S1]) :- insert(S,X,S1).
member(X,[X|_]).
member(X,[_|S]) :- member(X,S).
```

In this version, both sets and sequences are represented as simple lists, treated appropriately according to context. In particular, the programmer was aware that elements are only ever added to one end of the plan, making back-to-back lists a waste of time. It would be very difficult to deduce the validity of these optimisations automatically. (Indeed, they might be incorrect if its predicates were called from a separate program.)

The automatic translation scheme can be improved by some simple optimisations. The greatest source of inefficiency in the translated program is that each potential solution must be tested by solved, which evaluates the set representation of final_state anew each time it is called. In fact, the representation of final_state is constant. It is not hard to determine when a predicate is constant. By substituting expanded constants wherever they are used, the translated program is made twice as fast, making it only a factor of 2 slower than the hand-written version and 60 times faster than the interpreted version.

Another useful optimisation is to make special cases of singleton sequences and sets. Rather than append a new state to the plan using the concatenation operator, &&, it is faster to use the front_last predicate defined earlier. Similarly, in the case of the singleton sets appearing in ferry_object, it is better to replace join by insert, and omit by delete, defined as follows:

```
delete(set(S1),X,set(S3)) :- !,delete_set(S1,X,S3).
delete(S1,X,set(S3)) :-
        setof(X1,(apply(S1,X1),not(X1=X2)),S3).
insert(set(S),X,set(S1)) :- !,insert_set(S,X,S1).
insert(S1,X2,set(S3)) :-
        setof(X1,(apply(S1,X1);X1=X2),S3).
```

where delete_set and insert_set are defined as above.

These optimisations leave the translated version only 60% slower than the hand-written one, and about 75 times faster than the interpreted one.

11   Other data representations

Prolog lists have several drawbacks: only the head of a list may accessed efficiently, it is only possible to add elements at the head of a list, and lists must be processed sequentially. Even though a back-to-back list used as a queue has constant amortised cost per operation, backtracking over a worst-case operation may cause the average cost per operation to become proportional to the length of the list [8]. It is important to use data structures with better worst-case behaviours.

Lists do not offer fast random access to elements of large sets or sequences. Random access is best supported by hash tables. Unfortunately, although some Prolog implementations use hashing internally, it is costly to implement updateable hash tables in Prolog.

A workable alternative is to use balanced search trees. Balanced trees offer $O(\log N)$ time for operations on individual elements, and $O(N)$ time for operations on the whole set, such as union, intersection, etc. One structure that satisfies these requirements is the α-balanced tree, a form of weight-balanced binary tree. Each node of an α-balanced tree stores an element of the set, links to its left and right subtrees, and its weight, i.e., the total number of nodes in the subtrees rooted at the node in question. When the weights of its left and right subtrees exceed a certain ratio, typically 3:1, each node's subtree is balanced by rotation, similarly to AVL trees. A similar representation is useful for sequences. For any subtree, the terms preceding the root are stored in its left subtree, and the terms following it are stored in its right subtree. If the weight of the left subtree of the root is N, then the root itself must represent the $(N + 1)$th term in its subtree. This makes it easy to find any term at random. It also allows terms to be added to the head or tail of a sequence—or at any other position—in time $O(\log N)$. Relations are perhaps best represented as search trees whose elements form a pair: a domain value, and a search tree of its corresponding codomain values. Such a structure would allow a relation to be applied to an argument in time $O(\log N)$.

It would be desirable for every data object to have a canonical representation, so that converting from one form to another could be avoided, and equality could be tested by unification. Unfortunately, the author knows of no way to do this that permits efficient operations on sequences.

Since the example program given here deals only with small sets, representation issues make little difference to its efficiency. At the time of writing, no experiments have been made to compare different data representations.

12   Sets as types

The material in this section concerns type checking. As yet, RL does not have any means of type checking, and this area of its design is still the subject of speculation. As the author pointed out in an earlier paper [5], relational programs are difficult to debug because, when a relation yields no result, the computer cannot tell if this is the programmer's intention, or if it results from an error: for example, by trying to apply a relation on strings to an integer. Any type error of this kind on the programmer's part inevitably leads to a program that yields no result, and it is necessary to resort to tedious debugging to discover where things went wrong.

Most modern programming languages have means of declaring the types of variables and relations in such a way that type errors can be discovered by the compiler. This means that the algebra of types has to be complete and consistent, and indeed, verifying type correctness must also be efficient. Type checking not only aids the programmer, it also lets the compiler deduce statically how objects will be represented, and saves the overhead of finding their representations at execution time. Some languages have extremely sophisticated type algebras, e.g., Haskell [2]. Indeed, learning to use their type systems correctly may prove more tedious than learning their programming features.

Unfortunately, complete compile-time checking of types does not seem consistent with a relational language. A relation is defined from one set to another. The type of a relation is the cartesian product of its source and target sets. Relations can be program objects or data objects. Therefore their source and target sets may be unknown until execution time. Since they can be variables, they may also need to be passed as arguments.

A type therefore becomes an arbitrary and possibly variable set of values. In a language that already allows operations on sets, it seems unreasonable that its operations on types should be in any way different. Within a relational language, we ought to regard types as first-class objects. This has the advantage that the programmer can use ordinary set operations to manipulate them. But, it follows that it is becomes impossible to check types statically.

However, although it might not be possible to determine the actual members of a set statically, it may be possible to determine their representation. A future possibility is for the translator itself to infer representations, using Milner style type inference, for example [3,7].

The approach to types in developing RL will be that types are sets, and that is that. This removes what the author considers is a syntactical blemish of most programming languages, in that their means of constructing types are different from their means of constructing data or programs. However, the other side of the coin is that whatever can be defined as a set can be a type. RL allows sets to be defined procedurally, e.g., the set of prime numbers, and finite sets to be defined as data objects, e.g., the set of words read from a file. This means that type checking must be done at execution time. This causes difficulty during translation, as the translator often cannot tell what kind of data structure to expect.

For example, sequences are special cases of relations, and relations are special cases of sets. A relation operating on sets cannot tell, in general, what data structure to build as an output. A program may construct a relation on the integers that proves to be a sequence. It may be better to express it in the specialised form of a sequence rather than as a general set of pairs. On the other hand, that a set of pairs form a sequence may be a coincidence. It would not pay to test every set to see if it was a relation or test every relation to see if it was a sequence; it would be time-consuming and might gain nothing. The best choice of representation depends on how the result will be used later.

However, if the programmer knows that a set of pairs is intended to be a sequence, and will later be used as one, it would pay to convert it into one. Such an operation would have no meaning in relational algebra, because it does not affect the abstract relation in any way, and merely affects its internal representation. However, as an aid to efficiency, the language syntax now includes a unary form of the '?' operator, which in its binary form denotes a test for set membership. The notation '?S' denotes the identity relation on the set S: its input and output are the same abstract object—provided they belong to S. If they do, its output will be represented in the most efficient way that elements of S can be. For example, ?seq is an identity relation on sequences, and converts its input to a back-to-back list—or whatever the preferred representation for sequences happens to be.

What happens if the input is not a member of S? In that case, the situation is diagnosed as a run time error, and the erroneous input is reported. In other words, the ?S notation provides run-time type checking. This resolves a serious problem encountered when debugging RL programs: most programming errors arise from trying to apply a relation to the wrong kind of input. The relation is therefore inapplicable to its input argument. But inapplicability is normal behaviour for some kinds of relations, so it is not possible to tell that an error has occurred. (A similar problem occurs in Prolog: predicates fail when they are logically false, but they also fail if they are badly written or misused.)

A future potential of the ?S notation is to extend it to different data representations of the same abstract objects. For example, suppose sets can be represented either as ordered lists or as search trees, and their best representation depends on context. Then ?ord_set might convert a set to ordered list form, whereas ?tree_set might convert it to search tree form. At the level of relational algebra, these two relations are both vacuous.

There is a difficulty with this idea, concerning modularity. RL allows the programmer to define two or more relations with the same name, but which accept different types of input. This kind of overloading is common in other programming languages, and it would seem especially foolish to forbid it in a relational language, where arguments should be free to map to several values. Suppose there are two relations called add, one operating on vectors and the other on matrices. Suppose both begin by checking the types of their inputs. If the input is a pair of matrices, the vector add will detect a type error, and if the input is a pair of vectors, the matrix add will detect a type error. Either relation is valid separately, but their combination is faulty. We would only want an error to be diagnosed when the input was neither a pair of matrices nor a pair of vectors. This means that all the relations in a program with the same name have to be considered as a whole.

The obvious way to deal with this problem is to create extra rules as follows:

```
add((X,Y),Z) :- matrix(X),matrix(Y),matrix(Z),!,fail.
add((X,Y),Z) :- vector(X),vector(Y),vector(Z),!,fail.
add((X,Y),Z) :- write(add((X,Y),Z)),write(' type error'),nl.
```

the intention being that no error would be reported unless an argument failed to match both type patterns. These rules would need to be placed after all other rules for add.

Type checking is a two-edged sword. Determining the best representations for data objects can be expected to speed program execution, but checking for type errors at execution time is bound to slow it. It therefore seems wise, in the long run, to distinguish these two aspects carefully. The ideal situation is, wherever possible, for execution time checks to be removed once a program has been debugged.

References

1. Backus J. (1978) Can Programming be Liberated from the Von Neumann Style? Communications of the ACM, 21(8):613–641
2. Bird R., Scruggs T.E., Mastropieri M.A. (1998) Introduction to Functional Programming Using Haskell. (Prentice Hall)
3. Cattrall D.M. (1992) The Design and Implementation of a Relational Programming System. PhD Thesis, Dept. of Computer Science, University of York
4. Dwyer B. (1994) Programming Using Binary Relations: a proposed programming language. Technical Report 94-04, Dept. of Computer Science, University of Adelaide
5. Dwyer B. (1995) LIBRA: A Lazy Interpreter of Binary Relational Algebra. Technical Report 95-10, Dept. of Computer Science, University of Adelaide. (Also available via http://www.cs.adelaide.edu.au/~dwyer.)
6. Gabber E. (1990) Developing a Portable Parallelizing Pascal Compiler in Prolog. In: Sterling L. (Ed.) The Practice of Prolog, 109–136
7. Milner R. (1978) A theory of type polymorphism in programming. Journal of Computer and System Sciences, 17(3):348–375
8. O'Keefe R.A. (1990) The Craft of Prolog. MIT Press, Cambridge, Mass.
9. Potter B., Sinclair J. and Till D. (1991) An Introduction to Formal Specification and Z. Prentice-Hall
10. Sanderson J.G. (1980) A Relational Theory of Computing. Lecture Notes in Computer Science 82, Springer-Verlag Berlin

Chapter 3
A Calculus for Program Construction Based on Fork Algebras, Design Strategies and Generic Algorithms

Marcelo F. Frias[1] and Gabriel A. Baum[2] and Armando M. Haeberer[3]

[1] Department of Computer Science
  Universidad de Buenos Aires
  República Argentina
  mfrias@dc.uba.ar[†]
[2] LIFIA, Facultad de Informática
  Universidad Nacional de La Plata
  C.C.11, Correo Central, 1900, La Plata
  Provincia de Buenos Aires, República Argentina
  gbaum@sol.info.unlp.edu.ar
[3] Departamento de Informática
  Pontifícia Universidade Católica do Rio de Janeiro
  Rua Marquês de São Vicente 225, 22453–900
  Rio de Janeiro, RJ, Brazil
  armando@inf.puc-rio.br

Abstract. At the end of Chapter 4 of the RelMiCS book [11] an application of fork algebras as the basis for a calculus for program construction is outlined. In this paper we make a detailed presentation of the calculus as well as present some examples. We present a methodology for program construction based on the first-order theory of fork algebras. In this theory we will describe program design strategies, for instance case analysis, trivialization, divide-and-conquer and others. Using these strategies, from generic specifications (i.e., parameterized specifications) we will derive parametric algorithms. We will also provide conditions that will help in finding the parameters of the generic algorithms from the parameters in the specifications. We assume the reader is acquainted with the terminology and notation for relation and fork algebras, as well as with their basic properties as they were presented in the RelMiCS book [11].
Keywords: program construction, design strategies, genetic algorithms, fork algebras

1 Introduction

The most problematic part of the process of software development is debugging. Usually, after a program is considered to be finished by the programmer,

[†] Research partially supported by LIFIA, Universidad Nacional de la Plata, República Argentina.

a long time passes before the program is fully operational. This is due to the fact that most programmers tend to do mistakes when programming. When run for the first time, their programs usually do not terminate, or return incomprehensible results. Even when a program is accepted by the team of programmers as a fine working program, usually the performance needs to be improved. Improving the performance results in code modification, and a new need for testing the program. Opposed to the previous image is the notion of *formal program construction*. In a formal setting we can reason about logical or algebraic properties of programs that are difficult or impossible to express in an informal setting. At the heart of formal program construction is the ability to calculate programs in much the same way as a mathematician solves a set of equations or proves constructively a theorem. As a consequence, a formally constructed program is correct by construction with respect to its specifications, and its derivation is a proof of its correctness.

A particular class of formalisms for program construction are those based on formal calculi. These formalisms have a logical basis. Specifications are formulas, and a certain subset of those formulas are considered to have an algorithmic meaning and thus interpreted as programs from functional, logic, or imperative programming languages. Derivation rules resemble inference rules from logical frameworks.

Fork algebras arose in computer science when looking for a calculus for program construction based on binary relations. Programs are to be thought as the relation they establish between input and output data. Functional calculi have been extensively used for program construction [8,9,12,23], but their specification language is not declarative enough. Specifications are partial recursive functions (and thus programs in functional languages), that are optimized along the derivation process. Unfortunately, finding the functional specifications is not always easy, and also a gap wider than desirable is left between the original problem and its specification. Relations present some advantages over functions. Relations allow some operations, as the converse and complement, that are not even defined in functional frameworks. These operations make relations to be more expressive than functions, and thus relational frameworks allow for more declarative specifications. Relations have been used in program construction for some time. In [1,2,10,14], relations are introduced using a categorical approach, and used for defining an algebraic framework for program construction. In [7] and the references therein, the relational calculus is used for the construction of graph algorithms. In [24,25], a framework for program construction based on relations (not necessarily binary ones) is presented, with applications in the derivation of graph and pointer algorithms. Other applications of binary relations in Computer Science are reported in the book [11].

In this paper we present a calculus for program construction based on fork algebras and generic algorithms. The equational calculus of fork algebras has been used in program construction for some time [4,16–18]. Here we use the first-order theory of fork algebras as our formalism. First-order formulas over relations are used in order to describe design strategies (as case analysis, trivialization, divide-and-conquer, backtracking, etc.). Generic specifications using parameters describe a class of problems rather than a single problem. When the parameters satisfy enough properties, then it is possible to find a generic algorithm (also containing parameters) solving the whole class of problems. The methodology that we present, allows to derive generic algorithms following some design strategies, starting from generic specifications. We present examples showing also how to derive generic algorithms according to the presented strategies from some generic specifications.

2   Arithmetical properties, relational implication and notation

We begin this section by introducing the notion of a *filter*. Filters are partial identities, i.e., relations F satisfying the condition $F \sqsubseteq \mathbb{I}$. The reason why they are called *filters* is because they can be used as strainers, filtering the information that reaches the input of a relation. For example, if F is a filter and R is an arbitrary relation, $F;R$ restricts the input of R to F. There is a clear relationship between filters from algebras of binary relations and sets. A filter F univocally characterizes a set, namely, the set $\{x : xFx\}$. Also, given a set S, it univocally characterizes a filter, namely, the binary relation $\{\langle x, x \rangle : x \in S\}$. We will denote the filter associated to a set S by $\mathbb{I}_S$. Given a filter F, by $\neg F$ we denote the term $\overline{F} \sqcap \mathbb{I}$. Notice that if $F = \mathbb{I}_S$ for some set S, then $\neg F = \mathbb{I}_{\overline{S}}$, the filter associated to the complement of the set S.

Next is presented an operation on binary relations called *relational implication*. As we will see in Section 6, the relational implication is closely related to the specification of problems in fork algebras. The abstract definition of the relational implication of relations R and S, is given by the equality

$$R \to S = \overline{R;\overline{S^{\smile}}}, \tag{1}$$

while its set theoretical definition is given by

$$R \to S = \{\langle x, y \rangle : \forall z\, (x\,R\,z \Rightarrow y\,S\,z)\}.$$

In Fig. 1 we give a graphical representation of the relational implication. The pair $\langle x, y \rangle$ belongs to the relation $R \to S$ if the image set of x via R (represented by the small circle inside C) is contained in the image set of y via S, the last represented by the medium sized circle inside C.

From (1) it is immediate that the relational implication is definable in terms of the left residue.

Notice that from the definition of the relational implication given in (1), the following property follows directly:

$$(P \sqcup Q) \to R = (P \to R) \sqcap (Q \to R) . \tag{2}$$

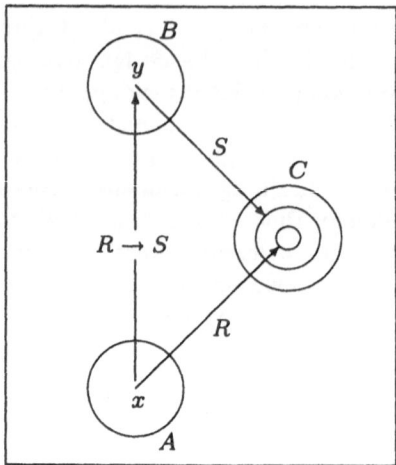

Fig. 1. The *relational implication.*

Finally, we present a useful property of the operator fork whose proof is given in [17]. For all R, S, T and U,

$$(R \triangledown S) \, ; (T \otimes U) = (R;T) \triangledown (S;U) \; . \tag{3}$$

3 Representability, expressiveness and program construction

Let us recall the representation theorem for fork algebras, already presented as Thm. 4.3.15 of the RelMiCS book [11].

Theorem 1. *Every abstract fork algebra is representable, i.e., given an abstract fork algebra $\mathfrak{A}$, there exists a proper fork algebra $\mathfrak{B}$ and an isomorphism $h : \mathfrak{A} \to \mathfrak{B}$.*

As a consequence of Thm. 1, the first-order theories of AFA and PFA are the same, and thus a natural semantics can be attributed to first-order formulas over abstract relations in terms of binary relations. This is a very important property in a calculus for program construction. The equivalence between the first-order theories of PFA and AFA guarantees that any first-order property valid about proper fork algebras can be proved syntactically from the axioms describing abstract fork algebras. This has a direct application in program construction. Let us consider a derivation of an algorithm from a relational specification S_0. The derivation has a shape $S_0, S_1, \ldots, S_k$, where for all i, $1 \le i \le k$, S_i is obtained from $S_0, \ldots, S_{i-1}$ by means of the derivation rules. If S_k still is not a satisfactory algorithmic expression, then further steps must be performed. If resorting to thinking about binary relations shows that a valid first-order property allows to pass from S_k to a new expression E (which is closer to an adequate algorithmic expression), then the representation theorem guarantees that a syntactic proof $S_k, S_{k+1}, \ldots, E$ exists that allows to reach the formula E from S_k. This shows that the heuristics arising from thinking about *concrete* binary relations along the process of program derivation using *abstract* fork algebras can be proved and used syntactically within the calculus. Another important property stems from the fact that only finitely many axioms are necessary for describing the class of abstract fork algebras. Notice that the previous reasoning does not apply to relation algebras without a fork operator. The validity of a formula in the algebras of binary relations does not imply its validity in the class of relation algebras (some relation algebras are not representable). This implies that some formulas (for instance derivation steps) that are valid about concrete binary relations are not derivable in the relational calculus. Also, the finiteness of the set of axioms allows to simplify the process of program derivation by using proof assistants. Of course there are other ways to obtain representability of relation algebras without using the fork operator. For instance, relation algebras satisfying the *point axiom* [29] are representable. Since the point axiom is not equational, then adding the fork operator is more appropriate when aiming to an equational calculus.

Regarding the expressiveness of fork algebras, it was proved [19] that first-order theories can be interpreted as equational theories in fork algebras. We present the expressiveness theorem (Thm. 4.3.6 of [11]) without proof. The complete proof appears in [19].

Theorem 2. *There exists a recursive mapping T mapping first-order sentences to fork algebra terms such that for any set of first-order sentences Γ and any first-order sentence α we have*

$$\Gamma \vdash \alpha \iff \{T(\gamma) = \mathbb{T} : \gamma \in \Gamma\} \vdash_\nabla T(\alpha) = \mathbb{T}.$$

The symbol $\vdash_\nabla$ in Thm. 2 is to be understood as provability in equational logic under the theory of abstract fork algebras.

Thm. 2 shows that a wide class of problems (at least those that can be described in first-order logic) can be specified in the equational calculus of fork algebras. Moreover, the abstract relational specification can be obtained algorithmically from the first-order specification by using the mapping T. Once again, this result does not hold when the relational calculus is considered in place of the fork calculus. It was proved by Korselt (the proof was published in [21] in 1915) that first-order properties requiring more than three variables for being expressed do not have suitable translations into the relational calculus. Therefore, the specifications of many computational problems cannot be captured in the relational calculus.

4   Adding program design strategies within the scope of the calculus

In programming in general, examples of design strategies include case analysis, trivialization, divide and conquer, backtracking, and many more [10], [26], [30], [31]. In our methodology, we will use the first-order language of fork algebras to express such design strategies (recall that from Thm. 1 and the discussion after it, formulas from the first-order theory of fork algebras have a standard semantics in terms of binary relations). A trivial example of a design strategy is case analysis (C_A). A problem is said to be solved using this strategy if the domain of the problem can be partitioned, let us say, in k parts $D_1, \ldots, D_k$, and we find k algorithms $A_1, \ldots, A_k$ such that A_i solves the given problem when its domain is restricted to the part D_i. This can be more simply and formally stated by the following formula over relations:

$$C\_A(R, R_1, \ldots, R_k) \iff$$

$$\bigwedge_{1 \leq i < j \leq k} dom\,(R_i) \sqcap dom\,(R_j) = \bot \;\wedge\; R = \bigsqcup_{i=1}^{k} R_i. \qquad (4)$$

The strategy of trivialization ($Triv$) is a particular instance of case analysis where one of the subproblems is assumed to be easy to solve. Easy subproblems are for example those whose solution does not depend on the original problem (non-recursive parts), or for which a solution is at hand. We then have

$$Triv(R, R_0, R_1, \ldots, R_k) \iff C\_A(R, R_0, R_1, \ldots, R_k) \wedge Easy(R_0). \qquad (5)$$

The relations $R_0, R_1, \ldots, R_k$ are usually determined by properties of the problem domain. In general, domains allow for "natural" partitions (empty and nonempty lists, trees of height 1 or greater, etc.). In [26, pp. 201–202], these partitions are obtained by introducing tautologies. Hence, the following heuristic can be used in order to determine relations $R_0, R_1, \ldots, R_k$.

Heuristic 1 Let D be a domain (type) characterized by the partial identity $\mathbb{I}_D$. Assume there are identities $\mathbb{I}_0, \mathbb{I}_1, \ldots, \mathbb{I}_k$ such that $\mathbb{I}_D = \mathbb{I}_0 \sqcup \mathbb{I}_1 \sqcup \cdots \sqcup \mathbb{I}_k$. In order to find the problem (relation) R_i, $1 \leq i \leq k$, define $R_i = \mathbb{I}_i ; R$, provided $Easy(\mathbb{I}_0 ; R)$ holds.

The strategy of recomposition ($Recomp$) is defined by the formula

$$Recomp(R, Split, Q_1, \ldots, Q_k, Join) \iff$$
$$R = Split ; (Q_1 \otimes \cdots \otimes Q_k) ; Join, \qquad (6)$$

where the relations $Split$ and $Join$ stand for programs so that the first one effectively decomposes the data, and the latter combines the results of $Q_1, \ldots, Q_k$ in order to provide a solution for R.

By joining the strategies of recomposition and trivialization, we obtain the following formalization of divide-and-conquer

$$D\&C(R, R_0, Split, Q_1, \ldots, Q_k, Join) \iff$$
$$\exists Q\,(Triv(R, R_0, Q) \;\wedge\; Recomp(Q, Split, Q_1, \ldots, Q_k, Join)), \qquad (7)$$

where the variable R may appear inside some of the terms $Q_1, \ldots, Q_k$, but does not affect the term R_0.

Generally, relations $Q_1, \ldots, Q_k$ will be either $\mathbb{I}$ or the relation R itself. This is supported for example by Smith [30] in his schema of divide-and-conquer algorithms. How to find the parameters for the $D\&C$ strategy is then explained by the following heuristic.

Heuristic 2 Among the relations $Q_1, \ldots, Q_k$, those that will take the value R are obtained by foldings of the definition of R. After no more foldings are possible, the remaining relations are to be set to $\mathbb{I}$. If we are heading correctly towards a divide and conquer algorithm, in this point we should have in front a term that approximately looks like

$$S_0 \,;\, (S_1 \,;\! R \,;\! J_1 \otimes \cdots \otimes S_i \,;\! R \,;\! J_i \otimes T_{i+1} \otimes \cdots \otimes T_k)\,;\, J_0,$$

where R does not occur in any of $T_{i+1}, \ldots, T_k$. The last step is rewriting T_m $(i < m \le k)$ as $S_m \,;\! J_m$, with S_m the "Split" part and J_m the "Join" part. Finally, let $Split := S_0\,;\,(S_1 \otimes \cdots \otimes S_k)$ and $Join := (J_1 \otimes \cdots \otimes J_k)\,;\, J_0$.

Program design strategies are also incorporated, for instance, in KIDS [32,33]. In KIDS, design strategies are specified by first-order theories. This forbids using quantifiers over problems (relations) as in the definition of divide-and-conquer (7). The use of these quantifiers allows: (a) to combine strategies in order to define new ones, and (b) to define strategies in a more natural way. Each strategy comes with an associated explanation about how to construct a program solving the original problem. It is easy to see how the previously given strategies induce the structure of the programs. For example, it is clear from the definition of case analysis that whenever $C\_A(R, R_0, R_1)$ holds, we can infer that $R = R_0 \sqcup R_1$, thus giving a program (equation) of the desired shape solving the problem R. In the same way, when $D\&C(R, R_0, Split, Q_1, \ldots, Q_k, Join)$ holds, we have a program with shape $R = R_0 \;\sqcup\; Split\,;(Q_1 \otimes \cdots \otimes Q_k)\,;Join$ solving R.

Notice that design strategies are in general described by formulas of the form

$$Strat(R, X_1, \ldots, X_n) \quad \iff \quad Strat\_Definition(R, X_1, \ldots, X_n), \quad (8)$$

where $Strat$ is a predicate symbol and $Strat\_Definition$ is a formula (involving the relational variables $R, X_1, \ldots, X_n$) that defines the strategy $Strat$.

Let us denote by $Theory(D_1), \ldots, Theory(D_m)$ the relational specifications [5,6] of the domains of a generic problem GP. Assume that a generic specification $GS(P_1, \ldots, P_k)$ for GP is available. Then, deriving a generic algorithm GA for solving the generic problem GP using a strategy $Strat$ defined as in (8) requires finding relational terms $T_1(P_1, \ldots, P_k), \ldots, T_n(P_1, \ldots, P_k)$ such that

$$Theory(D_1), \ldots, Theory(D_m), GS(P_1, \ldots, P_k) \vdash_{\mathsf{AFA}}$$
$$Strat\_Definition(GP, T_1(P_1, \ldots, P_k), \ldots, T_n(P_1, \ldots, P_k)). \qquad (9)$$

Notice that the algorithms characterized by the strategies are as a matter of fact equations. In order to find terms $T_1(P_1, \ldots, P_k), \ldots, T_n(P_1, \ldots, P_k)$ we will resort to equational reasonings using the axioms of fork algebras, plus equations describing the domains $D_1, \ldots, D_m$ [6,22]. The general strategy we will use for deriving recursive algorithms will be *Unfolding/Folding* [13].

The terms $T_1(P_1, \ldots, P_k), \ldots, T_n(P_1, \ldots, P_k)$ required in (9) and found as described in the previous paragraph, are either algorithms if they have algorithmic meaning, or can be considered as relational specifications of simpler problems. If we add further properties about the parameters $P_1, \ldots, P_k$, then we obtain a more concrete specification S from $GS(P_1, \ldots, P_k)$. If we now derive (using this same methodology) algorithms A_i $(1 \leq i \leq n)$ for the terms $T_i(P_1, \ldots, P_k)$ using the newly added properties, then from the generic algorithm $GA(T_1(P_1, \ldots, P_k), \ldots, T_n(P_1, \ldots, P_k))$ we obtain a more concrete algorithm A (by setting $A := GA(A_1, \ldots, A_n)$) computing the relation specified by S (see Fig. 2).

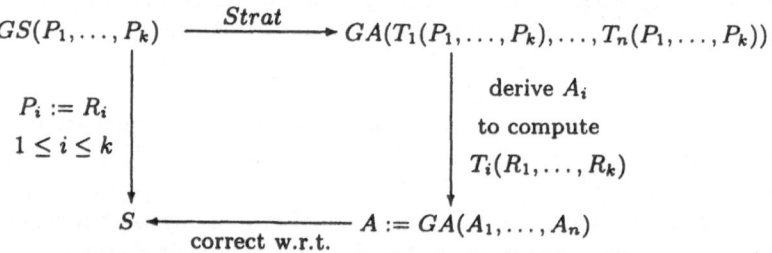

Fig. 2. Derivation of generic and concrete algorithms.

5   A methodology for program construction

In this section we present the outlines of a methodology for program construction based on fork algebras using generic algorithms (program schemes). As we will show in the next section, there is a useful relationship between the structure or form of a generic relational specification and a generic algorithm (a set of parameterized "algorithmic" equations) to compute this specification.

For explaining the methodology, we will assume that a library of generic specifications and generic algorithms derived from those specifications is available. Of course this library can be initially empty, and also several algorithms derived using different strategies can be related to the same specification. Given a new problem P to be solved, the starting point of our method is a formal specification F_P of the problem P. In our case, we will use as the specification language first-order logic with equality because it is a simple formal language that is taught in most computer science courses. The next step is finding a relational specification S for P, as well as choosing a design strategy $Strat$ to be used. In order to obtain S, we can proceed in one of the following two ways. Applying Thm. 2, from the first-order specification F_P and using the mapping T we will obtain a relational term $T(F_P)$ that captures the meaning of problem P. Unfortunately, the term resulting of applying the mapping T is not always very adequate with respect to the process of program derivation. The second method (the one we will use here), consists on reducing the first-order formula F_P into an equation S using the set-theoretical definition of the relational operators. Notice that given a formula, there are many ways in which this reduction can be done.

At this point, two possibilities arise. Either there is a generic problem G whose relational specification GS subsumes S and for which an algorithm GA has been derived according to the strategy $Strat$, or there is not. In the positive case, GS is instantiated in order to make it equivalent to S, and the instantiation is then used to instantiate the generic algorithm GA to a specific algorithm A solving the problem P. If there is a generic specification GS that subsumes S, but no generic algorithm for GS according to the strategy $Strat$, then we recommend deriving a generic algorithm for GS according to the strategy $Strat$, and then proceed as in the first case. The last case is when there is no generic specification subsuming S. In this case (which occurs for example when you try to solve the first problem using the methodology), once a design strategy is chosen, there are mainly two ways to proceed. One way is to derive a specific algorithm A from the specification S according to the strategy $Strat$, and after that generalize both the specification and the derivation as much as possible. The other way is to generalize the specification first and derive a generic algorithm that will later be instantiated to solve the generic problem. The methodology is graphically explained in Fig. 3.

6   Example

In this section we will present a generic problem for which we will proceed as follows.

1. We will specify the problem in first-order logic, in a totally declarative manner.

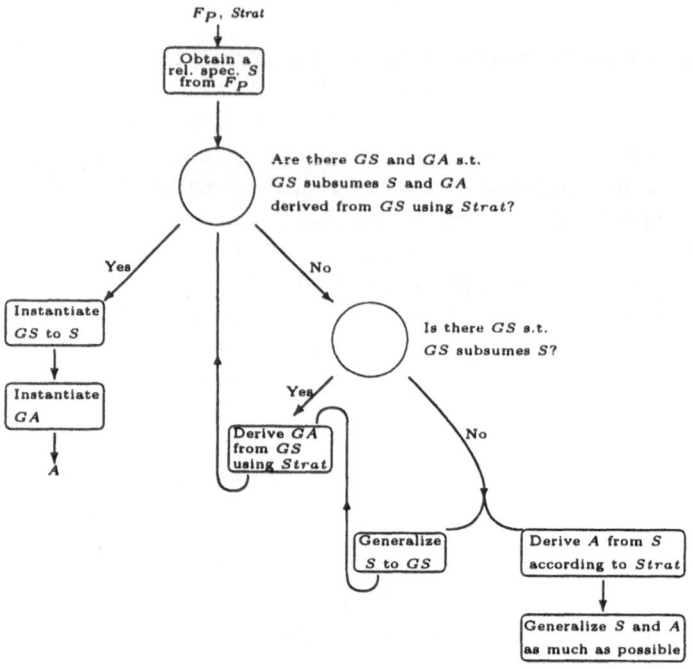

Fig. 3. The methodology for program derivation.

2. We will specify the problem with fork-algebraic equations obtained from the first-order specification.
3. We will derive a generic algorithm for the generic problem using the design strategies presented.
4. We will solve two specific problems by using the generic algorithm.

When a mathematician or computer scientist proves a theorem , she does it using convincing arguments rather than a formal calculus. It is nevertheless essential that these arguments are backed-up by a formal system. Similarly we could derive programs skipping some detail and shorten derivations considerably, but the intention of this paper is rather to show the adequacy of the underlying formalism. Also, these derivations are themselves constructive proofs of correctness of generic programs with respect to generic specifications. In this sense, the amount of effort invested in making (or understanding) complex derivations is largely compensated by their usefulness to design concrete programs. For the examples that will be presented we need to introduce the notion of *generator*. Intuitively, generators decompose structured data into simpler elements. Examples of generators are the relations that retrieve the constituent elements from structured data (elements from lists, sets, trees, etc.) or retrieve substructures (sublists, subsets, subtrees, etc.). Notice that in general generators are not functional.

Notation 1 *We will denote by Hd and Tl the functions that given a list $[e : l]$ retrieve the element e and the list l, respectively. By Cons we denote the function that given an element e and a list l produces as output the list $[e : l]$. By $\mathbb{I}_{L^k}$ we denote the filter over lists of length k, and by $\mathbb{I}_{L \succ k}$ the filter over lists of length greater than k. We will in general denote the constant relation whose output is the value v by C_v.*

For the example we will need the following definition.

Definition 1. A list l is a *contiguous sublist* of a list l' if there exist lists l_1 and l_2 such that $l' = l_1 \ \& \ l \ \& \ l_2$, where & denotes list concatenation.

Let us consider now the following generic problem.

> Given a list l, find the contiguous sublists l' of l satisfying (a) a condition c_1, and (b) l' is f-maximal with respect to all the contiguous sublists of l that satisfy the condition c_1 (f : **List(Int)** $\rightarrow$ **Int**, functional).

If we assume we already have a specification for the generator of contiguous sublists GCS, then the problem is specified by the following first-order formula.

$$l P l' \iff l \, GCS \, l' \wedge c_1(l') \wedge \forall l'' \, (l \, GCS \, l'' \wedge c_1(l'') \ \Rightarrow \ f(l') \succeq f(l'')) . \quad (10)$$

From the first-order specification given in (10), we immediately obtain the following abstract relational specification.

$$P = GCS;C_1 \ \sqcap \ (GCS;C_1 \ \rightarrow \ f;\succeq;f\breve{}) . \quad (11)$$

The generator of contiguous sublists GCS is specified by the following abstract relational equation

$$GCS = \mathbb{I}_{L^1} \ \sqcup \ \mathbb{I}_{L \succ 1};STA \ \sqcup \ \mathbb{I}_{L \succ 1};Tl;GCS, \quad (12)$$

where the relation STA is specified by the recursive equation

$$STA = \mathbb{I}_{L^1} \ \sqcup \ \mathbb{I}_{L \succ 1}; \ \overset{Hd}{\underset{C_{Nil}}{\nabla}} \ ;Cons \ \sqcup \ \mathbb{I}_{L \succ 1}; \ \overset{Hd}{\underset{Tl;STA}{\nabla}} \ ;Cons. \quad (13)$$

Intuitively, the relation STA generates the contiguous sublists that *start* in the head of the list, and thus, the process of generating all the contiguous sublists can be divided between generating the contiguous sublists starting in the head, and generating the contiguous sublists located in the tail of the list.

Since for lists of length zero or one the problem is easy, in order to derive a divide-and-conquer algorithm for this problem it suffices to find relations $Split$, Q_1, Q_2 and $Join$ such that $Recomp\,(\mathbb{I}_{L\succ 1};P, Split, Q_0, Q_1, Join)$ holds. Unfolding the specification of P given in (11),

$$\mathbb{I}_{L\succ 1};P = \mathbb{I}_{L\succ 1};\left(GCS;C_1 \;\sqcap\; \left(GCS;C_1 \;\rightarrow\; f;\succeq;f^{\smile}\right)\right). \tag{14}$$

If we now unfold the definition of GCS (see (12)) in (14), then

$$\mathbb{I}_{L\succ 1};P = (\mathbb{I}_{L\succ 1};STA \;\sqcup\; \mathbb{I}_{L\succ 1};Tl;GCS)\,;C_1$$
$$\sqcap\left((\mathbb{I}_{L\succ 1};STA \;\sqcup\; \mathbb{I}_{L\succ 1};Tl;GCS)\,;C_1 \;\rightarrow\; f;\succeq;f^{\smile}\right)$$
$$= (\mathbb{I}_{L\succ 1};STA;C_1 \;\sqcup\; \mathbb{I}_{L\succ 1};Tl;GCS;C_1)$$
$$\sqcap\left((\mathbb{I}_{L\succ 1};STA;C_1 \;\sqcup\; \mathbb{I}_{L\succ 1};Tl;GCS;C_1) \;\rightarrow\; f;\succeq;f^{\smile}\right).$$

By (2) and elementary Boolean algebra,

$$\mathbb{I}_{L\succ 1};P =$$
$$\mathbb{I}_{L\succ 1};STA;C_1 \;\sqcap\; \left(STA;C_1 \;\rightarrow\; f;\succeq;f^{\smile}\right) \;\sqcap\; \left(Tl;GCS;C_1 \;\rightarrow\; f;\succeq;f^{\smile}\right)$$
$$\sqcup\, \mathbb{I}_{L\succ 1};Tl;GCS;C_1 \;\sqcap\; \left(STA;C_1 \;\rightarrow\; f;\succeq;f^{\smile}\right)$$
$$\sqcap\, \left(Tl;GCS;C_1 \;\rightarrow\; f;\succeq;f^{\smile}\right). \tag{15}$$

Let us consider now the relation $MAXSTA$ defined by the equation

$$MAXSTA = STA;C_1 \;\sqcap\; \left(STA;C_1 \;\rightarrow\; f;\succeq;f^{\smile}\right). \tag{16}$$

We will assume the following:

$Ass_1 : C_1 = \mathbb{I}_{L^1} \;\sqcup\; \mathbb{I}_{L\succ 1};(Cons)^{\smile};(\mathbb{I}\otimes C_1)\,;C_2;Cons$, with $C_2 \sqsubseteq \mathbb{I}$,

$Ass_2 : f = \mathbb{I}_{L^1};C_0 \;\sqcup\; \mathbb{I}_{L\succ 0};(Cons)^{\smile};(g\otimes f);Add$, with $g \subseteq Int \times Int$ a functional relation,

$$Ass_3 :\quad \begin{matrix}\mathbb{I}\\\otimes\\STA;C_1\end{matrix}\;;C_2 = dom\left(\begin{matrix}\mathbb{I}\\\otimes\\MAXSTA\end{matrix}\;;C_2\right);\;\begin{matrix}\mathbb{I}\\\otimes\\STA;C_1\end{matrix}.$$

Hypothesis Ass_1 gives sufficient conditions for computing C_1. Hypothesis Ass_2 provides enough conditions for computing f. Finally, hypothesis Ass_3 gives a sufficient condition for dropping test C_2.

Let us define filters Fi_1 and Fi_2 by the conditions

$$Fi_1 = dom\left((f \otimes f;\preceq);2^{\smile}\right) \qquad \text{and} \qquad Fi_2 = dom\left((f;\preceq \otimes f);2^{\smile}\right).$$

We derived the following generic algorithm for solving problem P (the derivation is not included because of the lack of space):

$$P = \mathbb{I}_{L^1} \;\sqcup\; \mathbb{I}_{L\succ 1};MAXF;(Fi_1;\pi \;\sqcup\; Fi_2;\rho), \tag{17}$$

where $MAXF$ is characterized by the formula

$$D\&C \left(MAXF, \mathbf{I}_{L^2}; \begin{matrix} Hd \\ \nabla \\ Tl \end{matrix} ; \begin{matrix} J_{MAXSTA} \\ \nabla \\ \rho \end{matrix} , \mathbf{I}_{L>2}; \begin{matrix} Hd \\ \nabla \\ Tl \end{matrix} , \mathbf{I}, MAXF, \begin{matrix} \mathbf{I} \\ \otimes; J_{MAXSTA} \\ \pi \\ \nabla \\ \rho; (Fi_1; \pi \sqcup Fi_2; \rho) \end{matrix} \right).$$

(18)

The relation J_{MAXSTA} (the *join* part in a divide-and-conquer solution for $MAXSTA$) is defined by the conditions:

$$D_1 = dom\,(f; \preceq; \mathbb{I}_0), \quad D_2 = dom\,(f; \succeq; \mathbb{I}_0), \text{ and}$$

$$J_{MAXSTA} = C_2; \left(\begin{matrix} \mathbf{I} \\ \otimes \\ D_1; C_{Nil} \end{matrix} \sqcup \begin{matrix} \mathbf{I} \\ \otimes \\ D_2 \end{matrix} \right); Cons \sqcup \neg C_2; \begin{matrix} \mathbf{I} \\ \otimes \\ C_{Nil} \end{matrix}; Cons\,.$$

Formulas (17) and (18) induce the following programs.

```
Function P(l : List(Int)) : List(Int)
Var
    l₁, l₂ : List(Int),
Begin
    If  Length(l) = 1  Then
        ← l
    Else
        ⟨l₁, l₂⟩ ← MAXF(l),
        If   f(l₁) ⪰ f(l₂)  Then
            ← l₁
        Else
            ← l₂
        End If
    End If
End.

Function MAXF(l : List(Int)) : List(Int) × List(Int)
Var
    h : Int,
    t, o₁, o₂, l₁, l₂ : List(Int),
Begin
    If  Length(t) = 2 Then
        h := Hd(l),
        t := Tl(l),
        If  C₂(h, t) Then
            If  f(t) ≤ 0 Then
                o₁ := [h]
            Else
                o₁ := l
            End If
        Else
            o1 := [h]
```

```
        End If
        ← ⟨o₁, t⟩
    Else
        h := Hd(l),
        t := Tl(l),
        ⟨l₁, l₂⟩ := MAXF(t),
        If C₂(h, l₁) Then
            If f(l₁) ≤ 0 Then
                o₁ := [h]
            Else
                o₁ := [h : l₁]
            End If
        Else
            o₁ := [h]
        End If
        If f(l₁) ≿ f(l₂) Then
            o₂ := l₁
        Else
            o₂ := l₂
        End If
        ← ⟨o₁, o₂⟩,
    End If
End.
```

In the remaining part of this section we will derive algorithms for solving two problems whose specifications are instances of the generic problem P. The problems that we will use as examples are related to problems already studied in the literature. The first problem consists on finding the sublist with maximum sum. In [31] a divide-and-conquer algorithm for solving this problem is derived. The second problem consists on finding the longest plateau. An algorithm solving a weakened version of this problem – the input list is assumed to be sorted – is derived in [20] using the predicate transformer wp (weakest precondition).

6.1   Finding the contiguous sublists of maximum sum

The problem of finding a contiguous sublist of maximum sum was treated as a case study in [31]. In there, a divide-and-conquer algorithm is derived for solving this specific problem. The problem is informally specified as follows.

> Given a list l having integer numbers as elements, find a contiguous sublist of l with maximum sum.

This problem has a clear first-order specification given by the formula:

$$l\,MAXSUM\,l' \iff l\,GCS\,l' \wedge \forall l''\,(l\,GCS\,l'' \Rightarrow Sum(l') \succeq Sum(l'')),\quad (19)$$

where $Sum \subseteq List(Int) \times Int$ computes the sum of the elements of the list given as input. A relational specification for $MAXSUM$ is given by the following equation:

$$MAXSUM = GCS \sqcap \left(GCS \rightarrow Sum; \succeq; Sum^{\smile}\right). \tag{20}$$

If we take $C_1 := \mathbb{I}_{L^\bullet}$, then (20) has the same shape as (11). Assumptions Ass_1 and Ass_2 trivially hold. Regarding Ass_3, notice that

$$(\mathbb{I} \otimes STA; C_1); C_2 = (\mathbb{I} \otimes STA; \mathbb{I}); \mathbb{I} = (\mathbb{I} \otimes STA).$$

Notice also that since $dom\,(MAXSTA) = \mathbb{I}_{L \geq 1}$,

$$dom \begin{pmatrix} \mathbb{I} \\ \otimes & ; C_2 \\ MAXSTA \end{pmatrix} = dom \begin{pmatrix} \mathbb{I} \\ \otimes \\ MAXSTA \end{pmatrix} = \begin{matrix} \mathbb{I} \\ \otimes \\ \mathbb{I}_{L \geq 1} \end{matrix}.$$

Then,

$$dom \begin{pmatrix} \mathbb{I} \\ \otimes & ; C_2 \\ MAXSTA \end{pmatrix}; \begin{matrix} \mathbb{I} \\ \otimes \\ STA; C_1 \end{matrix} = \begin{matrix} \mathbb{I} \\ \otimes \\ \mathbb{I}_{L \geq 1} \end{matrix}; \begin{matrix} \mathbb{I} \\ \otimes \\ STA \end{matrix} = \begin{matrix} \mathbb{I} \\ \otimes \\ STA \end{matrix},$$

and Ass_3 holds.

If we now instantiate the relational algorithms given in (18) and (17), we have

$$MAXSUM = \mathbb{I}_{L^1} \sqcup \mathbb{I}_{L > 1}; MAXF; (Fi_1; \pi \sqcup Fi_2; \rho), \tag{21}$$

where

$$Fi_1 = dom \begin{pmatrix} Sum \\ \otimes & ; 2^{\smile} \\ Sum; \preceq \end{pmatrix} \quad \text{and} \quad Fi_2 = dom \begin{pmatrix} Sum; \preceq \\ \otimes & ; 2^{\smile} \\ Sum \end{pmatrix}.$$

The relation $MAXF$ is defined by

$$MAXF = \mathbb{I}_{L \geq 2};$$

$$\begin{matrix} Hd \\ \nabla; \\ Tl \end{matrix} \left[\begin{matrix} \mathbb{I} & J_{MAXSTA} \\ \otimes; & \nabla \\ \mathbb{I}_{L^1} & \rho \end{matrix} \sqcup \begin{matrix} \mathbb{I} \\ \otimes; \\ \mathbb{I}_{L>1} \end{matrix} \begin{matrix} \mathbb{I} \\ \otimes \\ MAXF \end{matrix}; \begin{pmatrix} \mathbb{I} \\ \otimes; J_{MAXSTA} \\ \pi \\ \nabla \\ \rho; (Fi_1; \pi \sqcup Fi_2; \rho) \end{pmatrix} \right], \tag{22}$$

where

$$J_{MAXSTA} = \begin{pmatrix} \mathbb{I} \\ \otimes \\ dom\,(Sum; \preceq; \mathbb{I}_0); C_{Nil} \end{pmatrix} \sqcup \begin{matrix} \mathbb{I} \\ \otimes \\ dom\,(Sum; \succeq; \mathbb{I}_0) \end{matrix}; Cons.$$

Equations (21) and (22) correspond to the algorithms below.

Function $MAXSUM(l : \text{List(Int)}) : \text{List(Int)}$
Var
    $l_1, l_2 : \text{List(Int)}$
Begin
   If $Length(l) = 1$ **Then**
     $\leftarrow l$
   Else
     $\langle l_1, l_2 \rangle := MAXS(l)$
     If $Sum(l_1) \succeq Sum(l_2)$ **Then**
       $\leftarrow l_1$
     Else
       $\leftarrow l_2$
     End If
   End If
End.

Function $MAXS$ is obtained by substituting Sum for f in function $MAXF$.

6.2   Finding the longest plateau

The problem we will solve in this section is a strengthened version of a problem used as example in [20]. Given a sorted list (the list being sorted is an assumption that simplifies solving the problem considerably), we look for the longest *plateau*, i.e., the longest contiguous sublist of the input list whose elements were all the same. We will drop the assumption of the input list being sorted, and will derive an algorithm for finding the longest plateau in an arbitrary list of integers. The problem is informally specified by the following sentence.

Given a list l, find the longest plateau p in l.

The problem is specified by the following first-order formula:

$$l\,LPLATEAU\,p \quad \Longleftrightarrow \quad l\,GCS\,p \,\wedge\, Plateau(p)$$
$$\wedge\, \forall p'\,(l\,GCS\,p' \wedge Plateau(p') \;\Rightarrow\; Length(p) \succeq Length(p')), \qquad (23)$$

where the unary predicate *Plateau* is defined by the formula

$$Plateau(p) \quad \Longleftrightarrow \quad \forall x \forall y\,(p\,Has\,x \wedge p\,Has\,y \;\Rightarrow\; x = y).$$

A relational specification for the problem *LPLATEAU* (obtained from (23)) is given by the equation

$$LPLATEAU = $$
$$GCS;Plateau \,\sqcap\, \left(GCS;Plateau \;\rightarrow\; Length;\succeq;Length^{\smile} \right), \qquad (24)$$

where the relation *Plateau* is defined by the recursive equation

$$Plateau = \mathbb{I}_{L \leq 1} \sqcup \mathbb{I}_{L > 1}; (Cons)\check{}\; ; \begin{array}{c} \mathbb{I} \\ \otimes \\ Plateau \end{array} ; dom \begin{pmatrix} \mathbb{I} \\ \otimes \; ; 2\check{} \\ Hd \end{pmatrix} ; Cons.$$

Notice that Eq. (24) has the same shape as Eq. (11). It is not difficult to check that defining

$$C_1 = Plateau \qquad \text{and} \qquad C_2 = \begin{array}{c} \mathbb{I} \\ \otimes \\ \mathbb{I}_{L^0} \end{array} \sqcup dom \begin{pmatrix} \mathbb{I} \\ \otimes \; ; 2\check{} \\ Hd \end{pmatrix},$$

Ass_1–Ass_3 are true.

If we now instantiate the relational algorithms given in (18) and (17),

$$LPLATEAU = \mathbb{I}_{L^1} \sqcup \mathbb{I}_{L \geq 1}; MAXF; (Fi_1; \pi \sqcup Fi_2; \rho), \qquad (25)$$

where

$$Fi_1 = dom \begin{pmatrix} Length \\ \otimes \; ; 2\check{} \\ Length; \preceq \end{pmatrix} \quad \text{and} \quad Fi_2 = dom \begin{pmatrix} Length; \preceq \\ \otimes \; ; 2\check{} \\ Length \end{pmatrix}.$$

The relation *MAXF* is defined by

$$MAXF =$$

$$\begin{array}{c} Hd \\ \mathbb{I}_{L \geq 2}; \nabla \; ; \\ Tl \end{array} \left[\begin{array}{cccc} \mathbb{I} & J_{MAXSTA} \\ \otimes \; ; & \nabla \\ \mathbb{I}_{L^1} & \rho \end{array} \; \sqcup \begin{array}{cc} \mathbb{I} & \mathbb{I} \\ \otimes \; ; & \otimes \\ \mathbb{I}_{L > 1} & MAXF \end{array} ; \begin{pmatrix} \mathbb{I} \\ \otimes \; ; J_{MAXSTA} \\ \pi \\ \nabla \\ \rho; (D_3; \pi \sqcup D_4; \rho) \end{pmatrix} \right], \qquad (26)$$

where

$$J_{MAXSTA} =$$

$$C_2; \begin{pmatrix} \mathbb{I} \\ \otimes \\ dom\,(Length; \preceq; \mathbb{I}_0)\,; C_{Nil} \end{pmatrix} \sqcup \begin{array}{c} \mathbb{I} \\ \otimes \\ dom\,(Length; \succeq; \mathbb{I}_0) \end{array} ; Cons$$

$$\sqcup \; \neg C_2; \begin{array}{c} \mathbb{I} \\ \otimes \\ C_{Nil} \end{array} ; Cons.$$

Notice that $dom\,(Length; \preceq; \mathbb{I}_0) = \mathbb{I}_{L^0}$ and $dom\,(Length; \succeq; \mathbb{I}_0) = \mathbb{I}_{L \geq 0}$. Then

$$J_{MAXSTA} = C_2; \begin{pmatrix} \mathbb{I} & \mathbb{I} \\ \otimes & \sqcup & \otimes \\ \mathbb{I}_{L^0} & \mathbb{I}_{L \geq 0} \end{pmatrix} ; Cons \sqcup \neg C_2; \begin{array}{c} \mathbb{I} \\ \otimes \\ C_{Nil} \end{array} ; Cons$$

$$= C_2; \begin{array}{c} \mathbb{I} \\ \otimes \\ \mathbb{I}_{L \geq 0} \end{array} ; Cons \sqcup \neg C_2; \begin{array}{c} \mathbb{I} \\ \otimes \\ C_{Nil} \end{array} ; Cons.$$

Since $C_2 = \begin{matrix}\mathbb{I}\\\otimes\\\mathbb{I}_{L^0}\end{matrix} \sqcup dom\begin{pmatrix}\mathbb{I}\\\otimes\ ;2^\smallsmile\\Hd\end{pmatrix}$, $\neg C_2 = \begin{matrix}\mathbb{I}\\\otimes\\\mathbb{I}_{L>0}\end{matrix} ;\neg dom\begin{pmatrix}\mathbb{I}\\\otimes\ ;2^\smallsmile\\Hd\end{pmatrix}$. Then,

$$\begin{matrix}\mathbb{I}\\\otimes\\\mathbb{I}_{L^1}\end{matrix} ;J_{MAXSTA} =$$

$$\begin{matrix}\mathbb{I}\\\otimes\\\mathbb{I}_{L^1}\end{matrix} ;\underbrace{\left(dom\begin{pmatrix}\mathbb{I}\\\otimes\ ;2^\smallsmile\\Hd\end{pmatrix} \sqcup \neg dom\begin{pmatrix}\mathbb{I}\\\otimes\ ;2^\smallsmile\\Hd\end{pmatrix} ;\begin{matrix}\mathbb{I}\\\otimes\\C_{Nil}\end{matrix}\right)}_{T} ;Cons. \qquad (27)$$

Notice also that

$$(\mathbb{I}\otimes\mathbb{I}_{L>0}) ;J_{MAXSTA} = (\mathbb{I}\otimes\mathbb{I}_{L>0}) ;T. \qquad (28)$$

Thus, by (3), (27) and (28),

$$MAXF =$$
$$\begin{matrix}Hd\\\mathbb{I}_{L\geq2}; \nabla ;\\Tl\end{matrix}\left[\begin{matrix}\mathbb{I}\ \mathbb{I}\\\otimes ;\nabla\\\mathbb{I}_{L^1}\ \rho\end{matrix}\ \sqcup\ \begin{matrix}\mathbb{I}\\\otimes ;\\\mathbb{I}_{L>1}\end{matrix}\ \begin{matrix}\mathbb{I}\\\otimes\\MAXF\end{matrix} ;\begin{pmatrix}\mathbb{I}\\\otimes\\\pi\\\nabla\\\rho;(D_3;\pi \sqcup D_4;\rho)\end{pmatrix}\right]\begin{matrix}T\\;\otimes.\\\mathbb{I}\end{matrix} \qquad (29)$$

Equations (25) and (29) correspond to the algorithms below.

Function $LPLATEAU(l : \text{List(Int)}) : \text{List(Int)}$
Var
    $l_1, l_2 : \text{List(Int)}$
Begin
   If $Length(l) = 1$ **Then**
     $\leftarrow l$
   Else
     $\langle l_1, l_2\rangle := MAXF(l)$
     If $Length(l_1)\succeq Length(l_2)$ **Then**
       $\leftarrow l_1$
     Else
       $\leftarrow l_2$
     End If
   End If
End.

Function $MAXF(l : \text{List(Int)}) : \text{List(Int)} \times \text{List(Int)}$
Var
    $h : \text{Int}$
    $t, o_1, o_2, l_1, l_2 : \text{List(Int)}$
Begin

```
    h := Hd(l)
    t := Tl(l)
    If Length(t) = 1 Then
        o₂ := t
        l₁ := t
    Else
        ⟨l₁, l₂⟩ := MAXF(t)
        If Length(l₁) ⪰ Length(l₂) Then
            o₂ := l₁
        Else
            o₂ := l₂
        End If
    End If
    If h = Hd(l₁) Then
        o₁ := [h : l₁]
    Else
        o₁ := [h]
    End If
End.
```

7   Comparison with previous work

The notion of generic algorithm is not new. Already in 1985 the wide spectrum language CIP-L [3] allowed to work with *program schemes*. Also, program design strategies were incorporated as *transformation rules*. The advantage of our calculus is its completeness, which leads to a theorem showing that given any two program schemes P_1 and P_2 with the same semantics, it is possible to derive their equivalence.

In [24,27,28] a framework for program construction based on an *algebra of formal languages* is presented. In [28] these algebras are used for deriving generic algorithms for the treatment of graphs. The operators from the algebras are defined in set-theory using variables over "*words*" besides variables over languages. From these set-theoretical definitions, the author derives some valid properties only involving variables that range over formal languages, but, opposed to the fork algebra case, there is no proof of whether these properties axiomatize the algebras or not. Also, variables ranging over words are used in proofs (something that is avoided in fork algebras by using only variables over relations), and reasoning in set-theory is carried on.

In [30,31] some strategies are presented aiming to help in the design of divide-and-conquer algorithms. A program scheme describing an arbitrary divide-and-conquer algorithm is given, and the strategies are used for finding the adequate program pieces. Notice that since no complete calculus is given, then the author reasons in first-order logic using variables over individuals. This can be avoided in fork algebras. Also, the lack of such calculus makes the author to find some of the missing parts using his intuition. This can be seen for example in the derivation of the *MIN* algorithm in [30] p. 45–46, where the *Split* operator and the subproblems *Id* and *MIN* are fixed by hand, and the *Join* part is derived. In our case, once the generator is fixed (something we believe equivalent to choosing the *Split* operator), the subproblems *Id* and *MIN* are found by unfolding and folding in fork algebras, and the *Join* is obtained in the process of satisfying the predicate *D&C*.

In [10] an approach similar to ours is presented. Relations are not introduced in an algebraic manner, but rather using *allegories* [15], a concept from category theory. Emphasis is also placed on algorithm design strategies, but, unlike the case in fork algebras, the strategies fall out of the scope of the calculus. Algorithm design strategies are described in plain English, making reference to the shape of specifications. Even though formulas as the ones used in the fork calculus for describing strategies fall within the mathematical language adopted in [10], there is an important difference that must be emphasized. An essential characteristic of the fork calculus is the representability theorem for fork algebras (Thm. 1). This theorem guarantees that first-order formulas describing strategies have a natural semantics in terms of binary relations. The corresponding theorem for the categorical framework is weaker, since it is only applied to Horn clauses. In the fork algebraic case, moving from an equational calculus to a first-order calculus allowed to include the strategies within the syntactic calculus. Thus, a specification using the methodology proposed in this paper will include the design strategies chosen, and several design strategies can be combined in a specification at a formal level. A feature that also distinguishes both frameworks is the background required for mastering the process of program construction. While in the categorical framework a fairly non-trivial amount of category theory is required, in the fork algebraic framework only first-order logic, equational reasoning and basic set-theory for understanding binary relations is required.

8   Conclusions

We have presented a calculus for program construction based on fork algebras that has some very nice features. First, the calculus is point free and complete with regards to the standard semantics chosen. Second, generic problems (rather than particular ones) are specified and programs solving the whole classes can be derived. Third, the calculus allows for a formal description of algorithm design strategies. Summing up, we have described a methodology for program construction within this calculus.

References

1. Backhouse R.C., de Bruin P.J., Malcolm G., Voermans E. and van der Woude J. (1991) Relational Catamorphisms. In: B. Möller (Ed.) Constructing Programs from Specifications, North Holland, 287–318

2. Backhouse R.C. and Hoogendijk P. (1993) Elements of a Relational Theory of Datatypes. Formal Program Development, IFIP TC2/WG 2.1 State-of-the-Art Report, LNCS 755, Springer–Verlag, 7–42
3. Bauer F.L., Berghammer R., Broy M., Dosch W., Geiselbrechtinger F., Gnatz R., Hangel E., Hesse W., Krieg–Brückner B., Laut A., Matzner T., Möller B., Nickl F., Partsch H., Pepper P., Samelson K., Wirsing M. and Wössner H. (1985) The Wide Spectrum Language CIP–L, LNCS 183, Springer–Verlag
4. Baum G.A., Frias M.F., Haeberer A.M. and Martínez López P.E. (1996) From Specifications to Programs: A Fork–algebraic Approach to Bridge the Gap. In: Proceedings of MFCS'96, LNCS 1113, Springer-Verlag, 180–191
5. Berghammer R., Gritzner T.F. and Schmidt G. (1993) Prototyping Relational Specifications Using Higher-Order Objects. In: Heering J., Meinke K., Möller B. and Nipkow T. (Eds.), Higher-Order Algebra, Logic and Term Rewriting, 1st. International Workshop, HOA'93, LNCS 816, Springer–Verlag, 56–75
6. Berghammer R. and Schmidt G. (1993) Relational Specifications. In: Rauszer C. (Ed.), Algebraic Logic, Banach Center Publications 28, Polish Academy of Sciences
7. Berghammer R. and von Karger B. Algorithms from Relational Specifications. Chapter 9 of [11]
8. Bird R. (1986) Transformational Programming and the Paragraph Problem. Science of Computer Programming, 6(2):159–189
9. Bird R. and de Moor O. (1993) List Partitions. Formal Aspects of Computing, 5(1):67–78
10. Bird R. and de Moor O. (1997) Algebra of Programming. Prentice Hall
11. Brink C., Kahl W. and Schmidt G. (Eds.) (1997) Relational Methods in Computer Science. Springer Wien–New York
12. Burstall R.M. and Darlilngton J. (1977) A Transformation System for Developing Recursive Programs. Journal of the ACM, 24(1):44–67
13. Darlington J. (1975) Applications of Program Transformation to Program Synthesis. In: Proceedings of the International Symposium on Proving and Improving Programs, Arc-et-Senans, France, July 1-3, 133–144
14. Doornbos H., van Gasteren N. and Backhouse R.C. (1997) Programs and Datatypes. Chapter 10 of [11]
15. Freyd P.J. and Ščedrov A. (1990) Categories, Allegories. Mathematical Library 39, North Holland
16. Frias M.F., Baum G.A. and Haeberer A.M. (1996) Adding Design Strategies to Fork Algebras. In: Perspectives of System Informatics, LNCS 1181, 214–226
17. Frias M.F., Baum G.A. and Haeberer A.M. (1998) Representability and Program Construction within Fork Algebras. Logic Journal of the IGPL, 6(2):229–259
18. Frias M.F., Baum G.A. and Haeberer A.M. (1997) Fork Algebras in Algebra, Logic and Computer Science. Fundamenta Informaticae, 32:1–25
19. Frias M.F. and Orłowska E. (1998) Equational Reasoning in Non–Classical Logics. Journal of Applied Non Classical Logic, 8(1–2),.
20. Gries D. (1981) The Science of Programming. Texts and Monographs in Computer Science, Springer–Verlag
21. Löwenheim L. (1915) Uber Möglichkeiten im Relativkalkul. Mathematische Annalen 76:447–470
22. Martínez–López P.E. and Baum G.A. (1998) Fork Algebraic Datatypes. Logic Journal of the IGPL, 6(4):531–543

23. Meertens L. (1987) Algorithmics - Toward Programming as a Mathematical Activity. In: De Bakker J.W., Hazewinkel M. and Lenstra J.K. (Eds.) Mathematics and Computer Science, Vol. 1 of CWI Monographs, 3–42, North Holland
24. Möller B. (1991) Relations as a Program Development Calculus. In: Möller B. (Ed.) Constructing Programs from Specifications, North–Holland, 373–397
25. Möller B. (1993) Derivation of Graph and Pointer Algorithms. Formal Program Development, IFIP TC2/WG 2.1 State-of-the-Art Report, LNCS 755, Springer–Verlag, 123–160
26. Partsch H.A. (1990) Specification and Transformation of Programs. A Formal Approach to Software Development. Texts and Monographs in Computer Science, Springer–Verlag
27. Russling M. (1996) Deriving a Class of Layer-Oriented Graph Algorithms. Science of Computer Programming, 26:117–132
28. Russling M. (1996) Deriving General Schemes for Classes of Graph Algorithms, AMNS 13, Augsburg
29. Schmidt G. and Ströhlein T. (1985) Relation Algebras – Concept of Points and Representability. Discrete Mathematics, 54:83–92
30. Smith D.R. (1985) Top-Down Synthesis of Divide-and-Conquer Algorithms. Artificial Intelligence, 27:43–96
31. Smith, D.R. (1987) Applications of a Strategy for Designing Divide-and-Conquer Algorithms. Science of Computer Programming, 8:213–229
32. Smith D.R. (1990) KIDS: A Semi–Automatic Program Development System. IEEE Transactions on Software Engineering, Special Issue on Formal Methods, September
33. Smith D.R. (1991) KIDS – A Knowledge–Based Software Development System. In: Automating Software Design AAA/MIT Press, 483–514

Chapter 4
Processes as Relations

Michael Winter[1] and Peter Kempf[2]

[1] Department of Computer Science
University of the Federal Armed Forces Munich
85577 Neubiberg, Germany
thrash@informatik.unibw-muenchen.de
[2] Razorsis
Bleichenbrücke 10
20354 Hamburg, Germany
peter.kempf@razorsis.de

Abstract. In this paper we give a relation-algebraic model of processes. All standard operations (including parallel composition/interleaving) of the Calculus of Communicating Systems CCS are interpreted by purely relational terms without any inductive methods. We also introduce the notion of a relational bisimulation which leads to a canonical representative of a bisimulation-class of processes.
Keywords: process calculi, bisimulation, CCS, relational semantics

1 Introduction

The standard model for the Calculus of Communicating Systems CCS is the synchronization tree model [4,8], i.e., operational trees modulo bisimulation. One of the drawbacks of this approach is that there is no canonical representative of a bisimulation class and that the definition of interleaving requires inductive methods.

Our relational approach introduces a category of transition graphs with graph homomorphisms. On this category a notion of bisimulation is established, and it is proven that a bisimulation class, seen as a subcategory, has a terminal object which serves as a canonical representative of this class. We will interpret the standard operations of CCS: prefixing, relabelling, hiding, sum, interleaving by purely relational methods as functors on our category. Every process term $P[X]$ has therefore an associated functor $F(X)$. The semantics of a recursive process definition $X = P[X]$ is defined to be the terminal object of the bisimulation class of the final F-coalgebra.

The paper is structured as follows: Based on some fundamentals on heterogeneous relation algebras introduced in the second section we define a category $\mathcal{G}$ of labelled graphs and graph homomorphisms over a given relation algebra in Section 3.

A main contribution of this paper is the introduction of the notion of a relational bisimulation on $\mathcal{G}$ in Section 4. It is proven by purely relational means that every equivalence class of bisimilar graphs has a terminal representative.

In Section 5 we define the standard operations of process calculi as suitable functors on this category. Thereby, the interleaving functor $| : \mathcal{G} \times \mathcal{G} \to \mathcal{G}$ corresponding to the parallel composition of two processes is defined without any inductive methods (e.g. using the expansion law [4]). Furthermore, we show that the transition rules associated with each operation are satisfied.

For the reason of brevity it is not possible to prove all theorems in this paper. We only give the idea, and for the details we refer to [10]. Furthermore, we assume that the reader is familiar with basic notions of the theory of heterogeneous relation algebras and allegories (cf. [2,5,7]). We use the notation from [5].

2   Heterogeneous relation algebras

In this section we recall some fundamentals on heterogeneous relation algebras.

Definition 1. A (heterogeneous abstract) relation algebra is a locally small category $\mathcal{R}$ consisting of a class $\mathrm{Obj}_\mathcal{R}$ of objects and a set $\mathcal{R}[A, B]$ of morphisms for all $A, B \in \mathrm{Obj}_\mathcal{R}$ (we also use the notation $R : A \leftrightarrow B$ to indicate that $R \in \mathcal{R}[A, B]$). The morphisms are usually called relations. Composition is denoted by ";" and identities are denoted by $\mathbb{I}_A \in \mathcal{R}[A, A]$. In addition, there is a totally defined unary operation $\check{}_{AB} : \mathcal{R}[A, B] \longrightarrow \mathcal{R}[B, A]$ between the sets of morphisms, called conversion. The operations satisfy the following rules:

1. Every set $\mathcal{R}[A, B]$ carries the structure of a complete atomic boolean algebra with operations $\sqcup_{AB}, \sqcap_{AB}, \overline{}_{AB}$, zero element $\bot\!\!\!\bot_{AB}$, universal element $\top\!\!\top_{AB}$, and inclusion ordering $\sqsubseteq_{AB}$.
2. The Schröder equivalences

$$Q; R \sqsubseteq_{AC} S \iff Q\check{}; \overline{S} \sqsubseteq_{BC} \overline{R} \iff \overline{S}; R\check{} \sqsubseteq_{AB} \overline{Q}$$

   hold for relations $Q : A \leftrightarrow B, R : B \leftrightarrow C$ and $S : A \leftrightarrow C$.
3. The Tarski rule

$$R \neq \bot\!\!\!\bot_{AB} \implies \top\!\!\top_{CA}; R; \top\!\!\top_{BD} = \top\!\!\top_{CD}$$

   holds for all $R \in \mathcal{R}[A, B]$ and $C, D \in \mathrm{Obj}_\mathcal{R}$.

All the indices of elements and operations are usually omitted for brevity and can easily be reinvented.

One might ask for the greatest solution of $Q; X \sqsubseteq R$. Using the Schröder equivalences one gets $X = \overline{Q\check{}; \overline{R}}$. This operation is called the right residual. By duality one defines the left residual

$$Q \backslash R := \overline{Q\check{}; \overline{R}}, \qquad S/T := \overline{\overline{T}; S\check{}}.$$

A symmetric version of the residuals is the symmetric quotient

$$\mathrm{syQ}(Q, R) := Q\backslash R \sqcap Q^{\smile}/R^{\smile}.$$

By definition this relation is the greatest solution of the inclusions $Q; X \sqsubseteq R$ and $X; R^{\smile} \sqsubseteq Q^{\smile}$.

As usual we define the concept of mappings.

Definition 2. A relation $R \in \mathcal{R}[A, B]$ is called

1. univalent (or partial function) iff $R^{\smile}; R \sqsubseteq \mathbb{I}_B$,
2. total iff $\mathbb{I}_A \sqsubseteq R; R^{\smile}$,
3. injective iff $R^{\smile}$ is univalent,
4. surjective iff $R^{\smile}$ is total,
5. a mapping iff it is univalent and total.

We also use the notation $f : A \rightarrow B$ to indicate that f is a mapping in $\mathcal{R}[A, B]$.

If $Q : A \leftrightarrow B$ is univalent the equation $(R \sqcap S; Q^{\smile}); Q = R; Q \sqcap S$ is valid for suitable R and S, and if Q is total we have $Q; \mathbb{T}_{BC} = \mathbb{T}_{AC}$. A proof of these properties can be found in [7].

Another important class of relations are equivalence relations.

Definition 3. A relation $R \in \mathcal{R}[A, A]$ is called

1. reflexive iff $\mathbb{I}_A \sqsubseteq A$,
2. symmetric iff $R^{\smile} \sqsubseteq R$,
3. transitive iff $R; R \sqsubseteq R$,
4. idempotent iff $R; R = R$,
5. an equivalence relation iff it is reflexive, transitive and symmetric.

The reflexive and transitive closure R^* of a relation R is defined as the least relation containing R which is both reflexive and transitive. It may be computed by $R^* = \bigsqcup_{i \in \mathbb{N}} R^i$ where $R^i := R; \ldots ; R$ (i times).

We now introduce the notion of unit objects which are the abstract version of singleton sets.

Definition 4. An object I is called a unit iff $\mathbb{I}_I$ is the greatest morphism in $\mathcal{R}[I, I]$ and for every object A there is at least one total morphism in $\mathcal{R}[A, I]$. $\mathcal{R}$ is called unitary iff it has a unit.

The unit I may also be characterized as a terminal object in the subcategory of mappings, and is, hence, unique up to isomorphism. Following the categorical notion of elements, we define a point as follows.

Definition 5. A mapping $x : I \rightarrow A$ is called a point.

One might be interested in the set of all points included in an arbitrary relation. The so-called point axiom guarantees that this set is not empty. It may be formulated as follows:

Point Axiom: *For every relation $Q \neq \bot$ there are two points x, y such that $x^{\smile}; y \sqsubseteq Q$.*

Notice, that the point axiom implies representability [6].

The relational description of pairing is the relational product [5,7]. This construction corresponds to the categorical product in the subcategory of mappings.

Definition 6. An object $A \times B$ together with two relations $\pi \in \mathcal{R}[A \times B, A]$ and $\rho \in \mathcal{R}[A \times B, B]$ is called a relational product of A and B iff

$$\pi^{\smile}; \pi = \mathbb{I}_A, \qquad \rho^{\smile}; \rho = \mathbb{I}_B,$$
$$\pi^{\smile}; \rho = \mathbb{T}_{AB}, \qquad \pi; \pi^{\smile} \sqcap \rho; \rho^{\smile} = \mathbb{I}_{A \times B}.$$

$\mathcal{R}$ has relational products iff for every pair of objects the relational product exists.

The relational product of two objects is unique (up to isomorphism) [11]. We use the following notations

$$<P, Q> := P; \pi^{\smile} \sqcap Q; \rho^{\smile}, \qquad R \times S := <\pi; R, \rho; S>,$$

whenever the projections exist. It is easy to see that

$$<P, Q>; <R, S>^{\smile} \sqsubseteq P; R^{\smile} \sqcap Q; S^{\smile}.$$

The validity of the converse inclusion is called the sharpness problem of relational products. A set of sufficient conditions for sharpness can be found in [1]. Notice, that sharpness implies the following equalities

$$<P, Q>; (R \times S) = <P; R, Q; S>,$$
$$(P \times Q); (R \times S) = (P; R \times Q; S).$$

However, if P is total we have

$$<P, Q>; \rho = P; \pi^{\smile}; \rho \sqcap Q = P; \mathbb{T} \sqcap Q = Q$$

and analogously $<P, Q>; \pi = P$ if Q is total.

The relational description of disjoint unions is the relational sum [5,11]. This construction corresponds to the categorical product[1]. Here we want to generalize this concept to not necessarily finite sets of objects.

---

[1] By conversion, a relation algebra is self-dual. Therefore a product is also a co-product and hence a biproduct.

Definition 7. Let $\{A_i \mid i \in I\}$ be a set of objects indexed by a set I. An object $\sum_{i \in I} A_i$ together with relations $\iota_j \in \mathcal{R}[A_j, \sum_{i \in I} A_i]$ for all $j \in I$ is called a relational sum of $\{A_i \mid i \in I\}$ iff for all $i, j \in I$ with $i \neq j$ the following holds

$$\iota_i; \breve{\iota_i} = \mathbb{I}_{A_i}, \qquad \iota_i; \breve{\iota_j} = \perp\!\!\!\perp_{A_i A_j}, \qquad \bigsqcup_{i \in I} \breve{\iota_i}; \iota_i = \mathbb{I}_{\sum_{i \in I} A_i}.$$

$\mathcal{R}$ has relational sums iff for every set of objects the relational sum does exist.

For a set of two objects $\{A, B\}$ this definition corresponds to usual the definition of the relational sum. We use the following notations

$$\bigvee_{i \in I} P_i := \bigsqcup_{i \in I} \breve{\iota_i}; P_i, \qquad \sum_{i \in I} R_i := \bigvee_{i \in I} R_i; \iota_i,$$

whenever the injections exist. In the binary case we also write ι, κ instead of ι_1, ι_2, $[P_1, P_2]$ instead of $\bigvee_{i \in \{1,2\}} P_i$ and $R_1 + R_2$ instead of $\sum_{i \in \{1,2\}} R_i$. It is easy to verify that

$$\iota_j; \bigvee_{i \in I} P_i = P_j, \qquad\qquad \iota_j; \sum_{i \in I} R_i = R_j; \iota_j,$$

$$(\bigvee_{i \in I} P_i); Q = \bigvee_{i \in I} P_i; Q, \qquad (\sum_{i \in I} R_i); (\bigvee_{i \in I} P_i) = \bigvee_{i \in I} R_i; P_i.$$

As known, categorical products and hence relational sums are unique up to isomorphism. Furthermore, every relation algebra may be embedded into one with relational sums (cf. [2,9]).

As in set theory, relational products distribute over arbitrary sums. The induced isomorphism is defined by

$$\text{distr} := <\bigvee_{i \in I} \pi_i, \sum_{i \in I} \rho_i> : \sum_{i \in I} A \times B_i \to A \times \sum_{i \in I} B_i.$$

Given a symmetric idempotent (also known as a partial equivalence relation) one might consider the object of (existing) equivalence classes and the corresponding partial function mapping each element to its equivalence class.

Definition 8. A relation $S : A \leftrightarrow A$ is called a split iff there is an object B and a relation $R : B \leftrightarrow A$ such that

$$R^{\smile}; R = S, \qquad R; R^{\smile} = \mathbb{I}_B.$$

It can be shown that the object B in the definition above is also unique up to isomorphism (cf. [2,9]).

3   Labelled graphs

Throughout this paper let $\mathcal{R}$ be a unitary heterogeneous relation algebra with a fixed object L from $\mathcal{R}$ such that the relational product $L \times A$ for every object A exists[2]. Furthermore, we suppose that every symmetric idempotent is a split. As shown in [2,9], every relation algebra can be embedded into another one such that the latter property holds.

In contrast to the synchronization tree approach, we model processes by labelled graphs, also called transition graphs. For example, the recusive defined process $P = c.b.a.P + a.(b.0 \mid c.0)$ may be modeled by the following graph.

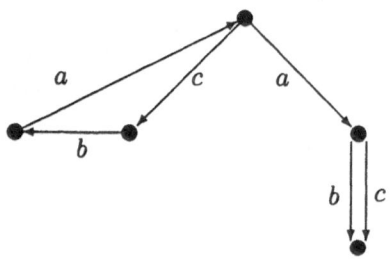

We consider a labelled graph on a set of nodes Z as a relation from Z to $L \times Z$. To obtain a convenient category we will consider suitable transition preserving (relational) homomorphisms [5].

Definition 9. The category $\mathcal{G}$ is defined as follows:

1. An object of $\mathcal{G}$ is a pair (G, w) consisting of a relation $G : Z \leftrightarrow L \times Z$ and a point $w : I \to Z$. $G = (G, w)$ is called a L-graph with root w over the state space Z.
2. A morphism $f : G_1 \to G_2$ is a mapping $f : Z_1 \to Z_2$ in $\mathcal{R}$ such that

$$G_1; (\mathbb{I}_L \times f) \sqsubseteq f; G_2 \quad \text{and} \quad w_1; f = w_2.$$

f is called a homomorphism from G_1 to G_2.

An easy verification shows that $\mathcal{G}$ is indeed a category.

In the category $\mathcal{G}$ a subobject describes a subgraph starting at the same root. To model a transition $P \xrightarrow{a} P'$ we are interested in subgraphs such that the new root is successor of the original root.

Definition 10. Let $a : I \to L$ be a point. An injective morphism f from $G_1 : Z_1 \leftrightarrow L \times Z_1$ to $G_2 : Z_2 \leftrightarrow L \times Z_2$ with

$$f; G_2 = G_1; (\mathbb{I}_L \times f) \quad \text{and} \quad w_1; f \sqsubseteq w_2; G_2; (a\breve{\ }; a \times \mathbb{I}_{Z_2}); \rho$$

is called a transition (in resp. with a) $f : G_1 \xrightarrow{a} G_2$. We write $G_1 \xrightarrow{a} G_2$ if such a morphism exists.

---

[2] This requirement gives us sharpness, but do not imply representability (cf. [1,5]).

Notice, that a transition morphism is not a morphism of the category $\mathcal{G}$ (but of $\mathcal{R}$). Furthermore, the direction of arrows is reversed. Intuitively, $G_1 \overset{a}{\rightarrowtail} G_2$ indicates that G_1 is an a-derivative of G_2. For example, the process P defined above may reduce (by an a-action) to $b.0 \mid c.0$. This situation is modeled by the following a-transition f.

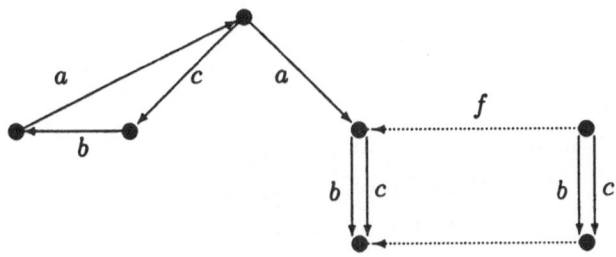

Within a graph there may be an edge targetting at the root. For several purposes we need to seperate the root from the rest of the graph in the sense that there are no edges of this kind.

Definition 11. Suppose $\mathcal{R}$ has relational sums. Then the extension $\text{ext}(G) = (\text{ext}(G), \text{ext}(w))$ of a graph $G = (G, w)$ is defined by

1. $\text{ext}(G) := [w; G, G]; (\mathbb{I}_L \times \kappa) : \text{I} + Z \leftrightarrow L \times (\text{I} + Z)$,
2. $\text{ext}(w) := \iota : \text{I} \leftrightarrow \text{I} + Z$.

In our example we gain the following graph.

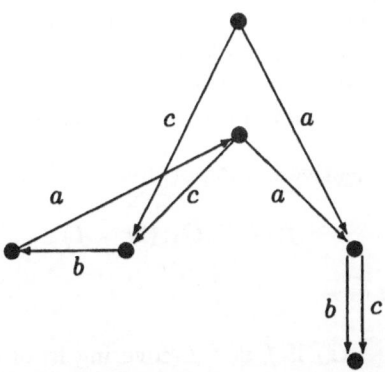

In the next section we will show that G and $\text{ext}(G)$ are bisimular. For the moment we have to be satisfied with the following lemma.

Lemma 1. Let $g : G_1 \overset{a}{\rightarrowtail} G_2$ be a transition morphism. Then the mapping $g; \kappa : Z_1 \rightarrow \text{I} + Z_2$ is a transition morphism from G_1 to $\text{ext}(G_2)$ with $g; \kappa; \text{ext}(w_2)^{\smile} = \mathbb{1}$.

Proof. Notice, that the composition of two injective mappings is a injective mapping again. The calculations

$$
\begin{aligned}
g; \kappa; \text{ext}(G_2) &= g; \kappa; [w_2; G_2, G_2]; (\mathbb{I}_L \times \kappa) \\
&= g; G_2; (\mathbb{I}_L \times \kappa) \\
&= G_1; (\mathbb{I}_L \times g); (\mathbb{I}_L \times \kappa) \\
&= G_1; (\mathbb{I}_L \times g; \kappa)
\end{aligned}
$$

and

$$
\begin{aligned}
w_1; g; \kappa \sqsubseteq\ & w_2; G_2; (a\check{\ }; a \times \mathbb{I}_{Z_2}); \rho; \kappa \\
&= w_2; G_2; (a\check{\ }; a \times \mathbb{I}_{Z_2}); (\mathbb{I}_L \times \kappa); \rho \\
&= w_2; G_2; (a\check{\ }; a \times \kappa); \rho \\
&= w_2; G_2; (\mathbb{I}_L \times \kappa); (a\check{\ }; a \times \mathbb{I}_{Z_2}); \rho \\
&= \iota; [w_2; G_2, G_2]; (\mathbb{I}_L \times \kappa); (a\check{\ }; a \times \mathbb{I}_{Z_2}); \rho \\
&= \text{ext}(w_2); \text{ext}(G_2); (a\check{\ }; a \times \mathbb{I}_{Z_2}); \rho
\end{aligned}
$$

show that $g; \kappa$ is indeed a transition morphism. The required property follows from

$$
g; \kappa; \text{ext}(w_2)\check{\ } = g; \kappa; \iota\check{\ } = g; \bot\!\!\!\bot = \bot\!\!\!\bot. \qquad \square
$$

4   Relational bisimulation

An important class of equivalence relations on processes are strong bisimulations. We are now going to establish a corresponding notion on $\mathcal{G}$. First we modify the definition of a covering [5] of two graphs. We want to allow a covering to identify two subgraphs which are identically labelled. This reflects the fact that the corresponding processes are bisimular.

Definition 12. A surjective homomorphism f from G_1 to G_2 with

$$
f; G_2 \sqsubseteq G_1; (\mathbb{I}_L \times f)
$$

is called a *L-covering*.

We write $f : G_1 \overset{\approx}{\to} G_2$ if f is a L-covering from G_1 to G_2, $G_1 \overset{\approx}{\to} G_2$ if such a morphism exists and $G_1 \approx G_2$ if there is a G_3 such that $G_1 \overset{\approx}{\to} G_3$ and $G_2 \overset{\approx}{\to} G_3$.

As mentioned in the last section there is a L-covering f from $\text{ext}(G)$ to G. This morphism identifies the new with the old root of the graph. In our example the states at the top of the graph are mapped to the original root.

Lemma 2. $\text{ext}(G) \overset{\approx}{\to} G$.

Proof. Consider the surjective mapping $[w, \mathbb{I}_Z] : I + Z \to Z$. Then we have

$$
\begin{aligned}
[w, \mathbb{I}_Z]; G &= [w; G, G] \\
&= [w; G, G](\mathbb{I}_L \times \mathbb{I}_Z) \\
&= [w; G, G](\mathbb{I}_L \times \kappa; [w, \mathbb{I}_Z]) \\
&= [w; G, G](\mathbb{I}_L \times \kappa); (\mathbb{I}_L \times [w, \mathbb{I}_Z]) \\
&= \mathrm{ext}(G); (\mathbb{I}_L \times [w, \mathbb{I}_Z])
\end{aligned}
$$

and

$$
\mathrm{ext}(w); [w, \mathbb{I}_Z] = \iota; [w, \mathbb{I}_Z] = w. \qquad \square
$$

The identification of subgraphs can be seen as a reduction process. In the next lemma we show that this process is confluent. The required graph G_4 is just the graph which is obtained from G_1 and the equivalence relation induced by the L-coverings $f : G_1 \xrightarrow{\approx} G_2$ and $g : G_1 \xrightarrow{\approx} G_3$.

Lemma 3. *If $G_1 \xrightarrow{\approx} G_2$ and $G_1 \xrightarrow{\approx} G_3$ then there is a G_4 such that $G_2 \xrightarrow{\approx} G_4$ and $G_3 \xrightarrow{\approx} G_4$.*

Proofsketch. Suppose $f : G_1 \xrightarrow{\approx} G_2$ and $g : G_1 \xrightarrow{\approx} G_3$. Then the relation $A := (f; f^{\smile} \sqcup g; g^{\smile})^*$ is an equivalence relation on Z_1. Futhermore, suppose R splits A. Then $R^{\smile}$ is a surjective mapping. Define

$$
\begin{aligned}
G_4 &:= R; G_1; (\mathbb{I} \times R^{\smile}) \\
w_4 &:= w_1; R^{\smile} \\
h &:= f^{\smile}; R^{\smile} \\
k &:= g^{\smile}; R^{\smile}.
\end{aligned}
$$

These definitions will work. $\qquad \square$

In the last lemma we have shown that the identification process of subgraphs is confluent. Furthermore, as we will show this process is terminating. In the language of categories this property is expressed by the existence of suitable terminal objects.

Given a graph G we denote with $\mathcal{G}_G$ the subcategory of $\mathcal{G}$ which objects are all graphs $G' \approx G$ and morphisms are L-coverings.

Theorem 1. *The category $\mathcal{G}_G$ has a terminal object.*

Proofsketch. Consider the operation[3]

$$
R \mapsto (G^{\smile} \backslash (\mathbb{I}_L \times R); G^{\smile}) \sqcap (G; (\mathbb{I}_L \times R)/G) = \overline{G; \overline{(\mathbb{I}_L \times R); G^{\smile}}} \sqcap \overline{G; (\mathbb{I}_L \times R)}; G^{\smile}
$$

---

[3] The definition of this operation and its greatest fixpoint A was motivated by a simular definition in [3].

on $\mathcal{R}[Z, Z]$. It is monotonic (wrt. $\sqsubseteq$) and has a greatest fixpoint A. This fixpoint is an equivalence relation. Suppose R splits A. Then we define

$$G_t := R; G; (\mathbb{I}_L \times R^{\smile}),$$
$$w_t := w; R^{\smile}.$$

$R^{\smile}$ is a L-covering from G to G_t. Furthermore, suppose there is another $f : G \stackrel{\approx}{\to} G_t$. Then $f; f^{\smile}$ is an equivalence relation and a pre-fixpoint of the operation above and hence included in A. A little computation shows that $f = R^{\smile}$. Given a G' such that $g : G \stackrel{\approx}{\to} G'$ we define $h := g^{\smile}; R^{\smile}$. This relation is indeed the unique L-covering from G' to G_t. Finally, if $k : G'' \stackrel{\approx}{\to} G'$ (and hence $G \approx G''$), then the relation $k; h$ is the unique L-covering from G'' to G_t. This implies that G_t is a terminal object of $\mathcal{G}_G$.   □

In contrast to the tree approach this terminal object can be taken as a canonical representation of its equivalence class.

The below theorem shows that $\mathcal{G}$ provides convenient models for processes.

Theorem 2. *If the point-axiom is valid, then the relation $\approx$ is a strong bisimulation with respect to $\stackrel{a}{\longmapsto}$.*

Given $G_1 \approx G_2$ and $G_1' \stackrel{a}{\longmapsto} G_1$ the idea of the proof is reflected by the following diagram:

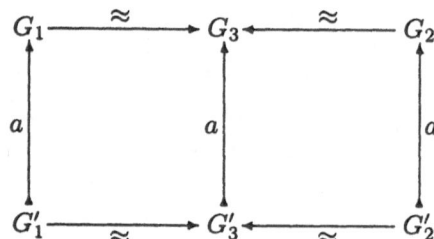

The existence of G_2' and G_3' is guaranteed by the following lemma.

Lemma 4. *1. If $G_1' \stackrel{a}{\longmapsto} G_1$ and $G_1 \stackrel{\approx}{\to} G_3$ then there is a G_3' such that $G_1' \stackrel{\approx}{\to} G_3'$ and $G_3' \stackrel{a}{\longmapsto} G_3$;*

2. If $G_2 \stackrel{\approx}{\to} G_3, G_3' \stackrel{a}{\longmapsto} G_3$ and the point-axiom is valid then there is a G_2' such that $G_2' \stackrel{a}{\longmapsto} G_2$ and $G_2' \stackrel{\approx}{\to} G_3'$.

Proofsketch.

1. Suppose f is a a-transition from G_1' to G_1 and g is a L-covering from G_1 to G_3. Then the relation $A := g^{\smile}; f^{\smile}; f; g$ is a partial identity on Z_3. Suppose that h splits A. Then h is an injective mapping and we define

$$G_3' := h; G_3; (\mathbb{I}_L \times h^{\smile}),$$
$$w_3' := w_1'; f; g; h^{\smile},$$
$$k := f; g; h^{\smile}.$$

Then h is a a-transition from G_3' to G_3 and k is a L-covering from G_1' to G_3'.

2. Suppose f is a L-covering from G_2 to G_3, and g is a a-transition from G_3' to G_3. Then the relation $A := f; g^\smile; g; f^\smile \sqcap \mathbb{I}_{Z_2}$ is a partial identity on Z_2. Suppose h splits A and define

$$G_2' := h; G_2; (\mathbb{I}_L \times h^\smile),$$
$$w_2' \text{ as a point contained in } w_3'; f; g^\smile,$$
$$k := h; f; g^\smile.$$

Here the point axiom is used to obtain the root w_2'. In general, the relation $w_3'; f; g^\smile$ is not univalent. Again, h is a a-transition from G_2' to G_2 and k is a L-covering from G_2' to G_3'.   □

5 $\mathcal{G}$ as a model of processes

Now, we want to define functors corresponding to the standard operations of CCS. Furthermore, we show that every transition rule associated with each operation is fulfilled.

Definition 13. Suppose $\mathcal{R}$ has relational sums, and let $a : I \to L$ be a point. The prefixing functor $P_a : \mathcal{G} \to \mathcal{G}$ is defined by

1. $P_a(G) := [<a, w>, G]; (\mathbb{I}_L \times \kappa) : I + Z \leftrightarrow L \times (I + Z),$
2. $P_a(w) := \iota : I \to I + Z,$
3. $P_a(f) := \mathbb{I}_I + f,$

for $G : Z \leftrightarrow L \times Z, w : I \to Z$ and homomorphism f.

The transition rule associated with the prefixing is just the simple axiom

$$\frac{\overline{}}{a.P \xrightarrow{\ a\ } P}.$$

$P_a(G)$ is, by definition, the graph containing a new root and exactly one transition from this new root to old one via the label a.

Lemma 5. P_a is a functor such that $G \xrightarrow{\ a\ } P_a(G)$.

Proofsketch. The required a-transition is just κ.   □

Relabelling and hiding are simular operations, i.e., hiding is a relabelling with a partial identity. This implies that both operations can be described by a common class of functors.

Definition 14. Let $l : L \leftrightarrow L$ be univalent. Then the functor $F_l : \mathcal{G} \to \mathcal{G}$ is defined by

1. $F_l(G) := G; (l \times \mathbb{I}_Z)$,
2. $F_l(w) := w$,
3. $F_l(f) := f$,

for $G : Z \leftrightarrow L \times Z, w : I \to Z$ and homomorphism f.

Given a relabelling function f and a set $\mathcal{L}$ of labels, the corresponding transition rules are

$$\frac{P \xrightarrow{a} P'}{P[f] \xrightarrow{f(a)} P'[f]} \qquad\qquad \frac{P \xrightarrow{a} P'}{P \backslash \mathcal{L} \xrightarrow{a} P' \backslash \mathcal{L}} \quad a \notin \mathcal{L}.$$

The second rule indicates that hiding has to be interpreted by $F_{\overline{l \cap \mathbb{I}}}$ where l is the partial identity induced by $\mathcal{L}$.

Lemma 6. F_l is a functor such that

1. if l is total then $G_1 \xrightarrow{a} G_2$ implies $F_l(G_1) \xrightarrow{a;l} F_l(G_2)$,
2. if $l \sqsubseteq \mathbb{I}_L$ then $G_1 \xrightarrow{a} G_2$ and $a\breve{\ };a \sqcap l = \bot\!\!\!\bot$ implies $F_{\overline{l \cap \mathbb{I}}}(G_1) \xrightarrow{a} F_{\overline{l \cap \mathbb{I}}}(G_2)$.

Proofsketch. In both cases the a-transition g from G_1 to G_2 is also one from $F_l(G_1)$ to $F_l(G_2)$ resp. from $F_{\overline{l \cap \mathbb{I}}}(G_1)$ to $F_{\overline{l \cap \mathbb{I}}}(G_2)$. $\qquad\square$

The sum operation of CCS is defined for arbitary sets I of processes. In our framework a set of objects (resp. morphisms) is represented by a function from I to the objects (resp. morphisms) of $\mathcal{G}$. For simplicity we use a tuple-like notation $(\ldots, G_i, \ldots)$.

Definition 15. Suppose $\mathcal{R}$ has relational sums. Let I be a set and $\mathcal{I}$ the induced discrete category. The functor $S_I : \mathcal{G}^{\mathcal{I}} \to \mathcal{G}$ is defined by

1. $S_I(\ldots, G_i, \ldots) := R; (\sum_{i \in I} \text{ext}(G_i)); \text{distr}; (\mathbb{I}_L \times R\breve{\ })$,
2. $S_I(\ldots, w_i, \ldots) := (R; \bigvee_{i \in I} \text{ext}(w_i)\breve{\ })\breve{\ }$,
3. $S_I(\ldots, f_i, \ldots) := R; (\mathbb{I}_I + \sum_{i \in I} f_i); R\breve{\ }$,

where $R : C \leftrightarrow \sum_{i \in I} I + Z_i$ resp. $R' : C' \leftrightarrow \sum_{i \in I} I + Z'_i$ splits the equivalence relation

$$S := (\bigsqcup_{i,j \in I} \iota_i\breve{\ }; \text{ext}(w_i)\breve{\ }; \text{ext}(w_j); \iota_j) \sqcup \mathbb{I}_{\sum_{i \in I} I + Z_i}$$

$$\text{resp. } S' := (\bigsqcup_{i,j \in I} \iota_i\breve{\ }; \text{ext}(w'_i)\breve{\ }; \text{ext}(w'_j); \iota_j) \sqcup \mathbb{I}_{\sum_{i \in I} I + Z'_i}.$$

The sum of a set of graphs is, roughly, given by the disjoint union of the graphs and identifying all separated roots. Associated with the sum operation is the following transition rule

$$\frac{P_i \xrightarrow{a} P'_i}{\sum_{i \in I} P_i \xrightarrow{a} P'_i}.$$

Lemma 7. *For any set I the construction S_I is a functor such that $G'_i \overset{a}{\rightarrowtail} G_i$ implies $G'_i \overset{a}{\rightarrowtail} S_I(\ldots, G_i, \ldots)$.*

Proofsketch. Suppose $h : G'_i \overset{a}{\rightarrowtail} G_i$. By Lemma 1 there is $g : G'_i \overset{a}{\rightarrowtail} \mathrm{ext}(G_i)$ such that $g; \mathrm{ext}(w_i)^{\smile} = \perp\!\!\!\perp$. Then the mapping $g; \iota_i; R^{\smile}$ is a a-transition from G'_i to $S(\ldots, G_i, \ldots)$. $\square$

Notice, that using just G_i instead of $\mathrm{ext}(G_i)$ does not give an adequate definition of the sum operation. Consider the processes $P_1 = a.P_1$ and $P_2 = b.0$. They are modeled by the graphs:

$$G_1 \qquad\qquad G_2$$

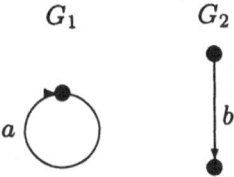

Not using the extension of G_1 and G_2 we would gain the following graph.

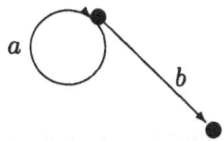

This graph seen as a process may produce the stream ab, which is not in the behaviour of $P_1 + P_2$.

Last but not least we define the interleaving functor.

Definition 16. Suppose $\mathcal{R}$ has relational products. Then the interleaving functor $| : \mathcal{G} \times \mathcal{G} \to \mathcal{G}$ is defined by

1. $G_1 \mid G_2 := (\pi; G_1; (\mathbb{I} \times \pi^{\smile}) \sqcap \rho; \rho^{\smile}; \rho^{\smile}) \sqcup (\pi; \pi^{\smile}; \rho^{\smile} \sqcap \rho; G_2; (\mathbb{I} \times \rho^{\smile}))$:
   $Z_1 \times Z_2 \leftrightarrow L \times (Z_1 \times Z_2)$,
2. $w_1 \mid w_2 := <w_1, w_2>$,
3. $f_1 \mid f_2 := f_1 \times f_2$,

for $G_1 : Z_1 \leftrightarrow L \times Z_1, G_2 : Z_2 \leftrightarrow L \times Z_2$ and a homomorphism f.

By definition the state space of $G_1 \mid G_2$ is the product $Z_1 \times Z_2$. The next picture shows an example of the interleaving of two graphs.

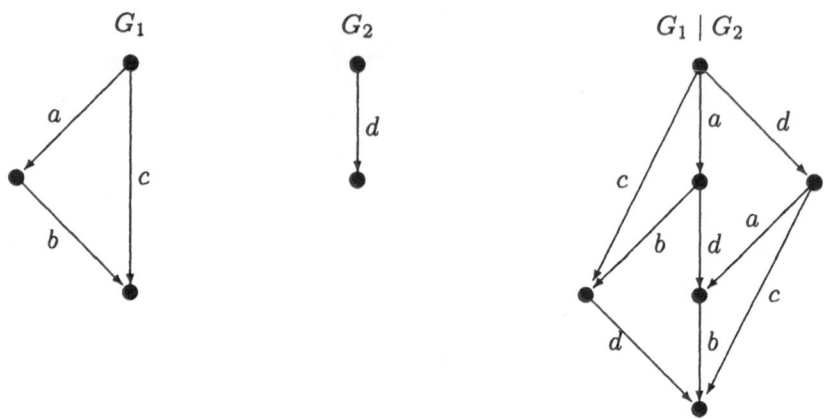

The transition rule associated with interleaving is

$$\frac{P \xrightarrow{a} P'}{P \mid Q \xrightarrow{a} P' \mid Q} \qquad \frac{Q \xrightarrow{a} Q'}{P \mid Q \xrightarrow{a} P \mid Q'}.$$

The commutativity of relational products implies that our definition of the interleaving lead to a commutative functor. Therefore, it is sufficient to consider the first rule.

Lemma 8. $\mid$ *is a functor such that* $G_1 \xrightarrow{a} G_2$ *implies* $G_1 \mid G_3 \xrightarrow{a} G_2 \mid G_3$.

Proofsketch. The required a-transition is given by the function $(f \times \mathbb{I})$ for a $f : G_1 \xrightarrow{a} G_2$. $\qquad\qquad\square$

We have not introduced a notion of communication. As usual this can be done by splitting L into $L_i + L_o + \mathrm{I}$ of input resp. output labels and a distinguished symbol τ.

6   Conclusion

We established a categorical model of process calculi based on abstract relation algebra. The main advantage of this approach is the existence of a canonical representation of an equivalance class by its terminal object.

Considering concrete relations, the representative of the interpretation of a process built up by finite summation (but arbitrary recursion) is a finite graph. The equality (up to isomorphism) of finite graphs is decidable and thus implies the decidability of strong bisimulation of such processes. This result corresponds to the theory of finite state machines. But notice, that our graphs are not necessarily finite. As an example consider the graph $S_{\mathbb{N}}(P_0(\emptyset), P_1(\emptyset), P_2(\emptyset)\ldots)$ where $0, 1, 2, \ldots$ are the points induced by the natural numbers.

References

1. Desharnais J. (1997) Monomorphic characterization of n-ary direct products. In: Third International Seminar on the Use of Relational Methods in Computer Science, Participant's Proceedings, University of Tunis II, Tunesia
2. Freyd P., Scedrov A. (1990) Categories, Allegories. North-Holland
3. Kawahara Y., Mori M. (2000) Hennesy Milner Properties in Dedekind Categories. Manuscript
4. Milner R. (1989) Communication and Concurrency. Prentice Hall
5. Schmidt G., Hattensperger C., Winter M. (1997) Heterogeneous Relation Algebras. In: Relational Methods in Computer Science, Advances in Computing, 45–63 Springer
6. Schmidt G., Ströhlein T. (1985) Relation Algebras — Concept of Points and Representability, Discrete Math. 54:83–92
7. Schmidt G., Ströhlein T. (1989) Relationen und Graphen. Springer; English version: Relations and Graphs. Discrete Mathematics for Computer Scientists, EATCS Monographs on Theoret. Comput. Sci., Springer (1993)
8. Winskel G. (1984) Synchronization Trees. Theoret. Comput. Sci. 34
9. Winter M. (1998) Strukturtheorie heterogener Relationenalgebren mit Anwendung auf Nichtdetermismus in Programmiersprachen. Dissertationsverlag NG Kopierladen GmbH, München
10. Winter M., Kempf P. (1998) Relational Semantics for Processes. Report Nr. 1998-01, Fakultät für Informatik, Universität der Bundeswehr München
11. Zierer H. (1991) Relation Algebraic Domain Constructions. Theoret. Comput. Sci. 87:163–188

Part II

Relational Constraints

Chapter 5
A Tableaux Procedure for the Implication Problem for Association Rules

Wendy MacCaull*

Department of Mathematics, Statistics and Computer Science
St. Francis Xavier University
PO Box 5000, Antigonish, NS, B2G 2W5, Canada
wmaccaul@stfx.ca

Abstract. Using a relational approach, we investigate the implication problem for association rules for contexts with 1. We provide sufficient conditions on the relations in an information frame with semistrong relations for the construction of a context with 1. We develop a Rasiowa/Sikorski-style relational calculus which is sound and complete for the implication problem for association rules. We show that this implication problem is decidable.
Keywords: data dependencies, association rules, relational semantics, tableaux deduction

1   Introduction

A database consists of objects and information about each object with respect to a number of attributes. In dependency theory, the idea is to relate attributes in a database to other attributes, so we may use the database more efficiently. A large number of dependencies have been described and studied over the years (see [1] and [17]). An area of study in database theory currently under intense investigation is the analysis of contexts, of importance in concept analysis (see [18]). A context is a database such that all attribute values are either 0 or 1. An association rule between two sets of attributes in a context is a database dependency. Associations have many important applications, for example, for making medical diagnoses and designing marketing strategies.

A relational formulation of functional and other dependencies was developed in [15], using the notion of *indiscernibility relation*, and a relational calculus for dependency theory was developed in [5]. The need for the development of the proof theory for this calculus was articulated in [5], and some progress in this direction was made (in [5]). In [8], we develop the relational proof theory for several kinds of dependencies, using a Rasiowa/Sikorski-style tableaux method of proof.

---
* Supported by the Natural Sciences and Engineering Research Council of Canada and by the St. Francis Xavier University Council for Research

Recently, Rough Set Theory has led to the study of a host of relations, in addition to the indiscernibility relations, for reasoning about incomplete information; this collection of relations is known as *information relations* and relational databases are here referred to as *information systems*. They give rise to the so-called *information frames*, that is, frames each having one (or more) set(s) of information relations parameterized by subsets of a set. A classification of sets of relations parameterized by subsets of a set has been made. Of particular interest are the sets of *strong relations*, exemplified by the indiscernibility relations. Theoretical foundations for the study of information relations in general have been developed and the study of information logics has ensued. The recent book, *Incomplete Information: Rough Set Analysis*, edited by Orłowska [13], contains much of the state of the art knowledge about Rough Set Theory. The approach we take in this paper may be generalized easily to deal with any of the information relations found in [13].

In this paper we focus on association rules in contexts with 1 (see [11]). We use the notion of *association relation* in order to discuss association rules. Though these relations are relations parameterized by subsets of a set, they have neither the *strong* property nor the *weak* property common to many information relations thus far studied in the literature (see [3], [4] and [13]). They have some of the properties of strong relations, which leads us to introduce the notion of *semistrong relations*. Lack of strongness leads us to the problem of informational representability, necessary for completeness of our deduction method. A discussion of informational representability with respect to several kinds of relations may be found in [16]. We give sufficient conditions to allow us to prove the required informational representability result. This will allow us to give a tableaux deduction procedure which is sound and complete in the desired sense. We develop a decision procedure for the implication problem for association rules. We end the paper with a discussion of further applications of these techniques and outline some directions for research.

2   Preliminaries

Definition 1. An **information system** is a four-tuple $S = (X, A, \{V(a) : a \in A\}, f)$, where X is a set (of objects); A is a set (of attributes); for each $a \in A$, $V(a)$ is the set of values, and for each $x \in X$, and $a \in A$, $f(x, a) \subseteq V(a)$.

The study of information systems has led to the study of relations parameterized by subsets of a set (see [3], [13]). The first of these, the **indiscernibility relations**, R_P^{ind}, for each $P \subseteq A$, are defined as follows: $(x, y) \in R_P^{ind}$ iff $\forall a \in P$, $f(x, a) = f(y, a)$. A database is an information system: using indiscernibility relations, one may express many dependencies from database theory (see [15]). For example:

Functional Dependency $\rightarrow$: $P \rightarrow Q$ holds in a database iff $\forall x, y \in X$, if $f(x, a) = f(y, a)$, $\forall a \in P$ then $f(x, a) = f(y, a)$, $\forall a \in Q$.

Using indiscernibility relations, we may express functional dependency as follows: (see [15]):

$$P \rightarrow Q \text{ iff } R_P^{ind} \subseteq R_Q^{ind}.$$

Lemma 1. *Given an information system S, the following hold for all $P \subseteq A$:*
(i) each R_P^{ind} is an equivalence relation;
(ii) $R_P^{ind} \cap R_Q^{ind} = R_{P \cup Q}^{ind}$;
(iii) $R_\emptyset^{ind} = X \times X$.

The proof of the above lemma is easy to establish. Using the jargon from the literature, (ii) implies that the indiscernibility relations R_P^{ind} are **standard** (see [4]) and (ii) and (iii) together imply that the indiscernibility relations R_P^{ind} are **strong relations** (see [13]).

Our goal here is to study association rules in contexts with 1.

Definition 2. A **context** is an information system, $(X, A, \{V(a) : a \in A\}, f)$, such that for all $a \in A$, $V(a) = \{0, 1\}$. Let 1_A be an object such that: for all $a \in A$, $f(1_A, a) = 1$. A **context with** 1 is a context with an object 1_A.

An association rule is a dependency for contexts with 1 defined as follows:

Association rule $=>$: $P => Q$ iff $\forall x \in X$, if $\forall a \in P$, $f(x, a) = 1$, then, $\forall a \in Q$, $f(x, a) = 1$.

Definition 3. In a context with 1, define the binary relation R_P^{as} as $\{(x, y) | \forall a \in P \ f(x, a) = 1 \text{ if and only if } \forall a \in P \ f(y, a) = 1\}$. Call R_P^{as} an **association relation**.

The following Proposition shows that we may express association rules using association relations:

Proposition 1. *Let $(X, A, \{V(a) : a \in A\}, f, 1_A)$ be a context with 1, and let $P, Q \subseteq A$. Then:*

$$P => Q \text{ iff } R_P^{as} = R_{P \cup Q}^{as}.$$

Proof. Let us show that the above *if and only if* statement holds. Suppose $P => Q$. That $R_P^{as} \subseteq R_{P \cup Q}^{as}$ is obvious from the definitions. To show the reverse containment, suppose $(x, y) \in R_{P \cup Q}^{as}$. Then, for all $a \in P \cup Q$, $f(x, a) = 1$ iff for all $a \in P \cup Q$, $f(y, a) = 1$. Assume first that for all $a \in P$, $f(x, a) = 1$. We are assuming $P => Q$, so for all $a \in P \cup Q$, $f(x, a) = 1$. Since $(x, y) \in R_{P \cup Q}^{as}$, we may conclude that for all $a \in P \cup Q$, $f(y, a) = 1$.

Consequently, for all $a \in P$, $f(y,a) = 1$. Suppose now that for some $a \in P$, $f(x,a) \neq 1$. Then, for some $a \in P \cup Q$, $f(x,a) \neq 1$; and consequently, for some $a \in P \cup Q$, $f(y,a) \neq 1$. If $a \in P$, we may conclude $(x,y) \in R_P^{as}$. If $a \in Q$, then for some $a \in Q$, $f(y,a) \neq 1$. The association rule $P \Rightarrow Q$ then tells us that for some $a \in P$, $f(y,a) \neq 1$; again we may conclude $(x,y) \in R_P^{as}$.

Suppose now that $R_P^{as} = R_{P \cup Q}^{as}$, and that for all $a \in P$, $f(x,a) = 1$. Therefore $(x,1) \in R_P^{as}$. Now either (1) for all $a \in P \cup Q$, $f(x,a) = 1$ or (2) for some $a \in P \cup Q$, $f(x,a) \neq 1$. However (2) gives a contradiction as follows: if (2) holds, we know that for some $a \in Q$, $f(x,a) \neq 1$. Thus $(x,1) \notin R_{P \cup Q}^{as}$. Consequently $(x,1) \notin R_P^{as}$, which is a contradiction. Therefore (1) holds, which implies that for all $a \in Q$, $f(x,a) = 1$. We conclude that $P \Rightarrow Q$. □

Lemma 2. *In a context with 1:*
   (i) each R_P^{as} is an equivalence relation;
   (ii) $R_P^{as} \cap R_Q^{as} \subseteq R_{P \cup Q}^{as}$;
   (iii) $R_\emptyset^{as} = X \times X$.

The proofs of (i)-(iii) are easy to establish. In (ii), equality in general does not hold, as the following simple example shows:

Example

$$
\begin{array}{cc}
 & P \;\; Q \\
\begin{array}{c} x \\ y \\ 1 \end{array} & \left(\begin{array}{cc} 1 & 0 \\ 0 & 1 \\ 1 & 1 \end{array} \right).
\end{array}
$$

Definition 4. Let A be a set and for each $P \subseteq A$, let R_P be a binary relation on a set X. We say that the relations R_P are **semistrong relations** iff the following hold:
   (i) for each $P, Q \subseteq A$, $R_P \cap R_Q \subseteq R_{P \cup Q}$;
   (ii) $R_\emptyset = X \times X$.

As with all dependencies, given some association rules, one usual goal is to deduce others.

3   A relational deduction apparatus

We adopt a formal setup similar to that of [3] and [4]. The language for information systems, LIS, consists of: a (countably infinite) set, A_{par}, of atomic parameters; a set, C_{par}, of (complex) parameters defined by induction in the following manner: atomic parameters are parameters and if P and Q are parameters then PQ is a parameter; a relational constant **P** for each (complex) parameter, P, a (distinguished) relational constant **1**; and the connectives $\cup$,

∩, ; →, and ¬. (The bold face analog of a complex parameter will be the relational constant corresponding to that parameter; i.e., **PQ** will be the relational constant corresponding to parameter PQ.) Formulas of LIS consist of the set of relational constants closed under the connectives. We shall write all our formulas using boldface; relational constants will be denoted by letters at the end of the alphabet (**P**, **Q**, **S**, etc.). Arbitrary LIS-formulas will be denoted by letters near the beginning of the alphabet (**F**, **G**, etc.). Motivated by the discussion in [5], we write **F** ⊃ **G** as shorthand for $(1; ¬\mathbf{F}; 1) \cup (\mathbf{G})$. As we shall see below, this allows us to use LIS to express entailment. In what follows, the connective ¬ takes precedence over the connective ; which takes precedence over the connective → which takes precedence over the other connectives (the associativity of composition of relations allows us to be ambiguous in LIS and write $(1; ¬\mathbf{F}; 1)$). The language $RLIS$ is LIS augmented with a (countable) list of variables (which we shall refer to as *objects*) $x, y, z, \ldots$ and a constant (designated object) 1. Formulas of $RLIS$ are of the form $x\mathbf{F}y$, where **F** is a formula of LIS.

We use this formal setup, which differs, somewhat, to that used in [5], for the following reasons: (1) it allows us express the axioms for associations in a format that is similar to that used by the database community and (2) it is analogous to that found in Balbiani and Orłowska (see [3] and [4]) who describe a hierarchy of modal logics which include modal operators corresponding to relations parameterized by subsets of a set. This formal setup requires the use of a map called *set*, from C_{par} into $2^{A_{par}}$, the set of subsets of A_{par}, defined by induction as follows: for every atomic parameter S, $set\ S = \{S\}$ and for every $P, Q \in C_{par}$, $set\ (PQ) = set\ P \cup set\ Q$.

Definition 5. An **information frame** is a structure of the form **K** $=$ (X, Par, R), where X is a set (of objects), Par is a (finite) set (of parameters) and R is a map from 2^{Par} to the set of binary relations on X. If each $R(P)$ is an equivalence relation, then we say that we have a **frame with equivalence relations**. We shall say that the frame is **semistrong** if and only if for every P and $Q \subseteq Par$, $R(P) \cap R(Q) \subseteq R(P \cup Q)$ and $R(\emptyset) = X \times X$. (If, in addition, the frame satisfies the condition $R(P \cup Q) \subseteq R(P) \cap R(Q)$, we say that the frame is **strong**.)

Remark 1. It is well known that any information system S gives rise to a strong information frame $\mathbf{K}_S$ with equivalence relations; the objects of the information system comprise the set X, and, for each $P \subseteq A$, $R(P)$ is the the indiscernibility relation R_P^{ind} from the information system. Analogously, using association relations, any context with 1 gives rise to a semistrong frame with equivalence relations where, for each $P \subseteq A$, $R(P)$ is the association relation R_P^{as}.

Definition 6. Given an information frame **K**, let m be a map from A_{par} to Par, extended to the *set* - map from C_{par} to 2^{Par}, so that for $S \in A_{par}$,

$m(S) = \{S\}$ and for complex parameters P and Q, $m(PQ) = m(P) \cup m(Q)$ (we are identifying the elements of A_{par} with those of Par). If we then suppose we have another map also (by abuse of notation) called m, from the set of relational constants to the image of the map R, defined as: $m(\mathbf{P}) = R(m(P))$ and $m(\mathbf{1}) = R(\emptyset)$, then m is called an **assignment** on **K**. The pair $\mathcal{M} = (\mathbf{K}, m)$ is called a **relational model** on (the information frame) **K**. Given formulas, **F** and **G**, extend the assignment m so that $m(\mathbf{F} \cap \mathbf{G}) = m(\mathbf{F}) \cap m(\mathbf{G})$; $m(\mathbf{F} \cup \mathbf{G}) = m(\mathbf{F}) \cup m(\mathbf{G})$; $m(\mathbf{F} \to \mathbf{G}) = m(\neg \mathbf{F}) \cup m(\mathbf{G})$, $m(\neg \mathbf{F}) = m(\overline{\mathbf{F}})$, and $m(\mathbf{F}; \mathbf{G}) = m(\mathbf{F}); m(\mathbf{G})$ (where the connectives on the right hand side of each equality is the relational connective - intersection, union, complement and composition). Given an information frame **K**, a formula **F** of LIS is **satisfied** by the model $\mathcal{M}$ if $m(\mathbf{F}) = X \times X$, and it is **valid** in **K** if it is satisfied by all the models.

Given an information frame, **K**, and model, $\mathcal{M}$, a **valuation** v of objects in $\mathcal{M}$ is a map from the set of objects of $RLIS$ into X. A formula $x\mathbf{F}y$ is **satisfied** by v in $\mathcal{M}$ iff $(v(x), v(y)) \in m(\mathbf{F})$; the formula $x\mathbf{F}y$ is **satisfied by the model** $\mathcal{M}$ iff $x\mathbf{F}y$ is satisfied by all valuations in $\mathcal{M}$. Finally $x\mathbf{F}y$ is **valid** in **K** iff it is satisfied by all the models $\mathcal{M}$. A **sequence**, S, of **formulas of** $RLIS$ **is valid in an information frame** if and only if for every relational model $\mathcal{M}$ and for every valuation v, there is a formula in S which is satisfied by v. A sequence, S, of formulas of $RLIS$ is **valid in a class Ω of information frames** iff it is valid in each frame in Ω.

The following is clear from the definitions:

Theorem 1. *The LIS-formula* **F** *is valid in an information frame* **K** *if and only if the RLIS-formula* $x\mathbf{F}y$ *is valid in* **K**.

A relational proof system for the logic $RLIS$ consists of rules that apply to finite sequences of $RLIS$ - formulas. Thus they are of the form $\frac{H}{J}$ or $\frac{H}{J_1 \quad J_2 \quad \cdots \quad J_n}$ where $H, J, J_1, ..., J_n$ are finite sequences of formulas. $\frac{H}{J}$ is an **admissible rule** for a class of information frames Ω in the case that H is valid in the class Ω if and only if J is valid in the class Ω; the rule $\frac{H}{J_1 \quad J_2 \quad \cdots \quad J_n}$ is admissible for the class Ω in the case that H is valid in Ω if and only if J_1 and J_2 and ... and J_n are valid in Ω. There are two kinds of rules - **decomposition rules** which enable us to decompose a formula into simpler formulas and **specific rules** which enable us to modify a sequence of formulas. The connectives determine the decomposition rules, and conditions on the relations determine the specific rules. For this proof system, special sequences, called **axiomatic sequences**, take the place of axioms. They are sequences that are valid in the class of frames under consideration. Any sequence containing all the formulas of an axiomatic sequence (in any order) is valid.

Relational deduction is a semantic tableaux method of proof: if **F** is the formula from LIS whose validity is in question, we place $x\mathbf{F}y$ at the root and generate a tree by applying deduction rules (each of which yields a sequence of formulas or branches to yield several sequences of formulas) until all branches close (meaning we have reached a valid sequence on each branch) or there is an open branch. If all branches close, the formula is valid (by virtue of the fact that the rules are admissible and closure of a branch occurs only when a valid sequence is obtained). In this case we say that the tableau is closed and **F** is *tableaux provable*. If a branch is open we may build countermodel which is an information frame (see, for example, [13], and references therein). Though we speak of *tableaux proofs*, we recognize that this process is, in fact, a validity-checker rather that a proof generator. Our goal here is completeness with respect to information systems, not merely information frames so before giving the formal definition of the deduction system, we need to take a detour to investigate the problem of informational representability.

4 Informational representability

Suppose we are given a class of information frames, Ω, and a property, φ, of information systems from a certain class Ψ, expressible in a formula φ' of LIS. For example, the property φ could be: the pair of functional dependencies $P \rightarrow Q$ and $Q \rightarrow T$ implies the functional dependency $P \rightarrow T$, which is expressible in LIS, using the formula φ': $(\mathbf{P} \rightarrow \mathbf{Q}) \cap (\mathbf{Q} \rightarrow \mathbf{T}) \supset (\mathbf{P} \rightarrow \mathbf{T})$. Tableaux completeness of the relational deduction system corresponding to Ω tells us that if φ' is not tableaux provable, then we can construct an information frame in Ω such that φ' is not valid. The question that we need to answer is: can we construct an *information system S* such that φ does not hold in S? This kind of question is termed *informational representability*: given an information frame in Ω, can we construct an information system which is in Ψ with *the same* (in the appropriate sense) properties. With an affirmative answer to this question and results of the next section, we will be able to show that:

$$\vdash \varphi' \text{ iff } \varphi \text{ holds in all information systems in } \Psi$$

where $\vdash$ denotes tableaux provability (with deduction corresponding to Ω). In [16], we find the construction of an information system from an information frame such that the indiscernibility relations, parameterized by subsets of attributes from the information system which may be defined on the objects of the information system, are precisely the relations in the frame with which we started. Indeed, such representability results are demonstrated for frames with several kinds of information relations, including frames with diversity relations and frames with tolerance relations.

To get the informational representability result for frames with semistrong equivalence relations (which analogous to that for frames with strong relations as shown in [16]), we must augment the axioms of semistrong information frames.

Theorem 2. *(Informational representability of contexts with 1) Let* $\mathbf{K} = (X, Par, R, 1)$ *be an information frame with a designated element* $1 \in X$. *Suppose for all* $P \subseteq Par$ *the relations* $R(P)$ *are semistrong equivalence relations satisfying the axioms:*

$(As1)$ $(x, y) \in R(P)$ *iff* $(x, 1) \in R(P)$ *and* $(y, 1) \in R(P)$ *or* $(x, 1) \in \overline{R}(P)$ *and* $(y, 1) \in \overline{R}(P)$;

$(As2)$ *for each* $S \in Par$, *and each* $P \subseteq Par$, $(x, 1) \in \overline{R}(\{S\})$ *implies* $(x, 1) \in \overline{R}(P \cup \{S\})$.

Then we can construct a context with 1, *such that* $R_P^{as} = R(P)$, *for all* $P \subseteq Par$.

Proof. Given a frame $(X, Par, R, 1)$ with semistrong equivalence relations that satisfy $(As1)$ and $(As2)$, we construct a context with 1, $(X, A, \{V(a) : a \in A\}, f, 1)$, as follows: Let A be the set Par. For each $x \in X$ and each $a \in A$, define $f(x, a) = 1$ iff $(x, 1) \in R(\{a\})$. Clearly $(1, 1) \in R(\{a\})$, since $R(\{a\})$ is reflexive. So $f(1, a) = 1$. We need to show that each $R(P)$ is the association relation R_P^{as}; i.e., for each $P \subseteq A$, $(x, y) \in R(P)$ iff for all $a \in P$, $f(x, a) = f(y, a) = 1$, or there exist $a_1, a_2 \in A$ such that $f(x, a_1) \neq 1$ and $f(y, a_2) \neq 1$.

First, we concentrate on subsets of parameters with only one element. and show that for all $a \in A$, $R(\{a\}) = R_{\{a\}}^{as}$. By $(As1)$, $(x, y) \in R(\{a\})$ iff $(x, 1) \in R(\{a\})$ and $(y, 1) \in R(\{a\})$ or $(x, 1) \in \overline{R(\{a\})}$ and $(y, 1) \in \overline{R(\{a\})}$ iff $f(x, a) = 1$ and $f(y, a) = 1$ or $f(x, a) \neq 1$ and $f(y, a) \neq 1$ iff $(x, y) \in R_{\{a\}}^{as}$.

Using the above, we now show that for all $P \subseteq A$, $R(P) = R_P^{as}$. First suppose $(x, y) \in R_P^{as}$. By definition of association relation, $(x, y) \in R_P^{as}$ iff either (1) for all $a \in P$, $(x, 1) \in R_{\{a\}}^{as}$ and $(y, 1) \in R_{\{a\}}^{as}$ or (2) there exist $a_1, a_2 \in P$, $(x, 1) \in \overline{R_{\{a_1\}}^{as}}$ and $(y, 1) \in \overline{R_{\{a_2\}}^{as}}$. Suppose (1): for all $a \in P$, $(x, 1) \in R_{\{a\}}^{as}$ and $(y, 1) \in R_{\{a\}}^{as}$. Then, by the above for all $a \in P$, $(x, 1) \in R(\{a\})$ and $(y, 1) \in R(\{a\})$, so for all $a \in P$, $(x, 1) \in R(\{a\})$. The relations are semistrong so we may conclude that $(x, y) \in R(P)$. Suppose (2): there exist $a_1, a_2 \in P$ such that $(x, 1) \in \overline{R_{\{a_1\}}^{as}}$ and $(y, 1) \in \overline{R_{\{a_2\}}^{as}}$. Thus there exist $a_1, a_2 \in P$, $(x, 1) \in \overline{R(\{a_1\})}$ and $(y, 1) \in \overline{R(\{a_2\})}$. By $(As2)$, $(x, 1) \in \overline{R(P)}$ and $(y, 1) \in \overline{R(P)}$ so, by $(As1)$, $(x, y) \in R(P)$.

Now suppose $(x, y) \notin R_P^{as}$. Then, either (1) $(x, 1) \in R_P^{as}$ and $(y, 1) \notin R_P^{as}$ or (2) $(x, 1) \notin R_P^{as}$ and $(y, 1) \in R_P^{as}$. If (1), then $(x, 1) \in R_P^{as}$ implies, by the argument in the previous paragraph, that $(x, 1) \in R(P)$; if $(y, 1) \notin R_P^{as}$, semistrongness implies there is $a \in P$ such that $(y, 1) \notin R_{\{a\}}^{as}$ so $(y, 1) \notin R(\{a\})$; consequently, $(y, 1) \in \overline{R(\{a\})}$ so, by $(As2)$, $(y, 1) \in \overline{R(P)}$. Then $(x, 1) \in R(P)$ and $(y, 1) \notin R(P)$; the fact that $R(P)$ is an equivalence relation allows us to conclude that $(x, y) \notin R(P)$, which is what we wanted to show. If (2) holds, a similar argument leads us to the same conclusion. $\square$

Definition 7. An information frame with semistrong equivalence relations satisfying conditions ($As1$) and ($As2$) of the above theorem is called a **frame with association relations**; denote such a frame by $\mathbf{K}^{as}$.

5   The deduction rules

The relational deductive system consists of the well known decomposition rules for the connectives. We shall use a shorthand for the rules and suppress sequences that occur both above and below the line: for example, the first rule below is shorthand for $\dfrac{H,x(F\cap G)y,J}{H,xFy,J \quad H,xGy,J}$, where H and J are finite sequences of $RLIS$ - formulas. An object is said to be **restricted** if it does not appear in any formula above the line. (Otherwise, if an object appears below the line, it must appear in some formula above the line.) The decomposition rules below are called *core* deduction rules.

Core Deduction Rules:

($\cap$) $\dfrac{x(F\cap G)y}{xFy \qquad xGy}$

($\neg\cap$) $\dfrac{x\neg(F\cap G)y}{x\neg Fy, x\neg Gy}$

($\cup$) $\dfrac{x(F\cup G)y}{xFy, xGy}$

($\neg\cup$) $\dfrac{x\neg(F\cup G)y}{x\neg Fy \qquad x\neg Gy}$

($\rightarrow$) $\dfrac{x(F\rightarrow G)y}{x\neg Fy, xGy}$

($\neg\rightarrow$) $\dfrac{x\neg(F\rightarrow G)y}{xFy \qquad x\neg Gy}$

($;$) $\dfrac{x(F;G)y}{xFu,x(F;G)y \qquad uGy,x(F;G)y}$ (u, any object)

($\neg;$) $\dfrac{x\neg(F;G)y}{x\neg Fu,u\neg Gy}$ (u, a restricted object)

Axiomatic sequences:

Any sequence containing the following as a subsequence, for any LIS-formula **F**:

$$xFy, x\neg Fy.$$

We now list the specific rules which correspond to conditions assumed to hold on the relations in the frame. The relations on the frame are assumed to be association relations, that is, semistrong equivalence relations, satisfying $(As1)$ and $(As2)$. Consequently, we need the following specific rules (in (ref), x and $\mathbf{P}$ must occur in some formula above the line):

Rules for Equivalence Relations:

(ref) $\dfrac{}{x \neg \mathbf{P}x}$;

(sym) $\dfrac{x \neg \mathbf{P}y}{x \neg \mathbf{P}y, y \neg \mathbf{P}x}$;

$(trans)$ $\dfrac{x \neg \mathbf{P}y, y \neg \mathbf{P}z}{x \neg \mathbf{P}y, y \neg \mathbf{P}z, x \neg \mathbf{P}z}$.

Rules for Semistrong Relations:

$(\neg S)$ $\dfrac{x \neg \mathbf{P}_2 y, x \neg \mathbf{P}_3 y}{x \neg \mathbf{P}_2 y, x \neg \mathbf{P}_3 y, x \neg \mathbf{P}_1 y}$ (set $P_1 = $ set $P_2 \cup$ set P_3);

(SS) $\dfrac{}{\bar{x} \neg 1 y}$.

Association Rules:

$(as1 \Rightarrow)$ $\dfrac{x \neg \mathbf{P}y}{x \neg \mathbf{P}y, x \neg \mathbf{P}1, y \neg \mathbf{P}1 \qquad\qquad\qquad x \neg \mathbf{P}y, x\mathbf{P}1, y\overline{\mathbf{P}1}}$;

$(as1 \Leftarrow (a))$ $\dfrac{x \neg \mathbf{P}1, y \neg \mathbf{P}1}{x \neg \mathbf{P}y, x \neg \mathbf{P}1, y \neg \overline{\mathbf{P}1}}$;

$(as1 \Leftarrow (b))$ $\dfrac{x\mathbf{P}1, y\mathbf{P}1}{x \neg \mathbf{P}y, x\mathbf{P}1, y\overline{\mathbf{P}1}}$;

$(as2)$ $\dfrac{x \neg \mathbf{P}S1}{x \neg \mathbf{P}S1, x \neg \mathbf{P}1, x \neg S1}$ where $\mid$ set $S \mid = 1$.

The first 3 association rules are required because we assume the condition $(As1)$. The last rule is required because we assume the condition $(As2)$ (the form of the rule used here was chosen so that the theorem prover could incorporate the mechanism to prevent reapplication rules (see Section 6, below) and thus get decidability.) All of the rules above can be shown to be admissible for information frames with association relations. As an example let us show that the rule $(as2)$ is admissible.

Lemma 3. *The rule $(as2)$ is admissible for the class of information frames with association relations; that is, the top sequence is valid in the class of information frames with association relations if and only if the bottom sequence is valid in the class of information frames with association relations.*

Proof. Clearly if the top sequence is valid, then the bottom sequence is valid. Suppose the bottom sequence is valid. Let $\mathbf{K}$ be a frame with association relations and let $\mathcal{M} = (\mathbf{K}, m)$ be a model. Then either $(x, 1) \notin R(m(PS))$ or $(x, 1) \notin R(m(P))$ or $(x, 1) \notin R(m(S))$ (which is to say: $(x, 1) \notin R(\{S\})$). If $(x, 1) \notin R(m(P))$ then by the semistrong condition, we can show that for some $S' \in m(P), (x, 1) \notin R(\{S'\})$. Let $S \in A_{par}$. Then $m(P) \cup \{S\} \subseteq Par$. By $(As2)$, $(x, 1) \notin R((m(P) \cup \{S\}) \cup \{S'\})$; therefore, $(x, 1) \notin R(m(P) \cup \{S\})$. This is equivalent to saying $(x, 1) \notin R(m(PS))$. If $(x, 1) \notin R(\{S\})$, then $(As2)$ tells us that $(x, 1) \notin R(m(P) \cup \{S\})$, which is equivalent to saying $(x, 1) \notin R(m(PS))$. In all cases we conclude that $(x, 1) \notin R(m(PS))$; therefore, $(x, 1) \in m(\neg(\mathbf{PS}))$. We may conclude that $x\neg\mathbf{PS}1$ is valid. Therefore, the top sequence is valid. □

In many relational deductive systems, a rule referred to as (cut) is required to build countermodels and thus give completeness results. The general form of a (cut)-rule is of the form:

$$(cut)\,\frac{}{x\mathbf{F}y \qquad\qquad x\neg\mathbf{F}y}$$

where $\mathbf{F}$ is any *LIS*-formula and x and y are any objects. Such rules are easily seen to be admissible. We will use a restricted form of the (cut)-rule, which suffices to give completeness and at the same time allows us to show that the tableaux procedure is decidable.

The Restricted Cut Rule:

$$(cut)'\,\frac{}{x\mathbf{P}1 \qquad\qquad x\neg\mathbf{P}1}$$

where the object x and either of the formulas $y\mathbf{P}z$ or $y\neg\mathbf{P}z$ (for any objects y, z) appear on the branch. We shall see that the $(cut)'$-rule does not interfere with termination for the class of problems connected with the implication problem for association rules in the way that (cut)-rules often do. Other forms of restricted cut rules for other deductive systems appear in (Gabbay's) labelled deduction method (where the rule is called partial bivalence or analytic cut) and in description logic (where the rule is called semantic branching).

Definition 8. A **complete tableau** is a tableau such that every rule that can be applied has been applied. (This means, for example, that rules like $(\neg;)$ and (ref) are applied for all objects on the branch.)

6   Soundness, completeness, decidability

Definition 9. Let *DAR* denote the deduction system consisting of: core deduction rules, $(\neg S)$, (SS), (ref), (sym), $(trans)$, $(as1 =>)$, $(as1 <= (a))$, $(as1 <= (b))$, $(as2)$ and $(cut)'$ and the axiomatic sequences mentioned in Section 5. Say **F** is **DAR-provable** if a *DAR*-tableau with xFy at the root, closes. If there is an open branch on a complete *DAR*-tableau for **F**, we say that **F** is **not DAR-provable**.

Theorem 3. *(Soundness) If the LIS-formula* **F** *is DAR-provable, then* **F** *is valid in information frames with association relations; i.e., for every information frame* **K** *with association relations and every model* $\mathcal{M}$ *of* **K**, $\mathcal{M}$ *satisfies* **F**.

Proof. The proof follows from Theorem 1 and the fact that the deduction rules are admissible in frames with association relations and the axiomatic sequences are valid in all information frames. □

Before stating the next theorem we nee the following definition:

Definition 10. An *RLIS*-formula is called **indecomposable** if it is of the form xSy or $x\neg Sy$ (any objects x, y), for S an atomic parameter, or of the form $x\neg 1y$.

Theorem 4. *(Completeness) If the LIS-formula* **F** *is not DAR-provable, then we can construct an information frame with association relations,* **K**, *and a model* $\mathcal{M}$ *of* **K** *that does not satisfy* **F**.

Proof. This proof follows the general format for completeness proofs for relational deduction systems, such as that found in [8], [9] and [10] and in several papers by Orłowska (see references in [14]). Assume the *LIS*-formula **F** is not *DAR*-provable; therefore there is an open branch, br, on a complete tableau. Let *ind* be the set of indecomposable formulas occurring in vertices of br and let *br* be the set of all formulas on br. If an indecomposable formula occurs on a vertex of br, then it occurs on every successor of that vertex. Define an information frame $\mathbf{K} = (X_{br}, Par_{br}, R_{br})$ and a model $\mathcal{M}_{br} = (\mathbf{K}_{br}, m_{br})$ as follows: The set of objects on the branch will be the set X_{br}. The set of parameters, Par_{br}, is the set $\{S_1, S_2, ..., S_n\}$, such that the relational constant S_i, corresponding to an atomic parameter, appears on the branch. (This will be a finite set because each *RLIS*-formula uses a finite number of relational constants. Each relational constant corresponds to a complex parameter and a complex parameter involves a finite number of atomic parameters.) For each nonempty $Q \subseteq \{S_1, S_2, ..., S_n\}$, let $R_{br}(Q)$ be $\{(x, y) : x\neg Qy \in br \}$. (For example, if $Q = \{S_1, S_2\}$, then $\mathbf{Q} = \mathbf{S_1 S_2}$.)

Tableaux rules guarantee that relations $R_{br}(Q)$ are equivalence relations: First, by (ref), $x\neg \mathbf{Q}_{br}x \in br$ so $(x, x) \in R_{br}(Q)$; second, suppose $(x, y) \in$

$R_{br}(Q)$; then $x \neg \mathbf{Q}_{br} y \in br$ so by (sym), $y \neg \mathbf{Q}_{br} x \in br$ so $(y, x) \in R_{br}(Q)$; finally, suppose $(x, y) \in R_{br}(Q)$ and $(y, z) \in R_{br}(Q)$; then $x \neg \mathbf{Q}_{br} y$ and $y \neg \mathbf{Q}_{br} z \in br$; by $(trans)$, we know $x \neg \mathbf{Q}_{br} z \in br$, and we may conclude that $(x, z) \in R_{br}(Q)$.

Tableaux rules also guarantee that this is a frame with semistrong relations: suppose $(x, y) \in R_{br}(Q) \cap R_{br}(T)$; then both $x \neg \mathbf{Q} y$ and $x \neg \mathbf{T} y \in br$. By $(\neg S)$, $x \neg (\mathbf{Q} \cup \mathbf{T}) y \in br$, so $(x, y) \in R_{br}(Q \cup T)$. Finally, let $R_{br}(\emptyset) = \{(x, y) : x \neg 1 y \in br\}$.

All that remains is to verify $(As1)$ and $(As2)$. To verify $(As1)$, we first consider the *only if* part. Suppose $(x, y) \in R_{br}(P)$; then $x \neg \mathbf{P} y \in br$. By $(as1 =>)$ either (a) both $x \neg \mathbf{P} 1$ and $y \neg \mathbf{P} 1 \in br$ or (b) both $x \mathbf{P} 1$ and $y \mathbf{P} 1 \in br$. If (a) holds, then $(x, 1) \in R_{br}(P)$ and $(y, 1) \in R_{br}(P)$ and we are done. If (b) holds, since the branch is open, it is not the case that either of $x \neg \mathbf{P} 1$ or $y \neg \mathbf{P} 1$ is on the branch; so $(x, 1) \notin R_{br}(P)$ and $(y, 1) \notin R_{br}(P)$.

Now let us prove the *if* part of $(As1)$. Suppose $(x, 1) \in R_{br}(P)$ and $(y, 1) \in R_{br}(P)$; then $x \neg \mathbf{P} 1$ and $y \neg \mathbf{P} 1 \in br$. By $(as1 <= (a))$, $x \neg \mathbf{P} y \in br$, so $(x, y) \in R_{br}(P)$. Now suppose $(x, 1) \notin R_{br}(P)$ and $(y, 1) \notin R_{br}(P)$. Then $x \neg \mathbf{P} 1$ is not on the branch and $y \neg \mathbf{P} 1$ is not on the branch. By the $(cut)'$-rule, $x \mathbf{P} 1$ and $y \mathbf{P} 1 \in br$. By $(as1 <= (b))$, $x \neg \mathbf{P} y \in br$. Thus $(x, y) \in R_{br}(P)$. This concludes the proof that the relations satisfy $(As1)$.

To prove the relations on the frame satisfy $(As2)$, we suppose $S \in Par_{br}$ and $P \subseteq Par_{br}$ and $(x, 1) \in R_{br}(P \cup \{S\})$. Therefore, $x \neg \mathbf{PS} 1 \in br$. By $(as2)$, $x \neg \mathbf{S} 1 \in br$; consequently, $(x, 1) \in R_{br}(\{S\})$. We now have a frame with association relations.

The identity map m_{br} from A_{par} to Par_{br}, extended in the appropriate manner, satisfies the properties of being an assignment; thus $(\mathbf{K}_{br}, m_{br})$ is a relational model on the information frame.

Let v_{br} be the identity valuation. The indecomposable formulas are of the form xSy or $x \neg Sy$, S an atomic parameter, and the formula $x \neg 1 y$. A formula xSy is satisfied in the model $(\mathbf{K}_{br}, m_{br})$ by the identity valuation v_{br} iff $(x, y) \in R_{br}(\{S\})$. If $xSy \in br$, the fact that the branch is open tells us that $x \neg Sy$ is not on the branch so the formula is not satisfied. A formula $x \neg Sy$ is satisfied by the identity valuation v_{br} iff $(x, y) \notin R_{br}(\{S\})$. If $x \neg Sy \in br$, then $(x, y) \in R_{br}(\{S\})$ so the formula is not satisfied. Finally, $x \neg 1 y$ is not satisfied because $m_{br}(\neg 1) = \overline{R_{br}(\emptyset)}$, which is the empty set. So, no indecomposable formula is satisfied by the model.

To prove that the *LIS*-formula $\mathbf{F}$ is not valid, we shall show that $(\mathcal{M}_{br}, v_{br})$ does not satisfy $x\mathbf{F}y$. We argue by contradiction: Suppose the contrary and let $\mathcal{Z}$ be the set of formulas which occur in some vertex of br and are satisfied by $(\mathcal{M}_{br}, v_{br})$. $\mathcal{Z}$ is nonempty, because $x\mathbf{F}y$ is a member if it. We define the degree of an *LIS*-formula by:

$d(\mathbf{S}) = d(\neg \mathbf{S}) = d(\neg 1) = 1$, where S is an atomic parameter;

$d(\mathbf{PQ}) = d(\mathbf{P}) + d(\mathbf{Q})$, where PQ is a complex parameter;

$d(\neg \mathbf{F}) = d(\mathbf{F}) + 1$, where $\mathbf{F}$ is not a formula of the form $\mathbf{1}$ or of the form $\mathbf{S}$, for S an atomic parameter;

$d(\mathbf{F!G}) = max(d(\mathbf{F}), d(\mathbf{G})) + 1$, where ! is one of $\cup$, $\cap$, $\rightarrow$ or $;$.

Let $x\mathbf{F}'y$ be a formula in $\mathcal{Z}$ with the property that the degree of its corresponding LIS-formula is least among the degrees of the LIS-formulas corresponding to formulas in $\mathcal{Z}$. It must be indecomposable. But above, we showed that indecomposable formulas are not satisfied. This gives a contradiction.   □

Theorem 5. *The LIS-formula* $\mathbf{F} \supset \mathbf{G}$ *is DAR-provable, iff for every frame* $\mathbf{K}$ *with association relations and model* $\mathcal{M}$ *of* $\mathbf{K}$, *if* $\mathcal{M}$ *satisfies* $\mathbf{F}$ *then* $\mathcal{M}$ *satisfies* $\mathbf{G}$.

Proof. This follows from Theorem 3, Definition 5 and the fact that given an information frame $\mathbf{K}$, and model $\mathcal{M} = (\mathbf{K}, m)$, if $m(\mathbf{F}) = X \times X$, then $m(\mathbf{1}; \neg\mathbf{F}; \mathbf{1}) = \emptyset$; otherwise, $m(\mathbf{1}; \neg\mathbf{F}; \mathbf{1}) = X \times X$.   □

Definition 11. In what follows, we use the notation $\mathbf{P} => \mathbf{Q}$ to denote the LIS-formula $(\mathbf{P} \rightarrow \mathbf{PQ}) \cap (\mathbf{PQ} \rightarrow \mathbf{P})$.

Theorem 6. *(Soundness and completeness for the implication problem for association rules) The LIS-formula* $((\mathbf{P}_1 => \mathbf{Q}_1) \cap (\mathbf{P}_2 => \mathbf{Q}_2) \cap ... \cap (\mathbf{P}_n => \mathbf{Q}_n)) \supset (\mathbf{P} => \mathbf{Q})$ *is DAR-provable if and only if for every context with 1 if the association rules* $P_i => Q_i$ *hold, for all* $i = 1, ..., n$, *then the association rule* $P => Q$ *holds.*

Proof. First recall that $\mathbf{P}_i$, $\mathbf{Q}_i$, all i, $\mathbf{P}$ and $\mathbf{Q}$ denote relational constants. Let us first consider the *only if* part. If $((\mathbf{P}_1 => \mathbf{Q}_1) \cap (\mathbf{P}_2 => \mathbf{Q}_2) \cap ... \cap (\mathbf{P}_n => \mathbf{Q}_n)) \supset (\mathbf{P} => \mathbf{Q})$ is DAR-provable, then given any information frame $\mathbf{K}$, with association relations and any model $\mathcal{M} = (\mathbf{K}, m)$, if $\mathcal{M}$ satisfies $\mathbf{P}_1 => \mathbf{Q}_1$ and , ... , and $\mathbf{P}_n => \mathbf{Q}_n$, then $\mathcal{M}$ satisfies $\mathbf{P} => \mathbf{Q}$. Now, if $\mathbf{T}$ and $\mathbf{S}$ are relational constants, $\mathcal{M}$ satisfies $\mathbf{T} => \mathbf{S}$ if and only if $m(\mathbf{T}) = m(\mathbf{TS})$, which is true if an only if $R(m(T)) = R(m(T)) \cup R(m(S))$. So, for an information frame with semistrong equivalence relations $R(P)$, for all $P \subseteq Par$, if $R(P_i) = R(P_i \cup Q_i)$, all $i = 1, ..., n$, then $R(P) = R(P \cup Q)$. Let S be a context with 1, with association rules $P_1 => Q_1, ... , P_n => Q_n$. By Remark 1, associated to it is an information frame, $\mathbf{K}_S$, a frame with semistrong equivalence relations which satisfy the conditions $R(P_i) = R(P_i \cup Q_i)$, $i = 1, ..., n$. (The relations in the frame are, of course, the association relations, R_P^{as}.) If $P => Q$ does not hold, then $R(P) \neq R(P \cup Q)$. This last statement gives a contradiction.

Now let us look at the *if* part; we argue by the contrapositive. If the LIS-formula is not DAR-provable, Theorems 4 and 5 tell us we can construct an information frame with association relations, $\mathbf{K}^{as}$, and a model $\mathcal{M}$ of $\mathbf{K}^{as}$ such that $\mathcal{M}$ satisfies $(\mathbf{P}_1 => \mathbf{Q}_1) \cap (\mathbf{P}_2 => \mathbf{Q}_2) \cap ... \cap (\mathbf{P}_n => \mathbf{Q}_n)$ and

$\mathcal{M}$ does not satisfy $\mathbf{P} \Rightarrow \mathbf{Q}$. Since the valuation is the identity, we conclude that we have an information frame with association relations, $\mathbf{K}^{as}$, such that $R(P_i) = R(P_i \cup Q_i)$, for all $i = 1, ..., n$, but $R(P) \neq R(P \cup Q)$. Theorem 4.1 assures us that we can construct a context with 1 from $\mathbf{K}^{as}$, whose set of attributes coincides with the set of parameters from the frame $\mathbf{K}^{as}$, and such that for all subsets P of the attributes, $R_P^{as} = R(P)$. Consequently, $R_{P_i}^{as} = R_{P_i \cup Q_i}^{as}$ but $R_P^{as} \neq R_{P \cup Q}^{as}$. Therefore, in this context with 1, the association rules $P_i \Rightarrow Q_i$, $i = 1, ..., n$, all hold, but the association rule $P \Rightarrow Q$ does not hold. □

Theorem 7. *The implication problem for association rules is decidable.*

Proof. We shall outline a decision procedure for the implication problem for association rules; that is, we describe a procedure which takes as an input any $RLIS$-formula of the form $x(((\mathbf{P}_1 \Rightarrow \mathbf{Q}_1) \cap (\mathbf{P}_2 \Rightarrow \mathbf{Q}_2) \cap ... \cap (\mathbf{P}_n \Rightarrow \mathbf{Q}_n)) \supset (\mathbf{P} \Rightarrow \mathbf{Q}))y$ and always terminates after a finite number of steps so that either all branches on the tableaux are closed or there is an open branch on a complete tableaux. If all the branches are closed, we conclude that the formula is DAR-provable; if there is an open branch, we conclude that the formula is not DAR-provable. The key points which insure such termination are the following:

(1) there is only a finite number of parameters in the formula;

(2) only a finite number of objects is introduced on any tableau (3, in fact: $\{x, y, 1\}$); and

(3) only a finite number of applications of $(cut)'$ is possible.

Consequently, in the development of a tableaux there are only a finite number of ways to use any rule, so we are able to determine in a finite number of steps if a tableau is closed or has an open branch.

Before describing the procedure, we note that we must assume that the procedure has a mechanism to prevent unnecessary reapplications of specific rules. For example, once we apply (sym) on a branch to $x \neg \mathbf{P} y$ to get $x \neg \mathbf{P} y, y \neg \mathbf{P} x$, we don't wish to reapply (sym) on that branch to $x \neg \mathbf{P} y$. One mechanism to prevent reapplications of rules is to Gödel number $RLIS$-formulas and sequences of $RLIS$-formulas in the standard manner so that each formula has associated to it a unique integer (its Gödel number), and each sequence of formulas has associated to it a unique integer (its Gödel number). Then, for each branch and for each rule we keep a list consisting of Gödel numbers; each number on the list is the Gödel number of the sequence of formulas that correspond to an instance of the upper line of the specific rule corresponding to the list. (The order of the formulas in the sequence will affect the Gödel number of the sequence so in order to uniquely assign a Gödel number to an instance of the upper line of a rule, we first order the formulas, that is, write them so that they have increasing Gödel numbers.) The rules (ref) and $(cut)'$ are a little different - we keep track of the Gödel number of the sequence consisting of the Gödel numbers of the object and the parameter to which they are applied. By referring to the list for a particular specific rule, the theorem prover can determine if a particular application of that specific rule has already been made on that branch.

The procedure is as follows. We shall think of the procedure in broad terms as involving: object introduction; parameter introduction; and clause introduction (where the clauses are of the form of $x\mathbf{P}y$ or $x\neg\mathbf{P}y$).

1. We start by applying the decomposition rules to decompose the formula. First apply the decomposition rule ($\cup$), then the rule ($\cap$) and then the rule ($\rightarrow$); next apply the rule ($as1$) one time on each branch.

Application of the ($as1$)-rule will introduce the object 1 on each branch. At no point in the process that we are describing do we get a formula of the form $x\neg(\mathbf{F};\mathbf{G})y$, so there will never be any applications of the ($\neg$;)-rule. Consequently, no new objects are introduced by applications of that decomposition rule. After applying the ($as1$)-rule, as described above, we have finished introducing objects on the tableau.

2. Apply the (;)-rule to the first occurrance of (;) in the formula $x(1;\neg((\mathbf{P}_1 => \mathbf{Q}_1)\cap(\mathbf{P}_2 => \mathbf{Q}_2)\cap...\cap(\mathbf{P}_n => \mathbf{Q}_n));1)y$, using the object x. Repeat this with y and then with 1. Drop the formula $x(1;\neg((\mathbf{P}_1 => \mathbf{Q}_1)\cap(\mathbf{P}_2 => \mathbf{Q}_2)\cap...\cap(\mathbf{P}_n => \mathbf{Q}_n));1)y$ from all branches.

3. Apply the (;)-rule to the formula $v(\neg((\mathbf{P}_1 => \mathbf{Q}_1)\cap(\mathbf{P}_2 => \mathbf{Q}_2)\cap...\cap(\mathbf{P}_n => \mathbf{Q}_n));1)y$, for each $v \in \{x,y,1\}$, using the object x. Repeat this with y and with 1. Drop the formulas $v(\neg((\mathbf{P}_1 => \mathbf{Q}_1)\cap(\mathbf{P}_2 => \mathbf{Q}_2)\cap...\cap(\mathbf{P}_n => \mathbf{Q}_n));1)y$ from all branches.

4. Apply all other appropriate decomposition rules.

When this process is completed, no formula with binary connectives is at the terminal vertex of any branch, so no more applications of decomposition rules are possible.

5. The specific rules ($as2$), ($\neg S$) and (SS) introduce parameters. Apply these **parameter introduction** rules in the order listed, finishing with all possible applications of one rule before proceeding to the next, and looping back to the previous rules to check if new applications are made possible by the current rule.

This process will eventually stop, because the formula we began with has only a finite number of complex parameters, each comprised of a finite number of atomic parameters, and there are only 3 objects on a branch.

6. The remainder of the specific rules introduce clauses. Apply these **clause introduction** rules wherever possible in the order (ref), (sym),

(*trans*), (*as*1 =>), (*as*1 <= (*a*)), (*as*1 <= (*b*)) and (*cut*)'. Again loop back to the previous rules to see if new applications are possible before proceeding to the next rule . (For example, if you are on (*trans*), once all applications of it have been made, check to see if new applications of (*sym*) are possible and then check if new applications of (*ref*) are possible then move down to (*sym*) and back up to (*ref*) and loop until you exit (*sym*) and proceed to (*trans*); if new applications of (*trans*) are possible repeat the looping process; continue until you exit (*trans*) and proceed to (*as*1 =>)).

There will be only a finite number of ways to apply any of these rules since the number of parameters and the number of objects is finite, so this looping process must eventually stop.

7. Return to the parameter introduction rules and make any new applications of these rules following the format given above. Follow this with new applications of the clause introduction rules, using the format given above. Continue looping.

Since the formula at the root of the tableau involves only a finite number, n, of atomic parameters, there will be at most 2^n parameters to introduce, so at some point, if the tableau has not already closed, when you loop back to the parameter introduction rules, all possible applications of these rules have been made.

Thus after a finite number of applications of rules, there are no new parameters to introduce, no new clauses to introduce and no new objects to introduce so the tableau either closes or is complete with an open branch.
□

7   Comments and future work

In this paper we have added association relations to the set of information relations and have initiated the study of dependencies in contexts with 1 via a relational deduction approach. We have also defined a new classification of relations parameterized by subsets of a set, the so called semistrong relations, and we have proved an informational representability theorem for semistrong equivalence relations with the added properties (*As*1) and (*As*2). Investigation into representability of the general set of semistrong relations remains to be done, as well as the investigation into the duality of information frames and algebras for frames with semistrong relations (see, for example, [16]).

The relational deduction method we discuss is an extremely general method that can be used to investigate many forms of dependencies for databases. We are currently investigating the tableaux method for difunctional dependencies (see [7]) which are useful in decomposing relational schemes which cannot otherwise be decomposed using the more traditional dependency theory, as well as ensuring data consistency and reducing data redundancy. Indeed, the method can be used to investigate generalized dependencies for all the information relations as listed in [13].

A big thrust today is in data mining where the goal is to *discover* dependencies in huge databases with many attributes. In many situations, study is focused on dependencies which are *less than perfect*; we may call these dependencies, *fuzzy dependencies*. By this we mean, for example, that an attribute's value is correctly determined by the value of a second attribute say 90% or maybe even 1% of the time. The inference technique here assumes perfect dependencies - and moreover, we must pick out the dependency we wish to question. Because of their great importance in marketing strategies and medical applications, associations have become the subject of intense investigation. A wide variety of counting and statistical methods have been used, to discover less than perfect, but still very important, associations among attributes, but many of them have shortcomings (see, for example [2]). A major problem, of course, is that when the number of attributes is large the number of subsets of attributes becomes enormous. One line of attack would be to develop a *multivalued* inferencing technique which will help direct the search for imperfect associations (and dependencies in general), possibly using graded techniques such as those considered by Gottwald (see [6]).

The reader interested in the automation of this deduction technique can consult [12] where we describe ReVAT an automated theorem prover based on this tableaux method.

Acknowledgements

I wish to thank Dirk van Gucht of Indiana University for introducing me to association rules and suggesting that I investigate association relations, and the referee for her or his valuable comments.

References

1. Abiteboul S., Hull R. and Vianu V. (1995) Foundations of Databases, Addison Wesley
2. Aggarwal C. and Yu P. (1998) A new framework for itemset generation. Proceedings of PODS 98 Principles of Database Systems, 18-24
3. Balbiani Ph. (1997) Axiomatization of Logics Based on Kripke Models with Relative Accessibility Relations. In: Orłowska E., (Ed.), Incomplete Information: Rough Set Analysis, Physica Verlag, 553-578
4. Balbiani Ph. and Orłowska E. (1999) A hierarchy of modal logics with relative accessibility relations. Journal of Applied Non-Classical Logics, 9:303-328
5. Buszkowski W. and Orłowska E. (1997) Indiscernibility-Based Formulation of Dependencies in Information Systems. In: Orłowska E., (Ed.), Incomplete Information: Rough Set Analysis, Physica Verlag, 298-320

6. Gottwald S. (1998) Many-valued logic, to appear. In: Hohle U., (Ed.), The Mathematics of Fuzzy Sets; A Handbook of Fuzzy Sets Methodology, Kluwer

7. Jaoua A., Belkhiter N., Ounalli H., Moukam T. (1996) Databases. In: Brink C., Kahl W. and Schmidt G., (Eds.), Relational Methods in Computer Science, Springer Verlag, 197 - 210

8. MacCaull W. (2000) A proof system for dependencies for information relations, to appear. Fundamenta Informaticae

9. MacCaull W. (1999) Relational tableaux for tree models, language models and information networks. In: Orłowska E., (Ed.), Logic at Work. A Memorial Tribute to Helena Rasiowa, Springer Physica Verlag, 354-382

10. MacCaull W. (1998) Relational semantics and a relational proof theory for full Lambek calculus. Journal of Symbolic Logic, 63:623-637

11. MacCaull W. (1998) A relational approach to association rules and functional dependencies. In: Orłowska E. and Szalas A., (Eds.), Proceedings of RelMiCS4, Fourth International Seminar on Relational Methods in Computer Science, Warsaw, Poland, 159-164

12. MacCaull W. and Spencer B. (2000) ReVAT: Relational Verification via Analytic Tableaux. Technical Report, Faculty of Computer Science, University of New Brunswick

13. Orłowska E. (1997) Introduction: What You Always Wanted to Know About Rough Sets. In: Orłowska E., (Ed.), Incomplete Information: Rough Set Analysis, Physica Verlag, 12-31

14. Orłowska E. (1996) Relational Foundations of Nonclassical Logics. In: Brink C., Kahl W. and Schmidt G., (Eds.), Relational Methods in Computer Science, Springer Verlag, 90-105

15. Orłowska E. (1987) Algebraic approach to database constraints. Fundamenta Informaticae, 10:57-66

16. SanJuan E. and Iturrioz L. (1997) Duality and informational representability of some information algebras, preprint

17. Ullman J. (1988) Database and Knowledge-Base Systems, Volume 1, Computer Science Press, Inc

18. Wille R. (1982) Restructuring Lattice Theory. In: Rival I., (Ed.), Ordered Sets, Reidel

Chapter 6
On a Static Verification of Integrity
Constraints in Relational Databases*

Jarosław Kachniarz[1] and Andrzej Szałas[2]

[1] Soft Computer Consultants
   34350 US 19N, Palm Harbor, FL 34684, USA
   jk@softcomputer.com
[2] Institute of Informatics
   Warsaw University
   ul. Banacha 2, 02-097 Warsaw, Poland
   szalas@mimuw.edu.pl

Abstract. The paper proposes a new approach to verification of integrity constraints in relational databases. According to the relational database paradigm, integrity constraints express certain conditions that should be preserved by all instances of a given database. Usually these conditions are checked dynamically, when the database is updated.

A static verification of integrity constraints, based on a technique of elimination of the second-order quantifiers is proposed and investigated in the current paper. The static approach allows one to verify whether given constraints have been preserved already during the database design phase. This results in better system performance, because no runtime checking is required when committing a statically verified transaction to the database.

Keywords: integrity constraints, relational databases, elimination of second-order quantifiers, verification of database transactions

1 Introduction

In this paper we present and discuss a new approach to verification of integrity constraints (*ICs*, for short) in relational databases. There are various definitions of integrity constraints in the literature. In [10,12] *ICs* are defined as formulas consistent with a given database, while in [9,11] *IC* is a theorem of the database. In [11] or [3], *ICs* are statements about contents of a database.

We accept a paradigm, according to which *IC* is a statement about database contents, expressed as classical first-order formulas (see also e.g. [1,4]) that are supposed to be satisfied by all possible instances of the database. In the existing implementations these conditions are checked dynamically during the database updates. In the case of software systems dealing with rapidly changing environment and reacting in real time, checking integrity

---

* Supported in part by the Wallenberg Foundation.

constraints after each update is usually unacceptable from the point of view of the required reaction time. Such situations are frequent in many artificial intelligence applications, including autonomous systems.

We propose a different approach, based on a static verification of *ICs*. We assume that the database can be modified only by well-defined procedures (later called transactions), supplied by database designers. In such a case the task of verification of *ICs* reduces to the following two steps:

1. verify that the initial contents of the database satisfies the defined constraints
2. verify that all transactions preserve the constraints.

If both above conditions hold, a simple induction, where point (1) is the first step and point (2) is the induction step, shows that all possible instances of the database preserve the *ICs*. In such a case runtime verification of *ICs* is no longer necessary. Of course, the database and transactions should be designed to satisfy the above conditions, because any violation of *ICs* is causing a transaction execution error.

Assume that $I(R_1, \ldots, R_n)$ is an *IC* involving relations (tables) $R_1, \ldots, R_n$ and is expressed as a classical first-order formula. In such a case the problem of checking the first of the above induction steps is in LOGSPACE and PTIME (see, e.g. [1,7]).

Consider a transaction, which modifies relations $R_1, \ldots, R_n$ giving as a result relations $R'_1, \ldots, R'_n$. The second of the steps mentioned earlier reduces to verification whether the following second-order formula is a tautology:

$$\forall R_1, \ldots, R_n[I(R_1, \ldots, R_n) \supset I(R'_1, \ldots, R'_n)].$$

In general this problem is totally undecidable. We shall show, however, that in numerous practical cases it can be reduced to decidable problems of acceptable complexity. The method is based on the Ackermann's lemma [2] and the algorithm of elimination of the second-order quantifiers published in [13], and improved in [5] (see also [6]). The algorithm of [5], called DLS, is implemented (see also Section 3).

A preliminary version of this paper has been published in [8].

2   Preliminaries

In this section we introduce the basic concepts and formulate the Ackermann's lemma. We deal with the first and the second-order classical logic with equality. In what follows, for any formula A and arbitrary expressions e, f, by $A(e \leftarrow f)$ we shall understand a formula obtained from A by substituting all occurrences of expression e by f. By $\top$ and $\perp$ we denote truth values "true" and "false", respectively. By $(e_1, \ldots, e_r) = (f_1, \ldots, f_r)$ we shall denote the formula $e_1 = f_1 \wedge \ldots \wedge e_r = f_r$.

Let us now define notions of relational database, integrity constraint, database update and transaction.

Definition 1. A *relational database DB*, is a first order structure

$$\langle U, r_1^{a_1}, \ldots, r_k^{a_k}, c_1, \ldots, c_l \rangle,$$

where

- U is a finite set
- for $1 \leq i \leq k$, $r_i^{a_i}$ is an a_i-ary relation on U, i.e. $r_i^{a_i} \subseteq U^{a_i}$
- $c_1, \ldots, c_l \in U$ are constants.

By a *signature* of DB we shall mean the signature consisting of relation symbols $R_1^{a_1}, \ldots, R_k^{a_k}$ and constant symbols $C_1, \ldots, C_l$ together with equality $=$.   □

Definition 2. By an *integrity constraint* in a relational database DB we shall mean any classical first-order formula over the signature of DB.   □

Definition 3. By an *update* of a relational database DB we shall mean an expression of one of the following forms:

- ADD $\bar{e}$ TO R,
- DELETE $\bar{e}$ FROM R,

where R is an k-ary relation of DB and $\bar{e}$ is a tuple of k elements.   □

The meaning of ADD and DELETE updates is rather obvious. Namely, ADD e TO R denotes adding a new tuple e to the relation R, whereas DELETE e FROM R denotes deleting e from R:

- (ADD e TO R)(R) $\equiv R \cup \{e\}$
- (DELETE e FROM R)(R) $\equiv R - \{e\}$.

From the logical point of view, the above updates are formula transformers defined as follows, where $A(R)$ is a formula:

$$\text{(ADD } e \text{ TO } R)(A(R(x))) \equiv A(R(x) \leftarrow (R(x) \vee x = e)) \tag{1}$$

$$\text{(DELETE } e \text{ FROM } R)(A(R(x))) \equiv A(R(x) \leftarrow (R(x) \wedge x \neq e)). \tag{2}$$

Definition 4. By a *transaction* on a relational database DB we shall mean any finite sequence of *updates* on DB.   □

For the sake of simplicity we consider only the updates of the form allowed in Definition 3. Observe, however, that any update can be defined my means of composition of ADD and DELETE updates. For example, tuple modification can be expressed as deleting the tuple and adding a new one.

The result of applying transaction T to formula A is defined as the composition of updates appearing in T and is further denoted by $T(A)$.

We are now ready to define correctness of transactions w.r.t. *ICs*. Observe that the definition simply adopts the corresponding notion well-known in the context of program verification.

Definition 5. Transaction T is *correct with respect to integrity constraint* $I(R_1, \ldots, R_k)$ iff the following implication:

$$I(R_1, \ldots, R_k) \supset T(I(R_1, \ldots, R_k))$$

is a tautology.   □

The following notions are necessary to formulate the lemma of Ackermann.

Definition 6. We say that a formula A is *positive* w.r.t. relational symbol R iff R appears under no negation sign in A (in negation normal form). We say that A is *negative* w.r.t. R iff all occurrences of R have the form $\neg R$ and $\neg R$ appears under no negation sign in A.   □

The Ackermann's lemma can be formulated as follows (see [2]).

Lemma 1 (Ackermann's Lemma). Let R be a relational symbol and $A(\bar{x}, \bar{z})$, $B(R)$ be formulas without second-order quantification. Let A contain no occurrences of R at all. Then the following equivalences hold:

- if $B(\neg R)$ is negative w.r.t. R, then

$$\exists R \forall \bar{x}[R(\bar{x}) \vee A(\bar{x}, \bar{z})] \wedge B(\neg R) \equiv B(\neg R \leftarrow A(\bar{x}, \bar{z})) \qquad (3)$$

- if $B(R)$ is positive w.r.t. R, then

$$\exists R \forall \bar{x}[\neg R(\bar{x}) \vee A(\bar{x}, \bar{z})] \wedge B(R) \equiv B(R \leftarrow A(\bar{x}, \bar{z})), \qquad (4)$$

where in the right-hand formulas the arguments $\bar{x}$ of A are to be substituted by the respective actual arguments of R (renaming the bound variables whenever necessary).   □

Remark 1. It is easily observable that the equivalence (4) of Lemma 1 is a dual form of (3) obtained by substituting all occurrences of the relational symbol R by $\neg R$. In what follows, we consider the first form only, assuming that the second one can easily be obtained by applying the above substitution.
□

3   The method

In this Section we formalize the substantial step of the proposed method, i.e. the verification of database transactions correctness as defined in Definition 5.

Let DB be a database, $I(R_1, \ldots, R_n)$ an IC and T be a transaction. Assume, that all formulas are expressed over the signature of DB.

According to Definition 5, in order to verify the correctness of transaction T, it suffices to prove, that the induction step expressed as the formula:

$$I(R_1, \ldots, R_k) \supset T(I(R_1, \ldots, R_k)) \qquad (5)$$

is a tautology. The proposed method is based on the fact, that formula (5) is a tautology iff the following second-order formula is a tautology, too:

$$\forall R_1 \ldots \forall R_k I(R_1, \ldots, R_k) \supset T(I(R_1, \ldots, R_k)). \tag{6}$$

In what follows we shall call formula (6) the *verification condition* for transaction T w.r.t. constraint I.

Now we can try to eliminate second-order quantifiers from (6) by applying Ackermann's lemma and obtaining as a result the formula without the relation symbols $R_1, \ldots, R_k$. It is now natural to raise the following questions:

1. When is the elimination of the second-order quantifiers possible?
2. Can the elimination of the second-order quantifiers be done automatically?
3. When can the correctness of the resulting formula be verified automatically?
4. What is the complexity of the method?

We shall answer these questions formulating conditions under which the elimination of the second-order quantifiers is guaranteed and results in a formula of a decidable theory. The method we propose is based on the technique of elimination of the second-order quantifiers which is automatic (see e.g. [5,13]) and already implemented[1]. The complexity of the method is discussed in Section 4.

In order to formulate the sufficient conditions that guarantee that the method works we have to define Ackermann's formulas[2] and universal Ackermann's formulas.

Definition 7. By an *Ackermann's formula w.r.t. relational symbols* $R_1, \ldots, R_k$ we shall mean:

1. any formula without symbols $R_1, \ldots, R_k$
2. any formula negative w.r.t. $R_1, \ldots, R_k$
3. any universally quantified disjunction of formulas of the form defined in the first item or literals, in which any symbol of $R_1, \ldots, R_k$ occurs at most once
4. any conjunction of the above formulas.   □

Definition 8. By an *universal Ackermann's formula w.r.t. relational symbols* $R_1, \ldots, R_k$ we shall mean any Ackermann's formula, where relational symbols $R_1, \ldots, R_k$ do not occur in the scope of existential quantifiers.   □

---

[1] The implementation of the DLS algorithm, made by J. Gustafsson is available via http://www.ida.liu.se/labs/kplab/project/dls/.
Information about another implementation, made by J. Kachniarz, and using software tool *Logic Engineer*, can be found in http://zls.mimuw.edu.pl/~szalas/cale/.

[2] We propose this term because of its correspondence to the Ackermann's lemma.

Example 1. Formulas $\neg R(x) \vee \neg R(y) \vee \neg S(z)$ and $R(x) \vee x \neq y \vee G(y)$ are Ackermann's formulas w.r.t. relational symbols R and S, but $R(x) \vee R(y) \vee \neg S(z)$ and $R(x) \vee S(y)$ are not. □

It is worth to emphasize here, that the introduced method works also for dual forms of Ackermann's formulas, where all relational symbols $R_1, \ldots, R_k$ are substituted by their negations (see Remark 1).

The following theorems are basic for the proposed method.

Theorem 1. For any integrity constraint $I(R_1, \ldots, R_k)$ of database DB, expressed as an universal Ackermann's formula w.r.t. $R_1, \ldots, R_k$ and any transaction T modifying at most relations $R_1, \ldots, R_k$, it is possible to eliminate the second-order quantifiers from the formula:

$$\forall R_1 \ldots \forall R_k I(R_1, \ldots, R_k) \supset T(I(R_1, \ldots, R_k)) \qquad (7)$$

applying the Ackermann's lemma[3]. Moreover, the resulting formula does not contain relation symbols $R_1, \ldots, R_k$ and its signature is included in the signature of DB. □

Proof. Consider formula

$$\forall R_1 \ldots \forall R_k I(R_1, \ldots, R_k) \supset T(I(R_1, \ldots, R_k)),$$

where I is an universal Ackermann's formula and T is a transaction. In order to apply the lemma of Ackermann we first negate this formula and obtain:

$$\exists R_1 \ldots \exists R_k I(R_1, \ldots, R_k) \wedge \neg I'(R_1, \ldots, R_k), \qquad (8)$$

where I' denotes the result of application of transaction T to I (i.e. the result of substitution of $R_i's$ by expressions of the form given in equations (1) or (2) corresponding to transaction updates). Since I' is obtained from universal Ackermann's formula I, relation symbols $R_1, \ldots, R_k$ do not appear in I' within the scope of existential quantifiers. In the next step move negation in formula (8) inside I'. Now relation symbols $R_1, \ldots, R_k$ do not appear in I' within the scope of universal quantifiers. Move all existential quantifiers binding variables occurring as parameters of $R_1, \ldots, R_k$ to the prefix of the formula. The resulting formula can now easily be transformed to the form required in the Ackermann's lemma and the second-order quantifiers can be eliminated (the algorithms of [5,13] easily do the job).

Observe also that the process of elimination of the second-order quantifiers based on the Ackermann lemma eliminates all occurrences of symbols $R_1, \ldots, R_k$ and does not introduce any new relation symbols (except $=$, which is assumed to be in the signature of database DB - see Definition 1). This proves the rest of the theorem. □

---

[3] Together with some simple equivalence preserving transformations, e.g. those listed in [5,13].

Theorem 2. Let $Th(Q_1, \ldots, Q_s, =)$ be a decidable first-order theory with a signature containing relational symbols $Q_1, \ldots, Q_s, =$. Let $I(R_1, \ldots, R_k)$ be an universal Ackermann's formula containing at most relation symbols $Q_1, \ldots, Q_s, =, R_1, \ldots, R_k$ and let T be a transaction modifying at most relations $R_1, \ldots, R_k$. Then it is decidable to verify whether the formula equivalent to:

$$\forall R_1 \ldots \forall R_k I(R_1, \ldots, R_k) \supset T(I(R_1, \ldots, R_k)),$$

obtained as in Theorem 1, is a theorem of $Th(Q_1, \ldots, Q_s)$.   □

Proof. Observe that, according to Theorem 1, the signature of the formula resulting from the process of elimination of the second-order quantifiers contains at most symbols $Q_1, \ldots, Q_s, =$. By assumption, $Th(Q_1, \ldots, Q_s, =)$ is decidable. Thus it is decidable whether the resulting formula is a theorem of $Th(Q_1, \ldots, Q_s)$.   □

Since the classical equality theory is decidable, the following corollary holds.

Corollary 1. Let Th be the decidable first-order equality theory with signature containing only symbol $=$. Let $I(R_1, \ldots, R_k)$ be an universal Ackermann's formula containing at most relational symbols $R_1, \ldots, R_k, =$ and let T be a transaction modifying relations $R_1, \ldots, R_k$. Then verification, whether the formula equivalent to:

$$\forall R_1 \ldots \forall R_k I(R_1, \ldots, R_k) \supset T(I(R_1, \ldots, R_k)),$$

obtained as in Theorem 1, is a tautology, is decidable.   □

4   The complexity

Let us now discuss the complexity of the proposed method.

If the integrity constraints are in the prefix and in the conjunctive normal form, then the elimination of quantifiers from a verification condition results, in the worst case, in a formula of length $O(n^2 + m)$, where n is the size of the integrity constraint and m is the size of the transaction[4]. Observe that usually the integrity constraints either are in this form, or can easily be transformed to it. However, in the worst case, the transformation of verification conditions to the form required in the Ackermann's lemma can result in an exponential blow up of the size of the formula.

The substantial complexity is hidden in deciding whether the resulting formula is a tautology (or a theorem of some theory). Even decidable theories are often of high complexity. On the other hand, one can observe, that the size of *ICs* and transactions is often relatively small. Moreover, the verification process is off-line. Thus the problem of checking whether the resulting formulas are tautologies or theorems has often an acceptable complexity.

---

[4] In many practical cases the result is even smaller than $(n + m)$.

It is also worth noting that there are many possible optimizations of the method. For example, instead of formulating integrity constraints as long conjunctions of formulas it is much better to define many integrity constraints defined as single conjuncts. One can sometimes reduce the complexity also by splitting transactions into smaller parts and verify each part separately.

5 Examples

The following examples illustrate the proposed method.

Example 2 (Mutual exclusion).
   Let's consider a database containing mutually exclusive relations $M(x)$, meaning that x is a male and $F(x)$, meaning that x is a female. No person can be both male and female, so the IC expressing this property can be defined as the following formula:

$$I(M, F) \equiv \forall x[\neg M(x) \vee \neg F(x)],$$

which is an universal Ackermann's formula.
   Consider transaction T moving a person a from F to M relation:

ADD a TO M; DELETE a FROM F.

Then $T(M(x)) \equiv M(x) \vee x = a$ and $T(F(x)) \equiv F(x) \wedge x \neq a$. According to the proposed method, the verification condition for integrity constraint I can be expressed as:

$$\forall F \forall M \forall x[\neg F(x) \vee \neg M(x)] \supset \forall z[\neg(F(z) \wedge z \neq a) \vee \neg(M(z) \vee z = a)]. \tag{9}$$

In order to transform formula (9) to a form suitable for the Ackermann's lemma, we first have to negate it (after the elimination of the second-order quantifiers, we shall negate the result obtaining a formula equivalent to (9)):

$$\exists F \exists M \forall x[\neg M(x) \vee \neg F(x)] \wedge \exists z[(F(z) \wedge z \neq a) \wedge (M(z) \vee z = a)].$$

Applying the Ackermann's lemma to eliminate the second-order quantifier $\exists M$ we obtain formula:

$$\exists F \exists z[(F(z) \wedge z \neq a) \wedge (\neg F(z) \vee z = a)]. \tag{10}$$

In order to apply Ackermann's lemma and eliminate $\exists F$, we have to transform the formula (10) to the form[5]:

$$\exists z \exists F \forall y(F(y) \vee y \neq z) \wedge z \neq a \wedge (\neg F(z) \vee z = a).$$

---

[5] Observe that algorithms of [5,13] do it automatically.

The application of the Ackermann's lemma results now in the formula:

$$\exists z[z \neq a \wedge (z \neq z \vee z = a)].$$

After negating it we obtain the formula:

$$\forall z[z = a \vee (z = z \wedge z \neq a)],$$

equivalent to (9) and being an obvious tautology (which can be verified automatically). □

Example 3 (Conditional uniqueness).

Let a database DB contain two relations: $W(x, y)$ meaning that y is x's wife and $M(x)$ meaning that x obeys the monogamy law. We can formulate an integrity constraint as follows: "if x and y are a couple and x obeys the monogamy law than x has only one wife, i.e. a tuple (x, y) occurs in the relation W at most once". It can be expressed formally as the following formula:

$$I(W, M) \equiv \forall x \forall y[(W(x, y) \wedge M(x)) \supset \forall z(W(x, z) \supset z = y)],$$

or equivalently:

$$I(W, M) \equiv \forall x \forall y[\neg W(x, y) \vee \neg M(x) \vee \forall z(\neg W(x, z) \vee z = y)],$$

which is an universal Ackermann's formula.

Consider a "divorce" transaction T deleting the tuple (a_1, a_2) from the relation W. Of course,

$$T(W) = W(x, y) \wedge (x, y) \neq (a_1, a_2).$$

The verification condition for T has then the following form:

$$\forall W \forall M \forall x \forall y[(W(x, y) \wedge M(x) \supset \forall z(W(x, z) \supset z = y))] \supset \quad (11)$$
$$[\forall x' \forall y'[(W(x', y') \wedge (x', y') \neq (a_1, a_2) \wedge M(x')) \supset$$
$$\forall z'((W(x', z') \wedge (x', z') \neq (a_1, a_2)) \supset z' = y')].$$

After some simple equivalence preserving transformations the negated verification condition has the form:

$$\exists W \exists M \forall x[\neg M(x) \vee \forall y(\neg W(x, y) \vee \forall z(\neg W(x, z) \vee z = y))] \wedge$$
$$[\exists x' \exists y' W(x', y') \wedge (x', y') \neq (a_1, a_2) \wedge M(x') \wedge \exists z'(W(x', z') \wedge (x', z')$$
$$\neq (a_1, a_2) \wedge z' \neq y')].$$

Applying the Ackermann's lemma we eliminate the second-order quantifier $\exists M$:

$$\exists W \exists x' \exists y'[W(x', y') \wedge (x', y') \neq (a_1, a_2) \wedge$$
$$\forall y(\neg W(x', y) \vee \forall z(\neg W(x', z) \vee z = y)) \wedge \exists z'(W(x', z') \wedge (x', z')$$
$$\neq (a_1, a_2) \wedge z' \neq y')].$$

This formula can easily (and, in fact, automatically) be transformed to the form:

$$\exists x'\exists y'\exists z'\exists W[\forall x,y(W(x,y)\vee((x,y)\neq(x',y')\wedge(x,y)\neq(x',z')))\wedge(x',y')$$
$$\neq(a_1,a_2)\wedge\forall y(\neg W(x',y)\vee\forall z(\neg W(x',z)\vee z=y))\wedge(x',z')$$
$$\neq(a_1,a_2)\wedge z'\neq y'].$$

Applying the Ackermann's lemma to eliminate $\exists W$ we obtain:

$$\exists x'\exists y'\exists z'(x',y')\neq(a_1,a_2)\wedge\forall y(((x',y)\neq(x',y')\wedge(x',y)\neq(x',z'))\vee \qquad (12)$$
$$\forall z(((x',z)\neq(x',y')\wedge(x',z)\neq(x',z'))\vee z=y))\wedge(x',z')\neq(a_1,a_2)\wedge z'\neq y'].$$

In order to prove unsatisfiability of this formula one can use existing theorem provers. For example, one can transform the formula (12) into the following equisatisfiable set of clauses, using standard techniques (where a,b,c are new Skolem constants):

$$a\neq a_1\vee b\neq a_2$$
$$y\neq b\vee z\neq b\vee z=y$$
$$y\neq b\vee z\neq c\vee z=y$$
$$y\neq c\vee z\neq b\vee z=y \qquad (13)$$
$$y\neq c\vee z\neq c\vee z=y$$
$$a\neq a_1\vee z\neq a_2$$
$$c\neq b \qquad (14)$$

Now clauses (13) and (14) lead to contradiction (with y substituted by b and z substituted by c). Thus the verification condition (11) is a tautology, i.e. transaction T is correct w.r.t. I and does not need a runtime verification. □

The following example illustrates application of the method in the case of integrity constraints not being in the form of universal Ackermann's formulas.

Example 4 (1-1 relationship).
Consider database DB containing two relations (tables) $R(x)$ and $S(x,z)$ being in 1-1 relationship, i.e. for every tuple from table R there exists one and only one appropriate tuple in table S and vice versa. It is worth emphasizing here, that the leading commercial relational database management systems practically do not provide effective mechanisms to enforce this constraint.

The 1-1 integrity constraint can be formalized as conjunction of the following two formulas:

$$I_1(R,S)\equiv\forall x[R(x)\supset\exists zS(x,z)] \qquad (15)$$

and

$$I_2(R,S)\equiv\forall x\forall y\forall z[(R(x)\wedge S(x,y)\wedge S(x,z))\supset y=z]. \qquad (16)$$

Although the formula (15) is not an universal Ackermann's formula, it will be possible to eliminate second order quantifiers using the Ackermann's lemma.

Consider the transaction T adding the tuple e to the relation R and the tuple (e, f) to the relation S:

ADD (e) TO R; ADD (e, f) TO S.

According to the proposed method, we have to verify whether the following second-order formulas are tautologies:

$$\forall R \forall S[\forall x(R(x) \supset \exists z S(x, z)) \supset \forall x((R(x) \lor x = e) \supset \exists z(S(x, z) \lor (x, z)$$
$$= (e, f))] \tag{17}$$

and

$$\forall R \forall S[\forall x \forall y \forall z((R(x) \land S(x, y) \land S(x, z)) \supset y = z) \supset \tag{18}$$
$$\forall x \forall y \forall z(((R(x) \lor x = e) \land (S(x, y) \lor (x, y) = (e, f)) \land (S(x, z) \lor (x, z)$$
$$= (e, f))) \supset y = z).$$

Observe that IC expressed as the formula (16) can easily be transformed to an universal Ackermann's formula. Thus one can try to verify it automatically using the method we propose.

The more interesting case is the IC expressed as the formula (15) which cannot be represented as an universal Ackermann's formula. However, as we shall show, the technique we have proposed still works in this case. Consider the negation of the formula (17):

$$\exists R \exists S[\forall x(\neg R(x) \lor \exists z S(x, z)) \land \exists x'((R(x') \lor x' = e) \land \forall z'(\neg S(x', z') \land (x', z')$$
$$\neq (e, f))]. \tag{19}$$

We apply Ackermann's lemma to eliminate quantifier $\exists R$ and obtain:

$$\exists S[\exists x'((\exists z S(x', z) \lor x' = e) \land \forall z'(\neg S(x', z') \land (x', z') \neq (e, f))]. \tag{20}$$

In order to apply Ackermann's lemma we transform the formula into the following equivalent form (algorithms presented in [5,13] do this automatically):

$$\exists x' \exists S[(\exists z S(x', z) \lor x' = e) \land \forall z' \forall x''(\neg S(x'', z') \lor x'' \neq x') \land \forall z'(x', z')$$
$$\neq (e, f))]. \tag{21}$$

Now the application of the Ackermann's lemma results in:

$$\exists x'[(\exists z x' \neq x' \lor x' = e) \land \forall z'(x', z') \neq (e, f))], \tag{22}$$

which after immediate simplification is equivalent to:

$$\exists x'[x' = e \land (x' \neq e \lor \forall z'(z' \neq f))], \tag{23}$$

which is equivalent to $\perp$. Thus the original condition (17) is a tautology and the correctness of transaction T w.r.t. integrity constraint (15) is completed.
$\square$

6   Conclusions

The commercially available RDBMSs[6] supply us with very advanced technologies, but almost ignore the problem of integrity constraints. These systems practically offer only rather simple constraints within one tuple, uniqueness and primary-foreign key relationships. On the other hand, the development of the computer aided system engineering (CASE) tools and object-oriented techniques requires means for specifying more subtle integrity constraints.

Modern RDBMSs provide the security features allowing us to define a list of transaction (procedures in Java or PL/SQL) permitted on the database. The other updates can be forbidden, e.g. in the Example 2 one could define procedures: addMale, addFemale and verify them against transactions like deleteMale, deleteFemale or changeSex. In the case of successful verification, dynamic checking of those constraints during runtime is no longer necessary.

To avoid complex and time-consuming checking of *ICs* during the runtime, we proposed a new, static approach to integrity constraint verification in relational databases. Our approach can easily be automated. In fact, the DLS algorithm of elimination of the second-order quantifiers has already been implemented. We also proved, that in the case of integrity constraints expressed as the universal Ackermann's formulas, the success of applying the techniques based on the elimination of the second-order quantifiers is guaranteed. Moreover, according to the Theorems 1, 2 and the Corollary 1, in many practical cases the proposed method leads to the decidable first-order theories. As shown in the Example 4, the method works also for some formulas not in the universal Ackermann's form, but the elimination of the second-order quantifiers is no longer guaranteed[7].

It is worth emphasizing here that - in the more general case of *ICs* not defined as universal Ackermann's formulas - a similar technique of partial elimination of the second-order quantifiers can be considered as an optimization technique, because the elimination of any second-order quantifier reduces the number of relations appearing in the constraint. This problem is a subject of a research being currently carried out by the authors.

References

1. Abiteboul S., Hull R., Vianu V. (1996) Foundations of Databases. Addison-Wesley Pub. Co.
2. Ackermann W. (1935) Untersuchungen über das Eliminationsproblem der mathematischen Logik. Mathematische Annalen, 110, 390-413

---

[6] Relational Database Management Systems.

[7] In fact, it is easily observable that whenever the negated verification condition is an Ackermann's formula, then the elimination of the second-order quantifiers is still guaranteed.

3. Chakravarthy U.S., Grant J., Minker J. (1987) Foundations of Semantic Query Optimization for Deductive Databases. In: Minker J. (Ed.) Foundations of Deductive Databases and Logic Programming, Morgan Kaufmann Pub., Inc.

4. Colomb R.M. (1998) Deductive Databases and Their Applications. Taylor & Francis Ltd.

5. Doherty P., Łukaszewicz W., Szałas A. (1997) Computing Circumscription Revisited. A Reduction Algorithm. Journal of Automated Reasoning, 18, 3:297-336

6. Doherty P., Łukaszewicz W., Szałas A. (1999) Declarative PTIME Queries for Relational Databases using Quantifier Elimination. Journal of Logic and Computation, 9, 97:737-758

7. Ebbinghaus H-D., Flum J. (1995) Finite Model Theory. Springer-Verlag

8. Kachniarz J., Szałas A. (1999) On a Certain Approach to Static Verification of Integrity Constraints in Relational Databases. In: Proc. of Conf. on Applications of Mathematics in Computer Science and Economy, Olsztyn, 123-134. In Polish

9. Lloyd J., Topor W. (1985) A Basis for Deductive Database Systems. Journal of Logic Programming, 2, 2:93-109

10. Kowalski R. (1978) Logic for Data Description. In: Minker J. (Ed.) Logic and Data Bases, Plenum Press

11. Reiter R. (1988) On Integrity Constraints. In: Proc. of the 2nd Conf. on the Theoretical Aspects of Reasoning about Knowledge, 97-111, Morgan Kaufmann Pub., Inc.

12. Sadri F., Kowalski R. (1987) A Theorem Proving Approach to Database Integrity. In: Minker J. (Ed.) Foundations of Deductive Databases and Logic Programming, Morgan Kaufmann Pub., Inc.

13. Szałas A. (1993) On the Correspondence between Modal and Classical Logic. An Automated Approach. Journal of Logic and Computation, 3:605-620

Part III

Relations in Linguistics and Spatial Reasoning

Chapter 7
Contact Relation Algebras

Ivo Düntsch

School of Information and Software Engineering
University of Ulster
Newtownabbey, BT 37 0QB, N. Ireland
I.Duentsch@ulst.ac.uk

Abstract. Contact relation algebras (CRAs), introduced in [25], arise from the study of "part–of" and "contact" relations rooted in mereology and have applications, for example, in qualitative spatial reasoning. We give an overview of the origins of CRAs and numerous examples.
Keywords: mereology, relation algebra, spatial reasoning

1 Introduction

Contemporary qualitative spatial reasoning (QSR) is based largely on the relational and topological properties of regions. A basic role is played by the binary "part – of" and "contact" relations, from which many others can be defined. The formal study of "part – of" relations goes back to [38], a Polish mathematician, who, together with Twardowski, Łukasiewicz, and his sole doctoral student Tarski, formed the core of the Lwów – Warsaw school of Logic and Philosophy, which

> "... in the 20s – 30s of this century made the University of Warsaw perhaps the most important research centre in the world for formal logic" [10].

Mereology, the "Science of parts", is a part of S. Leśniewski's work on the foundations of Mathematics, developed from about 1915 onwards [38]. It is not the purpose of this article to go into the details and ramifications of this system, but we refer the reader instead to [41,39,54] or [52,40]. Mereology was later taken up by [37], though for a different reason; formally, their calculus and Leśniewski's system are the same. [13] generalised mereology and based the relational part of his "Calculus of Individuals" on a "connection" or "contact" relation which first appeared in the works of [18] and [44]. In spatial reasoning, "mereology" is today frequently used synonymously with the study of connection, and Leśniewski's original system is referred to as "classical mereology" (CM), see [27].

A "connection" or "contact" relation is a reflexive and symmetric binary relation with the additional property that each element of the domain is determined by those elements with which it is in contact. From a contact relation between circles in the Euclidean plane the relations pictured in Figure 2 can be defined [18,13]. These relations also form the basis of the investigations of [26] and [49].

Recently, composition based reasoning with binary relations has been of interest to the QSR community [49,8,6,7], and the expressive power, consistency and complexity of relational reasoning have become an object of study.

It has been known for some time, that the expressiveness of reasoning with basic operations on binary relations is equal to the expressive power of the three variable fragment of first order logic [57]. Thus, it seems worthwhile to use methods of relation algebras, initiated by [56], to study contact relations in their own right, and then explore their expressive power with respect to various topological domains.

In this paper, we give an overview of the basic properties of contact relations and their algebras, and explore their expressive power on simple domains; most of the material is drawn from [24,25].

2   Binary relations and their algebras

A binary relation on a set U is a subset of $U \times U$. If $R, S \subseteq U \times U$, and $x, y, z \in U$, we will usually write xRy for $\langle x, y \rangle \in R$, and $xRySz$ for xRy and yRz. The *range of x in R* is the set

$$Rx \overset{\text{def}}{=} \{ y \in U : xRy \}.$$

We denote the set of all binary relations on U by $Rel(U)$; clearly, $Rel(U)$ is a Boolean algebra under the usual set operations $\cap, \cup, -$ with smallest element $\emptyset$ and largest element $V \overset{\text{def}}{=} U \times U$. We also consider the following operations on $Rel(U)$:

$$R \circ S \overset{\text{def}}{=} \{ \langle x, y \rangle : (\exists z \in U)[xRzSy] \}, \text{ Composition} \tag{1}$$

$$R^{\smile} \overset{\text{def}}{=} \{ \langle x, y \rangle : yRx \}. \qquad \text{Converse} \tag{2}$$

An additional distinguished constant is the identity relation $1'$. The structure

$$\langle Rel(U), \cap, \cup, -, \emptyset, V, \circ, \smile, 1' \rangle$$

is called the *full algebra of binary relations on U*. Any subalgebra of $Rel(U)$ is called an *algebra of binary relations* (BRA). We usually identify algebras with their base set and write $A \leq Rel(U)$ if A is a subalgebra of $Rel(U)$. $A \leq Rel(U)$ is called *integral*, if $1'$ is an atom of A. If $\{ R_i : i \in I \} \subseteq Rel(U)$, then $\langle R_i \rangle_{i \in I}$ is the subalgebra of $Rel(U)$ generated by $\{ R_i : i \in I \}$.

If $R \in Rel(U)$, then its *residual $R \setminus R$* is the largest $S \in Rel(U)$ for which $R \circ S \subseteq R$. The residual is equationally definable as

$$R \setminus R = -(R^{\smile} \circ -R), \tag{3}$$

and one can also show that

$$x(R \setminus R)y \iff R^{\smile}x \subseteq R^{\smile}y. \tag{4}$$

Furthermore,

Lemma 1. *[48]* $R \setminus R$ *is reflexive and transitive.*

The expressiveness of BRAs corresponds to a fragment of first order logic, and the following fundamental result is due to A. Tarski [57]:

Proposition 1. *If $R_0, \ldots, R_k \in Rel(U)$, then $\langle R_0, \cdots, R_k \rangle$ is the set of all binary relations on U which are definable in the (language of the) relational structure $\langle U, R_0, \ldots, R_k \rangle$ by first order formulas using at most three variables, two of which are free.*

In certain domains, BRA expressiveness is even stronger: We call a BRA $A \leq Rel(U)$ *first order closed*, if every relation definable in the first order structure $\langle U, A \rangle$ is an element of A.

If a BRA $A \leq Rel(U)$ is complete and atomic – in particular, if A is finite –, then each nonzero element is a sum of atoms, and relational composition can be be described by a matrix such as Table 1, whose rows and columns are labelled by the atoms and an entry $\langle P, Q \rangle$ is the set of atoms contained in $P \circ Q$. If A is integral, we omit column and row $1'$.

For example, the algebra determined by Table 1 has the atoms PP, $PP^{\smile}$, PO, DC, $1'$; we see that PO and DC are symmetric relations, and that $1'$ is an atom. The entry, for example, at position $\langle PP^{\smile}, PP \rangle$ means that

$$PP^{\smile} \circ PP = -DC = PP \cup PP^{\smile} \cup PO \cup 1'.$$

Table 1. Open circle algebra C_o

$\circ$	PP	$PP^{\smile}$	PO	DC
PP	PP	V	$-P^{\smile}$	DC
$PP^{\smile}$	$-DC$	$PP^{\smile}$	$PP^{\smile}, PO$	$-P$
PO	PP, PO	$-P$	V	$-P$
DC	$-P^{\smile}$	DC	$-P^{\smile}$	V

If $\mathcal{R} = \{ R_i : i \in I \}$ is a partition of $Rel(U)$ such that $\mathcal{R}$ is closed under converse, and $R_i \subseteq 1'$ or $R_i \cap 1' = \emptyset$ for all $i \in I$, we define the *weak composition* of $\mathcal{R}$ as the mapping $\circ_w : \mathcal{R} \times \mathcal{R} \to 2^{\mathcal{R}}$ such that for all $i, j \in I$

$$S \in R_i \circ_w R_j \stackrel{\text{def}}{\iff} S \cap (R_i \circ R_j) \neq \emptyset. \tag{5}$$

Table 2. Interval relations

before:	$\{\langle [q,r], [q',r'] \rangle : q < r < q' < r', q, r, q', r' \in \mathbb{R} \}$
meets:	$\{\langle [q,r], [q',r'] \rangle : q < r = q' < r', q, r, q', r' \in \mathbb{R} \}$
overlaps:	$\{\langle [q,r], [q',r'] \rangle : q < q' < r < r', q, r, q', r' \in \mathbb{R} \}$
starts:	$\{\langle [q,r], [q',r'] \rangle : q = q' < r < r', q, r, q', r' \in \mathbb{R} \}$
ends:	$\{\langle [q,r], [q',r'] \rangle : q' < q < r = r', q, r, q', r' \in \mathbb{R} \}$
contains:	$\{\langle [q,r], [q',r'] \rangle : q < q' < r' < r, q, r, q', r' \in \mathbb{R} \}$

Just as in the case of $\circ$, we can determine composition tables for $\circ_w$. Note that $R_i \circ R_j \subseteq R_i \circ_w R_j$; if equality holds everywhere, i.e. when $\circ = \circ_w$, we call the weak composition table *extensional*.

An abstract relation algebra (RA) is a structure

$$\langle A, +, \cdot, -, 0, 1, \circ, \breve{}, 1' \rangle$$

of type $\langle 2, 2, 1, 0, 0, 2, 1, 0 \rangle$ which satisfies for all $a, b, c \in A$,

1. $\langle A, +, \cdot, -, 0, 1 \rangle$ is a Boolean algebra (BA).
2. $\langle A, \circ, \breve{}, 1' \rangle$ is an involuted monoid, i.e.
   (a) $\langle A, \circ, 1' \rangle$ is a semigroup with identity $1'$,
   (b) $a^{\breve{}\breve{}} = a$, $(a \circ b)^{\breve{}} = b^{\breve{}} \circ a^{\breve{}}$.
3. The following conditions are equivalent:

$$(a \circ b) \cdot c = 0, \quad (a^{\breve{}} \circ c) \cdot b = 0, \quad (c \circ b^{\breve{}}) \cdot a = 0. \tag{6}$$

Each BRA is an RA with the obvious operations, but not vice versa [42]. If A is an abstract RA, a *representation of A* is a BRA isomorphic to A.[1]

For the arithmetic and other properties of BRAs we invite the reader to consult [12] or [32,33].

3   Relations of time and space

[2] has presented a set of 13 relations which characterise the possible relations between convex intervals of time.[2] These are the six relations of Table 2, their converses, and the identity. They are the atoms of an integral BRA on the set of all closed intervals on the real line; its composition table can be found in e.g. [36]. We observe that, in this model, the basic object in the ontology of time is the interval, as opposed to a point, and we invite the reader to consult [3] for a discussion of this issue.

If we want to extend the time interval relations to, say, two dimensional Euclidean space, a natural domain to choose is the set $\mathfrak{C}$ of closed disks. In

---

[1] This is more special than the usual definition, but it will suffice for our purposes.
[2] A logic of time was independently given by [9], see also [44].

Fig. 1. Interval relations

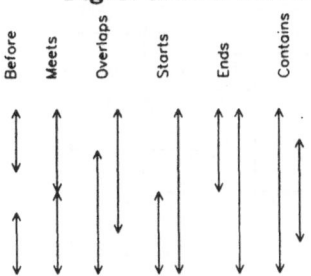

space, we do not have the direction of the real line any more, and thus, for example, we cannot distinguish between the "starts" and the "ends" relations, and between the "before" relation and its converse. In this spirit, we obtain the spatial relations which are defined in Table 3, and pictured in Figure 2.

Table 3. Circle relations

Disconnected (DC)	$: \{\langle a,b\rangle : a \cap b = \emptyset\}$
Externally connected (EC)	$: \{\langle a,b\rangle : a \cap b \neq \emptyset,\ int(a \cap b) = \emptyset\}$
Partial overlap (PO)	$: \{\langle a,b\rangle : a \not\subseteq b,\ b \not\subseteq a,\ int(a \cap b) \neq \emptyset\}$
Tangential proper part (TPP)	$: \{\langle a,b\rangle : a \subsetneq b,\ Fr(a) \cap Fr(b) \neq \emptyset\}$
Nontangential proper part (NTPP):	$\{\langle a,b\rangle : a \subseteq int(b)\}$.

There, $int(a)$ is the topological interior of a, and $Fr(a)$ its boundary, i.e.

Fig. 2. Circle relations

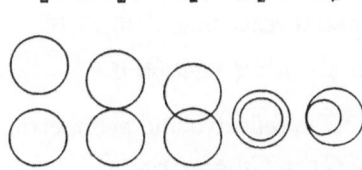

$Fr(a) = a \cap -int(a)$. We note that DC, EC, and PO are symmetric, while TPP and $NTPP$ are not; this gives us the additional circle relations $TPP^{\smile}$ and $NTPP^{\smile}$. Along with $1'$, they are the atoms of a BRA C_c on $\mathfrak{C}$ whose composition is given in Table 4 [25]. C_c is isomorphic to the subalgebra of $\mathcal{I}$ generated by the union of the "before" relation and its converse, but its circle

Table 4. Closed circle algebra $\mathcal{C}_c$

∘	TPP	$TPP^{\smile}$	$NTPP$	$NTPP^{\smile}$	PO	EC	DC
TPP	PP	$-(NTPP \cup NTPP^{\smile})$	$NTPP$	$-P$	$-P^{\smile}$	EC, DC	DC
$TPP^{\smile}$	$1', TPP,$ $TPP^{\smile}, PO$	$PP^{\smile}$	$PP^{\smile}, PO$	$NTPP^{\smile}$	$PP^{\smile}, PO$	$PP^{\smile}, PO, EC$	$-P$
$NTPP$	$NTPP$	$-P^{\smile}$	$NTPP$	1	$-P^{\smile}$	DC	DC
$NTPP^{\smile}$	$PP^{\smile}, PO$	$NTPP^{\smile}$	$-(EC \cup DC)$	$NTPP^{\smile}$	$PP^{\smile}, PO$	$PP^{\smile}, PO$	$-P$
PO	PP, PO	$-P$	PP, PO	$-P$	1	$-P$	$-P$
EC	PP, PO, EC	$EC \cup DC$	PP, PO	DC	$-P^{\smile}$	$-(NTPP \cup NTPP^{\smile})$	$-P$
DC	$-P^{\smile}$	DC	$-P^{\smile}$	DC	$-P^{\smile}$	$-P^{\smile}$	1

representation cannot be embedded into any representation of $\mathcal{I}$: Consider the square and its diagonals in Figure 3, and label the sides of the square with PO and its diagonals with DC. This network cannot be satisfied in any representation of $\mathcal{I}$ [36], but it can be satisfied in the closed circle algebra.

Fig. 3. Satisfiable circle network

4   Contact relation algebras

Contact relations first arose in the works of [18] and [58]. Subsequently, [13] used a "connection" relation to extend the mereological part of the calculus of Leśniewski. It is nowadays customary to talk about "contact" instead of "connection" relations (just as [18] did), in order to avoid confusion with the unary topological predicate "connected". Contact relations are the backbone of current qualitative spatial reasoning [5,30,15,14].

$C \in Rel(U)$ is called a *contact relation* if

$$C \text{ is reflexive and symmetric} \tag{7}$$

$$Cx = Cy \iff x = y. \tag{8}$$

It was shown by [25] that the extensionality axiom (8) can be replaced by the RA term equation

$$C \setminus C \text{ is a partial order.} \tag{9}$$

In the sequel, we will write P for $C \setminus C$, and set $PP = P \cap -1'$.

A *contact relation algebra* (CRA) is an RA which is generated by a non–identity contact relation. For a first example, consider the closed circle algebra C_c of Table 4: If we set

$$C \stackrel{\text{def}}{=} 1' \cup TPP \cup TPP^\smile \cup NTPP \cup NTPP^\smile \cup PO \cup EC, \qquad (10)$$

then $P = C \setminus C = 1' \cup TPP \cup NTPP$ is set inclusion, and C generates C_c.

If $\mathfrak{C}_o$ is the set of all open circles in the Euclidean plane, and $aCb \stackrel{\text{def}}{\Longleftrightarrow} a \cap b \neq \emptyset$ for $a, b \in \mathfrak{C}_o$, then the BRA C_o generated by C has the composition given in Table 1 with $C = 1' \cup PP \cup PP^\smile \cup PO$. This algebra is also known as the *containment algebra* [36]; it is isomorphic to the subalgebra of C_c generated by P, and isomorphic to the subalgebra of $\mathcal{I}$ generated by the union of "precedes" and "meets" and their converses. The interval algebra $\mathcal{I}$ itself, however, is not a CRA.

In the rest of this section we will present several small CRAs from [25]. This will show that CRAs do not only arise from spatial contexts. First, however, we want to express the circle relations of Table 3 by relation algebraic terms obtained from C:

$$
\begin{array}{llll}
O & = P^\smile \circ P & \text{overlap} & (11) \\
PO & = O \cdot -(P + P^\smile) & \text{partial overlap} & (12) \\
EC & = C \cdot -O & \text{external contact} & (13) \\
TPP & = PP \cdot (EC \circ EC) & \text{tangential proper part} & (14) \\
NTPP & = PP \cdot -TPP & \text{non–tangential proper part} & (15) \\
DC & = -C & \text{disconnected} & (16) \\
\text{We will also set} \quad CP & = P \cup P^\smile, & \text{comparable} & (17) \\
DR & = -O & \text{discrete.} & (18)
\end{array}
$$

We will keep these definitions throughout the rest of the paper.

Even though a contact relation C need not be equal to O, it will always contain O [25].

The smallest CRA is the algebra known as $\mathcal{N}_1$ [16]; it has four atoms, and its composition is given in Table 5. Clearly, $C = P^\smile \circ P = P \cup P^\smile$ is symmetric and reflexive, and P is a partial order. Finally,

$$C \setminus C = -(C \circ DC) = -((P \cup P^\smile) \circ DC) = -(DC \cup P^\smile) = P.$$

The first concrete representation of $\mathcal{N}_1$ was given by [19]. A picture of the order derived from a slightly different representation of $\mathcal{N}_1$, given in [4], is shown in Figure 4. There, P is a fractal–like structure with a copy of $\mathbb{Q}$ as its stem, and branching at each point into two copies of $\mathbb{Q}$.

120   Ivo Düntsch

Fig. 4. An ordering for $\mathcal{N}_1$

Fig. 5. The algebra $\mathcal{N}_1$

$\circ$	PP	$PP^{\smile}$	DC
PP	PP	1	DC
$PP^{\smile}$	$-DC$	$PP^{\smile}$	$PP^{\smile}, DC$
DC	PP, DC	DC	1

In $\mathcal{N}_1$, we have $C = O$. Contrary to this, the algebra $\mathcal{C}_c$ satisfies

$$O = P^{\smile} \circ P = P \cup PO,$$

and thus,

$$EC = C \cap -O \neq \emptyset.$$

A minimal example for this situation should have the five atoms $1'$, PP, $PP^{\smile}$, EC, and DC. Such a CRA is given in Table 5; we note that in this algebra O is not a contact relation. A representation of S_0 is as follows: Let

Table 5. The algebra S_0

$\circ$	PP	$PP^{\smile}$	EC	DC
PP	PP	$PP, PP^{\smile}, 1'$	EC, DC	DC
$PP^{\smile}$	$PP, PP^{\smile}, 1'$	$PP^{\smile}$	EC	EC, DC
EC	EC	EC, DC	$PP, PP^{\smile}, 1'$	$PP^{\smile}$
DC	EC, DC	DC	PP	$PP, PP^{\smile}, 1'$

$$S = \left\{ \frac{a}{3^k} : a \lneq 3^k, a \text{ odd}, k = 1, 2, 3, \ldots \right\},$$

$$T = \left\{ \frac{a}{3^k} : 0 \leq a \lneq 3^k, a \text{ even}, k = 1, 2, 3, \ldots \right\}.$$

It is not hard to see that

$$S \cap T = \emptyset, \ S, T \cong \mathbb{Q}, \tag{19}$$

S and T are dense in each other, (20)

$$x \in S \Rightarrow x = \inf\{ y \in T : x \lneq y \} = \sup\{ y \in T : y \lneq x \}, \tag{21}$$

$$x \in T \Rightarrow x = \inf\{ y \in S : x \lneq y \} = \sup\{ y \in S : y \lneq x \},, \tag{22}$$

$$x \in S \Longleftrightarrow 1 - x \in T. \tag{23}$$

Fig. 6. Tangent circles

Fig. 7. The tangent closed circle algebra $\mathcal{T}_c$

$\circ$	PP	$PP^\smile$	PO	DC
PP	PP	CP	$-CP$	DC
$PP^\smile$	CP	$PP^\smile$	PO	$-CP$
PO	PO	$-CP$	V	$-P$
DC	$-CP$	DC	$-P^\smile$	V

Now, we let $\langle S_0, \leq \rangle, \langle S_1, \leq \rangle$ be two disjoint copies of $\langle S, \leq \rangle$, $U = S_0 \cup S_1$, and let P be extension of the orders on the S_i to U. Furthermore,

$$x E C y \iff x \in S_i, y \in S_{i+1} \text{ and } 1 - x \lneq y,$$
$$x D C y \iff x \in S_i, y \in S_{i+1} \text{ and } 1 - x \gneq y.$$

Here, $i \in \{0, 1\}$, and addition is mod 2. The RA generated by $C = P \cup P^\smile \cup EC$ is just S_0.

Finally, we present two CRAs which arise from tangent circle orders. These structures are studied in the field of preference relations [1,28], and the CRAs were first presented by [22]. Let $\mathfrak{C}_c^t$ be the set of all open circles in the Euclidean plane which are tangent to the x–axis from above; an example is pictured in Figure 6. If $aCb \overset{\text{def}}{\iff} a \cap b \neq \emptyset$, then C is a contact relation with P being set inclusion. The CRA generated by C is given in Table 7. We observe that, unlike in the closed circle algebra $\mathcal{C}_c$, C loses the ability to express that two circles are tangential to each other. It is therefore somewhat surprising, that in the domain $\mathfrak{C}_o^t$ of open circles tangent to the x–axis, tangentiality is RA expressible: Suppose that $aCb \iff a \cap b \neq \emptyset$ in $\mathfrak{C}_o^t$. It is not hard to show that C is a contact relation on $\mathfrak{C}_o^t$ with P being set inclusion. Let $aNTDb$ iff $cl(a) \cap cl(b) = \emptyset$. Observe that $NTD \subsetneq DC$, and set $TD \overset{\text{def}}{=} DC \cap -NTD$. Then, $aTDb$ iff a and b are tangential to each other. It can now be shown that

$$PP \circ DC = NTD,$$

and thus, TD and NTD are RA definable. The composition of the CRA generated by C on $\mathfrak{C}_o^t$ is given in Table 6.

Note that $\mathcal{T}_c$ is isomorphic to the subalgebra of $\mathcal{T}_o$ generated by $C' = C \cup TD$. Obviously,

$$aC'b \iff cl(a) \cap cl(b) \neq \emptyset.$$

5   Mereological structures

The basic relation between individuals x, y in Leśniewski's mereology is

$$x \text{ is an ingredient of } y,$$

Table 6. The tangent open circle algebra $\mathcal{T}_o$

$\circ$	PP	$PP^{\smile}$	PO	TD	NTD
PP	PP	CP	$-CP$	NTD	NTD
$PP^{\smile}$	CP	$PP^{\smile}$	PO	PO	PO, DC
PO	PO	$-CP$	V	$PP^{\smile}, PO, DC$	$PP^{\smile}, PO, DC$
TD	PO	NTD	PP, PO, DC	$-(PP \cup PP^{\smile})$	$-P$
NTD	PO, DC	NTD	PP, PO, DC	$-P^{\smile}$	V

which we write as $x$ingr$y$. From ingr, several other relations are defined:

$$x\text{pt}y \iff x\text{ingr}y \text{ and not } x = y \quad \text{"part of"} \tag{24}$$

$$x\text{ov}y \iff (\exists z)[z\text{ingr}x \text{ and } z\text{ingr}y] \quad \text{"overlaps"} \tag{25}$$

$$x\text{extr}y \iff (\forall z)[z\text{ingr}x \Rightarrow \neg \, z\text{ingr}y] \quad \text{"discrete"} \tag{26}$$

In RA terms, these become

$$\text{pt} = \text{ingr} \cap -1' \tag{27}$$

$$\text{ov} = \text{ingr}^{\smile} \circ \text{ingr} \tag{28}$$

$$\text{extr} = -\text{ov}. \tag{29}$$

There are two relational axioms:

$$x\text{ingr}y \iff (\forall z)[z\text{ov}x \Rightarrow z\text{ov}y] \tag{30}$$

$$\text{ingr is antisymmetric.} \tag{31}$$

(30) together with (4) implies that

$$\text{ingr} = \text{ov} \setminus \text{ov}, \tag{32}$$

and now, Lemma 1 tells us that ingr is reflexive and transitive, hence, with (31), it is a partial order. We can, alternatively, use ov as the basis relation, define ingr $\stackrel{\text{def}}{=}$ ov $\setminus$ ov, and take as axioms

$$\text{ov is reflexive and symmetric,} \tag{33}$$

$$\text{ingr is antisymmetric.} \tag{34}$$

These are exactly the axioms of a contact relation. If we rename ingr to P, pt to PP and ov to O, then we are in accordance with our earlier terminology, and O is a contact relation C with the additional property that

$$C = P^{\smile} \circ P. \tag{35}$$

In CM, C is definable by P, which is usually not true in the more general case.

The other part of mereology is "sum formation" or "fusion", which we define here according to [13], which, in the presence of (35), is equivalent to Leśniewski's definition. If X is a collection of objects and C a contact relation, then

$$x = \sum X \overset{\text{def}}{\Longleftrightarrow} (\forall y)[xCy \Longleftrightarrow (\exists z \in X)yCz]. \tag{36}$$

This is read as x is the fusion of X. Now, a model of mereology is a structure $\mathfrak{M} = \langle U, C, \sum \rangle$ such that C is a contact relation, and

For each nonempty $X \subseteq U$ the fusion $\sum X$ exists.   (37)

Note that this definition is not first order. If X in (37) is finite, we speak of a weak model of mereology. If C additionally satisfies (35), then $\mathfrak{M}$ is called a model of classical mereology.

In models of mereology, one can define the additional following operations:

$$1 \qquad = \sum \{ x : xCx \} \qquad \text{Universal element} \tag{38}$$
$$x^* \qquad = \sum \{ y : y(-C)x \} \qquad \text{Complement} \tag{39}$$
$$\prod X = \sum \{ z : zPx \text{ for all } x \in X \} \text{ Product} \tag{40}$$

Observe that * and $\prod$ are partial operations.

The structures arising arising from Lesniewŝki's classical mereology are the complete Boolean algebras with the 0 element removed, cf. [55], p. 16f; the part – of relation P is the Boolean ordering, and

$$xCy \Longleftrightarrow x \not\leq -y. \tag{41}$$

If B is an atomless complete Boolean algebra, then the extreme elements $0, 1$ are relationally definable; thus, we are only interested in the behaviour of the contact relation and its derivatives on the set $U = B \cap -\{0, 1\}$. Since P is the basic relation of classical mereology, there is only one RA associated to CM, when the Boolean algebra is atomless.

In addition to the relations defined by (11) – (16), we define the following relations:

$$T = -(P \circ P^{\smile}) = \{ \langle x, z \rangle : x + z = 1 \} \tag{42}$$
$$PON = PO \cap T = \{ \langle x, z \rangle : x(-CP)z,\ x \cdot z \neq 0,\ x + z \neq 1 \} \tag{43}$$
$$POD = PO \cap -T = \{ \langle x, z \rangle : x(-CP)z,\ x \cdot z \neq 0,\ x + z = 1 \} \tag{44}$$
$$DN = DC \cap -T = \{ \langle x, z \rangle : x \cdot z = 0,\ x + z \neq 1 \} \tag{45}$$
$$DD = DC \cap T = \{ \langle x, z \rangle : x \cdot z = 0,\ x + z = 1 \} \tag{46}$$

The composition of the CRA $\mathcal{G}$ generated by P is given in Table 7.

Table 7. The algebra $\mathcal{G}$

$\circ$	O				D	
	PP	$PP^{\smile}$	PON	POD	DN	DD
PP	PP	$-(POD\cup DD)$	PP,PON,DN	PP,PO,D	DN	DN
$PP^{\smile}$	$1',O$	$PP^{\smile}$	$PP^{\smile},PO$	POD	$PP^{\smile},PO,D$	POD
PON	PP,PO	$PP^{\smile},PON,DN$	1	PP,PO	$PP^{\smile},PON,DN$	PON
POD	POD	$PP^{\smile},PO,D$	$PP^{\smile},PO$	$1',O$	$PP^{\smile}$	$PP^{\smile}$
DN	PP,PO,D	DN	PP,PON,DN	PP	$-(POD\cup DD)$	PP
DD	POD	DN	PON	PP	$PP^{\smile}$	$1'$

In the algebra $\mathcal{G}$, there are two possibilities to define a contact relation: We can take either $C = O$ or $C = O \cup DD$. In both cases, $P = C \setminus C$. In the first case, (35) is also fulfilled, so that we obtain a model of classical mereology. If $C = O \cup DD$, then we do not obtain a model of mereology, since in such models, a region is never in contact with its complement. At any rate, whenever a CRA generated by C assumes an underlying atomless Boolean algebra with the Boolean ordering as the "part – of" relation (such as the RCC discussed below), then the relations of $\mathcal{G}$ must be present, and $O \subseteq C$.

The algebraic part of a model of mereology need not be a Boolean algebra without a smallest element. [11] have shown the following:

Proposition 2. *If $\langle L, +, \cdot, - \rangle$ is a complete orthocomplemented lattice, then*

$$xCy \Longleftrightarrow x \not\leq -y$$

defines a contact relation, and the fusion is just the lattice join. Conversely, if $\langle U, C, \sum \rangle$ is a model of mereology, we let $U' = U \cup \{0\}$, where $0 \notin U$. Then, $\langle U', C, \sum \rangle$ is a complete orthocomplemented lattice with the lattice join being the fusion, and the other operations given by (39) and (40), extended by $\prod X = 0$ whenever $\prod X$ does not exist in U, and $0^* = 1$, $1^* = 0$.

Any CRA A for mereology must split DC into DD and DN. If A is a not a model of classical mereology, i.e. if $C \neq O$, then $EC = C \cap -O \neq \emptyset$. A minimal model for this situation is as follows: Let E_0, E_1 be two copies of the real interval $(0,1)$ ordered as usual by $\leq$, and set $E = E_0 \cup E_1$, $E^+ = E \cup \{1\}$. Order E^+ by

$$xPy \Longleftrightarrow x,y \in E_i \text{ and } x \leq y, \text{ or } y = 1.$$

In the following, addition is modulo 2. We let $m : E \to E$ be defined in such a way that, if $x \in E_i$, then $m(x)$ is the value of x in E_{i+1}. Now, the relation C defined on E by

$$\langle x, y \rangle \in C \Longleftrightarrow x \not\leq (1 - m(x)) \tag{47}$$

defines a contact relation, and

$$PP = \; \leqq$$
$$O = P^\smile \circ P = P + P^\smile + 1',$$
$$EC = C \setminus O = \{\, \langle x, y \rangle : y \geqq 1 - m(x) \,\},$$
$$DD = -[(-P^\smile \circ DC) \cup (P^\smile \circ C)] = \{\, \langle x, y \rangle : y = 1 - m(x) \,\},$$
$$DN = DC \cap -DD = \{\, \langle x, y \rangle : y \lessgtr 1 - m(x) \,\}$$

The composition of the RA S_1 generated by C is given in Table 9. We call S_1 a *scale algebra*, since x is related to its complement like a scale, as indicated in Figure 8. As indicated by the lines, the element x in the left copy is linked to $1 - x$ in the right copy by DD, to anything above $1 - x$ in the right copy by EC, to anything below $1 - x$ in the right copy by DN.

Fig. 8. An ordering for S_1 **Fig. 9.** The scale algebra S_1

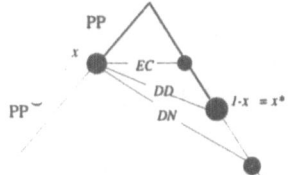

$\circ$	PP	$PP^\smile$	EC	DN	DD
PP	PP	CP	$-CP$	DN	DN
$PP^\smile$	CP	$PP^\smile$	EC	EC, DC	EC
EC	EC	$-CP$	CP	$PP^\smile$	$PP^\smile$
DN	EC, DC	DN	PP	CP	PP
DD	EC	DN	PP	$PP^\smile$	$1'$

Our final example of this section exhibits a model of mereology where EC splits according to whether $x + y = 1$ or not. Let S_i, $i < 4$ be disjoint copies of the rational interval $(0, 1)$. The mapping m is defined from

$$m : \begin{cases} S_0 \to S_1, \\ S_1 \to S_0, \\ S_2 \to S_3, \\ S_3 \to S_2. \end{cases}$$

and m puts $x \in (0, 1)$ onto its twin in the other component. We now define

$$xPPy \iff x, y \in S_i \text{ and } x \leqq y,$$
$$xDDy \iff y = 1 - m(x),$$
$$xENy \iff 1 - m(x) \leqq y,$$
$$xDNy \iff 1 - m(x) \geqq y,$$
$$xEDy \iff y \text{ is in a component different from that of } x \text{ or } DD(x).$$

If $C = -(DN \cup DD)$, then S_2 is isomorphic to the algebra generated by C. We have not been able to find an intuitive spatial explanation of this

Table 8. Algebra S_2 with complement and split EC

∘	PP	$PP^\smile$	EN	ED	DN	DD
PP	PP	$PP, PP^\smile, 1'$	EN, DC	ED	DN	DN
$PP^\smile$	$PP, PP^\smile, 1'$	$PP^\smile$	EN	ED	EN, DC	EN
EN	EN	EN, DC	$PP, PP^\smile, 1'$	ED	$P^\smile$	$P^\smile$
ED	ED	ED	ED	$-ED$	ED	ED
DN	EN, DC	DN	PP	ED	$PP, PP^\smile, 1'$	PP
DD	EN	DN	PP	ED	$PP^\smile$	$1'$

Fig. 10. An ordering for S_2

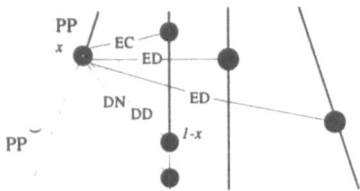

situation. The composition of S_2 is shown in Table 8, and an indication of the atoms of S_2 is given in Fig. 10.

We can also have $ED \circ ED = 1$; in this case, we need (at least) six components, and, otherwise, use the same definitions as for S_2. Figure 10 is to be interpreted similarly to Figure 8: In addition, x in the leftmost copy is related to any y in the two rightmost copies by ED.

6   The region connection calculus

The Region Connection Calculus (RCC) was introduced by [49] as a vehicle for reasoning about spatial phenomena, and has since received some prominence. It uses a contact relation C which fulfils Clarke's axioms (7) and (8).

A model for the RCC consists of a base set $U = R \cup N$, where R, N are disjoint, a distinguished $u \in R$, a unary operation $- : R_0 \to R_0$, where $R_0 \stackrel{\text{def}}{=} R \setminus \{u\}$, a binary operation $+ : R \times R \to R$, another binary operation $\cdot : R \times R \to R \cup N$, and a binary relation C on R.

The RCC axioms are as follows:

RCC 1. $(\forall x \in R)xCx$
RCC 2. $(\forall x, y \in R)[xCy \Rightarrow yCx]$
RCC 3. $(\forall x \in R)xCu$
RCC 4. $(\forall x \in R, y \in R_0)$,
  (a) $\langle x, -y \rangle \in C \Longleftrightarrow \neg\, xNTPPy$

(b) $\langle x, -y \rangle \in O \iff \neg\ xPy$

RCC 5. $(\forall x, y, z \in R)[\langle x, y + z \rangle \in C \iff xCy \text{ or } xCz$

RCC 6. $(\forall x, y, z \in R)[\langle x, y \cdot z \rangle \in C \iff (\exists w \in R)(wPy \text{ and } wPz \text{ and } xCw)]$

RCC 7. $(\forall x, y \in R)[x \cdot y \in R \iff xOy]$

RCC 8. If xPy and yPx, then $x = y$.

We shall in the sequel assume without loss of generality that $N = \{0\}$, and, to avoid trivialities, we suppose that $|R| \geq 2$. Axioms RCC 1, RCC 2, RCC 5 and RCC 8 show that $\langle R, C, + \rangle$ is a weak model of mereology. It is, however, not a model of mereology in the sense of Section 5, since it has a different definition of complement: In the RCC models, each proper region x is connected to its complement $-x$, which is impossible in models of mereology. Still

Proposition 3. *[53,25]*

Each model of the RCC axioms is a Boolean algebra with $N = \{0\}$.

In the original RCC, the circle relations of Table 3

$$1', TPP, TPP^\smile, NTPP, NTPP^\smile, PO, EC, DC \tag{48}$$

are considered base relations in a system called RCC8, and the weak composition table presented by [49] is shown in Table 9.

Table 9. RCC8 weak composition table

$\circ_w$	DR		C				
			O				
			PP			$PP^\smile$	
	DC	EC	PO	TPP	NTPP	$TPP^\smile$	$NTPP^\smile$
DC	1	DR, PO, PP	DR, PO, PP	DR, PO, PP	DR, PO, PP	DC	DC
EC	DR, PO, $PP^\smile$	1', DR, PO, TPP, $TPP^\smile$	DR, PO, PP	DR, PO, PP	EC, PO, PP	PO, PP	DR	DC
PO	DR, PO, $PP^\smile$	DR, PO, $PP^\smile$	1	PO, PP	PO, PP	DR, PO, $PP^\smile$	DR, PO, $PP^\smile$
TPP	DC	DR	DR, PO, PP	PP	NTPP	1', DR, PO, TPP, $TPP^\smile$	DR, PO, $PP^\smile$
NTPP	DC	DC	DR, PO, PP	NTPP	NTPP	DR, PO, PP	1
$TPP^\smile$	DR, PO, $PP^\smile$	EC, PO, $PP^\smile$	PO, $PP^\smile$	1', PO, TPP, $TPP^\smile$	PO, PP	$PP^\smile$	$NTPP^\smile$
$NTPP^\smile$	DR, PO, $PP^\smile$	PO, $PP^\smile$	PO, $PP^\smile$	PO, PP	PO, $PP^\smile$	$O \cup 1'$	$NTPP^\smile$	$NTPP^\smile$

It was asked in [8], when the RCC8 table has an extensional interpretation, i.e. when it can be interpreted as the composition table of a CRA. Table 4 shows that the closed circle algebra $\mathcal{C}_c$ provides such an interpretation.

Since each RCC model is a Boolean algebra B, we can restrict our investigations to $U \stackrel{\text{def}}{=} B \cap - \{0, 1\}$. Then, as with $\mathcal{G}$, PO splits into PON and POD, and DC splits into DN and Boolean complement DD as defined in

(43) – (46). Since each region is connected to its complement, and we want to reserve DC for the "disconnected" relation, we use different names as follows:

$$DC \overset{\text{def}}{=} -C = DN \text{ of } (45) \tag{49}$$

$$ECD \overset{\text{def}}{=} DD \text{ of } (46) \tag{50}$$

$$ECN \overset{\text{def}}{=} EC \cap -ECD \Longleftrightarrow xECy \text{ and } x + y \neq u, \tag{51}$$

[23] have shown that $ECN \circ TPP \leq POD$, and thus, POD splits into

$$PODZ \overset{\text{def}}{=} ECD \circ NTPP \tag{52}$$

$$PODY \overset{\text{def}}{=} POD \setminus (ECD \circ NTPP). \tag{53}$$

The resulting system, RCC11, has the weak composition given in Table 10. For cells containing $=$, the RCC axioms together with general RA properties imply that equality holds; for cells containing $\neq$, there is a model in which the composition is strictly smaller than the cell entry. In this way, we indicate in which cells the composition may be weak, and when it is not. Indeed, it turns out that a CRA model of the RCC relations has at least 25 atoms [23].

A standard RCC model is the Boolean algebra $RO(X)$ of regular open sets of a connected regular topological space $\langle X, \tau \rangle$, where for $x, y \in RO(X)$,

$$xCy \overset{\text{def}}{\Longleftrightarrow} cl(x) \cap cl(y) \neq \emptyset. \tag{54}$$

The question was raised in [8] in which situations a composition table for the CRA associated with a model of RCC is first order closed. The following necessary conditions was established by [24]. For this, recall that a Boolean algebra B is homogeneous, if every nontrivial relative algebra $B \restriction b$ is isomorphic to B, see [35].

Proposition 4. *If A is a first order closed CRA obtained from an RCC model, then the underlying Boolean algebra B is homogeneous.*

A subset of the circle relations, namely,

$$1', DR, PO, PP, PP^{\smile}$$

has received some attention, and is usually called RCC5 [34,6]. It arises from disregarding the split of C into O and EC, and PP into TPP and $NTPP$; in other words, one adds the additional axiom $C = O$.

Restricting relations to the non–extremal elements of a model, we arrive at seven relations and a weak composition table which has an extensional interpretation as the CRA $\mathcal{G}$ generated by the order of an atomless Boolean algebra.

Table 10. The RCC 11 weak composition

$\circ_w$	TPP	TPP⌣	NTPP	NTPP⌣	PON	PODY	PODZ	ECN	ECD	DC
TPP	TPP, NTPP	1', TPP, TPP⌣, PON, ECN, DC,≠	NTPP,=	TPP⌣, NTPP⌣, PON, ECN, DC,≠	TPP⌣, NTPP⌣, PON, ECN, DC	TPP, PON, PODY, ECN, ECD	TPP, PON, PODZ	ECN, DC	ECN,=	DC,=
TPP⌣	1', TPP, TPP⌣, PON, PODZ	TPP⌣, NTPP⌣	TPP, PON, PODZ	NTPP⌣,=	TPP⌣, PON, PODZ	PODY, PODZ	PODZ	TPP⌣, NTPP⌣, PON, ECN, ECD,≠	PODY	TPP⌣, PON, ECN, DC
NTPP	NTPP,=	TPP, PON, DC,≠	NTPP	1', TPP, TPP⌣, NTPP, NTPP⌣, PON, DC,=	TPP, PON, ECN, DC	TPP, PON, ECN, DC	TPP, PON, PODZ, ECD, DC	DC,=	DC,=	DC
NTPP⌣	TPP⌣, NTPP⌣, PON, PODZ	NTPP⌣,=	1', TPP, TPP⌣, NTPP, NTPP⌣, PON, PODZ,=	NTPP⌣	TPP⌣, NTPP⌣, PON, PODZ,=	PODZ	PODZ	TPP⌣, NTPP⌣, PON, PODZ	PODZ	TPP⌣, PON, PODY, PODZ, ECD, DC,=
PON	TPP, PON, PODZ	TPP⌣, NTPP⌣, PON, ECN, DC	TPP, PON, PODZ	TPP⌣, NTPP⌣, PON, DC,=	1', TPP, TPP⌣, NTPP, NTPP⌣, PON, PODY, PODZ, ECN, ECD, DC,=	TPP, PON, PODY, PODZ	TPP, PON, PODZ	NTPP⌣, PON, ECN, DC,≠	PON,=	TPP⌣, PON, ECN, DC,=
PODY	PODY, PODZ	TPP⌣, NTPP⌣, PON, PODY, ECN, ECD	PODZ	TPP⌣, NTPP⌣, PON, ECN, DC	TPP⌣, NTPP⌣, PON, PODZ, ECN, ECD, DC,=	1', TPP, TPP⌣, PON, PODY, PODZ	TPP, PON, PODZ	TPP⌣, NTPP⌣, PON, DC,≠	TPP⌣	NTPP⌣
PODZ	PODZ	TPP⌣, PON, PODY, PODZ	PODZ	TPP⌣, NTPP⌣, PON, PODY, ECN, ECD, DC	TPP⌣, PON, PODZ	TPP, PON, PODZ	1', TPP, TPP⌣, NTPP, NTPP⌣, PON, PODZ	NTPP⌣, PON, PODY	NTPP⌣	NTPP⌣
ECN	TPP, PON, NTPP⌣, PODY, ECN, ECD	ECN, DC	TPP, PON, PODZ	DC,=	TPP, PON, ECN, DC	TPP, NTPP	NTPP	1', TPP, TPP⌣, PON, ECN, DC	TPP,=	TPP⌣, NTPP⌣, PON, ECN, DC
ECD	PODY,=	ECN,=	PODZ,=	DC	PON,=	TPP,=	NTPP,=	TPP⌣,=	1',=	NTPP⌣,=
DC	TPP, PON, ECN, DC	DC,=	TPP, PON, PODZ, ECD, DC,=	DC	TPP, PON, DC,=	NTPP,=	NTPP,=	TPP, PON, DC,=	NTPP⌣, NTPP,=	1', TPP, TPP⌣, NTPP, NTPP⌣, PON, ECN, DC

7   Summary and outlook

We have given a survey of the origins and many examples of contact relations and their algebras. We have shown how spatial relations among open or closed circles are naturally obtained from the one–dimensional interval relations. "Part–of" and "contact" relations arising in mereology were the motivating factor in defining contact relation algebras (CRAs). We have given small examples for these algebras, and also explored CRAs which arise from the RCC, a well known mechanism for spatial reasoning.

There are many avenues which can be followed, and, to conclude, we present the questions raised in [25]:

- For which partial orders P is there a contact relation C such that $P = C \setminus C$? When can C be chosen as $P^\smile \circ P$?
- Investigate the complexity of CRAs. This is an important question, relating to the feasibility of relational reasoning in QSR [8]. There have been investigations for the interval algebra and its relatives [43,36,31], as well as for RA-like structures related to the RCC [50,51,34]. In connection with the different representations of subalgebras of the interval algebra, it is also of interest to investigate the network satisfaction problem for the given algebras and their representations [31].
- Find the CRAs for standard ontologies of mereo-topology and their expressiveness. These include the standard model of the RCC as the collection of all nonempty regular closed sets on a regular connected spaces, as well as the polygonal algebras of [46,47]. It is shown by [23] that such a CRA must contain at least 25 atoms.
- Look at vagueness of spatial regions. This seems especially important for applications such as geographical information systems [59]. The rough relations of [17] and [20], or the uncertainty approach of [21] may come in useful. It should also be worthwhile to investigate the connections of rough mereology [45] to this problem.

Acknowledgement

I should like to thank the participants of RelMiCS 4 and its organiser, Ewa Orłowska, for providing a stimulating atmosphere from which the current work received many inspirations.

References

1. Abbas M. and Vincke P. (1996) Tangent circle orders: Numerical representation and properties. Journal of Multi–Criteria Decision Analysis, 5
2. Allen J.F. (1983) Maintaining knowledge about temporal intervals. Communications of the ACM, 26(11):832–843

3. Allen J.F. (1984) Towards a general theory of action and time. Artificial Intelligence, 23:123–154
4. Andréka H., Givant S. and Németi I. (1994) The lattice of varieties of representable relation algebras. Journal of Symbolic Logic, 59:631–661
5. Asher N. and Vieu L. (1995) Toward a geometry of common sense: A semantics and a complete axiomatization of mereotopology. In: Mellish C. (Ed.), IJCAI 95, Proceedings of the 14th International Joint Conference on Artificial Intelligence
6. Bennett B. (1997) Logical representations for automated reasoning about spatial relationships. Doctoral dissertation, School of Computer Studies, University of Leeds
7. Bennett B. (1998) Determining consistency of topological relations. Constraints, 3:213–225
8. Bennett B., Isli A. and Cohn A. (1997) When does a composition table provide a complete and tractable proof procedure for a relational constraint language? In: IJCAI 97, Proceedings of the Workshop of Spatial Reasoning
9. van Benthem J. (1983) The logic of time. Reidel
10. Betti A. (1997) Stanisław Leśniewski. http://www.fmag.unict.it/PolPhil/Lesnie/Lesnie.html
11. Biacino L. and Gerla G. (1991) Connection structures. Notre Dame Journal of Formal Logic, 32:242–247
12. Chin L. and Tarski A. (1951) Distributive and modular laws in the arithmetic of relation algebras. University of California Publications, 1:341–384
13. Clarke B.L. (1981) A calculus of individuals based on 'connection'. Notre Dame Journal of Formal Logic, 22:204–218
14. Cohn A.G. (1997) Qualitative spatial representation and reasoning techniques. Research report, School of Computer Studies, University of Leeds
15. Cohn A.G., Bennett B., Gooday J. and Gotts N.M. (1997) Qualitative spatial representation and reasoning with the region connection calculus. Geoinformatica, 13:1–42
16. Comer S. (1983) A remark on chromatic polygroups. Congressus Numerantium, 38:85–95
17. Comer S. (1993) On connections between information systems, rough sets, and algebraic logic. In: Rauszer C. (Ed.), Algebraic Methods in Logic and Computer Science, 28 of Banach Center Publications, 117–124. Polish Academy of Science, Warszawa
18. de Laguna T. (1922) Point, line and surface as sets of solids. The Journal of Philosophy, 19:449–461
19. Düntsch I. (1991) Small integral relation algebras generated by a partial order. Period. Math. Hungar., 23:129–138
20. Düntsch I. (1994) Rough relation algebras. Fundamenta Informaticae, 21:321–331
21. Düntsch I. and Gediga G. (1997) Relation restricted prediction analysis. In: Sydow A. (Ed.), Proc. 15th IMACS World Congress, Berlin, 4, 619–624, Berlin. Wissenschaft und Technik Verlag
22. Düntsch I. and Roubens M. (1999) Tangent circle algebras. Submitted for publication
23. Düntsch I., Schmidt G. and Winter M. (2000) A necessary relation algebra for mereotopology. Studia Logica. To appear

24. Düntsch I., Wang H. and McCloskey S. (1999a) A relation algebraic approach to the Region Connection Calculus. Theoretical Computer Science. To appear
25. Düntsch I., Wang H. and McCloskey S. (1999b) Relation algebras in qualitative spatial reasoning. Fundamenta Informaticae, 39:229–248
26. Egenhofer M. and Franzosa R. (1991) Point–set topological spatial relations. International Journal of Geographic Information Systems, 5(2):161–174
27. Eschenbach C. and Heydrich W. (1995) Classical mereology and restricted domains. Internat. J. Human–Computer Studies, 43:723–740
28. Fodor J. and Roubens M. (1997) Parametrized preference structures and some geometrical interpretation. Journal of Multi–Criteria Decision Analysis, 6:253–258
29. Gotts N.M. (1996a) An axiomatic approach to topology for spatial information systems. Research Report 96.25, School of Computer Studies, University of Leeds
30. Gotts N.M. (1996b) Topology from a single primitive relation: Defining topological properties and relations in terms of connection. Research Report 96.23, School of Computer Studies, University of Leeds
31. Hirsch R. (1997) Expressive power and complexity in algebraic logic. Journal of Logic and Computation, 7(3):309–351
32. Jónsson B. (1982) Varieties of relation algebras. Algebra Universalis, 15:273–298
33. Jónsson B. (1991) The theory of binary relations. In: Andréka H., Monk J.D. and Németi I. (Eds.), Algebraic Logic, 54 of Colloquia Mathematica Societatis János Bolyai, 245–292. North Holland, Amsterdam
34. Jonsson P. and Drakengren T. (1997) A complete classification of tractability in RCC-5. Journal of Artificial Intelligence Research, 6:211–222
35. Koppelberg S. (1989) General Theory of Boolean Algebras, 1 of Handbook on Boolean Algebras. North Holland
36. Ladkin P.B. and Maddux R.D. (1994) On binary constraint problems. Journal of the ACM, 41:435–469
37. Leonard H.S. and Goodman N. (1940) The calculus of individuals and its uses. Journal of Symbolic Logic, 5:45–55
38. Leśniewski S. (1927 – 1931). O podstawach matematyki. Przeglad Filozoficzny, 30–34
39. Leśniewski S. (1983) On the foundation of mathematics. Topoi, 2:7–52
40. Link G. (1998) Algebraic Semantics in Language and Philosophy, 74 of CSLI Lecture Notes. Center for the Study of Language and Information, Stanford
41. Luschei E.C. (1962) The Logical Systems of Leśniewski. North Holland, Amsterdam
42. Lyndon R.C. (1950) The representation of relational algebras. Annals of Mathematics (2), 51:707–729
43. Nebel B. and Bürckert H.-J. (1993) Reasoning about temporal relations: A maximal tractable subclass of Allen's interval algebra. Research Report RR-93-11, German Research Center for Artificial Intelligence (DFKI), Saarbrücken, Germany
44. Nicod J. (1924) Geometry in a sensible world. Doctoral thesis, Sorbonne, Paris. English translation in *Geometry and Induction*, Routledge and Kegan Paul, 1969

45. Polkowski L. and Skowron A. (1996) Rough mereology: A new paradigm for approximate reasoning. International Journal of Approximate Reasoning, 15:333–365
46. Pratt I. and Schoop D. (1998) A complete axiom system for polygonal mereotopology of the real plane. Journal of Philosophical Logic, 27(6):621–658
47. Pratt I. and Schoop D. (1999) Expressivity in polygonal, plane mereotopology. Journal of Symbolic Logic. To appear
48. Pratt V.R. (1990) Dynamic algebras as a well-behaved fragment of relation algebras. In: Algebraic Logic and Universal Algebra in Computer Science, LNCS 425, 77–110, Ames, Iowa, June 1988. Springer-Verlag
49. Randell D.A., Cohn A. and Cui Z. (1992) Computing transitivity tables: A challenge for automated theorem provers. In: Proc CADE 11, 786–790. Springer Verlag
50. Renz J. and Nebel B. (1997) On the complexity of qualitative spatial reasoning: A maximal tractable fragment of the Region Connection Calculus. In: IJCAI 97, Proceedings of the 15th International Joint Conference on Artificial Intelligence
51. Renz J. and Nebel B. (1998) Efficient methods for qualitative spatial reasoning. In: Prade H. (Ed.), Proceedings of the 13th European Conference on Artificial Intelligence, ECAI'98, 562–566. Wiley
52. Simons P. (1987) Parts. A Study in Ontology. Clarendon Press, Oxford
53. Stell J. (1997) Personal communication, October 30, 1997
54. Surma S.J., Srzednicki J.T., Barnett D.I. and Ricky V.F. (Eds.) (1992) Stanisław Leśniewski: Collected works.
55. Tarski A. (1935) Zur Grundlegung der Boole'schen Algebra, I. Fundamenta Mathematicae, 24:177–198
56. Tarski A. (1941) On the calculus of relations. Journal of Symbolic Logic, 6:73–89
57. Tarski A. and Givant S. (1987) A formalization of set theory without variables, 41 of Colloquium Publications. Amer. Math. Soc., Providence
58. Whitehead A.N. (1929) Process and reality. MacMillan, New York
59. Worboys M. (1998) Imprecision in finite resolution spatial data. Geoinformatica, 2(3):257–280

Chapter 8
Relations Old and New

Joachim Lambek

Department of Mathematics and Statistics
McGill University
805 Sherbrooke Street West, Montreal, QC H3A 2K6, Canada

Abstract. We note that (binary) relations on a set form a (partially) ordered monoid with involution, which is also residuated and complete, hence a *quantale*. Relations between sets form an ordered category with involution. If $\rho : A \not\rightarrow B$ and $\sigma : B \not\rightarrow C$, one defines $\sigma\rho : A \not\rightarrow C$ by

$$c(\sigma\rho)a \Leftrightarrow \exists_{b \in B}(c\sigma b \vee b\rho a),$$

for all $a \in A$ and $c \in C$, and $\rho^\vee : B \not\rightarrow A$ by

$$a\rho^\vee b \Leftrightarrow b\rho a.$$

The partial order between relations $A \not\rightarrow B$ is defined elementwise.

We shall discuss some appearances of relations in anthropology, linguistics, computer science, algebra and category theory.

Keywords: relational calculus, anthropology, linguistics, cathegory theory, relation algebras

1 Kinship relations

If there is such a thing as prehistoric mathematics, it is surely the algebra of kinship relations. *Consanguineous* kinship relations are generated as monoid with involution by a single relation P of parenthood. We adopt the convention that xPy is read "x's parent is y" rather than "x is a parent of y", and write $P^\vee = C$, where $C = child$. One avoids PC, which is the disjoint union of the identity relation I and $S = sibling$. S is symmetric, but neither transitive nor reflexive, not having been introduced by a modern mathematician. One also avoids CP, the disjoint union of I and $\Sigma = spouse$, which is crucial for discussing *affine relations*, to be excluded from the present discussion. One also avoids $SP \subseteq P$, $CS \subseteq C$ and SS, the disjoint union of I and S. This leaves P^{m+1}, $P^m SC^n$ and C^{n+1} where m, n are natural numbers. These *kinship descriptions* may be generated by the rewrite rules:

$$R \rightarrow P, S, C, PR, RC.$$

We may decompose I into the disjoint union of two subrelations M and F, denoting equality between males and females respectively. In English, gender is expressed only at the end of a kinship description:

$$R\# \rightarrow RM\#, RF\#.$$

We have written # for a blank space. Basic English consanguineous kinship terms are then introduced as follows (between blank spaces):

$$PM \rightarrow father \qquad PF \rightarrow mother$$
$$CM \rightarrow son \qquad CF \rightarrow dauther$$
$$SM \rightarrow brother \qquad SF \rightarrow sister$$
$$PSM \rightarrow uncle \qquad PSF \rightarrow aunt$$
$$SCM \rightarrow nephew \quad SCF \rightarrow niece$$
$$PSCM \rightarrow cousin \quad PSCF \rightarrow cousin$$

Gender is irrelevant only for cousins; note however that French distinguishes between *cousin* and *cousine* or German between *Vetter* and *Base*. Iterated Ps and Cs are translated with the help of *grand* and *great #*, as in $PPM \rightarrow$ *granfather*, $CCCF \rightarrow$ *great#granddauther*. Note, however, that French distinguishes between *grand(e)* and *petit(e)*. For a fuller discussion of English kinship terminology, see [15], where one may also find an explanation why some dialects of English have *grandnephew* but *great # uncle*.

In many languages gender is expressed not only at the end of a kinship description. In Hindi for example [3] one distinguishes between

$$PMSM \rightarrow t\bar{a}y\bar{a} \text{ or } ch\bar{a}ch\bar{a}$$

(depending on whether the uncle is older or younger that the father) and

$$PFSM \rightarrow m\bar{a}m\bar{a},$$

also between

$$PMSF \rightarrow bu\bar{a} \text{ or } ph\bar{u}ph\bar{\imath}$$

and

$$PFSF \rightarrow maus\bar{\imath}.$$

In some languages even the ego's sex is relevant, that is, gender may have to be expressed at the beginning of a kinship description. Thus, in the language of the Trobriand islanders [4], one distinguishes between

$$MSF \rightarrow luta$$

and

$$FSF \rightarrow tuwa \text{ or } bwada$$

(depending on whether the sibling is older or younger than ego).

In many languages, the kinship descriptions are not as freely generated as at first sight in English, but are subject to certain *reduction* rules. For example, Hindi has the rule $PSC \rightarrow S$, according to which cousins are regarded as siblings. Even English has the optional rules $PSC^2 \rightarrow PSC$ and $P^2SC \rightarrow PSC$, according to which ith cousins j times removed may be called cousins. At some stage of its development, Lain had reduction rules

$C^2 \to SC$ and $P^2 \to PS$, according to which *nepos*, originally meaning "grandson", came to mean "nephew" and gave rise to this English word, and *avunculus*, originally meaning "granddaddy", came to mean "uncle" and gave rise to this English word. Anglosaxon had separate words for $PMSM$ and $PFSM$.

Let us pause for a moment to ask: what is an i-th cousin j times removed? One looks at the kinship description $P^{m+1}SC^{n+1}G$, where $G = M$ of F, and calculates

$$i = Min(m, n) + 1, j = |m - n|.$$

It seems that aunt Agatha, the only member of the family who understands this concept, has studied primitive recursive functions!

Reduction rules play an even more prominent role in many languages of interest to anthropologists. For example, the language of the Trobriand islanders had rules, extracted by Lounsbury [22] from data gathered by Malinowski [23]:

$$PMSF \to PMPF, \quad FSMC \to FCMC,$$

$$PGSG \to PG, \quad GSGC \to GC \ (G = M, F),$$

with a resulting collapse of the kinship terminology, and not surprisingly, $PFC \to S$. But, curiously, PMC was not conceived as a kinship description at all, leading some anthropologists to the view that the role of the father in reproduction was not recognized. More realistically, in view of Trobriand women's promiscuous behaviour, it may have been the identity of the father that was not recognized.

For example, Malinowski [23] had observed that what for us is a first cousin might be called by any of the following kinship terms:

tuwa, bwada, luta, latu, tabu, tama,

whose primary meanings were:

older sibling of same sex, younger $\cdots$, sibling of opposite sex,

child, grandparent or grandchild, father

respectively. Not surprisingly, Leach [20] dismissed Malinowski's interpretation of his data by declaring the underlying logic to be utterly incomprehensible. It was to answer this criticism that Lounsbury [22] devised his reduction rules, which enabled him to calculate all the kinship terms belonging to the kinship descriptions

$$G_1PG_2SG_3CG_4,$$

where the G_i are M or F, among others.

For example,

$$G_1PMSFCG_4 \to G_1PMPFCG_4 \to G_1PMSG_4,$$

using the rules $PMSF \rightarrow PMPF$ and $PFC \rightarrow S$. Now, there are two cases: when $G_4 = M$, one continues thus:

$$\rightarrow G_1 PM \rightarrow tama,$$

using the rule $PMSM \rightarrow PM$; but when $G_4 = F$, one immediately translates this into *tabu*.

Similarly, one calculates

$$G_1 PFSMCG_4$$

to be *latu* when $G_1 = M$ and *tabu* when $G_1 \neq G_4$, while

$$G_1 PMSMCG_4 \rightarrow G_1 PMCG_4$$

turns out to be undefined.

To quote Chomsky [8]: "[Kinship systems] may be the kind of mathematics you can create if you don't have formal mathematics. The Greeks made up number theory, others made up kinship systems."

2   Syntactic calculus

While kinship grammars may be seen as miniature models of grammars in general, namely production grammars or generative grammars, relations enter the field of linguistics yet through another door.

Inasmuch as the ordered monoid of relations on a set is *residuated*, one can define operations / (*over*) and \ (*under*) such that

$$RS \leq T \Leftrightarrow R \leq T/S \Leftrightarrow S \leq R\backslash T,$$

by stipulating that

$$x(T/S)y \Leftrightarrow \forall_z (ySz \Rightarrow xTz),$$

$$y(R\backslash T)z \Leftrightarrow \forall_x (xRy \Rightarrow xTz).$$

Years ago [13], I had proposed the residuated monoid generated by certain basic types ($s = sentence$, $n = name$, ...) as providing a hierarchy of syntactic types useful for the study of natural language, as illustrated by the sentence

John sees Jane today.

$$n\ (n\backslash s)/n\ n\ s\backslash s$$

Van Benthem [28] had suggested that relation algebras, viewed as residuated monoids, be studied as models of the syntactic calculus and Andréka and Mikulás [1] actually proved a completeness theorem for the synctatic calculus with respect to these models.

However, relation algebras have more structure. Not only is there an involution, the *converse*, but also a *dualizing object* 0 such that

$$(0/R)\backslash 0 = R = 0/(R\backslash 0)$$

making them models of the multiplicative fragment of *classical bilinear* logic. (For this too, a linguistic application has been studied by Claudia Casadio [7]). Moreover, $0/R = R\backslash 0$, hence they are models of *cyclic* bilinear logic, so named by Yetter [29]. Indeed, $x0y \Leftrightarrow x \neq y$, and one easily verifies that $0/R = \neg(R^\vee) = (\neg R)^\vee$, for which one usually writes $R^\perp$, so that $0 = I^\perp$, where I is the identity relation.

3   Recursive functions

Relations can be put to good use in various branches of mathematics. For example, the easiest way to define *partial recursive functions* $N \hookrightarrow N$ is as relations of the form $fg^\vee$, where f and g are primitive recursive functions and $g^\vee g \leq f^\vee f$. Moreover, $fg^\vee$ is then a *total* recursive function if and only if g is surjective, that is, $I \leq gg^\vee$.

Relations on N of the from $fg^\vee$ are precisely those whose graphs are enumerable by primitive recursive functions (or by total recursive functions for that matter). The relations whose graphs are recursively enumerable form a monoid under conjunction. For

$$(fg^\vee)(hk^\vee) = (fp)(kq)^\vee,$$

since the graph of $g^\vee h$ is evidently recursive, hence recursively enumerable, so that $g^\vee h = pq^\vee$, where p and q are primitive recursive functions. The relations whose graphs are recursively enumerable form an ordered monoid with involution.

4   Homomorphic relations

In algebra, equivalence relations compatible with given operations have always been studied as *congruence* relations. Most interesting here is the famous result of Maltsev: pairs of congruence relations in an algebra permute if and only if the algebra possesses a ternary operation m such that $mxyy = x$ and $myyz = z$. As Findlay [9] pointed out, this is also equivalent to saying thet every reflexive homomorphic relation is an congruence. A relation $\rho : A \nrightarrow B$ between algebras in a variety is said to be *homomorphic* if it is compatible with the operations, equivalently, if its graph is a subalgebra of $B \times A$.

Riguet [27] had called a relation ρ *difunctional* if $\rho\rho^\vee\rho = \rho$, and I pointed out [12] that the existence of a Maltsev operation is also equivalent to the assertion that all homomorphic relations between algebras of the variety are difunctional. This allows one to generalize a theorem, due to Goursat [11] for groups, to arbitrary Maltsev varieties: any homomorphic relation between algebras A and B is induced by an isomorphism between quotient algebras of subalgebras of A and B.

This theorem is easily seen to be equivalent to the Maltsev condition. However, in [14] I established a two-square lemma, which I considered to be a homological version of Goursat's theorem. It was pointed out by Carboni and Pedicchio that this lemma, when generalized to varieties (see Lemma 1 below), holds under more general conditions that those of Maltsev. They named these varietes "Goursat varietes", although Goursat himself was innocent of this concept. What is required is that, for any homomorphic relation ρ, $\rho\rho^\vee$ is tarnsitive, hence idempotent, that is, $\rho\rho^\vee\rho\rho^\vee = \rho\rho^\vee$. This is equivalent to the existence of a quaternary operation h satisfying the identities

$$hxxxy = y, \quad hxxyy = hyxyx.$$

Goursat varietes which are not already Maltsev varietes are not easy to come by. The first example of one was found by Mitschke [26]: weak implicational algebras with a binary operation $\Rightarrow$ satisfying

$$(y \Rightarrow y) \Rightarrow x = x, \quad (y \Rightarrow x) \Rightarrow x = (x \Rightarrow y) \Rightarrow y.$$

As I showed in [12], Goursat's theorem also yields the so-called butterfly lemma used by Zassenhaus to prove the Jordan-Hölder-Schreier theorem for *normal* series. All one has to do is to apply Goursat's theorem to homomorphic relations $\rho = \kappa\lambda$, where κ and λ are subcongruences, that is, homomorphic relations which are transitive and symmetric. Garret Birkhoff had already proved the J-H-S theorem for *principal* series usinfg congruence relations (see his book [5]).

5   The connecting homomorphism

Homomorphic relations other than transitive ones (order relations, congruences) and homomorphisms had been eschewed by algebraists until Mac Lane [24] showed that the easiest way to obtain the so-called *connecting homomorphism* in homological algebra was to look at the *zigzag* homomorphic relation

$$\varphi = ee^\vee fg^\vee hi^\vee jk^\vee k$$

and prove that it is a homomorphism, to wit, that $\varphi\varphi^\vee \leq 1$ and $1 \leq \varphi^\vee\varphi$. (From now on, the identity relation will be denoted by 1.). Here e, f, g, h, i, j and k are given homomorphisms between modules embedded in a diagram satisfying certain exactness and commutativity conditions, as in the following diagram:

$$
\begin{array}{c}
0 \\
\downarrow \\
A \;\rightarrow\; B \;\overset{e}{\cdots}\; P \;\rightarrow\; 0 \\
\downarrow \qquad \downarrow f \\
C \;\rightarrow\; D \;\overset{g}{\rightarrow}\; E \;\rightarrow\; 0 \\
\downarrow \qquad \downarrow h \qquad \downarrow \\
0 \;\rightarrow\; F \;\overset{i}{\rightarrow}\; G \;\rightarrow\; H \\
\downarrow j \qquad \downarrow \\
0 \;\rightarrow\; Q \;\overset{k}{\cdots}\; I \;\rightarrow\; J \\
\downarrow \\
0
\end{array}
$$

It is assumed that all rows and columns are exact and that all squares commute, and it is concluded that the sequence

$$ A \rightarrow B \overset{\varphi}{\rightarrow} I \rightarrow J $$

is exact.

This result may be extended to Gousat varietes, provided we suitably extend the notion of exactness and commutativity. Exactness is applied to *forks*:

$$
A \overset{f}{\underset{g}{\rightrightarrows}} B \overset{h}{\rightarrow} C, \quad D \overset{u}{\rightarrow} E \overset{v}{\underset{w}{\rightrightarrows}} F,
$$

called *left forks* and *right aforks* respectively. A left fork is *exact* if

$$ \mathrm{Im}(f, g) = \mathrm{Ker}\, h. $$

A right fork is *exact* if

$$ \mathrm{Im}\, u = \mathrm{Ker}(v, w), $$

where $\mathrm{Ker}(v, w) = \{e \in E \mid ve = we\}$ is the usual equalizer of v and w. For modules, this may be written

$$ \mathrm{Im}\, u = \mathrm{Ker}(v - w). $$

The appropriate generalization of commutativity will be discussed below.

Instead of repeating the above argument in the more general context, we shall sketch another proof, which generalizes that for groups in [14].

Lemma 1. *In any Goursat variety, if the two forks in the diagram*

$$
\begin{array}{ccc}
A \overset{}{\underset{}{\rightrightarrows}} B & \overset{f}{\rightarrow} & C \\
& \downarrow g & \\
D \overset{}{\underset{}{\rightrightarrows}} E & \overset{}{\underset{}{\rightrightarrows}} F
\end{array}
\qquad (1)
$$

are exact, then

$$\frac{Img \cap Imh}{gIm(A \underset{\rightarrow}{\rightarrow} B)g^\vee} \cong \frac{g^\vee Ker(E \underset{\rightarrow}{\rightarrow} F)}{Kerf \cup Kerg},$$

where the congruence relations in the denominators are assumed to be restricted to the algebras in the numerators.

The partially doubled squares in the diagram

$$
\begin{array}{ccccc}
A & \overset{\rightarrow}{\underset{\rightarrow}{}} & B & \overset{f}{\rightarrow} & C \\
\downarrow\downarrow & & \downarrow g & & \downarrow\downarrow \\
D & \vec{h} & E & \overset{\rightarrow}{\underset{\rightarrow}{}} & F
\end{array}
\qquad (2)
$$

are said to quasi-commute *if*

$$gIm(A \underset{\rightarrow}{\rightarrow} B)g^\vee = hIm(A \underset{\rightarrow}{\rightarrow} D)h^\vee$$

when restricted to Img ∩ Imh and if

$$g^\vee Ker(E \underset{\rightarrow}{\rightarrow} F) = f^\vee Ker(C \underset{\rightarrow}{\rightarrow} F)$$

respectively. We note that quasi-commutativity for modules is implied by the usual commutativity if parallel arrows are replaced by their difference.

The so-called *snake lemma* asserting the existence of a connecting homomorphism may be extended to arbitrary Goursat varietes by imposing appropriate exactness and quasi-commutativity conditions on the appropriate diagram. One way of proving it is with the help of Lemma 1. Indeed, a concise way of stating Lemma 1 for the diagram (2) is to say that the *image* of the first square is isomorphic to the *kernel* of the second. Now look at the following diagram:

$$
\begin{array}{ccccc}
& & \overset{\rightarrow}{\underset{\rightarrow}{}} & \overset{e}{\rightarrow} & P \\
& & \downarrow\downarrow\ 1\ \downarrow f & & \\
& & \overset{\rightarrow}{\underset{\rightarrow}{}}\ \overset{g}{\underset{}{}} & & \\
& & \downarrow\downarrow\ 3\ \downarrow\ 2\ \downarrow\downarrow & & \\
& & \overset{i}{\underset{}{}}\ \ \overset{\rightarrow}{\underset{\rightarrow}{}} & & \\
& & \downarrow j\ 4\ \downarrow\downarrow & & \downarrow \\
Q & \overset{k}{\rightarrow} & \overset{\rightarrow}{\underset{\rightarrow}{}} & & \rightarrow
\end{array}
$$

It is assumed that all rows and columns are exact, that all squares quasi-commute and that k, i and f are injections and j, g and e are surjections. (An arrow $f : A \to B$ is said to be an *injection* if $f^\vee f = 1_A$ and a *surjection* if $f f^\vee = 1_B$. One then concludes that

$$P \cong \operatorname{Im}(1) \cong \operatorname{Ker}(2) \cong \operatorname{Im}(3) \cong \operatorname{Ker}(4) \cong Q.$$

6 Relations in categories

Let $\mathcal{R}$ be an oredered category with involution. We shall think of the arrows $\rho : A \to B$ in $\mathcal{R}$ as relations. With $\mathcal{R}$ we shall associate two other categories $\mathcal{R}_0$ and $\bar{\mathcal{R}}$.

$\mathcal{R}_0$ is the full subcategory of $\mathcal{R}$ whose arrows: $f : A \to B$ satisfy

$$f f^\vee \leq 1_B, \quad 1_A \leq f^\vee f,$$

that is, for which $f^\vee$ is *right adjoint* to f. The order in $\mathcal{R}_0$ is seen to be discrete.

$\bar{\mathcal{R}}$ is the ordered category with involution whose objects are idempotent and symmetric relations in $\mathcal{R}$. In concrete situations, idempotency here follows from transitivity, hence the objects of $\bar{\mathcal{R}}$ may be described as *partial equivalence relations*. Its arrows $_\beta\rho_\alpha : \alpha \to \beta$ are induced by relations $\rho : A \to B$ in $\mathcal{R}$ satisfying $\beta\rho\alpha = \rho$. Composition and converses are defined in the obvious way and identity arrows are $_\alpha\alpha_\alpha : \alpha \to \alpha$. The forgetful functor $\bar{\mathcal{R}} \to \mathcal{R}$, which sends the object $\alpha : A \to A$ of $\bar{\mathcal{R}}$ onto A and the relation $_\beta\rho_\alpha : \alpha \to \beta$ onto $\rho : A \to B$ is faithful.

Exactness of forks in $\mathcal{R}_0$ is defined as in Sect. 5, provided we define:

$$\operatorname{Ker} h = h^\vee, \quad \operatorname{Im} h = h h^\vee,$$

and call $h^\vee h$ a *congruence*, $h h^\vee$ a *cocongruence*,

$$\operatorname{Im}(f, g) = \text{intersection of all congruences } k^\vee k \text{ containing } f g^\vee,$$

$$\operatorname{Ker}(f, g) = \text{join of all congruences } k k^\vee \text{ contained in } g^\vee f,$$

assuming that these exist. It may be useful here to adopt:

Postulate 1. For each object A of $\mathcal{R}$, $\operatorname{Hom}_\mathcal{R}(A, A)$ is a complete lattice.

If we assume that $\mathcal{R}$ satisfies the Goursat condition that, for any relation ρ, $\rho\rho^\vee$ is idempotent, we may reformulate Lemma 1 of Sect. 5 in a more general context.

Lemma 2. *If $\mathcal{R}$ satisfies the Goursat condition and (1) is a diagram in $\mathcal{R}_0$, then we have the following isomorphism in $\mathcal{R}_0$.*

$$g g^\vee h \operatorname{Im}(A \xrightarrow{} B) h^\vee g g^\vee \cong g^\vee g f^\vee \operatorname{Ker}(C \xrightarrow{} F) f g^\vee g.$$

Without the Goursat condition, in concrete situations, in which transitive and symmetric relations are necessarily idempotent, we may have recourse to Postulate 1 and replace the two sides of the above isomorphism by their transitive closures.

If we assume the Goursat condition for $\mathcal{R}$, we say that the partially doubled squares in (2) of Sect. 5 for $\mathcal{R}_0$ P *quasi-commute* if

$$hh^\vee g\mathrm{Im}(A \xrightarrow{\rightarrow} B)g^\vee hh^\vee = gg^\vee h^\vee \mathrm{Im}(A \xrightarrow{\rightarrow} B)h^\vee gg^\vee.$$

and

$$f^\vee fg\mathrm{Ker}(E \xrightarrow{\rightarrow} F)gf^\vee f = g^\vee gf^\vee \mathrm{Ker}(C \xrightarrow{\rightarrow} F)fg^\vee g$$

respectively. If we assume Postulate 1 instead, in concrete situations, we may again replace the two sides of each equation by their transitive closures.

Example 1. We recall that a category is *regular* in the same sense of Barr et al. [2], if it has finite limits, every kernel pair has a coequalizer and regular epis are stable under pullbacks; it is *exact* if all equivalence relations are kernel pairs.

If $\mathcal{R}$ is the ordered category of relations over a *regular* category $\mathcal{C}$, as in Barr et al. [2], then $\mathcal{C} = \mathcal{R}_0$ and $\bar{\mathcal{R}}_0$ is the *exact completion* of $\mathcal{R}$ (see Calenko et al. [6], Freyd and Scedrov [10] and McLarty [25]).

If $\mathcal{R}_0 = \mathcal{C}$ is a regular category, left forks and right forks are exact if and only if

$$\mathrm{coim}h = \mathrm{coeq}(f,g), \quad \mathrm{im}h = \mathrm{eq}(f,g)$$

respectively.

It is more difficult to express quasi-commutativity for regular categories without invoking zig-zac relations. For exact categories, one can presumably copy the definition for varietes following Lemma 1, which mildly invokes $g^\vee$, $h^\vee$ and $f^\vee$.

7   Partial equivalence relations

Partial equivalence relations are symmetric and transitive, but not necessarily reflexive. In concrete situations and in regular categories, they are also idempotent.

Lemma 3. *Each of the following assertions about relations (arrows in an ordered category $\mathcal{R}$ with involution) implies the next:*

1. *Every relation is representable in the form $gf^\vee$, where f and g are arrows in $\mathcal{R}_0$.*
2. *Every relation ρ is semi-difunctional: $\rho \leq \rho\rho^\vee\rho$.*

3. Every partial equivalence relation is a symmetric idempotent.

Proof. (1) $\Rightarrow$ (2). If $\rho = gf^\vee$ then $\rho = gf^\vee \leq gf^\vee fg^\vee gf^\vee = \rho\rho^\vee\rho$.

(2) $\Rightarrow$ (3) If $\alpha\alpha \leq \alpha$ and $\alpha^\vee \leq \alpha$ then $\alpha \leq \alpha\alpha^\vee\alpha \leq \alpha\alpha\alpha \leq \alpha\alpha$. $\square$

I have elsewhere [17] constructed a category $\mathcal{R}_0^{\mathrm{per}}$ as follows:

- its objects are partial equivalence relations;
- its arrows ${}_\beta\rho_\alpha : \alpha \to \beta$ are relations $\rho : A \to B$ such that $\rho\alpha\rho^\vee \leq \beta$ and $\alpha \leq \rho^\vee\beta\rho$;
- equality between arrows ${}_\beta\rho_\alpha$ and ${}_\beta\rho_\alpha$ is defined to mean $\rho\alpha\sigma^\vee \leq \beta$ or, equivalently, $\alpha \leq \rho^\vee\beta\sigma$.

Under the assumption (3) of Lemma 2, it is not difficult to see that $\mathcal{R}_0^{\mathrm{per}}$ is equivalent ro $\bar{\mathcal{R}}_0$. All one has to observe is that every arrow ${}_\beta\rho_\alpha$ in $\mathcal{R}_0^{\mathrm{per}}$ is equal to exactly one arrow ${}_\beta\bar{\rho}_\alpha$ in $\bar{\mathcal{R}}_0$, namely when $\bar{\rho} = \beta\rho\alpha$. Indeed, one easily verifies that $\bar{\rho}\bar{\rho}^\vee \leq \beta$ and $\alpha \leq \bar{\rho}^\vee\bar{\rho}$, as well as

$$\rho\alpha\bar{\rho}^\vee = \rho\alpha\rho^\vee\beta \leq \beta\beta \leq \beta.$$

If $\mathcal{R}_0$ is regular, all partial equivalence relations are induced by equivalence relations on subobjects [17], Prop. 3. Hence $\mathcal{R}_0^{\mathrm{per}}$ is equivalent to $\mathcal{R}_0^{\mathrm{eq}}$, whose objects are equivalence relations. According to Freyd and Scedrov [10] or McLarty [25], $\mathcal{R}_0^{\mathrm{eq}}$ is exact completion of $\mathcal{R}_0$.

Example 2. Let $\mathcal{R}$ be the ordered monoid of all relations on N whose graphs are recursively enumerable (see Sect. 3 above), so that $\mathcal{R}_0$ is the monoid of totally recursive functions $N \to N$. It is not difficult to show that any arrow ${}_\beta\rho_\alpha : \alpha \to \beta$ of $\mathcal{R}_0^{\mathrm{per}}$ is equal to the arrow ${}_\beta\varphi_\alpha : \alpha \to \beta$, where φ is the partial recursive function defined as follows:

$$\varphi x = \text{ smallest } y \text{ such that } y\rho x.$$

Indeed, one immediately verifies that

$$\varphi\alpha\varphi^\vee \leq \rho\alpha\rho^\vee \leq \beta.$$

To prove that $\alpha \leq \varphi^\vee\beta\varphi$ takes a bit longer [17].

Constructed thus, $\mathcal{R}_0^{\mathrm{per}}$ resembles the category PER, which plays a role in theoretical computer science [21]. The only difference is that PER has more objects than $\mathcal{R}_0^{\mathrm{per}}$: all partial equivalence relations on N are object of the former, while only those with recursively enumerable graphs are object of the latter, it being crucial to the intended applications that the set of objects of PER is closed under arbitrary intersections.

8 Summary

Binary relations play a prominent role in anthropological linguistics in connection with the algebra of kinship relations, while in categorial linguistics they enter only marginally as models of the syntactic calculus. Whereas, in mathematics, relations have been largely replaced by functions, we have seen that often the very definition of a function is greatly simplified by viewing it as a relation. this is so for recursive functions and for the connecting homomorphism in homological algebra. the best known relations in algebra are congruence relations, but other "homomorphic" relations also turn out to be useful in proving basic results such as the Zassenhaus Lemma. The construction of the connecting homomorphism has been generalized from module categories to other varietes and categories. Finally, relations are crucial for obtaining the exact completion of a regular category and for describing the category PER in theoretical computer science.

Acknowledgements

I wish to thanks the National Sciences and Engineering Research Council of Canada for partial support of this work, Ewa Orlowska for inviting me to the RELMICS 1998 meeting in Warsaw which prompted this paper, and the following for helpful comments: Peter Freyed, Peter Gumm and Mihaly Makkai.

References

1. Andréka H. and Mikulás S. (1993) The completeness of the Lambek calculus for relational semantics. J. of Logic, Language and Information 3:1–37
2. Barr M., Grillet P.A. and van Osdal D.H. (1971) Exact categories and categories of sheaves. Springer LNM 236
3. Bhargava M. and Lambek J. (1983) A production grammar for Hindi kinship terminology. Theoretical Linguistics 10:227–245
4. Bhargava M. and Lambek J. (1995) A rewrite system for the Western Pacific. Theoretical Linguistics 21:241–253
5. Birkhoff G. (1967) Lattice Theory. Amer. Math. Soc. New York
6. Calenko M.S., Gisin V.B. and Raikov D.A. (1984) Ordered categories with involution. Dissertations Mathematicae (= Rozprawy Matematyczne) 227:1–11
7. Casadio C. (2000) Noncommutative linear logic in linguistics. Manuscript
8. Chomsky N. (1979) Language and responsibility. Pantheon Books. New York
9. Findlay G.D. (1960) Reflexive homomorphic relations. Canad. Math. Bull. 3:131–132
10. Freyd P. and Scedrov A. (1990) Categories and allegories. North Holland, Amsterdam
11. Goursat É. Sur les substitutions orthogonales. Ann. Sci. École Normale Supérieure (3) 6:9–102

12. Lambek J. (1957) Goursat's theorem and the Zassenhaus lemma. Canad. J. Math. 10:45–56
13. Lambek J. (1958) The mathematics of sentence structure. Amer. Math. Monthly 65:154–169
14. Lambek J. (1964) Goursat's theorem and homological algebra. Can. Math. Bull. 7:597–608
15. Lambek J. (1986) A production grammar for English kinship terminology. Theoretical Linguistics 13:19–36
16. Lambek J. (1996) The butterfly and the serpent. In: Agliano P. and Ursini A. (Eds.) Logic and Algebra, Marcel Dekkert, New York, 161–179
17. Lambek J. (1997) Relations in operational categories. J. Pure and Applied Algebra 116:221–248
18. Lambek J. (2000) Diagram chasing in ordered categories with involution. J. Pure and Applied Algebra, to appear
19. Lambek J. (2000) Relations: binary relations in the social and mathematical sciences. In: Cantini A., Casari E., Minari P. (Eds.) Logic in Florence, Kluwer Academic Publishers, to appear
20. Leach E. (1958) Concerning Trobriand clans and the kinship category *tabu*. In: Goody J. (Ed.) The development cycle of domestic groups. Cambridge Papers on Social Anthropology 1, Cambridge University Press
21. Longo G., Moggi E. (1991) Constructive natural deduction and its "ω-set" interpretation. Math. Structures in Computer Science 1, 215–254
22. Lounsbury F.G. (1965) Another view of Trobriand kinship categories. In: Hammel E.A. (Ed.) Formal Semantics, American Anthropologist 67 (5) Part 2 142–185
23. Malinowski B. (1932) Sexual life of savages. 3rd edition. Routledge and Kegan Paul Ltd., London
24. Mac Lane S. (1961) An algebra of additive relations. Proc. Nat. Acad. Sci. USA 47(7):1043–1051
25. McLarty C. (1992) Elementary categories, elementary toposes. Claderon Press. Oxford
26. Mitschke A. (1971) Implication algebras are 3-permutable and 3-distributive. Algebra Universalis 1:182–186
27. Riguet J. (1950) Quelques propriétés des relations difonctionelles. C.R. Acad. Sci. Paris. Sér. I Math. 230:1999–2000
28. van Benthem J. (1991) Language in action. Elsevier
29. Yetter D.N. (1990) Quantales and (non-commutative) linear logic. J. Symbolic Logic 55:41–64

Chapter 9
Relational Models for the Nonassociative Lambek Calculus

Marek Szczerba

Faculty of Mathematics and Computer Science
Adam Mickiewicz University
ul. Matejki 48/49, 60-769 Poznań, Poland
psuam@amu.edu.pl

Abstract. We prove a theorem on representation of residuated groupoids in algebras of binary relations, which yields a strong completeness theorem for the nonassociative Lambek calculus. Relational models are of interest for dynamic interpretations of Lambek-style calculi [5]. We use techniques of labelled formulas [7], [5] to the nonassociative case.
AMS: 03G25, 08A99, 68S05.
Keywords: nonassociative Lambek calculus, relational algebra, residuated groupoid

1 The nonassociative Lambek calculus NL

1.1 Basic definitions

We define a language of the nonassociative Lambek calculus (NL). Let Pr be a nonempty set of *atomic types*; then by $T(Pr)$ we will denote the set of *types*, it is the smallest set containing Pr and closed under the following formation rule: if A, B are types, then $(A \cdot B)$, $(A \rightarrow B)$ and $(A \leftarrow B)$ are also types. Roman capital letters $A, B, C, \ldots$ will denote types and Greek capital letters $\Gamma, \Delta, \ldots$ finite, nonempty, bracketed strings of types, we will call them *terms*. (Formally, we can define terms inductively as elements of the smallest set containing $T(Pr)$ and closed under the following formation rule: if Γ, Δ are terms, then (Γ, Δ) is a term too.) We also use a standard notion of *subterm* of a given term. $\Gamma[B]$ denotes the term Γ with a distinguished occurrence of the type B. $\Gamma[\Delta]$ in the context of rule $\frac{\Gamma[B]}{\Gamma[\Delta]}$ denotes the term Γ with the term Δ substituted for the distinguished occurrence of B. *Sequents* are of the form $\Gamma \vdash A$.

Note, that we will use symbols $\cdot$, $\leftarrow$ and $\rightarrow$ in three different contexts: as propositional connectives $(A \cdot (B \rightarrow C))$, binary operations in residuated groupoids $(a \cdot (b \rightarrow c))$ and binary operations in relational residuated groupoids $(S \cdot (T \rightarrow U))$.

1.2   Axiomatization of the NL

$$(Ax) \quad A \vdash A,$$

$$(CUT) \quad \frac{\Gamma \vdash A \quad \Delta[A] \vdash B}{\Delta[\Gamma] \vdash B},$$

$$(\to L) \quad \frac{\Gamma[B] \vdash C \quad \Delta \vdash A}{\Gamma[\Delta, A \to B] \vdash C}, \qquad (\to R) \quad \frac{(A, \Gamma) \vdash B}{\Gamma \vdash A \to B},$$

$$(\leftarrow L) \quad \frac{\Gamma[B] \vdash C \quad \Delta \vdash A}{\Gamma[B \leftarrow A, \Delta] \vdash C}, \qquad (\leftarrow R) \quad \frac{(\Gamma, A) \vdash B}{\Gamma \vdash B \leftarrow A},$$

$$(\cdot L) \quad \frac{\Gamma[A, B] \vdash C}{\Gamma[A \cdot B] \vdash C}, \qquad (\cdot R) \quad \frac{\Gamma \vdash A \quad \Delta \vdash B}{\Gamma, \Delta \vdash A \cdot B}.$$

If X is a set of sequents, then by NL(X) we will denote the system NL enriched by the sequents from X as new axioms, and by $\Gamma \vdash_{\text{NL}(X)} A$ a sequent provable in NL(X).

If we add one more rule of inference,

$$(ASS) \quad \frac{\Gamma[A, (B, C)] \vdash D}{\Gamma[(A, B), C] \vdash D}$$

we obtain the axiomatization of the Lambek calculus, here denoted by L. The double bar in the (ASS) rule means that we can use it in proofs in both directions, from top to bottom and from bottom to top.

2   Models for the NL

Natural models for the nonassociative Lambek calculus are *residuated grou-poids* i. e. algebras of the form $\mathcal{G} = <G, \cdot, \to, \leftarrow, \leq>$ such that $\leq$ is a partial order, and three binary operations $\cdot, \leftarrow, \to$ satisfy equivalences:

$$(RES) \quad b \leq a \to c \iff a \cdot b \leq c \iff a \leq c \leftarrow b,$$

for all $a, b, c \in G$.

An *RG-model* is a pair $< \mathcal{G}, \varphi >$ such that $\mathcal{G}$ is a residuated groupoid, and $\varphi : T(Pr) \longmapsto G$ is a homomorphic extension of some mapping $\overline{\varphi} : Pr \longmapsto G$. One extends also the assignement φ to terms by setting $\varphi(\Gamma, \Delta) = \varphi(\Gamma) \cdot \varphi(\Delta)$. Sequent $\Gamma \vdash A$ is *true in the RG-model*, if $\varphi(\Gamma) \leq \varphi(A)$. For every set of sequents X, an *RG*-model is called a *model for* X, if all sequents from X are true in it.

For this class of models the following theorem holds (cf. [3]).

Theorem 1. *For every set of sequents* X, $\Gamma \vdash_{\text{NL}(X)} A$ *if and only if* $\Gamma \vdash A$ *is true in every RG-model for* X.

□

Another class of models for NL is formed by *relational residuated groupoids*, i. e. algebras of the form $\mathcal{G}(R) =< \mathcal{P}(R), \cdot, \rightarrow, \leftarrow, \subseteq>$ such that R is a binary relation, $\mathcal{P}(R)$ denotes the set of all subrelations of R, $\subseteq$ is an ordinary set inclusion, and the binary operations are defined as follows:

$$S \cdot T = \{< x, y >\in R | \exists z (< x, z >\in S, < z, y >\in T)\}, \tag{1}$$

$$S \rightarrow T = \{< x, y >\in R | \forall z (\text{if } < z, x >\in S \text{ and } < z, y >\in R, \tag{2}$$
$$\text{then } < z, y >\in T)\},$$

$$T \leftarrow S = \{< x, y >\in R | \forall z (\text{if } < y, z >\in S \text{ and } < x, z >\in R, \tag{3}$$
$$\text{then } < x, z >\in T)\}.$$

One can easily check that $\mathcal{G}(R)$ is a residuated groupoid. The notions of *RR-model*, sequent *true in RR-model* and *RR-model for* a set of sequents X are similar to those above, we just use $\mathcal{G}(R)$ instead of $\mathcal{G}$.

3 Remarks on the associative Lambek calculus

Note that if R is a transitive relation then definitions (1)–(3) are equivalent to:

$$S \cdot T = \{< x, y > | \exists z (< x, z >\in S, < z, y >\in T)\}, \tag{4}$$

$$S \rightarrow T = \{< x, y >\in R | \forall z (\text{if } < z, x >\in S \text{ then } < z, y >\in T)\}, \tag{5}$$

$$T \leftarrow S = \{< x, y >\in R | \forall z (\text{if } < y, z >\in S \text{ then } < x, z >\in T)\}. \tag{6}$$

Algebras with operations (4)–(6) were considered in [1]. They are models for the associative Lambek calculus. The transitivity of R, as shows the following fact, is not equivalent to the associativity of $\cdot$ defined by (1).

Fact 1 *There exists a non transitive binary relation R, such that $< \mathcal{P}(R), \cdot >$ is a semigroup.*

Proof. Let R' be a transitive binary relation. Let us define relation $R = R' \cup \{< x, y >, < y, z >\}$, where elements x, y, z are new (they do not belong to the field of R'). R is not transitive since $< x, z >\notin R$. Nevertheless we will show that operation $\cdot$ defined by (1) is associative, so $\langle \mathcal{P}(R), \cdot \rangle$ is a semigroup.

Let $S, T, U \in \mathcal{P}(R)$ and $< a, d >\in S \cdot (T \cdot U)$, so $< a, d >\in R$. But then by (1) there are pairs $< a, b >\in S$, $< b, c >\in T$, $< c, d >\in U$ such that $< b, d >\in R$. One can easily check that none of elements a, b, c, d is equal to x, y or z. So pairs $< a, b >$, $< b, c >$, $< c, d >$ belong to R', but R' is transitive, so $< a, c >\in R' \subseteq R$. Consequently $< a, d >\in (S \cdot T) \cdot U$. In a similar way one shows that $< a, d >\in (S \cdot T) \cdot U$ implies $< a, d >\in S \cdot (T \cdot U)$.

□

So we should find another property of binary relations which is equivalent to associativity of $\cdot$. A good one is expressed by (A). We call a binary relation R *associative*, if for every elements a, b, c, d the following condition holds:

$$\text{if } <a,b>, <b,c>, <c,d>, <a,d> \in R,$$

$$\text{then } <a,c> \in R \text{ iff } <b,d> \in R \qquad (A)$$

It is clear that every transitive relation is associative, but the converse does not hold. Relation R from the proof of the Fact 1 is associative (as none of elements a, b, c, d is equal to x, y or z) and not transitive.

Fact 2 *For every binary relation R and binary operation $\cdot$ defined by (1), $<\mathcal{P}(R), \cdot>$ is a semigroup if and only if relation R is associative.*

Proof. Implication from right to left is obvious. For the other direction we will show only one implication in (A), from left to right. Let $<a,b>, <b,c>, <c,d>, <a,d> \in R$ and $<a,c> \in R$. Define $S = \{<a,b>\}$, $T = \{<b,c>\}$, $U = \{<c,d>\}$, then $<a,d> \in (S \cdot T) \cdot U$, but $(S \cdot T) \cdot U = S \cdot (T \cdot U)$, so $<a,d> \in S \cdot (T \cdot U)$. Then, there exists x such that $<a,x> \in S$ and $<x,d> \in T \cdot U$. Since $S = \{<a,b>\}$, then $x = b$ and $<b,d> \in T \cdot U$ and consequently $<b,d> \in R$. $\square$

Note, that the associative Lambek calculus is complete with respect to RR-models $<\mathcal{G}(R), \varphi>$ such that the relation R is associative.

4   The representation theorem

Now we will show, via a representation theorem, that NL is complete with respect to the class of RR-models with the antisymmetric relation R (antisymmetric means: if $<x,y> \in R$ than $<y,x> \notin R$).

Theorem 2. *For every residuated groupoid $\mathcal{G}$, there exists a binary, antisymmetric relation R on some universe U such that $\mathcal{G}$ is isomorphically embeddable in the relational residuated groupoid. $\langle \mathcal{P}(R), \cdot, \leftarrow, \rightarrow, \subseteq \rangle$.*

Our proof of Theorem 2 uses methods of [5], but the non-associativity of R requires essential differences in constructions and proofs. We have to modify the notion of closed description and the definition of initial description D_X.

The key lemma is the following lemma, which states the existence of a canonical RR-model.

Lemma 1. *For every set of sequents X, with all atomic subtypes from Pr, there exists a binary, antisymmetric relation R on some universe U and a map $\overline{\varphi} : Pr \longmapsto \mathcal{P}(R)$ such that the sequents derivable in $NL(X)$ are precisely the sequents true in RR-model $< \mathcal{P}(R), \varphi >$.*

Having this lemma we can prove Theorem 2 in this way:

Let $\mathcal{G} =< G, \cdot, \rightarrow, \leftarrow, \leq >$ be a residuated groupoid. Let $Pr = \{p_g \mid g \in G\}$. Define $\mu : T(Pr) \mapsto G$ by $\mu(p_g) = g$. Let X be the set of all sequents (whose atomic types are in Pr) true in the model $< \mathcal{G}, \mu >$. By Lemma 1 we obtain model $< \mathcal{P}(R), \varphi >$ such that R is binary, antisymmetric relation. Next we define mapping $h : G \mapsto \mathcal{P}(R)$ by setting: $h(g) = \varphi(p_g)$, for $g \in G$. This mapping is the required monomorphism of $\mathcal{G}$ into $\mathcal{P}(R)$.

5   Proof of Lemma 1

Fix sets X and Pr. An ordered quadruple $< V, R, P, N >$ such that V is a set of *labels*, R is a binary, antisymmetric relation defined on V, and P, N are subsets of the set $LF(D)$ of all labelled types $ab : A$ such that $a, b \in V$, $< a, b >\in R$ and $A \in T(Pr)$, is called a *description*.

The description $D =< V, R, P, N >$ is said to be *consistent*, if $P \cap N = \emptyset$, and *closed*, if the following conditions holds:

$$\text{for every sequent } A_1 \vdash_{\text{NL}(X)} A \text{ and } a, b \in V, \\ \text{if } ab : A_1 \in P, \text{ then } ab : A \in P \qquad (*)$$

and

$$\text{for every sequent } A_1, A_2 \vdash_{\text{NL}(X)} A \text{ and } a_0, a_1, a_2 \in V, \\ \text{if } a_0 a_1 : A_1, a_1 a_2 : A_2 \in P \text{ and } < a_0, a_2 >\in R, \qquad (**) \\ \text{then } a_0 a_2 : A \in P.$$

Let $D =< V, R, P, N >$ be a description. Define the chain of sets $C_i(P)$, $i = 1, 2, \ldots$ such that $C_0(P) = P$ and $C_i(P)$ is the smallest set containing $C_{i-1}(P)$, and closed under the following rules:

$$\text{for every sequent } A_1 \vdash_{\text{NL}(X)} A \text{ and } a, b \in V, \\ \text{if } ab : A_1 \in C_{i-1}(P), \text{ then } ab : A \in C_i(P) \qquad (a)$$

and

$$\text{for every sequent } A_1, A_2 \vdash_{\text{NL}(X)} A, \text{ and } a_0, a_1, a_2 \in V, \\ \text{if } a_0 a_1 : A_1, a_1 a_2 : A_2 \in C_{i-1}(P) \text{ and } < a_0, a_2 >\in R, \qquad (b) \\ \text{then } a_0 a_2 : A \in C_i(P).$$

Then we define $C_D(P)$ as the sum of that chain, i. e. $C_D(P) = \bigcup_{i=1}^{\infty} C_i(P)$.

Fact 3 *For any set $P \subseteq LF(D)$, the description D' whose positive part is $C_D(P)$, and the remainder is as in D, is closed.*

Proof. As $(*)$ is obvious we will show $(**)$. Let $A_1, A_2 \vdash_{\text{NL}(X)} A$, $a_0, a_1, a_2 \in V$, $a_0 a_1 : A_1, a_1 a_2 : A_2 \in C_D(P)$, and $< a_0, a_2 >\in R$. Then there exists $i \in \mathbb{N}$ such that $a_0 a_1 : A_1, a_1 a_2 : A_2 \in C_i(P)$. By (b) we have $a_0 a_2 : A \in C_{i+1}(P)$ and consequently $a_0 a_2 : A \in C_D(P)$. □

Lemma 2. *For every description $D = < V, R, P, N >$, if $ab : A \in C_D(P)$, then there exist sequent $A_1, \ldots, A_n \vdash_{NL(X)} A$ and labels $a_0, \ldots, a_n \in V$ such that $a_0 = a$, $a_n = b$ and $a_{i-1}a_i : A_i \in P$, for every $1 \le i \le n$, and $< a_i, a_j > \in R$ for every pair $< i, j >$, ij such that $A_i, \ldots, A_j$ is a subterm of a term $A_1, \ldots, A_n$.*

Proof. We prove this lemma by induction, according to construction of $C_D(P)$.

As initial step C_0 is obvious, assume the lemma holds for C_k, and let $ab : A \in C_{k+1}(P)$. According to two ways of adding elements to $C_{k+1}(P)$ we have to consider two cases:

(a) there exists sequent $A_1 \vdash_{NL(X)} A$ such that $ab : A_1 \in C_k(P)$. By induction hypothesis we have sequent $B_1, \ldots, B_n \vdash_{NL(X)} A_1$ and labels $b_0, \ldots, b_n$ such that $b_0 = a$, $b_n = b$ and $b_{i-1}b_i : B_i \in P$, for every $1 \le i \le n$, and pairs $< b_i, b_j >$ obtained from subterms of a term $B_1, \ldots, B_n$ there are in R. Using (CUT) we obtain $B_1, \ldots, B_n \vdash_{NL(X)} A$.

(b) there exists sequent $A_1, A_2 \vdash_{NL(X)} A$ and label $c \in V$ such that $ac : A_1$, $cb : A_2 \in C_k(P)$. As in previous case we have sequents $B_1, \ldots, B_n \vdash_{NL(X)} A_1$, $C_1, \ldots, C_m \vdash_{NL(X)} A_2$ and labels $b_0, \ldots, b_n$, $c_0, \ldots, c_m$ such that $b_0 = a$, $b_n = c = c_0$, $c_m = b$ and $b_{i-1}b_i : B_i \in P$, $c_{j-1}b_j : C_j \in P$ for every $1 \le i \le n$, $1 \le j \le m$. Moreover, pairs $< b_i, b_j >$, $< c_k, c_l >$ obtained from subterms of terms $B_1, \ldots, B_n$ and $C_1, \ldots, C_m$ respectively there are in R. Using (CUT) to sequents $B_1, \ldots, B_n \vdash_{NL(X)} A_1$ and $A_1, A_2 \vdash_{NL(X)} A$ we obtain sequent $(B_1, \ldots, B_n), A_2 \vdash_{NL(X)} A$. Applying (CUT) to this sequent and $C_1, \ldots, C_m \vdash_{NL(X)} A_2$ we obtain sequent $(B_1, \ldots, B_n), (C_1, \ldots, C_m) \vdash_{NL(X)} A$. Finally every labelled type which occurs in antecedent of this sequent belongs to P. □

Lemma 3. *Let $D = < V, R, P, N >$ be a consistent and closed description, and let $ab : A \cdot B \in P$. Take a new label $c \notin V$ and define:*
$$V' = V \cup \{c\}$$
$$R' = R \cup \{< a, c >, < c, b >\}$$
$$P' = C_{D'}(P \cup \{ac : A, cb : B\})$$
$$N' = N$$
Then, $D' = < V', R', P', N' >$ is a consistent and closed description.

Proof. D' is closed by fact 3. The definition of P' is correct, although it refers to D' since V' and R' have been defined.

For consistency, notice that types labelled by pair $< a, c >$ or $< c, b >$ do not belong to N', so it suffices to prove the following lemma (by Q we denote the set $P \cup \{ac : A, cb : B\}$):

Lemma 4. *If $uv : C \in C_{D'}(Q)$ and $< u, v > \in R$, then $uv : C \in P$.*

Proof. By induction, according to construction of $C_{D'}(Q)$.

The lemma holds for $C_0(Q)$.

Assume, the lemma holds for $C_i(Q)$, and let $uv : C \in C_{i+1}(Q)$. We should consider two cases (see Fig. 1.)

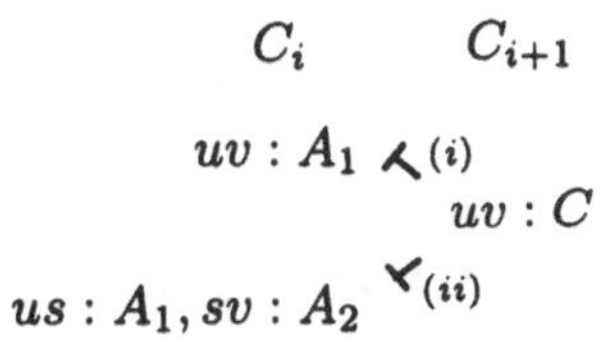

$$C_i \qquad C_{i+1}$$

$$uv : A_1 \; \swarrow^{(i)}$$
$$uv : C$$
$$us : A_1, sv : A_2 \; \nwarrow^{(ii)}$$

Fig. 1

(i) there exists a labelled type $uv : A_1 \in C_i(Q)$, such that $A_1 \vdash_{\text{NL}(X)} C$. But we assume that lemma holds for $C_i(Q)$, so $uv : A_1 \in P$ and, since P is closed, $uv : C \in P$.

(ii) there exist labelled types $us : A_1$, $sv : A_2 \in C_i(Q)$ such that $A_1, A_2 \vdash_{\text{NL}(X)} C$. If pairs $< u, s >$, $< s, v >$ belong to R we have $us : A_1$, $sv : A_2 \in P$ and since P is closed $uv : C \in P$. Otherwise we have $u = a$, $s = c$, $v = b$. Applying lemma 2 to description $< V', R', Q, N' >$ and labelled types $ac : A_1$, $cb : A_2$ we obtain (having in mind that in V' does not exists element z such that $< a, z >$, $< z, c > \in R'$) labelled types $ac : A_1'$, $cb : A_2' \in Q$ such that $A_1' \vdash_{\text{NL}(X)} A_1$, $A_2' \vdash_{\text{NL}(X)} A_2$. Moreover in Q we have only two types labelled by a pair with c, so $A_1' = A$, $A_2' = B$. We also have the following derivation:

$$\dfrac{\dfrac{A \vdash_{\text{NL}(X)} A_1 \quad B \vdash_{\text{NL}(X)} A_2}{\dfrac{A, B \vdash_{\text{NL}(X)} A_1 \cdot A_2}{A \cdot B \vdash_{\text{NL}(X)} A_1 \cdot A_2} (\cdot L)} (\cdot R) \quad \dfrac{A_1, A_2 \vdash_{\text{NL}(X)} C}{A_1 \cdot A_2 \vdash_{\text{NL}(X)} C} (\cdot L)}{A \cdot B \vdash_{\text{NL}(X)} C} (\text{CUT})$$

But by assumption of lemma 3 $ab : A \cdot B \in P$ and P is closed, so $ab : C \in P$.

$\square$

Lemma 5. *Let $D = < V, R, P, N >$ be a consistent, and closed description, and let $ab : A \to B \in N$. Take a new label $c \notin V$ and define:*
$$V' = V \cup \{c\}$$
$$R' = R \cup \{< c, a >, < c, b >\}$$
$$P' = C_{D'}(P \cup \{ca : A\})$$
$$N' = N \cup \{cb : B\}$$
Then $D' = < V', R', P', N' >$ is a consistent and closed description.

Proof. Here, lemma 4 holds trivially, as no pair from R can be obtained by composition, using $< c, a >$ or $< c, b >$. So, for consistency of D', it suffices to show that $cb : B \notin P'$. It is obvious for $C_0(P \cup \{ca : A\})$. Assume it is true for $C_i(P \cup \{ca : A\})$, and let $cb : B \in C_{i+1}(P \cup \{ca : A\})$ but then we should consider two cases (by Q we denote the set $P \cup \{ca : A\}$):

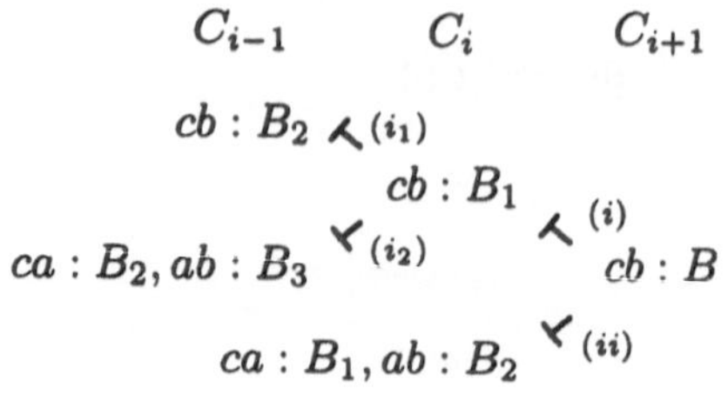

$$C_{i-1} \qquad C_i \qquad C_{i+1}$$

$$cb : B_2 \ (i_1)$$
$$cb : B_1$$
$$ca : B_2, ab : B_3 \quad (i_2) \qquad cb : B$$
$$ca : B_1, ab : B_2 \quad (ii)$$

Fig. 2

(i) there exists a labelled type $cb : B_1 \in C_i(Q)$ such that $B_1 \vdash_{\text{NL}(X)} B$

   (i_1) there exists a labelled type $cb : B_2 \in C_{i-1}(Q)$ such that $B_2 \vdash_{\text{NL}(X)}$ B_1, but using (CUT) we obtain $B_2 \vdash_{\text{NL}(X)} B$ and $cb : B \in C_i(Q)$. Contradiction.

   (i_2) there are labelled types $ca : B_2, ab : B_3 \in C_{i-1}(Q)$ such that $B_2, B_3 \vdash_{\text{NL}(X)} B_1$. Again using (CUT) we obtain $B_2, B_3 \vdash_{\text{NL}(X)} B$ and consequently $cb : B \in C_i(Q)$. Contradiction.

   (Above consideration is true for $i \geq 2$. For $i = 1$ it suffices to notice that in $C_0(Q)$ there is no type labelled by the pair $< c, b >$.)

(ii) there are labelled types $ca : B_1, ab : B_2 \in C_i(Q)$ such that $B_1, B_2 \vdash_{\text{NL}(X)}$ B. Since R is antisymmetric, there is no type in $LF(D')$ labelled by pair $< b, a >$. From lemma 2 applied to description $< V', R', Q, N' >$ and labelled type $ca : B_1$ we obtain sequent $B'_1 \vdash_{\text{NL}(X)} B$ such that $ca : B'_1 \in Q$. Moreover in Q there is only one type labelled by pair $< c, a >$ so $B'_1 = A$. We have also the following derivation:

$$\frac{\dfrac{A \vdash_{\text{NL}(X)} B_1 \quad B_1, B_2 \vdash_{\text{NL}(X)} B}{A, B_2 \vdash_{\text{NL}(X)} B} \text{(CUT)}}{B_2 \vdash_{\text{NL}(X)} A \to B} (\to\text{R})$$

But $ab : B_2 \in C_i(Q)$ so $ab : A \to B \in P'$. By lemma 4 we also have $ab : A \to B \in P$. Contradiction.

$\square$

Lemma 6. *Let $D = < V, R, P, N >$ be a consistent and closed description, and let $ab : B \leftarrow A \in N$. Take a new label $c \notin V$ and define:*
   $V' = V \cup \{c\}$
   $R' = R \cup \{< a, c >, < b, c >\}$
   $P' = C_{D'}(P \cup \{ac : A\})$
   $N' = N \cup \{bc : B\}$
Then $D' = < V', R', P', N' >$ is a consistent and closed description.

Proof. Similar to the previous Lemma. $\square$

Lemma 7. *Let* $D =< V, R, P, N >$ *be a consistent and closed description, and let* $ab : A \in LF(D), ab : A \notin P$. *Define:*

$$V' = V$$
$$R' = R$$
$$P' = P$$
$$N' = N \cup \{ab : A\}$$

Then $D' =< V', R', P', N' >$ *is a consistent and closed description.*

Let us define description D_X. For any sequent $A_1, \ldots, A_n \not\vdash_{NL(X)} A, n \geq 1$, we choose different labels $a_0, \ldots, a_n$ (different sequents are assigned different labels) and set:

$V =$ the set of all labels produced in this way;

$R =$ the set of all pairs $< a_{i-1}, a_i >$ plus the set of all pairs $< a_0, a_n >$ plus the set of all pairs $< a_k, a_l >, 0 \leq k < l \leq n$, such that $A_k, \ldots, A_l$ is a subterm of a term $A_1, \ldots, A_n$, where the labels appearing in the pairs are elements of V;

$P' =$ the set of all labelled types $a_{i-1}a_i : A_i$ obtained from the sequents defined above;

$N =$ the set of all labelled types $a_0 a_n : A$ obtained from the sequents defined above, $D_X =< V, R, C_{D_X}(P'), N >$.

Lemma 8. D_X *is a consistent and closed description.*

Proof. Of course relation R is antisymmetric. We will show the consistency of D_X. Suppose that there is a labelled type $ab : A \in C_{D_X}(P')$ and $ab : A \in N$. But labels assigned to different labelled types in N are different, so there exists sequent $A_1, \ldots, A_n \not\vdash_{NL(X)} A$ and the set of labels $a_0, \ldots a_n$, such that $a_0 a_1 : A_1, \ldots, a_{n-1} a_n : A_n \in P'$ and $a_0 = a$, and $a_n = b$. Moreover according to Lemma 2 there exist sequent $B_1, \ldots, B_m \vdash_{NL(X)} A$ and a set of labels $b_0, \ldots, b_m \in V$ such that $b_0 = a$, $b_n = b$ and $b_{i-1} b_i : B_i \in P'$ for every $1 \leq i \leq m$. As assignment of labels to types in P' is unique we obtain $m = n$, $b_i = a_i$ and $B_i = A_i$ for every $1 \leq i \leq n$. But then we have $A_1, \ldots, A_n \vdash_{NL(X)} A$. Contradiction. $\square$

A description $D =< V, R, P, N >$ is said to be *complete*, if $P \cup N = LF(D)$, and *witnessed*, if for all $a, b \in V$, the following conditions hold:

(W1) if $ab : A \cdot B \in P$, then $ac : A \in P$ and $cb : B \in P$, for some $c \in V$.

(W2) if $ab : A \rightarrow B \in N$, then $ca : A \in P$ and $cb : B \in N$, for some $c \in V$.

(W3) if $ab : B \leftarrow A \in N$, then $ac : A \in P$ and $bc : B \in N$, for some $c \in V$.

If $D =< V, R, P, N >$ and $D' =< V', R', P', N' >$ are descriptions such that $V \subseteq V', R \subseteq R', P \subseteq P', N \subseteq N'$, then we write: $D \sqsubseteq D'$.

Lemma 9. *For every consistent and closed description D, there exists a consistent, closed, complete and witnessed description D' such that* $D \sqsubseteq D'$.

Proof. (See [5].) Let $D =< V, R, P, N >$ be a consistent and closed description. Choose an infinite cardinal $\kappa \geq \text{card}(T(Pr) \cup V)$ and a set W, of new labels, such that $\text{card}(W) = \kappa$. We fix a transfinite sequence $(w_\xi)_{\xi \leq \kappa}$ of all labels from W (without repetitions). By $\mathcal{F}$ we denote the set of all formulas $ab : A$ such that $A \in T(pr)$ and $a, b \in V \cup W$. Clearly, $\text{card}(\mathcal{F}) = \kappa$, and we fix a transfinite sequence $(\gamma_\xi)_{\xi \leq \kappa}$, of all elements of $\mathcal{F}$, such that:

(CF) for all $\gamma \in \mathcal{F}$ and $\xi \leq \kappa$, there exists $\kappa \geq \zeta \geq \xi$ such that $\gamma = \gamma_\zeta$.

We define a transfinite chain of descriptions $(D_\xi)_{\xi \leq \kappa}$ with $D_\xi \sqsubseteq D_{\xi+1}$. The definition guarantees $V_\xi \subseteq V \cup W$ and $w_\xi \notin V_\xi$, for all $\xi \leq \kappa$.

Put $D_0 = D$. For limit ordinals $\lambda \leq \kappa$, define: $V_\lambda = \bigcup_{\xi \leq \lambda} V_\xi$, $R_\lambda = \bigcup_{\xi \leq \lambda} R_\xi$, $P_\lambda = \bigcup_{\xi \leq \lambda} P_\xi$, $N_\lambda = \bigcup_{\xi \leq \lambda} N_\xi$. We define $D_{\xi+1}$ on the basis of D_ξ. We take the labelled formula γ_ξ and consider several cases.

(I) $\gamma_\xi = ab : A \cdot B \in P_\xi$ and there is no $c \in V_\xi$ such that $ac : A, cb : B \in P_\xi$. We put $c = w_\xi$ and define $D_{\xi+1}$ as in lemma 3.

(II) $\gamma_\xi = ab : A \to B \in N_\xi$ and there is no $c \in V_\xi$ such that $ca : A \in P_\xi, cb : B \in N_\xi$. We put $c = w_\xi$ and define $D_{\xi+1}$ as in lemma 5.

(III) $\gamma_\xi = ba : B \leftarrow A \in N_\xi$ and there is no $c \in V_\xi$ such that $ac : A \in P_\xi, bc : B \in N_\xi$. We put $c = w_\xi$ and define $D_{\xi+1}$ as in lemma 6.

(IV) $\gamma_\xi \notin P_\xi \cup N_\xi$, $\gamma_\xi \in LF(D_\xi)$. We define $D_{\xi+1}$ as in lemma 7.

(V) In the remaining cases, we set $D_{\xi+1} = D_\xi$.

All descriptions D_ξ are consistent and closed. We define $D' = < V', R', P', N' >$, where $V' = \bigcup_{\xi \leq \kappa} V_\xi$, $R' = \bigcup_{\xi \leq \kappa} R_\xi$, $P' = \bigcup_{\xi \leq \kappa} P_\xi$, $N' = \bigcup_{\xi \leq \kappa} N_\xi$. Clearly, D' is consistent and closed. By the construction and (CF), D' is also witnessed and complete. $\qquad \square$

Lemma 10. *Let $D = < V, R, P, N >$ be a consistent, closed, complete and witnessed description. Let an assignment $\varphi : Pr \longmapsto P(R)$ be defined as follows:*

$$< a, b > \in \varphi(p) \text{ iff } ab : p \in P, \qquad (M1)$$

for all $a, b \in V$ and $p \in Pr$. Then, for all $a, b \in V$ and $A \in T(Pr)$:

$$< a, b > \in \varphi(A) \text{ iff } ab : A \in P. \qquad (M2)$$

Proof. Induction on the complexity of A, (For atomic types (M2) holds by (M1)).

Case $A = B \cdot C$. Assume $< a, b > \in \varphi(B \cdot C)$ so there exists $c \in V$ such that $< a, c > \in \varphi(B)$ and $< c, b > \in \varphi(C)$ but then $ac : B \in P$, $cb : C \in P$, we also have $B, C \vdash_{NL(X)} B \cdot C$ and D is closed so by (**) we obtain $ab : B \cdot C \in P$. Assume $ab : B \cdot C \in P$. As D is witnessed there exists $c \in V$ such that $ac : B \in P$ and $cb : C \in P$. Now we have $< a, c > \in \varphi(B)$, $< c, b > \in \varphi(C)$ and $< a, b > \in R$ so $< a, b > \in \varphi(B \cdot C)$.

Case $A = B \to C$. Assume $ab : B \to C \notin P$. By completeness of D $ab : B \to C \in N$ but D is also witnessed so there exists $c \in V$ such that $ca : B \in P$ and $cb : C \in N$, which yields $< c, a > \in \varphi(B)$ and $< c, b > \notin \varphi(C)$. Consequently $< a, b > \notin \varphi(B \to C)$. Assume $ab : B \to C \in P$, $< c, a > \in \varphi(B)$ and $< c, b > \in R$ which yields $ca : B \in P$. As $B, (B \to C) \vdash_{NL(X)} C$ and

D is closed we have $cb : C \in P$, which yields $< c, b > \in \varphi(C)$ this means that
$< a, b > \in \varphi(B \rightarrow C)$.

Case $A = B \leftarrow C$ is dual.   □

The lemmas of this section enable us to prove Lemma 1 formulated in Section 4.

Proof of Lemma 1. Consider the description D_X. From Lemma 8 it follows that D_X is consistent and closed, so by Lemma 9, there exists a description $D_X \sqsubseteq D$ which is consistent, closed, complete and witnessed. Let $D = <V, R, P, N >$. Define φ as in Lemma 10. We prove that sequents derivable in NL(X) are precisely the sequents true in RR-model $< \mathcal{P}(R), \varphi >$. Let $A_1, \ldots, A_n \vdash_{\text{NL}(X)} A$ and let $< a, b > \in \varphi(A_1) \cdot \ldots \cdot \varphi(A_n) = \varphi(A_1 \cdot \ldots \cdot A_n)$. From (M2) we have $ab : A_1 \cdot \ldots \cdot A_n \in P$ but $A_1 \cdot \ldots \cdot A_n \vdash_{\text{NL}(X)} A$ and D is closed so, by (*), $ab : A \in P$, again from (M2) we obtain $< a, b > \in \varphi(A)$. For the other direction let $A_1, \ldots, A_n \nvdash_{\text{NL}(X)} A$ so in D_X there are labels $a_0, \ldots, a_n \in V$ such that $a_{i-1}a_i : A_i \in P$, for $i = 1, \ldots n$, and $a_0 a_n : A \in N$. By (M2) $< a_{i-1}, a_i > \in \varphi(A_i)$ for $i = 1, \ldots, n$. Moreover, if $A_k, \ldots, A_l$ is a subterm of a term $A_1, \ldots, A_n$ then $< a_k, a_l > \in R$, so $< a_0, a_n > \in \varphi(A_1) \cdot \ldots \cdot \varphi(A_n)$. It means $\varphi(A_1) \cdot \ldots \cdot \varphi(A_n) \nsubseteq \varphi(A)$.   □

References

1. Andréka H. and Mikulás S. (1994) Lambek Calculus and its Relational Semantics: Completeness and Incompleteness. Journal of Logic, Language and Information 3:1–37
2. van Benthem J. (1991) Language in Action. Categories, Lambdas and Dynamic Logic. North-Holland Publ. Comp., Amsterdam
3. Buszkowski W. (1986) Completeness results for Lambek Syntactic Calculus. Zeitschrift für matematische Logik und Grundlagen der Mathematik 32:13–28
4. Buszkowski W. (1998) Algebraic structures in categorial grammar. Theoretical Computer Science 199:5–24
5. Buszkowski W. and Kołowska-Gawiejnowicz M. (1997) Representation of Residuated Semigroups in Some Algebras of Relations. Fundamenta Informaticae 31:1–12
6. Kandulski M. (1988) The non-associative Lambek Calculus. In: Buszkowski W., Marciszewski W. and van Benthem J. (Eds.), Categorial Grammar. John Benjamins, Amsterdam, 141–151
7. Kurtonina N. (1995) Frames and Labels. A modal analysis of categorial inference. ILLD Dissertation Series 1995-1998, Amsterdam
8. Lambek J. (1961) On the Calculus of Syntactic Types. In: Jakobson R. (Ed.), Structure of Language and Its Mathematical Aspects, AMS, Providence
9. Szczerba M. (1997) Representation Theorems for Residuated Groupoids. In: Retoré C. (Ed.), Logical Aspects of Computational Linguistics, Lecture Notes in Artificial Intelligence 1328, Springer, Berlin, 426–434
10. Venema Y. (1966) Tree Models and (Labelled) Categorial Grammar. Journal of Logic, Language, and Information 5:253–277

Part IV

Relations
and Uncertainty

Chapter 10
Coping with Semilattices of Relations in Logics with Relative Accessibility Relations

Stéphane Demri

Laboratoire LEIBNIZ - C.N.R.S.
46 Avenue Félix Viallet, 38031 Grenoble, France
demri@imag.fr

Abstract. We present a class of polymodal logics for which the set of terms indexing the modal connectives can be hierarchized in two levels: the set of Boolean terms and the set of terms built upon the set of Boolean terms. The semantical structures of the logics contains a family of binary relations that can be viewed a homomorphism between semilattices. Various results related to decidability, axiomatization and computational complexity are established by faithfully translating the logics into more standard modal logics. The paper is a short survey of results obtained by translation for various logics of the above kind from the literature.
Keywords: modal logic, relative operator, reduction

1 Introduction

The information logics derived from Pawlak's *information systems* [30] are polymodal logics such that the relations in the models correspond to relations derived from information systems. Let us recall the peculiarities of such logics. First, numerous propositional modal logics can be defined from semantical structures of the form $\mathcal{M} = \langle W, (R_a)_{a \in M}, V \rangle$ where W is a non-empty set, $(R_a)_{a \in M}$ is a family of binary relations over W, M is the set of modal expressions and V is a *meaning function* that is, for each propositional variable p, $V(p) \subseteq W$. The well-known propositional dynamic logic PDL (see e.g. [17]) uses this kind of semantical structures. In the sequel, such logics are called *standard modal logics*. By adding a Boolean dimension to the standard modal logics we obtain a class of logics (the logics with Relative Accessibility RElations or shorter, the "Rare-logics") that includes numerous information logics (see [24,25]). At the syntactical level, we replace the set of modal constants (upon which the set M of modal expressions is built) by a set of expressions of the form $r(\alpha)$ with $\alpha \in P$ where the set P is built upon a set $P_0 = \{\delta_i : i \in \omega\}$ of *parameter constants* and is closed under the Boolean operators $\cap, \cup, -$. The syntactic construction $r(.)$ announces a parameter expression. The semantical structures are of the form $\langle W, PAR, (\mathcal{R}_P)_{P \subseteq PAR}, V \rangle$ where PAR is a non-empty set of *parameters*, V also maps homomorphically every Boolean expression α to a subset of PAR and $V(r(\alpha)) = \mathcal{R}_{V(\alpha)}$ for any $\alpha \in P$. According to the algebraic properties of $(\mathcal{R}_P)_{P \subseteq PAR}$, different *types* of logics are defined (see e.g. [27,4,20]).

The main result of the paper states that there exist satisfiability-preserving transformations between Rare-logics and the corresponding standard modal logics (validity-preserving maps can be also designed). The translations are interesting for their own sake, for instance they help understanding what is brought by adding a Boolean dimension to a logic. By taking advantage of such translations, we provide a uniform framework to prove decidability for various Rare-logics from [24,27,26,2,4]. Moreover, we show how it can also help to define proof systems for the Rare-logics. Quantitative aspects about computational complexity are also briefly discussed.

As far as we know, the notion of Rare-logic appeared in the literature in [26] where various Rare-logics are described to model reasoning in the presence of incomplete information. Hilbert-style and Rasiowa-Sikorski-style calculi for some Rare-logics have been defined in [2,4,20]. Recently, in [6], a classification of logics with relative accessibility relations has been proposed. None of these works tackle the problem of relating Rare-logics with more standard modal logics in a systematic way. Moreover, in these works, decidability issues are not their concern. Decidability of information logics has been established in the past by using filtration-like and restriction-like techniques (see e.g. [33,7]). Here we use a different approach, we interpret a Rare-logic in a standard modal logic following the general framework established in [32].

The paper is organised as follows. In Section 2, we define the class of standard modal logics as well as the class of Rare-logics considered in the paper. In Section 3, we define general properties of semilattices and then show how they can be used to define satisfiability-preserving maps between Rare-logics and standard modal logics. In Section 4, we establish various decidability results whereas in Section 5 we provide a sufficient condition to prove that the satisfiability problem of a Rare-logic is in the complexity class **EXPTIME** (that is, it can be solved by a deterministic Turing machine in exponential-time with respect to the size of the input formulae). In Section 6, we propose a general recipe for defining proof systems for Rare-logics that is illustrated on a particular example. We round off the paper by open questions that are worth being investigated.

This paper is a full version of the extended abstract [8]. Most of the results of this paper can be extended to the case when nominals are allowed in the language (see [10,12]) or to the case when the accessibility relations of the semantical structures can be of arbitrary arity (see also [10]). Some other related works can be found in [10,9,11].

2   Modal logics

2.1   Language

Let $OP = \{\oplus_1, \ldots, \oplus_s\}$ be a (possibly empty) finite set of *operators* such that $\rho(\oplus_i) \in \omega \setminus \{0\}$ denotes the *arity* of $\oplus_i$. A set $\mathsf{M} = \{\mathsf{a}, \mathsf{b}, \ldots\}$ of *modal expressions* is the smallest set that contains a non-empty countable set M_0 of *basic modal expressions* and it is closed under OP with respect to the arity map ρ. A *modal language* L is defined as a pair $\langle\langle OP, \rho, \mathsf{M}_0, \mathsf{M}\rangle, \mathrm{For}_0\rangle$ where $\mathrm{For}_0 = \{\mathsf{p}, \mathsf{q}, \ldots\}$ is a countable set of propositional variables. The formulae φ of L are inductively defined as follows: $\varphi ::= \mathsf{p} \mid \varphi_1 \wedge \varphi_2 \mid \neg\varphi \mid [\mathsf{a}]\varphi$ for $\mathsf{p} \in \mathrm{For}_0$ and $\mathsf{a} \in \mathsf{M}$. The set of L-formulae is denoted **For**. Standard abbreviations include $\bot$, $\top$, $\langle\mathsf{a}\rangle$, $\vee$, $\Rightarrow$, $\Leftrightarrow$. We write $sub(\varphi)$ to denote the set of *subformulae* of the formula φ.

2.2 Kripke-style semantics

A *relation operation* g maps any set U to a mapping $g(U) : \mathcal{P}(U^{i_1}) \times \ldots \times \mathcal{P}(U^{i_n}) \to \mathcal{P}(U^{i_{n+1}})$ with $i_1, \ldots, i_{n+1} \geq 1$ and $i_1, \ldots, i_{n+1}$ do not depend on U. $\langle i_1, \ldots, i_{n+1}\rangle$ is the *profile* of g and n is its *arity*. We also require that if there is an 1-1 mapping $f : U \to U'$, then for any $\langle X_1, \ldots X_n\rangle \in \mathcal{P}(U^{i_1}) \times \ldots \times \mathcal{P}(U^{i_n})$,

$$f(g(U)(X_1, \ldots, X_n)) = g(U')(f(X_1), \ldots, f(X_n)))$$

An *operator interpretation* $\mathcal{I}$ maps the set OP into the set of relation operations such that for any $\oplus \in OP$ such that $\rho(\oplus) = n$, the profile of $\mathcal{I}(\oplus)$ is $\langle 2, \ldots, 2, 2\rangle$, an $n + 1$-tuple. A similar definition is used in [13]. An L-*frame* $\mathcal{F}$ is a pair $\langle W, (R_{\mathsf{a}})_{\mathsf{a}\in\mathsf{M}}\rangle$ such that W is a non-empty set and for any $\mathsf{a} \in \mathsf{M}$, $R_{\mathsf{a}} \subseteq W^2$. An L-*model* $\mathcal{M}$ *respecting some operator interpretation* $\mathcal{I}$ is a structure $\mathcal{M} = \langle W, (R_{\mathsf{a}})_{\mathsf{a}\in\mathsf{M}}, V\rangle$ such that $\langle W, (R_{\mathsf{a}})_{\mathsf{a}\in\mathsf{M}}\rangle$ is an L-frame, V is a map $V : \mathrm{For}_0 \to \mathcal{P}(W)$ and for any $\oplus(\mathsf{a}_1, \ldots, \mathsf{a}_n) \in \mathsf{M}$, $R_{\oplus(\mathsf{a}_1, \ldots, \mathsf{a}_n)} = \mathcal{I}(\oplus)(W)(R_{\mathsf{a}_1}, \ldots, R_{\mathsf{a}_n})$. The formula φ is *satisfied by the world* $u \in W$ *in* $\mathcal{M}$ iff $\mathcal{M}, u \models \varphi$ where the *satisfaction relation* $\models$ is inductively defined as follows:

1. $\mathcal{M}, u \models \mathsf{p} \overset{\text{def}}{\Leftrightarrow} u \in V(\mathsf{p})$, for any $\mathsf{p} \in \mathrm{For}_0$;
2. $\mathcal{M}, u \models \neg\varphi \overset{\text{def}}{\Leftrightarrow}$ not $\mathcal{M}, u \models \varphi$;
3. $\mathcal{M}, u \models \varphi \wedge \psi \overset{\text{def}}{\Leftrightarrow} \mathcal{M}, u \models \varphi$ and $\mathcal{M}, u \models \psi$;
4. $\mathcal{M}, u \models [\mathsf{a}]\varphi \overset{\text{def}}{\Leftrightarrow}$ for all $u' \in R_{\mathsf{a}}(u)$, $\mathcal{M}, u' \models \varphi$.

A formula φ is *true* in an L-model $\mathcal{M}$ (denoted by $\mathcal{M} \models \varphi$) $\overset{\text{def}}{\Leftrightarrow}$ for any $u \in W$, $\mathcal{M}, u \models \varphi$. φ is *valid* in an L-frame $\mathcal{F}$ (denoted by $\mathcal{F} \models \varphi$) $\overset{\text{def}}{\Leftrightarrow}$ $\mathcal{M} \models \varphi$ for any L-model based on $\mathcal{F}$.

2.3 Classes of logics

An L-*normal modal logic* $\mathcal{L}$ is defined as a triple $\langle L, \mathcal{I}, \mathcal{C}\rangle$ such that $\mathcal{I}$ is an operator interpretation and $\mathcal{C}$ is a class of L-models respecting $\mathcal{I}$. A *standard modal logic* is an L-normal modal logic such that the set of basic modal expressions is a countable (possibly finite) set $\mathsf{M}_0 = \{\mathsf{c}_0, \mathsf{c}_1, \ldots\}$ of constants. An L-formula φ is said to be $\mathcal{L}$-*valid* iff φ is true in all the $\mathcal{L}$-models. An L-formula

φ is said to be *$\mathcal{L}$-satisfiable* iff there exist an $\mathcal{L}$-model $\mathcal{M} = \langle W, (R_{\mathbf{a}})_{\mathbf{a}\in\mathsf{M}}, V\rangle$ and $u \in W$ such that $\mathcal{M}, u \models \varphi$. We say that ψ is a *logical $\mathcal{L}$-consequence* of φ (in symbols $\varphi \models_{\mathcal{L}} \psi$) $\overset{\text{def}}{\Leftrightarrow}$ for any $\mathcal{L}$-model $\mathcal{M}$, $\mathcal{M} \models \varphi$ implies $\mathcal{M} \models \psi$. As usual, we say that the modal logic $\mathcal{L}$ has the *finite model property* (fmp) iff each $\mathcal{L}$-satisfiable formula φ has an $\mathcal{L}$-model of finite cardinality.

A set of modal expressions is said to be *designed for Rare-logics* if each basic modal expression is of the form $r(\alpha)$ where α is a *parameter expression* and 'r' is an arbitrary symbol fixed in the rest of the paper. The set $\mathsf{P} = \{\alpha, \beta, \ldots\}$ of parameter expressions is the smallest set containing a countable set $\mathsf{P}_0 = \{\delta_i : i \in \omega\}$ of *parameter constants* and it is closed under the Boolean operators $\cap, \cup, -$. A P-*valuation* V is a map $V : \mathsf{P} \to \mathcal{P}(PAR)$ such that for any $\alpha_1, \alpha_2 \in \mathsf{P}$,

- $V(\alpha_1) \in \mathcal{P}(PAR)$; $V(-\alpha_1) = PAR \setminus V(\alpha_1)$;
- $V(\alpha_1 \cap \alpha_2) = V(\alpha_1) \cap V(\alpha_2)$; $V(\alpha_1 \cup \alpha_2) = V(\alpha_1) \cup V(\alpha_2)$.

For any $\alpha, \beta \in \mathsf{P}$ we write $\alpha \equiv \bot$ [resp. $\alpha \equiv \beta$, $\alpha \sqsubseteq \beta$] when for any P-valuation V, $V(\alpha) = \emptyset$ [resp. $V(\alpha) = V(\beta)$, $V(\alpha) \subseteq V(\beta)$]. The relations $\equiv$ and $\sqsubseteq$ are known to be decidable (by decidability of classical propositional logic for instance). Let L be a modal language designed for Rare-logics. An L-model $\mathcal{M} = \langle W, (R_{\mathbf{a}})_{\mathbf{a}\in\mathsf{M}}, V\rangle$ is said to be *designed for Rare-logics* $\overset{\text{def}}{\Leftrightarrow}$ there exist a non empty set PAR, a family $(\mathcal{R}_P)_{P\subseteq PAR}$ of binary relations over W and a P-valuation V' such that for any $\alpha \in \mathsf{P}$, $\mathcal{R}_{V'(\alpha)} = R_{r(\alpha)}$. Such a model $\mathcal{M}$ is denoted $\langle W, PAR, (\mathcal{R}_P)_{P\subseteq PAR}, V''\rangle$ where V'' is a map $V'' : (\mathsf{For}_0 \cup \mathsf{P} \cup \mathsf{M}) \to \mathcal{P}(PAR) \cup \mathcal{P}(W) \cup \mathcal{P}(W^2)$ such that the restriction of V'' to P is V', the restriction of V'' to For_0 is V and for any $\mathbf{a} \in \mathsf{M}$, $V''(\mathbf{a}) = R_{\mathbf{a}}$.

We write Fr^2 to denote the class of structures $\langle W, R\rangle$ where W is a non-empty set and $R \subseteq W^2$.

Definition 1. Let L be a modal language designed for Rare-logics. An L-normal modal logic $\mathcal{L} = \langle \mathsf{L}, \mathcal{I}, \mathcal{C}\rangle$ is said to be a *Rare-logic* iff there is a class $X \subseteq Fr^2$ such that $\mathcal{C}$ is the class of L-models $\mathcal{M} = \langle W, PAR, (\mathcal{R}_P)_{P\subseteq PAR}, V\rangle$ respecting $\mathcal{I}$ satisfying for any $\emptyset \neq P \subseteq PAR$, $\langle W, \mathcal{R}_P\rangle \in X$.

$\mathcal{L}$ is also written $\langle \mathsf{L}, \mathcal{I}, \mathcal{C}, X\rangle$. The main motivation for introducing the class of Rare logics comes from the theory of informations systems. During the last decade, the information logics derived from Pawlak's *information systems* [30] have been the object of quite active research. An *information system* can be seen as a structure $\langle OB, AT\rangle$ such that OB is a non-empty set of *objects*, AT is a non-empty set of *attributes* and each attribute $at \in AT$, is a mapping $at : OB \to \mathcal{P}(Val_{at})$ where Val_{at} is a non-empty set of *values*. For each object o and for each attribute at, $at(o)$ is the set of *possible* values of o with respect to the attribute at. This is at least one possible reading for $at(o)$ (one can think also about its conjunctive reading). Usually, $at(o)$ is assumed to be non-empty. Such structures are intended to capture some aspects of incomplete information. In that setting, various derived relations between objects can be

defined. We recall below the *indiscernibility* and *positive similarity* relations.
For any $o_1, o_2 \in OB$, $A \subseteq AT$,

- $o_1 ind(A) o_2 \overset{\text{def}}{\Leftrightarrow}$ for any $at \in A$, $at(o_1) = at(o_2)$;
- $o_1 sim(A) o_2 \overset{\text{def}}{\Leftrightarrow}$ for any $at \in A$, $at(o_1) \cap at(o_2) \neq \emptyset$.

$o_1 ind(A) o_2$ can be read as follows: the objects o_1 and o_2 cannot be distinguished modulo the set of attributes A. Similarly, $o_1 sim(A) o_2$ iff o_1 and o_2 are similar modulo A. The polymodal logics obtained from the information systems are multimodal logics such that the relations in the Kripke-style semantical structures correspond to relations between objects in the underlying information systems. Usually, such logics are supposed to perform reasoning about information systems. It is not clear to us that those logics satisfy their initial goal however they offer other remarkable properties. For instance, the accessibility relations in the models are interdependent; for instance, if $B \subseteq A \subseteq AT$, then $ind(A) \subseteq ind(B)$. Moreover, the set of modal terms can be hierarchized in two levels: the set of Boolean terms (interpreted as "sets of attributes") and the set of modal expressions (interpreted as "derived relations from information systems").

The main purpose of this work is to associate a standard modal logic with each Rare-logic in order to study the Rare-logic via properties of the standard modal logic. In general, the standard modal logics and the Rare-logics share neither the same type of modal language nor the same type of semantical structures. However, the main non-technical difference between these logics can be explained by the following observation. Two kinds of syntactic objects can be distinguished for standard modal logics: the modal expressions (interpreted as binary relations) and the formulas (interpreted as sets of worlds). In the Rare-logics, a third kind of syntactic objects is introduced: the parameter expression (interpreted as sets of attributes). This third component introduces new constraints on the semantical structures and this is our intention in this paper to show why this seemingly increase of complexity is sometime only superficial.

Definition 2. Let $\mathcal{L} = \langle L, \mathcal{I}, \mathcal{C}, X \rangle$ be a Rare-logic. The standard modal logic $\mathcal{L}_d$ from $\mathcal{L}$ is the structure $\langle L_d, \mathcal{I}_d, \mathcal{C}_d \rangle$ such that

- L_d is the modal language obtained from L by replacing $\{r(\alpha) : \alpha \in P\}$ by the set $\{c_i : i \in \omega\}$ of modal constants;
- $\mathcal{I}_d = \mathcal{I}$;
- for any L_d-model $\mathcal{M} = \langle W, (R_a)_{a \in M}, V \rangle$, $\mathcal{M} \in \mathcal{C}_d \overset{\text{def}}{\Leftrightarrow} \mathcal{M}$ respects $\mathcal{I}$ and the relations generated from $\{R_c : c \in M_0\}$ with intersection belong to X.

In [10, Part I], the definition of the standard modal logic from a Rare-logic is more involved and more general. Indeed, in the present paper, we only provide developments for a single (forthcoming) class of Rare-logics.

In this work, we shall consider algebras $\langle D, \sqcap \rangle$ of type $\langle 2 \rangle$ such that $\sqcap$ is commutative, associative, idempotent with a zero element e. In particular, any join-semilattice [resp. meet-semilattice] $\langle D, \leq \rangle$ with a bottom element $\perp$ [resp. with a top element $\top$], can be seen as an algebra of that kind by defining for any $a, b \in D$, $a \sqcap b \stackrel{\text{def}}{=} a \vee b$ [resp. $a \sqcap b \stackrel{\text{def}}{=} a \wedge b$]. Similarly, any algebra $\langle D, \sqcap \rangle$ of the above kind can be seen for instance as a join-semilattice by defining for any $a, b \in D$, $a \leq b \stackrel{\text{def}}{\Leftrightarrow} a \sqcap b = b$. By abusing our notation, we write $\langle D, \sqcap, e \rangle$ to denote the algebras of the above class and we call them *semilattices with zero element e*. Indeed, we shall mainly investigate Rare-logics for which the sets of relations of the models are semilattices with zero element. Indeed, we consider the case when the family $(\mathcal{R}_P)_{P \subseteq PAR}$ is exactly a map $g : \langle \mathcal{P}(PAR), \cup, \emptyset \rangle \to \langle \mathcal{P}(W^2), \sqcap, W^2 \rangle$ where

1. $\langle \mathcal{P}(PAR), \cup, \emptyset \rangle$ is the semilattice where $\cup$ is the set union;
2. $\langle \mathcal{P}(W^2), \sqcap, W^2 \rangle$ is a semilattice with zero element W^2;
3. $g(\emptyset) = W^2$;
4. g is an homomorphism, that is for any $P, P' \in \mathcal{P}(PAR)$, $g(P \cup P') = g(P) \sqcap g(P')$;
5. for any $P \subseteq PAR$, $\mathcal{R}_P = g(P)$.

In [22,19] algebraic structures similar to semilattices have been investigated in order to study the *dependence spaces* and information systems. Other conditions on the family $(\mathcal{R}_P)_{P \subseteq PAR}$ exist in the literature (see e.g. [14,28,20,4]). We concentrate here on Rare-logics $\mathcal{L} = \langle \mathrm{L}, \mathcal{I}, \mathcal{C}, X \rangle$ where there is an operator $\oplus_{\mathcal{L}} \in OP$ such that for any L-model $\mathcal{M} = \langle W, PAR, (\mathcal{R}_P)_{P \subseteq PAR}, V \rangle$, $\mathcal{M} \in \mathcal{C} \stackrel{\text{def}}{\Leftrightarrow}$

1. $\mathcal{M}$ respects $\mathcal{I}$ and for any $\emptyset \neq P \subseteq PAR$, $\langle W, \mathcal{R}_P \rangle \in X$;
2. $\mathcal{I}(\oplus_{\mathcal{L}})(W) = \sqcap$;
3. for any $P, P' \subseteq PAR$, $\mathcal{R}_{P \cup P'} = \mathcal{R}_P \sqcap \mathcal{R}_{P'}$;
4. $\mathcal{R}_\emptyset = W^2$.

As a consequence for such Rare-logics, the class X of modal frames is closed under $\sqcap$. The technical developments are done in this paper for these kinds of Rare-logics. Other classes are treated in [10, Part I].

Example 1. Let $LIR = \langle \mathrm{L}, \mathcal{I}, \mathcal{C}, X \rangle$ be the Rare-logic such that $OP = \{\cap, \cup^*\}$ (respectively interpreted as the intersection and the reflexive and transitive closure of the union on binary relations), X is the class of equivalence relations and $\sqcap$ is interpreted as the set intersection. The corresponding standard modal logic LIR_d is precisely the logic DAL defined in [15]. DAL is a standard (poly)modal logic where the modal terms are built upon the modal constants $\{c_i : i \in \omega\}$ and closed under $\cap$ and $\cup^*$. Furthermore, each c_i is interpreted as an equivalence relation.

Let $\mathcal{L}_d = \langle \mathrm{L}_d, \mathcal{I}_d, \mathcal{C}_d \rangle$ be a standard modal logic. We write $\mathcal{L}_d^{\mathsf{U}}$ to denote the modal logic obtained from $\mathcal{L}_d$ by adding the nullary modal operator U and the class of models is obtained from $\mathcal{C}_d$ by imposing that $R_U = W^2$ (see e.g. [16,18]). We denote by $\mathcal{L}_d^{U^-}$ the logic obtained from $\mathcal{L}_d^U$ by only allowing the occurrences of U of the form [U]. $\mathcal{L}_d^U$ is said to be U-*simplifiable* iff there is an effective procedure $f : \text{For} \to \text{For}$ such that for any $\varphi \in \text{For}$: the only occurrences of U in $f(\varphi)$ are in the context [U] and $f(\varphi) \Leftrightarrow \varphi$ is $\mathcal{L}_d^U$-valid. For instance, for the standard modal logic DAL -see Example 1 - DAL^U is U-simplifiable.

3   Satisfiability-preserving maps

3.1   Constructions on semilattices

Let L be a modal language designed for Rare-logics and let $\text{Mod} = \{c_i : i \in \omega\}$ be a countably infinite set of modal constants (intended to belong to the language of a standard modal logic). Let $\delta_1, \dots, \delta_n$ be elements of P_0. For any integer $k \in \{0, \dots, 2^n - 1\}$, we write α_k^* to denote the Boolean expression (also called a *component*) $\alpha_k^* \overset{\text{def}}{=} \alpha_1 \cap \dots \cap \alpha_n$ where for any $s \in \{1, \dots, n\}$, $\alpha_s \overset{\text{def}}{=} \delta_s$ if $bit_s(k) = 0$ ($bit_s(k)$ denoting the sth bit in the binary representation of k) otherwise $\alpha_s \overset{\text{def}}{=} -\delta_s$. For instance,

$$\alpha_{2^{n-1}-1}^* = -\delta_1 \cap \dots \cap -\delta_{n-1} \cap \delta_n$$

For any P-valuation V, $\{V(\alpha_k^*) : k \in \{0, \dots, 2^n - 1\}\}$ is a partition of PAR. For any parameter expression $\alpha \in P$ such that the only parameter constants occurring in α are in $\{\delta_1, \dots, \delta_n\}$, either $\alpha \equiv \bot$ or there is a unique non-empty set $Y = \{\alpha_{i_1}^*, \dots, \alpha_{i_l}^*\}$ such that $\alpha \equiv \alpha_{i_1}^* \cup \dots \cup \alpha_{i_l}^*$. There exists an effective procedure that computes Y in deterministic exponential-time in the size of α. Proposition 1 below states how to transform a family $(X_P)_{P \subseteq PAR}$ into a family $(Y_c)_{c \in \text{Mod}}$ when both families can be seen as the carrier sets of semilattices.

Proposition 1. *Let* $\delta_1, \dots, \delta_n$ *be* $n > 0$ *elements of* P_0, $\langle\{X_P : P \subseteq PAR\},$ $\sqcap, e\rangle$ *be a semilattice with zero element* e *and* V *be a P-valuation* $V : P \to$ $\mathcal{P}(PAR)$ *such that (H1)* $X_\emptyset = e$ *and (H2) for any* $P, P' \subseteq PAR$, $X_{P \cup P'} = X_P \sqcap X_{P'}$. *Then, there is a family* $(Y_c)_{c \in \text{Mod}}$ *such that*

(C1) $\{Y_c : c \in \text{Mod}\}$ *is a finite subset of* $\{X_P : P \subseteq PAR\}$;
(C2) *If* α *is a parameter expression built from the parameter constants* $\delta_1, \dots,$
      δ_n *such that* $\alpha \equiv \alpha_{i_1}^* \cup \dots \cup \alpha_{i_l}^*$, *then* $X_{V(\alpha)} = Y_{c_{i_1}} \sqcap \dots \sqcap Y_{c_{i_l}}$.

Proposition 2 below states how to transform a family $(Y_c)_{c \in \text{Mod}}$ into a family $(X_P)_{P \subseteq PAR}$ when both families can be seen as the carrier set of semilattices with zero element.

Proposition 2. *Let $\delta_1, \ldots, \delta_n$ be $n > 0$ elements of P_0, $\langle Y, \sqcap, e \rangle$ be a semilattice with zero element and $(Y_C)_{C \in M_{od}}$ be an indexed family of elements of Y. Then, there is a subalgebra of $\langle Y, \sqcap, e \rangle$ of the form $\langle \{X_P : P \subseteq PAR\}, \sqcap, e \rangle$ satisfying the conditions (H1)-(H2) from Proposition 1 and there is a P-valuation $V : P \to \mathcal{P}(PAR)$ such that*

(C1) $card(PAR) = 2^n$;

(C2) *If α is a parameter expression built from the parameter constants $\delta_1, \ldots, \delta_n$ such that $\alpha \equiv \alpha_{i_1}^* \cup \ldots \cup \alpha_{i_l}^*$, then $X_{V(\alpha)} = Y_{C_{i_1}} \sqcap \ldots \sqcap Y_{C_{i_l}}$.*

Proof. Let $\langle \langle \{X_P : P \subseteq PAR\}, \sqcap, e \rangle, V \rangle$ be the structure defined as follows:

- $PAR \overset{\text{def}}{=} \{0, \ldots, 2^n - 1\}$;
- $X_\emptyset \overset{\text{def}}{=} e$ and for any $\emptyset \neq P \subseteq PAR$, $X_P \overset{\text{def}}{=} \sqcap_{k \in P} Y_{C_k}$ ($\sqcap$ is commutative, associative and each P is finite);
- for any $s \in \{1, \ldots, n\}$, $V(\delta_s) \overset{\text{def}}{=} \{k \in PAR : bit_s(k) = 0\}$ (for the other parameter constants V is not constrained until V is a P-valuation which is always possible).

$\langle \langle \{X_P : P \subseteq PAR_i\}, e, \sqcap \rangle, V \rangle$ satisfies the required conditions. By way of example, let us check that the condition (C2) holds. First, observe that for any $k \in \{0, \ldots, 2^n - 1\}$, $V(\alpha_k^*) = \{k\}$.

$$
\begin{aligned}
X_{V(\alpha)} &= X_{V(\alpha_{i_1}^* \cup \ldots \cup \alpha_{i_l}^*)} \text{ (normal form of } \alpha) \\
&= X_{V(\alpha_{i_1}^*) \cup \ldots \cup V(\alpha_{i_l}^*)} \text{ (V is a P-valuation)} \\
&= X_{V(\alpha_{i_1}^*)} \sqcap \ldots \sqcap X_{V(\alpha_{i_l}^*)} \text{ (by (H2))} \\
&= X_{\{i_1\}} \sqcap \ldots \sqcap X_{\{i_l\}} \\
&= Y_{C_{i_1}} \sqcap \ldots \sqcap Y_{C_{i_l}} \text{ (by construction)}
\end{aligned}
$$

$\square$

In Proposition 1 and in Proposition 2 the X_P's and Y_C's are not necessarily relations. We are going to take advantage of these propositions when dealing with possible-world semantics for *polymodal modal* logics.

3.2   Normalization

Let φ be an L-formula such that $P_0(\varphi) \subseteq \{\delta_1, \ldots, \delta_n\}$ where $P_0(\varphi)$ is the set of parameter constants occurring in φ (the case when $P_0(\varphi) = \emptyset$ is omitted herein but it poses no extra difficulties). The first normal form of $r(\alpha)$, written $N_1(r(\alpha))$, is the basic modal expression $r(\alpha_{i_1}^* \cup \ldots \cup \alpha_{i_l}^*)$. It is similar to the canonical disjunctive normal form for the propositional calculus. In the case when $\alpha \equiv \perp$, $N_1(r(\alpha)) \overset{\text{def}}{=} r(\delta_1 \cap -\delta_1)$. We write $N_1(\varphi)$ to denote the formula obtained from φ by substituting each occurrence of $r(\alpha)$ by $N_1(r(\alpha))$. $N_1(\varphi)$ is unique modulo associativity and commutativity of $\cup$ and $\cap$ (which is harmless in the sequel). The technique of components has been firstly used for information logics by B. Konikowska (see e.g. [20]) in order to define Rasiowa-Sikorski proof systems for relative similarity logics. The second normal form of φ, written $N_2(\varphi)$, is the formula obtained from $N_1(\varphi)$ where each occurrence of $r(\alpha_{i_1}^* \cup \ldots \cup \alpha_{i_l}^*)$ has been substituted by $r(\alpha_{i_1}^*) \oplus_{\mathcal{L}} \ldots \oplus_{\mathcal{L}} r(\alpha_{i_l}^*)$. Obviously, $\varphi \Leftrightarrow N_2(\varphi)$ is $\mathcal{L}$-valid.

3.3   Satisfiability-preserving map

Let us define the mapping t from the set of $\mathcal{L}$-formulae into the set of $\mathcal{L}_d^{\mathsf{U}}$-formulae where $\mathcal{L}_d$ is the standard modal logic from $\mathcal{L}$ -see Definition 2. For any $\mathcal{L}$-formula φ, $t(\varphi)$ is obtained from $N_2(\varphi)$ by the following replacements of the basic modal expressions: $r(\delta_1 \cap -\delta_1)$ is replaced by U and $r(\alpha_k^*)$ is replaced by c_k for $k \in \{0, \ldots, 2^n - 1\}$ where $n = card(P_0(\varphi))$.

Example 2. Let $\mathcal{L}$ be the Rare-logic defined in Example 1 and φ be the $\mathcal{L}$-formula:

$$[r(\delta_1)]\mathsf{p} \wedge [r(\delta_1 \cap \delta_2)]\mathsf{q} \wedge [r(\delta_1 \cap \delta_2 \cap -\delta_1) \cup^* r(\delta_2)]\mathsf{p}$$

By definition, $t(\varphi) = [c_0 \cap c_2]\mathsf{p} \wedge [c_0]\mathsf{q} \wedge [\mathsf{U} \cup^* (c_0 \cap c_1)]\mathsf{p}$.

Proposition 3 below states that t is a satisfiability-preserving transformation from $\mathcal{L}$-satisfiability into $\mathcal{L}_d^{\mathsf{U}}$-satisfiability.

Proposition 3. *[10, Part I] φ is $\mathcal{L}$-satisfiable iff $t(\varphi)$ is $\mathcal{L}_d^{\mathsf{U}}$-satisfiable.*

The proof of Proposition 3 uses the semilattice structure of the family of relations of the models.

Proof. First assume that φ is $\mathcal{L}$-satisfiable. So there exist an $\mathcal{L}$-model

$$\langle W, PAR, (\mathcal{R}_P)_{P \subseteq PAR}, V \rangle$$

and $w \in W$ such that $\mathcal{M}, w \models \varphi$ and therefore $\mathcal{M}, w \models N_2(\varphi)$. The structure $\langle \{\mathcal{R}_P : P \subseteq PAR\}, \sqcap, W^2 \rangle$ and the map V satisfy the hypothesis of Proposition 1 with the set of parameter constants occurring in φ. If such a set is empty, φ is a formula of the classical propositional calculus and therefore the proposition trivially holds. Otherwise, by Proposition 1, there is a family $(Y_c)_{c \in M_0}$ satisfying the conditions (C1) and (C2) from Proposition 1. Let $\mathcal{M}'$ be the $\mathcal{L}_d^{\mathsf{U}}$-model $\langle W, (R_a)_{a \in M}, V' \rangle$ such that,

- for any $\mathsf{p} \in \mathsf{For}_0$, $V'(\mathsf{p}) \stackrel{\text{def}}{=} V(\mathsf{p})$;
- for any $c \in M_0$ $R_c \stackrel{\text{def}}{=} Y_c$;
- $R_{\oplus(a_1, \ldots, a_s)} \stackrel{\text{def}}{=} \mathcal{I}(\oplus)(W)(R_{a_1}, \ldots, R_{a_s})$ for $\oplus(a_1, \ldots, a_s) \in M$ (of $\mathcal{L}_d^{\mathsf{U}}$).

It is a routine task to check that $\mathcal{M}'$ is an $\mathcal{L}_d^{\mathsf{U}}$-model. Furthermore, for any $\alpha \in \mathsf{P}$ occurring in φ such that $\alpha \equiv \alpha_{i_1}^* \cup \ldots \cup \alpha_{i_l}^*$, $\mathcal{R}_{V(\alpha)} = R_{c_{i_1} \oplus_\mathcal{L} \ldots \oplus_\mathcal{L} c_{i_l}} = \mathcal{R}_{V N_2(\alpha)}$ and for any $\alpha \in \mathsf{P}$ such that $\alpha \equiv \bot$, $\mathcal{R}_{V(\alpha)} = R_{\mathsf{U}} = W \times W$. So $\mathcal{M}', w \models t(\varphi)$.

Now assume that $t(\varphi)$ is $\mathcal{L}_d^{\mathsf{U}}$-satisfiable. So there exist an $\mathcal{L}_d^{\mathsf{U}}$-model $\mathcal{M} = \langle W, (R_a)_{a \in \mathsf{M}}, V \rangle$ and $w \in W$ such that $\mathcal{M}, w \models t(\varphi)$. The restriction of $(R_a)_{a \in \mathsf{M}}$ to M_0, say $(R_c)_{c \in \mathsf{M}_0}$, satisfies the conditions (H1) and (H2) from Proposition 2. By Proposition 2, there is a structure $\langle \{\mathcal{R}_P : P \subseteq PAR\}, \sqcap, W^2 \rangle$ and a P-valuation $V'' : \mathsf{P} \to \mathcal{P}(PAR)$ such that

1. $\langle \{\mathcal{R}_P : P \subseteq PAR\}, \sqcap, W^2 \rangle$ is a semilattice with zero element W^2;
2. $\mathcal{R}_\emptyset = W^2$ and for any $P, P' \subseteq PAR$, $\mathcal{R}_{P \cup P'} = \mathcal{R}_P \sqcap \mathcal{R}_{P'}$;
3. $card(PAR) = 2^n$.

Let $\mathcal{M}' \stackrel{\text{def}}{=} \langle W, PAR, (\mathcal{R}_P)_{P \subseteq PAR}, V' \rangle$ be the $\mathcal{L}$-model such that

- V' restricted to P is the restriction of V'';
- for any $\mathsf{p} \in \mathsf{For}_0$, $V'(\mathsf{p}) \stackrel{\text{def}}{=} V(\mathsf{p})$;
- $V'(\oplus(\mathsf{a}_1, \ldots, \mathsf{a}_s)) \stackrel{\text{def}}{=} \mathcal{I}(\oplus)(W)(V'(\mathsf{a}_1), \ldots, V'(\mathsf{a}_s))$
  for any $\oplus(\mathsf{a}_1, \ldots, \mathsf{a}_s) \in \mathsf{M}$ (of $\mathcal{L}$).

It is easy to check that $\mathcal{M}'$ is an $\mathcal{L}$-model. Additionnally, for any $\alpha \in \mathsf{P}$ occurring in φ such that $\alpha \equiv \alpha_{i_1}^* \cup \ldots \cup \alpha_{i_l}^*$, $\mathcal{R}_{V(\alpha)} = R_{c_{i_1} \oplus_\mathcal{L} \ldots \oplus_\mathcal{L} c_{i_l}}$ and for any $\alpha \in \mathsf{P}$ such that $\alpha \equiv \bot$, $\mathcal{R}_{V(\alpha)} = R_{\mathsf{U}}$. So $\mathcal{M}', w \models \mathsf{N}_2[\varphi]$. □

Proposition 3 entails that $\mathcal{L}_d^{\mathsf{U}}$ is decidable only if $\mathcal{L}$ is decidable. Proposition 4 will help stating the converse.

Proposition 4. *There exists a polynomial-time many-one reduction (see e.g. [29]) from $\mathcal{L}_d^{\mathsf{U}}$-satisfiability into $\mathcal{L}$-satisfiability.*

The idea of the proof of Proposition 4 consists in defining a *reverse* map of t.

Using the construction of the proof of Proposition 3, one can prove the proposition below.

Corollary 1. *Let $\mathcal{L}$ be a Rare-logic from the class considered so far.*

1. $\mathcal{L}$-satisfiability is decidable iff $\mathcal{L}_d^{\mathsf{U}}$-satisfiability is decidable.
2. $\mathcal{L}$ has the finite model property iff $\mathcal{L}_d^{\mathsf{U}}$ has the finite model property.
3. Any $\mathcal{L}$-satisfiable formula φ has an $\mathcal{L}$-model such that $card(PAR) \le 2^{|\varphi|}$.
4. If $\mathcal{L}_d^{\mathsf{U}}$ is U-simplifiable, then $\mathcal{L}$-satisfiability is decidable iff $\mathcal{L}_d^{\mathsf{U}-}$ is decidable and $\mathcal{L}$ has the finite model property iff $\mathcal{L}_d^{\mathsf{U}-}$ has the finite model property.

Example 3. Let $\mathcal{L}$ be the Rare-logic $\langle L, \mathcal{I}, \mathcal{C}, X \rangle$ such that $OP = \{\cap, \cdot, ^*, \cup, ^{-1}\}$, $X = Fr^2$ and $\cap$ [resp. $\cdot$, *, $\cup$, $^{-1}$) is interpreted as the intersection (resp. composition, Kleene star, union, converse]. PDL with the operators $\cdot, ^*, \cup, ^{-1}, \cap$ (and without the test operator '?') is a fragment of $\mathcal{L}_d^{\mathsf{U}}$ and does not have the finite model property -see e.g. [34]. By Corollary 1, $\mathcal{L}$ does not have the finite model property.

The flexibility of the translations allows an extension when nominals are included in the language (see e.g. [10, Part II]) although it is technically more involved. So when Rare-logics can be translated into well-known modal logics, we may obtain straightforward results about the Rare-logics (decidability and possibly complexity upper bounds, ...).

4   Decidability

4.1   A logic of indiscernibility relations.

Indiscernibility (see Section 2.3) is a central concept to study relationships between objects in information systems [30]. The logic of indiscernibility relation LIR has been introduced in [28] and it has been defined in Example 1.

Proposition 5. *The LIR-satisfiability problem is decidable iff the DAL-satisfiability problem is decidable.*

Proof. (sketch) Since $\mathrm{LIR}_d^{\mathsf{U}}$ is U-simplifiable, by Corollary 1, LIR is decidable iff $\mathrm{LIR}_d^{\mathsf{U}-}$ is decidable. $\mathrm{LIR}_d^{\mathsf{U}-}$ is exactly the logic DAL defined in [15] to which is added the universal modal connective [U]. One can show that DAL (or equivalently LIR_d) is decidable iff $\mathrm{LIR}_d^{\mathsf{U}-}$ is decidable. Indeed, for any formulae φ, ψ, $\varphi \models_{LIR_d} \psi$ iff $[\mathrm{a}]\varphi \Rightarrow \psi$ is LIR_d-valid with a $\overset{\text{def}}{=} c_1 \mathsf{U}^* \ldots \mathsf{U}^* c_n$ and $\{c_1, \ldots, c_n\}$ is the set of modal constants occurring in $\{\varphi, \psi\}$. The other direction is shown in [10, Part II] by using some techniques from [16].   □

Decidability of DAL is open although various attempts to prove such a result can be found in the literature (see e.g. [1]). This fact is rather surprising considering that after all, DAL is similar to various other polymodal logics, among them the Propositional Dynamic Logic. It is not difficult to show that if PDL with converse and intersection is decidable (which is commonly conjectured in the literature) then DAL is also decidable. By contrast, the logic "LIR without U^*", say LIR', is known to be decidable. Indeed, LIR' is decidable iff $\mathrm{LIR}_d'^{\mathsf{U}-}$ is decidable. However, $\mathrm{LIR}_d'^{\mathsf{U}-}$ is decidable (see e.g. [9]). Consequently, the logic of indiscernibility relations defined in [25] is decidable.

4.2   A logic with knowledge operators.

The logic with knowledge operators LKO has been introduced in [27] to model reasoning in presence of incomplete information. The ontology from which are defined the semantical structures of LKO is alternative to the usual Kripke-style semantics. Indeed, the worlds in a model are not interpreted as knowledge states but as objects. Similarly, the relations are not interpreted as compatibility relations but as indiscernibility relations between objects with respect to sets of agents. The set of formulae of LKO is the smallest set that contains For_0 and it is closed under $\neg$, $\wedge$ and under the unary operators from $\{K(\alpha) : \alpha \in \mathrm{P}\}$ where P is a set of parameter expressions. An *LKO-model*

$$\mathcal{M} = \langle OB, AGT, (R_Q)_{Q \subseteq AGT}, V \rangle$$

is a structure such that:

1. OB is a non-empty set of *objects*; AGT is a non-empty set of *agents*;
2. for any $Q, Q' \subseteq AGT$, R_Q is an equivalence relation, $R_{Q \cup Q'} = R_Q \cap R_{Q'}$ and $R_{\emptyset} = OB \times OB$
3. V is a mapping $\text{For}_0 \cup \mathrm{P} \to \mathcal{P}(OB) \cup \mathcal{P}(AGT)$ such that $V(\mathrm{p}) \subseteq OB$ for any $\mathrm{p} \in \text{For}_0$ and V restricted to P is a P-valuation.

The satisfiability relation $\models$ is defined as usual, except for the following condition: $\mathcal{M}, w \models K(\alpha)\varphi \overset{\text{def}}{\Leftrightarrow}$ either for any $w' \in R_{V(\alpha)}(w)$, $\mathcal{M}, w' \models \varphi$ or for any $w' \in R_{V(\alpha)}(w)$, $\mathcal{M}, w' \models \neg\varphi$. $K(\alpha)\varphi$ can be interpreted by: the set α of agents knows whether φ holds (see e.g. [27]). The notion of LKO-validity, LKO-satisfiability, ..., are defined in the standard way. Let g be the mapping from the set of LKO-formulae into the set of LIR'-formulae such that

- $g(\mathrm{p}) \overset{\text{def}}{=} \mathrm{p}$ for any $\mathrm{p} \in \text{For}_0$; $g(\neg\varphi) \overset{\text{def}}{=} \neg g(\varphi)$;
- $g(\varphi \wedge \psi) \overset{\text{def}}{=} g(\varphi) \wedge g(\psi)$; $g(K(\alpha)\varphi) \overset{\text{def}}{=} [r(\alpha)]g(\varphi) \vee [r(\alpha)]g(\neg\varphi)$.

Proposition 6. *For any LKO-formula φ, φ has an LKO-model of the form $\langle OB, AGT, \ldots \rangle$ iff $g(\varphi)$ has an LIR'-model of the form $\langle OB, AGT, \ldots \rangle$.*

As a corollary, LKO-satisfiability problem is decidable. Moreover, it is possible to define a polynomial-time many-one reduction from LKO-satisfiability into LIR'-satisfiability using renaming techniques (see e.g. [21]).

4.3   Modal logics with a fixed set of parameters

The language L of the *modal logics for parameters* contains a *fixed* countable set PAR of parameters. The modal expressions of the language are the subsets of PAR. Hence, the modal operators are indexed by sets of parameters. Such logics have been considered for instance in [3,4]. To be precise, we shall not deal with sets but rather with a *finite representation* of certain sets. This representational aspect shall be emphasize when needed but this is really necessary since we wish to establish decidability results. For example, we want to be able to decide whether two sets that occur in a formula are equal, which seems to be a reasonable requirement.

By an L-*frame* (for such kinds of logics) we understand a pair $\langle W, (R_P)_{P \subseteq \text{PAR}} \rangle$ such that W is a non-empty set and for any $P \subseteq \text{PAR}$, R_P is a binary relation on W. By an L-model $\mathcal{M}$, we understand a triple $\langle W, (R_P)_{P \subseteq \text{PAR}}, V \rangle$ such that $\mathcal{F} = \langle W, (R_P)_{P \subseteq \text{PAR}} \rangle$ is an L-frame and V is a mapping $\text{For}_0 \to \mathcal{P}(W)$. The satisfiability relation is defined in the usual way. In this paper, by a *modal logic for parameters* $\mathcal{L}$, we understand (this is a restricted sense in comparison with the notion introduced in [4,10]) a triple $\langle \text{L}, X, \mathcal{C} \rangle$ such that

- L is a language for modal logics for parameters;
- X is a class of modal frames;
- $\mathcal{C}$ is the class of L-models such that for any $\mathcal{M} = \langle W, (R_P)_{P \subseteq \text{PAR}}, V \rangle$,
  1. $R_{\emptyset} = W^2$ and for any $P, P' \subseteq \text{PAR}$, $R_{P \cup P'} = R_P \cap R_{P'}$;
  2. for any $\emptyset \neq P \subseteq \text{PAR}$, $\langle W, R_P \rangle \in X$.

The notion of $\mathcal{L}$-satisfiability, $\mathcal{L}$-validity, logical $\mathcal{L}$-consequence etc, ... are defined in the usual way. Let $\mathcal{L}$ be a modal logic for parameters $\langle \text{L}, X, \mathcal{C} \rangle$. The Rare-logic $\text{RARE}(\mathcal{L}) = \langle \text{L}', \mathcal{I}', \mathcal{C}', X' \rangle$ is called the *Rare-logic from* $\mathcal{L}$ $\overset{\text{def}}{\Leftrightarrow}$

- L' is a language for Rare-logic such that $OP \overset{\text{def}}{=} \{\cap\}$ and $\mathcal{I}$ interprets $\cap$ as set intersection;
- $X' \overset{\text{def}}{=} X$;
- $\mathcal{C}'$ is the unique set of L'-models respecting $\mathcal{I}'$ making $\text{RARE}(\mathcal{L})$ a Rare-logic of the class considered so far.

Let $\mathcal{L}$ be a modal logic for parameters. Let φ be an L-formula such that the only *sets* occurring in φ are $X_1, \ldots, X_n$. For any integer $k \in \{0, \ldots, 2^n - 1\}$, we write X_k^* to denote the set

$$X_k^* \overset{\text{def}}{=} Y_1 \cap \ldots \cap Y_n$$

where for any $i \in \{1, \ldots, n\}$, $Y_i \overset{\text{def}}{=} X_i$ if $bit_i(k) = 0$ otherwise $Y_i \overset{\text{def}}{=} \text{PAR} \setminus X_i$. Hence, X_k^* is a *concrete* set (not a Boolean expression as done until now). The set $\{X_k^* : k \in \{0, \ldots, 2^n - 1\}, X_k^* \neq \emptyset\}$ is a partition of PAR. For each set X_i we shall associate a parameter constant δ_i. For any integer $k \in \{0, \ldots, 2^n - 1\}$, we write α_k^* to denote the Boolean expression $\alpha_k^* \overset{\text{def}}{=} \alpha_1 \cap \ldots \cap \alpha_n$ where for any $i \in \{1, \ldots, n\}$, $\alpha_i \overset{\text{def}}{=} \delta_i$ if $bit_i(k) = 0$ otherwise $\alpha_i \overset{\text{def}}{=} -\delta_i$. We write $t(\varphi)$ to denote the $\text{RARE}(\mathcal{L})$-formula obtained from φ by substituting $X_i \neq \emptyset$ by $t(X_i)$ defined below by

$$t(X_i) \overset{\text{def}}{=} r(\bigcup \{\alpha_k^* : k \in \{0, \ldots, 2^n - 1\}, X_k^* \neq \emptyset, bit_i(k) = 0\})$$

In the case when $X_i = \emptyset$, $\emptyset$ is substituted by $r(\delta_1 \cap -\delta_1)$. It is worth noting that since we have not yet fixed the *mode of representation* of the sets

$P \subseteq$ PAR, it might not be decidable to know whether $X_k^* = \emptyset$ or $X_i = \emptyset$. But, we can show that

Proposition 7. φ is $\mathcal{L}$-satisfiable iff $t(\varphi)$ is RARE($\mathcal{L}$)-satisfiable.

Proof. Let $\mathcal{M} = \langle W, (R_P)_{P \subseteq \text{PAR}}, V \rangle$ be an $\mathcal{L}$-model and $w \in W$ such that $\mathcal{M}, w \models \varphi$. Consider the RARE($\mathcal{L}$)-model $\mathcal{M}' = \langle W, \text{PAR}, (\mathcal{R}_P)_{P \subseteq \text{PAR}}, V' \rangle$ such that

- for any $P \subseteq$ PAR, $\mathcal{R}_P \stackrel{\text{def}}{=} R_P$;
- the restriction of V' to the set of propositional variables is V;
- for any $j \in \{1, \dots, n\}$, $V'(\delta_j) \stackrel{\text{def}}{=} X_j$.

Hence for any $j \in \{1, \dots, n\}$, $V'(t(X_j)) = X_j$. It is a routine task to check that $\mathcal{M}', w \models t(\varphi)$ and $\mathcal{M}'$ is a RARE($\mathcal{L}$)-model.

Now let $\mathcal{M}' = \langle W, PAR, (\mathcal{R}_P)_{P \subseteq PAR}, V' \rangle$ be a RARE($\mathcal{L}$)-model and $w \in W$ such that $\mathcal{M}', w \models t(\varphi)$. The set PAR *does not have to be equal to* PAR (fixed for $\mathcal{L}$). Consider the $\mathcal{L}$-model $\mathcal{M} = (W, (R_P)_{P \subseteq PAR}, V)$ such that

- V is the restriction of V' to the set of propositional variables;
- for any $k \in \{0, \dots, 2^n - 1\}$ and $x \in X_k^*$, $R_{\{x\}} \stackrel{\text{def}}{=} \mathcal{R}_{V'(\alpha_k^*)}$ and $R_\emptyset \stackrel{\text{def}}{=} W \times W$;
- for any $\emptyset \neq P \subseteq$ PAR, we write $\{X_{i_1}^*, \dots, X_{i_l}^*\}$ to denote the smallest set of non-empty sets (with respect to set inclusion) such that $P \subseteq X_{i_1}^* \cup \dots \cup X_{i_l}^*$. $\{X_{i_1}^*, \dots, X_{i_l}^*\}$ always exists and is unique. We define R_P as follows

$$R_P \stackrel{\text{def}}{=} \bigcap \{R_{\{x\}} : x \in X_{i_u}^*, u \in \{1, \dots, l\}\}$$

It is a routine task to check that the definition is correct. We can also show that for any $P, P' \subseteq$ PAR $R_{P \cup P'} = R_P \cap R_{P'}$. It remains to prove that $R_{X_{k'}} = \mathcal{R}_{V'(t(X_{k'}))}$ for $k' \in \{1, \dots, n\}$. First, for any $j \in \{0, \dots, 2^n - 1\}$, if $X_j^* \neq \emptyset$, then $R_{X_j^*} = \mathcal{R}_{V'(\alpha_j^*)}$.

$R_{X_j} = R_{\bigcup \{X_k^* : k \in \{0, \dots, 2^n - 1\}, bit_j(k) = 0, X_k^* \neq \emptyset\}}$
  (by definition of the X_k^*'s)
  $= \bigcap \{R_{X_k^*} : k \in \{0, \dots, 2^n - 1\}, bit_j(k) = 0, X_k^* \neq \emptyset\}$
  $= \bigcap \{\mathcal{R}_{V'(\alpha_k^*)} : k \in \{0, \dots, 2^n - 1\}, bit_j(k) = 0, X_k^* \neq \emptyset\}$
  (see the preliminary remark)
  $= \mathcal{R}_{V'(\bigcup \{\alpha_k^* : k \in \{0, \dots, 2^n - 1\}, bit_j(k) = 0, X_k^* \neq \emptyset\})}$
  ($\mathcal{M}'$ is a RARE($\mathcal{L}$)-model)
  $= \mathcal{R}_{V'(t(X_j^*))}$

$\square$

Corollary 2. *Let $\mathcal{L}$ be a modal logic for parameters. Let Z be a class of $\mathcal{L}$-formulae such that for any $\varphi \in Z$ it is decidable whether (see the notations above) (D1) X_i is empty where $X_1, \dots, X_n$ are representations of the sets occurring in φ and (D2) X_k^* is empty ($0 \leq k \leq 2^n - 1$). Then, if the corresponding Rare-logic RARE($\mathcal{L}$) has a decidable satisfiability problem, then the $\mathcal{L}$-satisfiability problem for the fragment Z is decidable.*

Let PAR $= \{p_1, p_2, \ldots\}$ be a countable set of parameters (not necessarily finite). A natural representation of the finite subset $\{p_1, \ldots, p_k\}$ of PAR is $\{^f p_1, \ldots, p_k\}^f$. '$\{^f$', '$\}^f$' and ',' are symbols of the language. Each cofinite subset PAR $\setminus \{p_1, \ldots, p_k\}$ can be represented by $\{^c p_1, \ldots, p_k\}^c$. '$\{^c$' and '$\}^c$' are symbols of the language. Let Z^{fc} be the set of $\mathcal{L}$-formulae such that only finite or cofinite sets of parameters occur and the representation above is used. Then Z^{fc} satisfies the hypothesis of Corollary 2. Moreover, if the representation of a set Y occurs in a formula, then the representation of the set PAR $\setminus Y$ can also occur in a formula of Z^{fc}. Similar classes of formulae have been considered for instance in [4].

By way of example we can state that

Proposition 8. *Let $\mathcal{L} = \langle L, X, C \rangle$ be a modal logic for parameters. $\mathcal{L}$-satisfiability restricted to some Z satisfying (D1) and (D2) in Corollary 2 is decidable when X is either the set of transitive frames or the set of reflexive and transitive frames.*

Other decidability results for logics with relative accessibility relations (involving nominals) can be found in [12].

5   Complexity

The map t defined in Section 3 may increase exponentially the size of formulae although the number of subformulae does not change. In this section, we provide a sufficient condition so that $\mathcal{L}$-satisfiability is in **EXPTIME**. That is, it can be solved by a deterministic Turing machine in exponential-time (see e.g. [29]).

Lemma 1. *Let φ be a formula.*

1. *$t(\varphi)$ can be computed in deterministic time $\mathcal{O}(2^{p_1(|\varphi|)})$ for some polynomial $p_1(.)$;*
2. *$card(sub(\varphi)) = card(sub(t(\varphi)))$;*
3. *$|t(\varphi)|$ is in $\mathcal{O}(2^{p_2(|\varphi|)})$ for some polynomial $p_2(.)$;*

The proof is by simple inspection of the definition of t.

Proposition 9. *Let $\mathcal{L}$ be a Rare-logic of the kind considered so far.*

1. *There is a polynomial-time many-one reduction from $\mathcal{L}_d^\cup$-satisfiability into $\mathcal{L}$-satisfiability.*
2. *If the $\mathcal{L}_d^\cup$-satisfiability can be solved by a deterministic Turing machine in time $\mathcal{O}(q_1(|\varphi|) + 2^{q_2(card(sub(\varphi)))})$ for some polynomials $q_1(.)$ and $q_2(.)$, then $\mathcal{L}$-satisfiability is in **EXPTIME**.*

Proof. (1) See Proposition 4. (2) We know that φ is $\mathcal{L}$-satisfiable iff $t(\varphi)$ is $\mathcal{L}_d^U$-satisfiable. By using Lemma 1, deciding whether φ is $\mathcal{L}$-satisfiable requires time in

$$\mathcal{O}(2^{p_1(|\varphi|)} + q_1(2^{p_2(|\varphi|)}) + 2^{q_2(card(sub(\varphi)))})$$

which is also in time $\mathcal{O}(2^{p(|\varphi|)})$ for some polynomial $p(.)$.   □

Corollary 3. *[9] LIR'-satisfiability and LKO-satisfiability are* **EXPTIME-***complete.*

To establish the complexity lower bounds, general results from [18] are used.

6   Proof systems for LKO

Proposition 3 is not only meaningful to prove decidability or the finite model property but it also helps to define proof systems for Rare-logics from proof systems for the corresponding standard modal logics. In the sequel, we concentrate on the logic LKO that can be equipped with Hilbert-style proof system [9]. Let $\mathcal{L}$ be a Rare-logic of the class studied so far and $\mathcal{L}_d^U$ be the corresponding standard modal logic. Assume that $\mathcal{L}_d^U$ is equipped with a proof system $\vdash^*$. A proof system $\vdash$ for $\mathcal{L}$ should first be able to simulate the normalization process. For instance, the following equivalences have to be encoded:

1. $[r(\alpha)]\mathbf{p} \Leftrightarrow [r(\beta)]\mathbf{p}$ when $\alpha \equiv \beta$;
2. $[r(\alpha \cup \beta)]\mathbf{p} \Leftrightarrow [r(\alpha) \oplus_{\mathcal{L}} r(\beta)]\mathbf{p}$.

For instance 1. and 2. above can be viewed as axiom schemes of Hilbert-style systems. The rest of the calculus $\vdash$ consists of $\vdash^*$ where only normalized formulae are admitted and the basic modal expressions of the form $r(\delta \cap -\delta)$ should play the role of U. By *normalized formula*, we mean a formula φ such that $N_2(\varphi) = \varphi$ modulo associativity and commutativity of $\cap$ and $\cup$. Then, in $\vdash$ the basic modal expressions of the form $r(\alpha_k^*)$ play the role of the modal constants c_k in $\vdash^*$. Although described at some informal level, this program can be easily implemented for particular logics and proof systems. This was first done in [20] for logics with relative similarity relations. This has been more systematically pursued for Hilbert-style proof systems in [10, Part II]. By way of example, the Hilbert-style proof system $\vdash_{lko}$ for the logic LKO is composed of the axiom schemes

- the tautologies of the Propositional Calculus;
- $K(\alpha)\mathbf{p} \Rightarrow K(\alpha')\mathbf{p}$ when $\alpha \sqsubseteq \alpha'$; $\varphi \wedge K(\alpha)\mathbf{p} \wedge K(\alpha)(\mathbf{p} \Rightarrow \mathbf{q}) \Rightarrow K(\alpha)\mathbf{q}$;
- $K(\alpha)(K(\alpha)\mathbf{p} \Rightarrow \mathbf{p})$; $K(\alpha)\mathbf{p} \Leftrightarrow K(\alpha)\neg\mathbf{p}$.

and of the inference rules

1. *modus ponens*: $\frac{\varphi \quad \varphi \Rightarrow \psi}{\psi}$;
2. *necessitation*: $\frac{\varphi}{K(\alpha)\varphi}$ for any $\alpha \in P$.

Proposition 10. *[9]* $\vdash_{lko} \varphi$ *iff* φ *is LKO-valid.*

Display Logic (DL) is a proof-theoretical framework introduced in [5] that admits a very general cut-elimination theorem. Moreover, DL generalises the structural language of Gentzen's sequents in a rather abstract way by using multiple complex structural connectives instead of Gentzen's comma. A display logic calculus for LKO can be found in [11].

7 Concluding remarks

In this paper, we have presented many-one reductions between satisfiability problems for Rare-logics and standard modal logics. Both directions have been investigated and in some sense, we have seen that the Rare-logics can be very similar to standard modal logics. The present short survey has been the opportunity to present results for particular classes of Rare-logics (because of lack of space the presentation of other classes had to be skipped but most of them can be found in [10]). When the standard modal logics corresponding to the Rare-logics are well-known, we get serious insights about the Rare-logics (decidability, axiomatization, complexity upper bounds, ...). Solving the following open questions will help solving similar questions for Rare-logics thanks to the translation presented here:

1. Axiomatization and decidability status of DAL (if PDL + converse and intersection is decidable then DAL is decidable);
2. Decidability of Combinatory PDL (CPDL) [31] with converse and intersection.

References

1. Archangelsky D. and Taitslin M. (1989) A logic for data description. In: Meyer A. and Taitslin M. (Ed.), Symposium on Logic Foundations of Computer Science, Pereslavl-Zalessky, 2–11. Springer-Verlag, Lecture Notes in Computer Science, Vol. 363, July
2. Balbiani Ph. (1996) A modal logic for data analysis. In: Penczek W. and Szalas A. (Ed.), 21st Symposium on Mathematical Foundations of Computer Sciences (MFCS'96), Kraków, 167–179. Lecture Notes in Computer Science, Vol. 1113, Springer-Verlag
3. Balbiani Ph. (1996) Modal logics with relative accessibility relations. In: Gabbay D. and Ohlbach H.J. (Ed.), Conference on Formal and Applied Practical Reasoning (FAPR'96), Bonn, 29–41. Springer-Verlag, June
4. Balbiani Ph. (1997) Axiomatization of logics based on Kripke models with relative accessibility relations. In: *[23]*, 553–578

5. Belnap N. (1982) Display logic. J. of Philosophical Logic, 11:375–417
6. Balbiani Ph. and Orlowska E. (1999) A hierarchy of modal logics with relative accessibility relations. J. of Applied Non-Classical Logics, special issue in the Memory of George Gargov, 9:303–328
7. Demri S. (1998) A class of decidable information logics. Theoretical Computer Science, 195(1):33–60
8. Demri S. (1998) Coping with semilattices of relations in logics with relative accessibility relations (extended abstract). In: Orlowska E. and Szałas A. (Ed.), 4th International Seminar on Relational Methods in Logic, Algebra and Computer Science, 43–47, September
9. Demri S. (1999) A logic with relative knowledge operators. J. of Logic, Language and Information, 8(2):167–185
10. Demri S. and Gabbay D. (2000) On modal logics characterized by models with relative accessibility relations: Part I and Part II. Studia Logica, To appear
11. Demri S. and Goré R. (2000) Display calculi for logics with relative accessibility relations. J. of Logic, Language and Information, 9(2):213–236
12. Demri S. and Konikowska B. (1998) Relative similarity logics are decidable: reduction to FO^2 with equality. In: JELIA'98, 279–293. Lecture Notes in Artificial Intelligence, Vol. 1489, Springer-Verlag
13. Demri S. and Orlowska E. (1999) Every finitely reducible logic has the finite model property with respect to the class of <>-formulae. Studia Logica, 62(2):177–200. Special issue edited by M.L. Dalla Chiara and D. Mundici. Selected papers in honour of Ettore Casari
14. Düntsch I. (1997) Rough sets and algebras of relations. In: [23], 95–108
15. Fariñas del Cerro L. and Orlowska E. (1985) DAL - A logic for data analysis. Theoretical Computer Science, 36:251–264
16. Goranko V. and Passy S. (1992) Using the universal modality: gains and questions. J. of Logic and Computation, 2(1):5–30
17. Harel D. (1984) Dynamic logic. In: Gabbay D. and Guenthner F. (Eds.), Handbook of Philosophical Logic, Volume II, 497–604. Reidel, Dordrecht
18. Hemaspaandra E. (1996) The price of universality. Notre Dame Journal of Formal Logic, 37(2):173–203
19. Järvinen J. (1997) Representation of information systems and dependences spaces, and some basic algorithms. Licentiate's thesis
20. Konikowska B. (1997) A logic for reasoning about relative similarity. Studia Logica, 58(1):185–226
21. Mints G. (1988) Gentzen-type and resolution rules part I: propositional logic. In: Martin-Löf P. and Mints G. (Eds.), International Conference on Computer Logic, Tallinn, 198–231. Springer Verlag, Lecture Notes in Computer Science, Vol. 417
22. Novotny M. (1997) Applications of dependence spaces. In: [23], 247–289
23. Orlowska E. (ed.) (1997) Incomplete Information: Rough Set Analysis. Studies in Fuzziness and Soft Computing. Physica-Verlag, Heidelberg
24. Orlowska E. (1984) Logic of indiscernibility relations. In: Skowron A. (Ed.), 5th Symposium on Computation Theory, Zaborów, Poland, 177–186. Lecture Notes in Computer Science, Vol. 208, Springer-Verlag
25. Orlowska E. (1984) Modal logics in the theory of information systems. Zeitschrift für Mathematik Logik und Grundlagen der Mathematik, 30(1):213–222

26. Orłowska E. (1988) Kripke models with relative accessibility and their applications to inferences from incomplete information. In: Mirkowska G. and Rasiowa H., (Ed.), Mathematical Problems in Computation Theory, 329–339. Banach Center Publications, Volume 21 PWN - Polish Scientific Publishers, Warsaw

27. Orłowska E. (1989) Logic for reasoning about knowledge. Zeitschrift für Mathematik Logik und Grundlagen der Mathematik, 35:559–568

28. Orłowska E. (1993) Reasoning with incomplete information: rough set based information logics. In: Alagar V., Bergler S. and Dong F. (Eds.), Incompleteness and Uncertainty in Information Systems Workshop, 16–33. Springer-Verlag, October

29. Papadimitriou Ch. (1994) Computational Complexity. Addison-Wesley Publishing Company

30. Pawlak Z. (1981) Information systems theoretical foundations. Information Systems, 6(3):205–218

31. Passy S. and Tinchev T. (1991) An essay in combinatory dynamic logic. Information and Computation, 93:263–332

32. Tarski A. (1953) Undecidable Theories. Studies in Logic and the foundations of Mathematics. North-Holland Publishing Company. In collaboration with A. Mostowski. and R. Robinson

33. Vakarelov D. (1991) Modal logics for knowledge representation systems. Theoretical Computer Science, 90:433–456

34. Vakarelov D. (1992) A modal logic for cyclic repeating. Information and Computation, 101:103–122

Chapter 11
A Relational Formalisation of a Generic Many–Valued Modal Logic

Beata Konikowska[1] and Ewa Orłowska[2]

[1] Institute of Computer Science
   Polish Academy of Sciences
   Ordona 21, 01-237 Warsaw, Poland
   beatak@ipipan.waw.pl
[2] Institute of Telecommunications
   Szachowa 1, 04-894 Warsaw, Poland
   orlowska@itl.waw.pl

Abstract. In the paper we define a generic many valued modal logic, in which modalities are defined in the most general way possible following the idea of Thomason. Both the valuation of formulae and the accessibility predicates — replacing the usual accessibility relations — can be many valued. We present two types of semantics of the logic: the standard (Kripke) one and a relational one. In connection with the latter, we define a special calculus of relations corresponding to the connectives and modalities of the logic, and we develop a complete deduction system in Rasiowa-Sikowski style for this calculus. We illustrate the results by applying our formalisation to the two-valued modalities of possibility and necessity, and to a general class of many-valued modal logics defined by Fitting.
Keywords: relational proof systems, many-valued logic, modal logic

1 Introduction

Relational formalisation of logics consists in interpreting formulae of non-classical logics as relations in an appropriate algebra of relations. Up to now, this approach has been applied with success to a variety of nonclassical logics, such as modal, temporal and intuitionistic logic, formalised via algebras of binary right ideal relations [5,6,11,14,15], substructural and relevant logics, represented with algebras of ternary relations [8,8,12], and finally many-valued logics, formalised with help of special n-ary relations called n-cubes [7]. The main motivation for relational formalisation is that it leads to a general framework for developing deduction means for a broad class of logics, providing a uniform treatment for a lot of different logics.

In this paper we extend the approach presented in [7] to many-valued modal logic. The latter notion is understood in a very general way. First, we assume that propositional variables are interpreted in a many-valued semantic range SR, which of course gives rise to a many-valued interpretation of formulae. Second, we replace the accessibility relations of two-valued modal logics with a many-valued accessibility predicate.

We consider a very broad, generic class of such logics, following the idea presented in [17], but going even further in generalizing the definition of many-valued modal logic. The logics we consider are polymodal ones. Each modality O_i is parametrized by two semantic functions helping to determine the value of $O_i A$ in a world w.

The first of them is a propositional function $f_{O_i} : SR^2 \to SR$ which evaluates the relationship between $R_i(w, w')$ and $I(w', A)$ for every $w' \in W$, where W is the set of possible worlds, R_i is the accessibility predicate for O_i and $I(w', A)$ is the interpretation of formula A in a world w'. The second is a quantifier-type function $g_{O_i} : \mathcal{P}(SR) \setminus \{\emptyset\} \to SR$, where $\mathcal{P}(SR)$ is the set of (necessarily finite) subsets of SR, assigning a single logical value to the set of values given by the function f_{O_i} for w' ranging over W.

To see the role of the latter function, note that in fact modality is restricted quantification. For example, the classical modality of necessity is universal quantification restricted to the set of worlds accessible from a given world, whereas the classical modality of possibility is existential quantification restricted to the latter set. Of course, in case of many-valued logics we have a big variety of quantifiers, each represented semantically by a function assigning a single value in SR to a subset of SR. Thus our function g_{O_i} is just a semantic counterpart of the many-valued quantifier underlying the modality O_i.

Clearly, the above definition encompasses a broad class of modalities, including various types of necessity, corresponding to $g_{O_i}(X) = \bigwedge X$, as well as various types of possibility, corresponding to $g_{O_i}(X) = \bigvee X$, if SR is a lattice, and $\bigwedge, \bigvee$ denote the g.l.b. and l.u.b. in that lattice.

For such a class of logics, we give relational formalisation via an algebra on n-ary relations called n-cubes, being a certain extension of the algebra considered in [7].

2 Syntax of the mv-modal language L and foundations of its semantics

Let us denote the mv-modal language we shall introduce here by L. The alphabet of L consists of:

- the set $VPROP$ of propositional variables;
- the set $\{c_1, \ldots, c_l\}$ of propositional connectives, with the arity of c_j equal to $i(j)$ for $j = 1, \ldots, l$;
- the set $\{O_1, \ldots, O_m\}$ of modal operators.

The set $FORM_L$ of *formulae* of the language L is the least set containing $VPROP$ and closed under all the connectives $c_1, \ldots, c_l$ as well as under all the modal operators $O_1, \ldots, O_m$.

The basis for semantics of our language is a fixed semantic range SR, being a finite algebra of logical values that the formulae of L can take. We assume that $SR = \{0, 1, \ldots, n - 1\}$, though the use of natural numbers for denoting the elements of SR does not in general imply that the latter elements are ordered linearly according to their numbers. We also assume that the designated values are $\{s, s + 1, \ldots, n - 1\}$, where $0 < s \leq n - 1$.

- With each propositional connective c_j we associate a *semantic function*

$$f_{c_j} : SR^{i(j)} \to SR$$

  representing the interpretation of connective c_j in the algebra SR.
- With each modality $\bigcirc_i$ we associate a binary propositional-like function,

$$f_{\bigcirc_i} : SR^2 \to SR$$

and a quantifier-like function

$$g_{\bigcirc_i} : \mathcal{P}(SR) \to SR.$$

These two functions are parameters determining the type of modality represented by $\bigcirc_i$.

3   Kripke semantics of the language L

The standard semantics of the language L of many-valued modal logic is defined in the usual Kripke style.

An *L-frame* is a pair

$$F = < W, \{R_i\}_{i=1}^{m} >$$

where:

- W is a nonempty set of possible worlds,
- for any i, $1 \leq i \leq m$, $R_i : W \times W \to SR$ is a many-valued binary *accessibility predicate* corresponding to the modality $\bigcirc_i$.

An *L-model* is a pair

$$M = < F, I >,$$

where $F = < W, \{R_i\}_{i=1}^{m} >$ is an L-frame, and

$$I : W \times VPROP \to SR$$

is an interpretation of propositional variables in possible worlds. As usual, $I(w, p)$ is interpreted as the value of variable p in world w.

The interpretation I is extended to all formulae in $FORM_L$ as follows:

1. $I(w, c_j(A_1, \ldots, A_{i(j)})) = f_{c_j}(I(w, A_1), \ldots, I(w, A_{i(j)}))$ for $j = 1, \ldots, l$;

2. $I(w, \bigcirc_i A) =$
$g_{\bigcirc_i}(\{f_{\bigcirc_i}(R_i(w, w'), I(w', A)) : w' \in W\})$ for $i = 1, \ldots, m$.

For any $i, 1 \le i \le m$, and any $k \in SR$, we denote

$$R_k^i = \{(w, w') \in W \times W : R_i(w, w') = k\}$$

In Kripke semantics of many-valued modal logic we introduce the so-called *meaning functions*

$$S_k : FORM_L \to \mathcal{P}(W),$$

$k \in SR$, with $S_k(A)$ representing the set of all worlds $w \in W$ in which the formula A takes the value k. The meaning functions are defined as follows:

- $S_k(p) = \{w \in W : I(w, p) = k\}$ for any $p \in VPROP$,
- $S_k(c_j(A_1, \ldots, A_{i(j)})) = \bigcup_{f_{c_j}(m_1, \ldots, m_{i(j)}) = k} \bigcap_{p=1}^{i(j)} S_{m_p}(A_p)$ for $j = 1, \ldots, l$,
- $S_k(\bigcirc_i A) =$
$\bigcup_{X \subseteq SR: g_{\bigcirc_i}(X) = k}[(W \setminus \bigcup_{r \in SR \setminus X} \bigcup_{f_{\bigcirc_i}(m_1, m_2) = r}(R_{m_1}^i)^{-1}(S_{m_2}(A)))$
$\cap \bigcap_{l \in X} \bigcup_{f_{\bigcirc_i}(n_1, n_2) = l}(R_{n_1}^i)^{-1}(S_{n_2}(A))]$

The last complicated clause concerning $\bigcirc_i A$ requires some explanation. Since

$$S_k(\bigcirc_i A) = \{w \in W : I(w, \bigcirc_i A) = k\},$$

then in view of the definition of $I(w, \bigcirc_i A)$ we have:

$S_k(\bigcirc_i A) =$
$\{w \in W : (\exists X \subseteq SR)[g_{\bigcirc_i}(X) = k \ \& \ \{f_{\bigcirc_i}(R_i(w, w'), I(w', A)) : w' \in W\}$
$= X\} = \{w \in W : (\exists X \subseteq SR)[(g_{\bigcirc_i}(X) = k)$
$\quad\quad \& \ (\forall w' \in W)(\exists l \in X)(f_{\bigcirc_i}(R_i(w, w'), I(w', A)) = l)$
$\quad\quad \& \ (\forall l \in X)(\exists w' \in W)(f_{\bigcirc_i}(R_i(w, w'), I(w', A)) = l))]$
$= \bigcup_{X \subseteq SR: g_{\bigcirc_i}(X) = k}\{w \in W : \neg(\exists w' \in W)(\exists r \in (SR \setminus X))(\exists m_1, m_2 \in SR)$
$\quad\quad (f_{\bigcirc_i}(m_1, m_2) = r \ \& \ R_{m_1}^i(w, w') \ \& \ w' \in S_{m_2}(A))\}$
$\quad\quad \cap\{w \in W : \forall l \in X)(\exists w \in W')(\exists n_1, n_2 \in SR)$
$\quad\quad (f_{\bigcirc_i}(n_1, n_2) = l \ \& \ R_{n_1}^i(w, w') \ \& \ w' \in S_{n_2}(A))\}]$
$= \bigcup_{X \subseteq SR: g_{\bigcirc_i}(X) = k}[(W \setminus \bigcup_{r \in SR \setminus X} \bigcup_{f_{\bigcirc_i}(m_1, m_2) = r}$
$\quad\quad (R_{m_1}^i)^{-1}(S_{m_2}(A)) \cap \bigcap_{l \in X} \bigcup_{f_{\bigcirc_i}(n_1, n_2) = l}(R_{n_1}^i)^{-1}(S_{n_2}(A))]$

The meaning functions S_k have the following basic properties, which we will use in building our n-cube algebra:

Proposition 1. *For any L-model $M = (F, I)$, and any formula A, the functions S_k satisfy the following conditions:*

(a) *If $k \ne r$, then $S_k(A) \cap S_r(A) = \emptyset$,*
(b) $\bigcup_{k \in SR} S_k(A) = W$.

Examples of the Kripke semantics for the classical modality of possibility and Fitting's many-valued modalities of possibility and necessity are discussed in Section 7.

4   Relational semantics of the language L

The relational semantics for the mv-modal language L is a certain extension of the relational semantics proposed in [7] for an arbitrary many-valued propositional logic.

Again, the semantics is based on a certain calculus of special n-ary relations called n-cubes, where n is the cardinality of the semantic range SR of L. However, this time we use a two-sorted calculus involving n-cubes over W and n-cubes over W^2, where W is a nonempty set corresponding to the set of worlds in Kripke semantics. As before, we employ the singleton $\{\emptyset\}$ as an "emptiness" marker. Namely, we want to avoid the situation when emptiness of the k-th component P_k of a cube relation $P = P_0 \times P_1 \times \cdots \times P_{n-1}$, which intuitively represents the set of worlds for which a given many-valued formula takes the value k, makes the whole relation empty. In such a case, we simply replace P_k by $\{\emptyset\}$.

The said relational calculus is a system

$$RE^L(W) =$$
$$< Rel(W), Rel(W^2), \{R_i^*\}_{i=1}^m, \{c_j\}_{j=1}^l, \{\bigcirc_i\}_{i=1}^m, \{J_k^1\}_{k=0}^{n-1}, \{J_k^2\}_{k=0}^{n-1} >,$$

where:

- $R_i^* \in Rel(W^2)$ for $i = 1, \ldots, m$;
- for $Y \in \{W, W^2\}$, $Rel(Y)$ is the set of n-cube relations over $Y \cup \{\emptyset\}$ (we assume that $\emptyset \notin W$), having the form

$$P = P_0 \times P_1 \times \cdots \times P_{n-1}$$

  such that the following conditions are satisfied:
  1. For any i, $0 \le i \le n-1$, $P_i \in \mathcal{P}(Y \cup \{\emptyset\}) \setminus \{\emptyset\}$, i.e. P_i is a nonempty subset of $Y \cup \{\emptyset\}$;
  2. If $i \ne j$, then $P_i \cap P_j \in \{\emptyset, \{\emptyset\}\}$, i.e. $P_i \cap P_j$ is either empty or equals $\{\emptyset\}$;
  3. $Y \subseteq \bigcup_{k=0}^{n-1} P_k$;
- $R_1^*, R_2^*, \ldots, R_m^*$, where $R_i^* \in Rel(W^2)$ for each i, are constants of the calculus corresponding to the accessibility predicates R_i in the Kripke semantics of L, i.e. we have

$$R_i^* = R_0^{*i} \times R_1^{*i} \times \cdots \times R_{n-1}^{*i}$$

  where R_k^{*i} corresponds to R_k^i in Kripke semantics.
- For any i, j, the operations $c_j, \bigcirc_i$ are functions on n-cube relations in $Rel(W)$ such that c_j is of arity $i(j)$ for $j = 1, \ldots, l$, and $\bigcirc_i$ is of arity 1 for $i = 1, \ldots, m$. Further, for $i = 1, 2$ and $k = 1, \ldots, n-1$, J_k^i is a unary operation on $Rel(W^i)$, where $W^1 = W$. The above operations are defined as follows:

(i) For any n-cube relations $P^1, \ldots, P^{i(j)} \in Rel(W)$ such that $P^k = P_0^k \times \cdots \times P_{n-1}^k$,

$$c_j(P^1, \ldots, P^{i(j)}) = Q_0 \times \cdots \times Q_{n-1},$$

where

$$Q_k = \bigcup_{f_{c_j}(m_1, \ldots, m_{i(j)})=k} P_{m_1}^1 \cap \cdots \cap P_{m_{i(j)}}^{i(j)}$$

if the above union is nonempty, and $\{\emptyset\}$ otherwise;

(ii) For any n-cube relation $P = P_0 \times \cdots \times P_{n-1} \in Rel(W^i)$,

$$J_k^i(P) = Q_0 \times \ldots \times Q_{n-1}$$

where

$$Q_{n-1} = P_k, \quad Q_0 = \bigcup_{l \neq k} P_l, \text{ and } Q_j = \{\emptyset\} \text{ for } j \neq 0, n-1.$$

(iii) For any n-cube relation $P = P_0 \times \cdots \times P_{n-1} \in Rel(W)$,

$$\bigcirc_i P = Q_0 \times \ldots \times Q_{n-1}$$

where

$$Q_k = \bigcup_{X \subseteq SR: g_{\bigcirc_i}(X)=k} [(W \setminus \bigcup_{r \in SR \setminus X} \bigcup_{f_{\bigcirc_i}(m_1,m_2)=r} (R_{m_1}^i)^{-1}(P_{m_2})) \cap \bigcap_{l \in X} \bigcup_{f_{\bigcirc_i}(n_1,n_2)=l} (R_{n_1}^i)^{-1}(P_{n_2})]$$

The role of the operations J_k^i is similar to that played by the J operators in Rosser-Turquette logics — that is why they are denoted with the same symbol. J_k^i behaves like a "selector" of the logical value k, and applied to a relation $P \in RE^L(W^i)$ partitions the set W into the sets P_k and $W^i - P_k$.

For the sake of simplicity, in the sequel we shall drop the superscript i in J_k^i, and use the same symbol J_k for denoting the respective operation on both $Rel(W)$ and $Rel(W^2)$.

Examples of the relational semantics for the classical modality of possibility and Fitting's many-valued modalities of possibility and necessity are discussed in Section 7.

It can be proved in a way analogous to that used in [7] that the following holds:

Proposition 2. *For any nonempty set W, the cube calculus $RE^L(W)$ defined above is an algebra.*

Denote by

$$RE^L = \{RE^L(W) : W \text{ is a nonempty set}\}$$

the class of all algebras of n-cube relations for an mv-modal logic L. A relational model for L is of the form

$$M = (RE^L(W), I_R),$$

where I_R is a relational interpretation of propositional variables, i.e. $I_R :$ $VPROP \to Rel(W)$. The function I_R is extended to the interpretation of all formulae from $FORM_L$ in M by interpreting the connectives c_j and modalities $\bigcirc_i$ as the corresponding operations in the algebra $RE^L(W)$, i.e. by taking

$$I_R(c_j(A_1, \ldots, A_{i(j)})) = c_j(I_R(A_1), \ldots, I_R(A_{i(j)}))$$
$$I_R(\bigcirc_i A) = \bigcirc_i I_R(A)$$

A formula A is said to be true in a relational model M, written $M \models A$, iff $I_R(A) = P_0 \times P_1 \times \cdots \times P_{n-1}$ is such that $\bigcup_{i=s}^{n-1} P_i \supseteq W$, where W is the universe underlying the cube algebra $RE^L(W)$.

5   The language L_R of the relational calculus RE^L

Our aim is to develop a deduction system for many-valued modal logic L based on the relational semantics described in the preceding section. The system will use relational formulae being the terms of our two-sorted relational algebra RE^L enriched with variables representing possible worlds.

Let us begin with introducing the basic notions.

Assume $VREL$ is a set of relational variables of equal cardinality with $VPROP$, and that $VWRD$ is a countable set of world variables.

We define the language L_R of relational calculus as follows.

The set $TERM_R$ of relational terms is a disjoint sum $TERM_R = TERM_R^1 + TERM_R^2$, where

$$TERM_R^2 = \{R_i : i = 1, 2, \ldots, m\} \cup \{J_k R_i : i = 1, \ldots, m, k = 0, 1, \ldots, n-1\}$$

and $TERM_R^1$ is the least set satisfying the following conditions:

1. $VREL \subseteq TERM_R^1$;
2. for any $j, 1 \le j \le l$, if $P_1, \ldots, P_{i(j)} \in TERM_R^1$, then $c_j(P_1, \ldots, P_{i(j)}) \in TERM_R^1$;
3. for any $k, 0 \le k \le n-1$, and any $i, 1 \le i \le m$, if $P \in TERM_R^1$, then $J_k P, \bigcirc_i P \in TERM_R^1$.

The set $FORM_R$ of relational formulae is a disjoint sum $FORM_R = FORM_R^1 + FORM_R^2$, where:

1. $FORM_R^1$ is the set of all expressions of the form $P(x)$ with $P \in TERM_R^1$, $x \in VWRD$;

2. $FORM_R^2$ is the set of all expressions of the form $Q(x,y)$ with $Q \in TERM_R^2, x, y \in VWRD$, i.e. the set of all expressions of the form $R_i(x,y)$, $J_k R_i(x,y)$, $i = 1, \ldots, m, k = 0, \ldots, n-1$.

Relational formulae will be denoted by lowercase Greek letters $\alpha, \beta, \ldots$. A model for the relational language L_R is a pair

$$M = < RE^L(W), I >$$

where $RE^L(W)$ is an algebra of n-cubes over a set W, and $I = < I_R, I_W >$ is a two-sorted interpretation, with $I_R : VREL \to Rel(W)$ being the interpretation of relational variables, and $I_W : VWRD \to W$ — the interpretation of world variables.

The interpretation I_R extends in a natural way to all relational terms, with the prerequisite that the constants $R_i \in TERM_R^2$ are interpreted as the constants $R_i^* \in Rel(W^2)$ in the algebra $RE^L(W)$.

The notion of satisfaction of a relational formula in a model is given by the following clauses:

- for any $P(x) \in FORM_R^1$, $M \models P(x)$ iff

$$I_W(x) \in \bigcup_{j=s}^{n-1} [I_R(P)]_j,$$

where Q_j denotes the j-th component of the n-cube $Q = Q_0 \times Q_1 \times \cdots \times Q_{n-1}$;
- for any $Q(x,y) \in FORM_R^2$, $M \models Q(x,y)$ iff

$$(I_W(x), I_W(y)) \in \bigcup_{j=s}^{n-1} [I_R(Q)]_j$$

A relational formula $\alpha \in FORM_R$ is said to be valid iff $M \models \alpha$ for each model M.

As we have said, we shall develop a deduction system for the relational language L_R rather than for the original language L itself. However, one can easily see that L can be equivalently embedded in the richer language L_R.

Let $\sigma : VPROP \to VREL$ be any 1-1 mapping of $VPROP$ onto $VREL$ (recall we assumed these sets to be of the same cardinality). Then σ can be extended to an 1-1 injection of $FORM_L$ into $TERM_R$ by defining

$$\sigma(c_j(A_1, \ldots, A_{i(j)})) = c_j(\sigma(A_1), \ldots, \sigma(A_{i(j)})), \qquad \sigma(\bigcirc_i A) = \bigcirc_i \sigma(A)$$

for any $i, j, 1 \leq i \leq m, 1 \leq j \leq l$, and any $A_1, \ldots, A_{i(j)} \in FORM_L$.

Now let $x \in VWRD$ be any world variable, and define

$$\sigma^*(A) = \sigma(A)(x)$$

for any $A \in FORM_L$. Then σ^* is a one-to-one mapping of $FORM_L$ into $FORM_R$. Moreover, we have

Lemma 1. *A formula $A \in FORM_L$ is valid iff the formula $\sigma(A) \in FORM_R$ is valid.*

Hence if we develop a complete deduction system for the relational language L_R, then we will also be able to use this system — via the trivial translation σ^* — as a deduction system for the original language L.

The deduction system DR^L for RE^L proposed here is of the Rasiowa-Sikorski type. It belongs to the family of natural deduction mechanisms in a broad sense of the word, and is dual to the tableaux formalism. The system consists of decomposition rules applied to finite sequences of relational formulae, and of what is called fundamental sequences. Decomposition rules lead from valid sequences to valid sequences, so they correspond to inference rules of a Hilbert-type system. Fundamental sequences are required to be valid, so they play the role of axioms.

Let us introduce first the necessary general preliminaries.

We say that a sequence $\Omega = \alpha_1, \alpha_2, \ldots, \alpha_k$ of relational formulae is valid in RE^L if for every model M of the relational language L_R there is an index $i, 1 \leq i \leq k$, such that $M \models \alpha_i$.

A decomposition rule of the DR^L system is a $(k+1)$-tuple $\Omega, \Omega_1, \ldots, \Omega_k$, where all the Ω's are sequences of relational formulae, written usually in the form

$$\frac{\Omega}{\Omega_1 \mid \Omega_2 \mid \ldots \mid \Omega_k}$$

Here Ω is called the conclusion of the rule, and $\Omega_1, \ldots, \Omega_k$ - premises of the rule. The rule is said to be sound if validity of its conclusion is equivalent to the validity of all its premises, i.e. Ω is valid iff all the Ω_i's are valid.

Now we can introduce the deduction system for the class RE^L of algebras of relations.

A fundamental sequence is a sequence containing either all the formulae $J_0\alpha, \ldots, J_{n-1}\alpha$ for some α, or the term $J_0 J_k J_l \alpha$ for some α, where $k \neq 0, n-1, l \in \{0, 1, \ldots, n-1\}$.

It is easy to check that each fundamental sequence is indeed valid.

To formulate the decomposition rules, we need the notion of an indecomposable sequence, intended to denote a very simple sequence that need not be decomposed any further.

A formula is said to be indecomposable if it is of one of the following forms:

- $J_k P(x)$ for some $k, 0 \leq k \leq n-1$, and some $P \in VREL$, $x \in VWRD$,
- $J_k R_i(x, y)$ for some i, k, with $0 \leq k \leq n-1, 1 \leq i \leq m$, and some $x, y \in VWRD$.

A sequence Ω is said to be indecomposable if each element of Ω is indecomposable.

Because the rules of our deduction system have to match a generic many-valued modal logic with arbitrary propositional connectives and the modalities defined in a very general way, they necessarily have to express rather involved relationships between the premise and conclusions. However, we do not assume that our logics features any particular kind of disjunction or conjunction, which are the basic tools for expressing such relationships. What we have at our disposal is only meta-disjunction represented by comma in the sequences of formulae and meta-conjunction represented by the branching | between the premises of a rule. However, neither the decomposition rule for an arbitrary connective c_j nor the decomposition rule for modality can be represented through non-nested metadisjunction and metaconjunction. In case of the former rule this problem can be overcome by breaking the rule into a finite sentence of subrules (see [Konikowska, Morgan, Orłowska 98]), but in case of the modality rule this is not feasible. Hence in order to represent these rules in a legible way we use in their notation special symbols for meta-disjunction and meta-conjunction $\vee$ and $\wedge$, which in the decomposition process are later "unwound" into the commas in sequences Ω and branchings | between individual conclusions according to the first two "meta-rules" in DR^L.

Multiple disjunctions and conjunctions will be denoted by $\bigvee$ and $\bigwedge$, respectively.

The decomposition rules of the deduction system DR^L are given below. In each of the rules we assume that the initial context sequence Ω' is indecomposable, i.e. we decompose the leftmost decomposable formula in the conclusion.

$(\vee)$
$$\frac{\Omega', \alpha \vee \beta, \Omega''}{\Omega', \alpha, \beta, \Omega''}$$

$(\wedge)$
$$\frac{\Omega', \alpha \wedge \beta, \Omega''}{\Omega', \alpha, \Omega'' \mid \Omega', \beta, \Omega''}$$

$(J\text{-in})$
$$\frac{\Omega', \alpha, \Omega''}{\Omega', J_s\alpha, \ldots, J_{n-1}\alpha, \Omega''}$$

where α is not of the form $J_k\beta$ for any $k, 0 \leq k \leq n-1, \beta \in FORM_R$;

(c_j)
$$\frac{\Omega', J_k c_j(P_1, \ldots, P_{i(j)})(x), \Omega''}{\Omega', \bigvee_{f_{c_j}(m_1, \ldots, m_{i(j)})=k} \bigwedge_{r=1}^{i(j)} J_{m_r} P_r(x), \Omega''}$$

$(\bigcirc_i)$
$$\frac{\Omega', J_k \bigcirc_i P(x), \Omega''}{\begin{array}{c}\Omega', \bigvee_{Z \subseteq SR: g_{\bigcirc_i}(Z)=k} [(\bigvee_{r \in Z} \bigvee_{f_{\bigcirc_i}(m_1, m_2)=r} J_{m_1} R_i(x, y_Z) \wedge J_{m_2} P(y_Z)) \\ \wedge \bigwedge_{p \in Z}(\bigvee_{f_{\bigcirc_i}(n_1, n_2)=p} J_{n_1} R_i(x, t_Z^p) \wedge J_{n_2} P(t_Z^p))], \Omega'', J_k \bigcirc_i P(x)\end{array}}$$

where each y_Z is a new variable in $VRWD$ with $y_Z \neq y_{Z'}$ for $Z \neq Z'$, and each t_Z^p is an arbitrary variable in $VWRD$.

$(J_0 J_r)$
$$\frac{\Omega', J_0 J_r P(x), \Omega''}{\Omega', J_0 P(x), \ldots, J_{r-1} P(x), J_{r+1} P(x), \ldots, J_{n-1} P(x), \Omega''}$$

for any $1 \leq r \leq n-2$,

$$\frac{\Omega', J_0 J_0 P(x), \Omega''}{\Omega', J_1 P(x), \ldots, J_{n-1} P(x), \Omega''}, \qquad \frac{\Omega', J_0 J_{n-1} P(x), \Omega''}{\Omega', J_0 P(x), \ldots, J_{n-2} P(x), \Omega''}$$

$(J_{n-1} J_r)$
$$\frac{\Omega', J_{n-1} J_r P(x), \Omega''}{\Omega', J_r P(x), \Omega''} \qquad \text{for any } r \in SR,$$

$(J_k J_r)$
$$\frac{\Omega', J_k J_r P(x), \Omega''}{\Omega', , \Omega''}$$

for any $r \in SR$, and any $k \neq 0, n-1$.

It can be easily shown that all the decomposition rules are sound in the strong sense defined above.

6   Completeness of the deduction system DR^L

Provability under the DR^L system is defined in terms of a deduction tree of a sequence of terms.

By a deduction tree of a sequence Ω we mean any tree $DT(\Omega)$ labelled with sequences of terms and constructed as follows:

1. The root of $DT(\Omega)$ is labelled with Ω.
2. If b labelled with Σ is an end vertex of a branch B of the tree constructed up to now, then:
   (a) we terminate branch B at b if Σ is either fundamental or indecomposable, or no rule applicable to Σ introduces a new formula[1];
   (b) otherwise, if $\dfrac{\Sigma}{\Sigma_1 \mid \Sigma_2 \ \ldots \ \mid \Sigma_k}$ is an instance of a rule in DR^L applicable to Σ and introducing a new term, we prolong the branch B by attaching to the vertex b new vertices $b_1, b_2, \ldots, b_k$, where b_i is labelled with Σ_i for each i.
3. $DT(\Omega)$ is a maximal tree constructed along these rules.

Evidently, each leaf of a decomposition tree is labelled with either a fundamental sequence or an indecomposable sequence. Indeed: if a label of a vertex is decomposable and non-fundamental, then there is a decomposition rule applicable to this sequence, and hence we can append a son or sons to the vertex, so it cannot be a leaf.

A decomposition tree is said to be a proof if it is finite and all its leaves are labelled with fundamental sequences

---

[1] A rule R applied to Σ introduces a new formula if one of the sequences Σ_i resulting from this application contains a term that is not an element of Σ.

A sequence Ω of terms (in particular, a single formula A) is said to be provable in DR^L, written $\vdash_{DR^L} \Omega$, if it has a decomposition tree that is a proof.

Let us dwell for a moment on the issue of finiteness of the decomposition tree $DT(\Omega)$, crucial from the viewpoint of the completeness proof given below.

Note that in the modality rule $(\bigcirc_i)$ we repeat the decomposed formula $J_k \bigcirc_i P(x)$ below the double line. This is a quite classical way of dealing with existential quantification — implicit in our generic modality $\bigcirc_i$ — in Rasiowa-Sikorski systems. Of course, such repetition can give rise to an infinite branch in the decomposition tree of a formula. In fact, this is the only rule that can give rise to such a branch. Indeed: all other rules except (J-in) replace the decomposed formula with a finite number of formulae of a strictly lower rank (complexity). In turn, the (J-in) rule is used only once on each formula $\alpha \in \Omega$ which is not of the form $J_k \beta$ — namely, when α is first decomposed (because no other rule is applicable to such an α). Following that use, all the formulae obtained out of α are of the $J_k \beta$ type, so (J-in) is no longer applicable.

Note also that rule $(\bigcirc_i)$ encodes a fairness principle for the decomposition process. Indeed: the repeated formula $J_k \bigcirc_i P(x)$ is shifted to the end of the sequence, which assures that we will not keep decomposing this formula infinitely many times without ever getting to the further part of the decomposed sequence. Moreover, clause 2 b) in the definition of the decomposition tree prevents applying the said rule more than one time with the same arbitrary variable t_z^P — because such an application would not introduce any new term into the sequence. Finally, the maximality clause 3. of that definition ensures that any infinite branch of the tree will contain the application of rule $(\bigcirc_i)$ for each choice of the arbitrary variable t_z^P. All these facts should be borne in mind when reading the completeness proof.

Of course, these safeguards could be made more precise by assuming that the choice of new and arbitrary variables in the modality rule is performed according to some predetermined order with additional conditions cutting down the size of the decomposition tree. The respective mechanism are well-known e.g. in the area of automatic deduction systems connected with tableaux, and discussing them here is outside the scope of this paper.

The completeness and soundness result for our deduction system is:

Proposition 3. *A sequence Ω is valid iff it is provable in DR^L, i.e.*

$$\models_{REL} \Omega \text{ iff } \vdash_{DR^L} \Omega$$

Proof. The backward implication $\vdash_{DR^L} \Omega \Rightarrow \models_{REL} \Omega$ (i.e. soundness) follows easily from finiteness of the decomposition tree $DT(\Omega)$ as well as from the soundness of decomposition rules and validity of the fundamental sequences. Indeed: if $\vdash_{DR^L} \Omega$, then each leaf of Ω is labelled by a fundamental — and hence valid — sequence. By the construction of $DT(\Omega)$, the label of each vertex is obtained from the labels of its sons by means of a backward application of a decomposition rule. Since each such rule leads from valid sequences to valid sequences in both directions, going upwards in the finite tree we can prove by induction that the sequence labeling each vertex is valid — which proves that Ω is valid as the label of the root.

The converse implication $\models_{REL} \Omega \Rightarrow \vdash_{DRL} \Omega$ is proved by contradiction: thus we show that $\nvdash_{DRL} \Omega$ implies $\nvDash_{REL} \Omega$. Suppose that Ω has no proof, and let $DT(\Omega)$ be any decomposition tree of Ω. Then, since this tree is not a proof, we have the two following cases:

Case 1: There exists a leaf b of $DT(\Omega)$ labelled with a non-fundamental sequence. By the construction of the decomposition tree, the sequence labelling the leaf b has to be indecomposable.

Case 2: The tree $DT(\Omega)$ is infinite. Then, since the tree is a finitely branching one, by Koenig's lemma it must contain an infinite branch B.

Consider the set Δ being the set of indecomposable formulae appearing in the sequence labelling the leaf b in the first case, and the set of all indecomposable formulae appearing in the labels of the vertices of the branch B in the second case. We shall construct a counter-model M for Δ.

Since Δ contains only indecomposable formulae, then each of its elements is of the form either $J_k P(x)$ or $J_k R_i(x, y)$, where $P \in VREL, x, y \in VWRD, 0 \leq k \leq n - 1, 1 \leq i \leq m$. We define a counter-model

$$M = < RE^L(W), I >$$

for Δ as follows. We put $W = VWRD$, and $I_W(x) = x$ for any $x \in VWRD$. Further, for any $P \in VREL$, we take

$$I_R(P) = P_0 \times P_1 \times \cdots \times P_{n-1}$$

where

$$P_k = \{x \in VWRD : \ k = Min\{l : J_l P \notin \Delta\}\}$$

Finally, we define the constant relations R_i^* in $Rel(W^2)$, $i = 1, 2, \ldots, m$, by

$$R_i = R_0^{*i} \times R_1^{*i} \times \cdots \times R_{n-1}^{*i},$$

where

$$R_k^{*i} = \{(x, y) : \ x, y \in VWRD \text{ and } \ k = Min\{l : J_l R_i(x, y) \notin \Delta\}\}$$

One can easily see that since Δ is non-fundamental, then for each $P \in VREL$ and each $x \in VWRD$ there exists exactly one $k, 0 \leq k \leq n - 1$ such that $x \in P_k$. Indeed: the minimum in the formula for P_k is a uniquely defined number, and if $J_l P(x) \notin \Delta$ for any l, then we have $x \in P_0$. This shows that $I_R(P)$ defined as above is an n-cube relation in $Rel(W)$. The same kind of argument shows that R_i^* is an n-cube relation in $Rel(W^2)$ for each $i, 1 \leq i \leq m$.

Since for any $\delta_i \in \Delta$ we have either $\delta_i = J_k P(x)$ or $\delta_i = J_k R_i(x, y)$ for some $x, y \in VWRD$ and some $P \in VREL, 0 \leq k \leq n-1, 1 \leq i \leq m$, in the above definition we obviously have $M \not\models \delta_i$.

In the first case, when Δ is the label of a leaf b of a finite $DT(\Omega)$, this obviously implies that Ω is not valid. Indeed: denote the (finite) branch containing b by B_b. Then the label of each vertex on B_b is obtained from the labels of its sons by means of some decomposition rules preserving the validity in both directions. Evidently, since the label Δ of the leaf b of B_b is not valid, this means that the labels of all the vertices on B are not valid. Since the label of the top vertex of B_b — the root — is Ω, this means that Ω is not valid, which ends the proof by contradiction.

In the second case, when Δ is the set of indecomposable formulae labelling the vertices of an infinite branch B of $DT(\Omega)$, we prove that all the formulae labelling vertices of B are not satisfied in M. We argue by induction on the rank of the formula, defined as a maximal depth of the nesting of operators in the formula. Formulae of rank 0 are decomposed using the rule $(J - in)$ into the indecomposable formulae in Δ, which are not satisfied in M. Further, assuming that all formulae of rank less or equal to k are not satisfied in M we prove that also formulae of rank k are not satisfied in M. The proof uses the equivalent character of the rules and maximality of the decomposition tree, and follows the same lines as an analogous part of the completeness proof of a Rasiowa-Sikorski system for classical logic in [16].

The conclusion is that Ω labeling the top vertex of B is not valid, which ends the proof by contradiction.   □

7   Examples

In this section we consider two examples of applying our formalisation to well-known modal logics: the first concerns standard two-valued modalities of possibility and necessity, the second - a general class of many-valued modal logics defined by Fitting.

7.1   Standard modalities in two-valued logic

Consider the case of standard modalities of possibility $\Diamond$ and necessity $\Box$ in two-valued modal logic with a single accessibility relation R. Thus $SR = \{0, 1\}$, the number of modalities is $m = 2$, $R_1 = R_2 = R$, and $\bigcirc_1 = \Diamond, \bigcirc_2 = \Box$.

Let us start with the modality of possibility. We claim that in the formalism we have introduced here $\Diamond$ is described by the functions $f_\Diamond = f_\wedge, g_\Diamond = g_\vee$, where by $f_\wedge$ we mean the truth function on SR corresponding to classical conjunction, and by $g_\vee$ - the truth function on $\mathcal{P}(SR)$ corresponding to supremum. For the sake of simplicity, below we shall write f, g instead of $f_\diamond$ and $g_\diamond$, and $\wedge, \vee$ instead of $f_\wedge, g_\vee$, respectively. The same simplification of notation will be employed in other examples.

Consistently with the notation we introduced earlier, we have for the Kripke semantics of our language

$$I(w, \diamond A) = \bigvee_{w \in W} R(w, w') \wedge I(w', A)$$

Now let us pass to the relational semantics. In this case it is based on 2-cube relations of the form $P = P_0 \times P_1 \in RE^L(W)$. Moreover, $RE^L(W)$ contains a single constant $R^* = R_0 \times R_1 \in Rel(W^2)$ representing the common accessibility relation for $\diamond$ and $\Box$.

Intuitively, for $k = 0, 1$, P_k represents the set of worlds in W in which a relational term P^* evaluating by P takes the value k. Analogously, for $i = 0, 1$, R_i is the set of pairs (w, w') for which the accessiblity relation R represented by R^* takes the value i. Taking

$$P = P_0 \times P_1, \qquad \diamond P = Q, \qquad Q = Q_0 \times Q_1$$

we have

$$Q_0 = \bigcup_{X \subseteq SR: \vee X = 0} [(W \setminus \bigcup_{r \in SR \setminus X} \bigcup_{m_1 \wedge m_2 = r} R_{m_1}^{-1}(P_{m_2})) \cap \bigcap_{l \in X} \bigcup_{n_1 \wedge n_2 = l} R_{n_1}^{-1}(P_{n_2})$$

In the above equality we have $X = \{0\}, SR \setminus X = \{1\}, r = 1, (m_1, m_2) = (1, 1), l = 0, (n_1, n_2) \in \{(0, 1), (1, 0), (0, 0)\}$, whence

$$Q_0 = (W \setminus R_1^{-1}(P_1)) \cap (R_0^{-1}(P_1) \cup R_1^{-1}(P_0) \cup R_0^{-1}(P_0))$$

Denoting

$$W' = R_0^{-1}(P_1) \cup R_1^{-1}(P_0) \cup R_0^{-1}(P_0) \tag{1}$$

we get

$$Q_0 = (W \setminus R_1^{-1}(P_1)) \cap W'$$

Moreover,

$$W' = \{w \in W : (\exists w' \in W)(R_0(w, w') \text{ or } w' \in P_0)\}$$

Hence

$$\begin{aligned}
Q_0 &= \{w \in W : (\forall w' \in W)(R_0(w, w') \text{ or } P_0(w'))\} \\
&\quad \cap \{w \in W : (\exists w' \in W)(R_0(w, w') \text{ or } P_0(w'))\} \\
&= \{w \in W : (\forall w' \in W)(R_0(w, w') \text{ or } P_0(w'))\} \\
&= \{w \in W : \neg(\exists w' \in W)(R_1(w, w') = 1 \ \& \ P_1(w'))\}
\end{aligned}$$

Further, we have

$$Q_1 = \bigcup_{X \subseteq SR: \vee X = 1} [(W \setminus \bigcup_{r \in SR \setminus X} \bigcup_{m_1 \wedge m_2 = r} R_{m_1}^{-1}(P_{m_2})) \cap \bigcap_{l \in X} \bigcup_{n_1 \wedge n_2 = l} R_{n_1}^{-1}(P_{n_2})]$$

From the above we get two possibilites for X: $X_1 = \{1\}, X_2 = \{0,1\}$. Denote by W_i the set in the square brackets corresponding to $X_i, i = 1, 2$. As for $X_1 = \{1\}$ we get $SR \setminus X_1 = \{0\}, r = 0, (m_1, m_2) \in \{(0,1),(1,0),(0,0)\}, l = 1, (n_1, n_2) = (1,1)$, then

$$W_1 = (W \setminus (R_0^{-1}(P_1) \cup R_1^{-1}(P_0) \cup R_0^{-1}(P_0))) \cap R_1^{-1}(P_1)$$

Thus

$$W_1 = (W \setminus W') \cap R_1^{-1}(P_1)$$

For $X_2 = \{0,1\}$ we get $S \setminus X_2 = \emptyset$, whence

$$W_2 = (W \setminus \emptyset) \cap \bigcap_{l \in \{0,1\}} \bigcup_{n_1 \wedge n_2 = 1} R_{n_1}^{-1}(P_{n_2})$$

Since for $l = 0$ we get $(n_1, n_2) \in \{(0,1),(1,0),(0,0)\}$ and for $l = 1 - (n_1, n_2) = (1,1)$, then

$$W_2 = W \cap (R_0^{-1}(P_1) \cup R_1^{-1}(P_0) \cup R_0^{-1}(P_0)) \cap R_1^{-1}(P_1)$$

Hence recalling the definition of W' we have

$$W_2 = W \cap W' \cap R_1^{-1}(P_1) = W' \cap R_1^{-1}(P_1)$$

Thus

$$Q_1 = (W \setminus W') \cap R_1^{-1}(P_1) \cup W' \cap R_1^{-1}(P_1) = R_1^{-1}(P_1)$$
$$= \{w \in W : (\exists w' \in W)(R_1(w, w') \ \& \ P_1(w'))\}$$

Obviously, considering the intuitive interpretation of P_i and R_i, this is an exact counterpart of the usual Kripke semantics for standard possibility.

Now let present the decomposition rules of the relational deduction system we developed in Section 6 for the considered modality. In the rules given below we use the symbols $\bigvee, \bigwedge$ to denote supremum and infimum in order to distinguish them from the same symbols denoting structural meta-disjunction and meta-conjunction. For the modality of possiblity we have:

$$\frac{\Omega', J_k \Diamond P(x), \Omega''}{\Omega', \Omega'', \bigvee_{Z \subseteq SR: \bigvee Z = k} [(\bigvee_{r \in Z} \bigvee_{m_1 \wedge m_2 = r} J_{m_1} R(x, yz) \wedge J_{m_2} P(yz))}$$
$$\overline{\wedge \bigwedge_{p \in Z}(\bigvee_{n_1 \wedge n_2 = p} J_{n_1} R(x, t_Z^p) \wedge J_{n_2} P(t_Z^p))], J_k \Diamond P(x)}$$

where $k = 1, 2$, each yz is a new variable in $VRWD$ with $yz \neq yz'$ for $Z \neq Z'$, and each t_Z^p is an arbitrary variable in $VWRD$.

For $k = 0$ we get $Z = \{0\}, p = r = 0, (m_1, m_2), (n_1, n_2) \in \{(0,1),(1,0),(0,0)\}$, which after simplifying the notation to $yz = y, t_Z^0 = z$ and recalling that $\bigvee_{i=1}^{s} \Omega_i = \Omega_1, \ldots, \Omega_s$ yields the rule

$$\frac{\Omega', J_0 \Diamond P(x), \Omega''}{\Omega', \Omega'', (J_0 R(x,y) \wedge J_1 P(y), J_1 R(x,y) \wedge J_0 P(y), J_0 R(x,y) \wedge J_0 P(y))}$$
$$\overline{\wedge (J_0 R(x,z) \wedge J_1 P(z), J_1 R(x,z) \wedge J_0 P(z), J_0 R(x,z) \wedge J_0 P(z)), J_0 \Diamond P(x)}$$

This can be unravelled to

$$\frac{\Omega', J_0 \Diamond P(x), \Omega''}{\Omega', \Omega'', J_0 R(x,y), J_1 P(y), J_1 R(x,y) \wedge J_0 P(y), J_0 R(x,y) \wedge J_0 P(y), rep}$$

$$\overline{\mid \Omega', \Omega'', J_0 R(x,z) \wedge J_1 P(z), J_1 R(x,z) \wedge J_0 P(z), J_0 R(x,z) \wedge J_0 P(z), rep}$$

where $rep = J_0 \Diamond P(x)$.

Obviously, since y is a new variable and z – an arbitrary variable, then to the left of the branching symbol | we have a branch corresponding to universal quantification, and to the right — to existential quantification over the same formulae. Intuitively, it means the existential branch can be dropped together with the repetition $J_0 \Diamond P(x)$ of the conclusion, which is useful only in the context of the existential branch by allowing a repeated choice of the arbitrary variable z. This would yield a simpler rule — but still a much more involved one than the usual decomposition rule for possibility.

However, this is a price of applying a generic decomposition rule for modality to a concrete modality: one is bound to get a rule much more complicated than a specific rule specially tailored to this particular modality. Such generic rules give a foolproof way of developing a complete deduction system for any many-valued modal logic in the considered class, but if we want to have a concise, effective system, we should either work with a concrete logic from a start or else reshape the concrete version of the generic system making use of the properties of a particular logic to make it more effective.

For $k = 1$ we get $Z_1 = \{1\}$ or $Z_2 = \{0,1\}$. The set Z_1 yields $r = p = 1, (m_1, m_2) = (n_1, n_2) = (1,1)$. The set Z_2 yields $r, p \in SR$; $r = 0$ yields $(m_1, m_2) \in \{(0,1),(1,0),(1,1)\}$, $r = 1$ yields $(m_1, m_2) = (1,1)$, and analogously for $p, (n_1, n_2)$. As a result, denoting $y_{Z_i} = y_i$ and $t^p_{Z_i} = t^p_i$, we get

$$\frac{\Omega', J_1 \Diamond P(x), \Omega''}{\Omega', \Omega'', J_1 R(x,y_1) \wedge J_1 P(y_1) \wedge J_1 R(x,z_1^1) \wedge J_1 P(z_1^1), (J_0 R(x,y_2) \wedge J_1 P(y_2),}$$

$$\overline{J_1 R(x,y_2) \wedge J_0 P(y_2), J_0 R(x,y_2) \wedge J_0 P(y_2), J_1 R(x,y_2) \wedge J_1 P(y_2))}$$

$$\overline{\wedge (J_0 R(x,z_0^2) \wedge J_1 P(z_0^2), J_1 R(x,z_0^2) \wedge J_0 P(z_0^2), J_0 R(x,z_0^2)) \wedge J_0 P(z_0^2))}$$

$$\overline{\wedge J_1 R(x,z_1^2) \wedge J_1 P(z_1^2), J_1 \Diamond P(x)}$$

Obviously, this rule can also be simplified: e.g., the sequence $J_0 R(x,y_2) \wedge J_1 P(y_2) \vee J_1 R(x,y_2) \wedge J_0 P(y_2) \vee J_0 R(x,y_2) \wedge J_0 P(y_2) \vee J_1 R(x,y_2) \wedge J_1 P(y_2)$ is always valid, so the subbranch starting with it can be simply deleted.

The reasons for such an intricate form of the rules is the same as before: adaptation of a generic rule that must necessarily be intricate to suit every modality in a very broad class to a concrete simple modality.

For the sake of brevity, we refrain from repeating the above detailed calculations for the case of necessity. Let us only remark that, according to our postulates, the semantic functions corresponding to that modality are $f_\Box = \to$ and $g_\Box = \bigwedge$, and corresponding deduction rules are:

$$\frac{\Omega', J_0 \Box P(x), \Omega''}{\Omega', \Omega'', J_1 R(x, y_1) \wedge J_0 P(y_1) \wedge J_1 R(x, z_0^1) \wedge J_0 P(z_0^1), (J_1 R(x, y_2) \wedge J_0 P(y_2),}$$

$$\frac{}{J_0 R(x, y_2) \wedge J_1 P(y_2), J_1 R(x, y_2) \wedge J_1 P(y_2), J_0 R(x, y_2) \wedge J_0 P(y_2))}$$

$$\frac{}{\wedge J_1 R(x, z_0^2) \wedge J_0 P(z_0^2) \wedge (J_0 R(x, z_1^2) \wedge J_1 P(z_1^2), J_1 R(x, z_1^2) \wedge J_1 P(z_1^2),}$$

$$\frac{}{J_0 R(x, z_1^2) \wedge J_0 P(z_1^2)), J_0 \Box P(x)}$$

and

$$\frac{\Omega', J_1 \Box P(x), \Omega''}{\Omega', \Omega'', (J_0 R(x, y) \wedge J_1 P(y), J_1 R(x, y) \wedge J_1 P(y), J_0 R(x, y) \wedge J_0 P(y))}$$

$$\frac{}{\wedge (J_0 R(x, z) \wedge J_1 P(z), J_1 R(x, z) \wedge J_1 P(z), J_0 R(x, z) \wedge J_0 P(z)), J_0 \Box P(x)}$$

7.2 Fitting's many-valued modal logic

Our next example is the many-valued modal logic mv-ML introduced in [3,4]. We follow the notational convention introduced in the preceding example.

The semantic range for the logic mv-ML is a finite Heyting algebra, say H. The Kripke model for the logic is of the form $M = (W, R, I)$, with W, I having the usual meanings, and R being an H-valued binary accessibility predicate on W, called accessibility relation. The interpretation of necessity formulae is defined by

$$I(w, \Box A) = \bigwedge_{w' \in W} (R(w, w') \to I(w', A))$$

where $\to$ is the relative pseudo-complement in H.

Thus, using the simplified notation defined in the previous subsection, the modality $\Box$ is defined by $f = \to, g = \bigwedge$, where $\bigwedge$ is the infimum in H.

The relational calculus features relations $P = \times_{k \in H} P_k \in Rel(W)$ together with the accessibility constant $R^* = \times_{k \in H} R_k \in Rel(W^2)$.

The operation of the relational calculus $RE^L(W)$ corresponding to modal necessity is defined by $\Box P = Q$, where

$$Q_k = \bigcup_{X \subseteq H : \bigwedge X = k} [(W \setminus \bigcup_{r \in H \setminus X} \bigcup_{m_1 \to m_2 = r} (R_{m_1})^{-1}(P_{m_2})) \cap$$

$$\bigcap_{l \in X} \bigcup_{n_1 \to n_2 = l} (R_{n_1})^{-1}(P_{n_2})]$$

The deduction rules for necessity are as follows:

$$\frac{\Omega', J_k \Box P(x), \Omega''}{\bigvee_{Z \subseteq H: \bigwedge Z=k} [(\bigvee_{r \in Z} \bigvee_{m_1 \to m_2 = r} J_{m_1} R(x, y_Z) \wedge J_{m_2} P(y_Z))}$$

$$\wedge \bigwedge_{p \in Z} (\bigvee_{n_1 \to n_2) = p} J_{n_1} R(x, t_Z^p) \wedge J_{n_2} P(t_Z^p)], J_k \Box P(x)$$

where each y_Z is a new variable in $VRWD$ with $y_Z \neq y_{Z'}$ for $Z \neq Z'$, and each t_Z^p is an arbitrary variable in $VWRD$.

In this case the rules are also a bit more complicated than those given in [7] — but again this follows from the fact that in the latter paper the rules were tailored to one concrete modality.

References

1. Carnielli W. (1987) Systematization of finite many-valued logics through the method of tableaux. Journal of Symbolic Logic 52(2):473–493
2. Carnielli W. (1991) On sequents and tableaux for many-valued logics. Journal of Non-Classical Logic 8(1):59–76
3. Fitting M.C. (1992) Many-valued modal logics. Fundamenta Informaticae, 15:235-254
4. Fitting M.C. (1992a) Many-valued modal logics II. Fundamenta Informaticae, 17:55-73
5. Frias M., Orłowska E. (1995) A proof system for fork algebras and its applications to reasoning in logics based on intuitionism. Logique et Analyse, 150-151-152:239-284
6. Frias M., Orłowska E. (1998) Equational reasoning in nonclassical logics. Journal of Applied Non-Classical Logics, 8(1-2):27-66
7. Konikowska B., Morgan C., Orłowska E. (1998) A relational formalisation of arbitrary many-valued logics. Journal of IGPL, 6(5):755-774
8. MacCaull W. (1997) Relational proof system for linear and other substructural logics. Logic Journal of the IGPL, 5(5)673-697
9. MacCaull W. (1998) Relational semantics and a relational proof theory for full Lambek calculus. Journal of Symbolic Logic, 63:623-637
10. Morgan Ch., Orłowska E. (1993) Kripke and relational-style semantics and associated tableau proof systems for arbitrary finite valued logics. Proceedings of the Workshop on Theorem Proving with Analytic Tableau and Related Methods, Marseille, France, 179-182
11. Orłowska E. (1988) Relational interpretation of modal logics. In: Andreka H., Monk D. and Nemeti I. (Eds.) Algebraic Logic. North Holland, Amsterdam, 443-471
12. Orłowska E. (1992) Relational proof system for relevant logics. Journal of Symbolic Logic 57:1425-1440
13. Orłowska, E. (1994) Relational semantics for nonclassical logics: Formulas are relations. In: Wolenski J. (Ed.) Philosophical Logic in Poland. Kluwer, Dordrecht, 167-186

14. Orłowska, E. (1995) Temporal logics in a relational framework, In: Bolc. L. and Szałas A. (Eds.) Time and Logic - a Computational Approach. University College London Press, 249-277
15. Orłowska, E. (1996) Relational proof systems for modal logics. In: Wansing H. (Ed.) Proof Theory of Modal Logics. Kluwer, Dordrecht, 55-77
16. Rasiowa H., Sikorski R. (1963) The Mathematics of Metamathematics, PWN, Warsaw
17. Thomason S.K. (1978) Possible worlds and many truth values. Studia Logica, 37:195-204

Chapter 12
An Application of Standard BAO Theory to Some Abstract Information Algebras*

Eric SanJuan and Luisa Iturrioz

Laboratoire de Mathématiques Discrètes (EA 619)
Université Claude Bernard
Lyon 1 - Bât 101, 69622 Villeurbanne cedex - France
sanjuan@jonas.univ-lyon1.fr,
luisa@jonas.univ-lyon1.fr

Abstract. We show how methods that were introduced by B. Jónsson and A. Tarski in the paper "Boolean algebras with operators" (1951) are useful to develop representational mechanisms of some abstract algebraic structures related to uncertainty.
Keywords: Boolean algebras with operators, canonical extensions, relational structures, information systems, Kripke frames

1   Introduction and overview

Information Systems, as defined by Pawlak in [9], give rise to algebraic structures which are Boolean algebras of subsets of *objects* with additional operators parametrized by subsets of *attributes*.

These algebras and their derived relational structures were introduced by Ewa Orlowska in [8], under the name of Information Algebras (IAs) and Information Frames (IFs). They provide an abstract framework for modeling incomplete information in a nonnumerical way and enable us to reach the two levels of information: properties (set of objects) and individual entities (objects).

We showed in [12] that IAs which are defined within the two paradigms of incompleteness manifested by indiscernibility or orthogonality, are entirely determined by an Information Frame. This fact allowed us to propose an informational representation of these concrete type of IAs.

The characterization of IAs determined by their derived frame is recalled here in Section 2.

In this paper we consider the IAs defined in [8] which are not exactly characterized by their linked frame and we develop the duality theory for some of them. These structures are not directly derived from a concrete database; they are theoretical generalizations. Duality theory between Boolean algebras

---

* Research realized in the framework of COST Action n# 15 (in Informatics) "Many-Valued Logics for Computer Science Applications"

with operators (BAOs) and relational structures is an important issue of the BAO theory introduced by B. Jónsson and A. Tarski in [6].

Following some methods in this theory, we consider in Section 3 canonical extensions of IAs. We base the definitions of these extensions on Stone duality to make explicit the links between constructions defined by B. Jónsson and A. Tarski, and those considered in the paragraph entitled Preliminaries of Duality Theory for IAs in [8].

In the last section, powerful results on identities preserved by canonical extensions in [6], are applied to some IAs.

2   Complete information algebras

This section is devoted to the duality issue between Information Algebras with complete operators and Information Frames.

General terminology. We will call **operator** any unary function on a Boolean algebra and any Boolean algebra with such operators will be referred to as a **BAO**. If the operators are normal and additive we will say that the BAO is **standard**.

Let B a complete Boolean algebra and $X \subseteq B$, we will denote $\sum X$ the least upper bound of X and $\prod X$ the greatest lower bound.

If f is an operator on B, we will denote by $f(X)$ the set $\{f(x) : x \in X\}$ and we will say that f is: **normal** iff $f(0) = 0$; **co-integral** iff $f(1) = 0$; **(completely) additive** iff for any finite (infinite) X: $f(\sum X) = \sum f(X)$; **(completely) co-multiplicative** iff for any finite (infinite) X: $f(\prod X) = \sum f(X)$; **complete** iff f is completely additive or completely co-multiplicative.
□

Ob-Algebras and Ob-Frames. Let Ob be a *nonempty* set of objects and Att a *finite* set of attributes. We will denote by $\wp(Ob)$ the complete and atomic Boolean algebra $B = (2^{Ob}, \cap, \cup, \neg, \emptyset, Ob)$ and by At_B the set of its atoms (i.e. the singletons). For any $P \subseteq Att$, let f_P be an operator on $\wp(Ob)$ and R_P a binary relation on Ob.

By Ob-**Algebra** we mean any BAO of the form:

$$\Delta = (\wp(Ob), \{f_P : P \subseteq Att\})$$

and by Ob-**Frame** any frame:

$$K = (Ob, \{R_P : P \subseteq Att\})$$

Let $\Delta = (\wp(Ob), \{f_P : P \subseteq Att\})$ be an Ob-Algebra. If for any $P \subseteq Att$, f_P is normal (respectively: additive, co-integral, co-multiplicative, complete) then Δ will be called normal (respectively: additive, co-integral, co-multiplicative, complete).

Information Algebras. Let Δ be an Ob-Algebra. We will denote by $\Delta\neg$ the Ob-Algebra $(\wp(Ob), \{f_{P\neg} : P \subseteq Att\})$.

Following [8] we define various classes of Ob-Algebras in an abstract way.

We say that Δ is **weak** if for any subset X of Ob we have $f_\emptyset(X) = \emptyset$ and $(\forall P, Q \subseteq Att)\ f_{P\cup Q}(X) = f_P(X) \cup f_Q(X)$.

We say that Δ is **strong** if for any *nonempty* subset X of Ob we have $f_\emptyset(X) = Ob$ and for any *singleton* $X = \{x\}$ of Ob we have $(\forall P, Q \subseteq Att)$ $f_{P\cup Q}(X) = f_P(X) \cap f_Q(X)$.

Moreover, following [8], we define four subclasses of Ob-Algebras. Thus Δ is:

- in **WN** iff Δ is weak normal and additive;
- in **SCN** iff $\Delta\neg \in WN$ (i.e. Δ is weak, co-integral and co-multiplicative);
- in **SN** iff Δ is strong normal and additive;
- in **WCN** iff $\Delta\neg \in SN$ (i.e. $\Delta\neg$ is strong, and Δ is co-integral and co-multiplicative).

By Information Algebra (**IA**) we mean any Ob-Algebra in one of the previous abstract subclasses.

In fact, the IA classes are characterized by the following statements, for any $P, Q \subseteq Att$,

$$\Delta \in WN \quad \text{iff} \quad \begin{cases} f_P \text{ is normal and additive} \\ (\forall x \in B)\ f_\emptyset(x) = 0 \\ (\forall x \in B)\ f_{P\cup Q}(x) = f_P(x) \cup f_Q(x) \end{cases}$$

$$\Delta \in SCN \quad \text{iff} \quad \begin{cases} f_P \text{ is co-integral and co-multiplicative} \\ (\forall x \in B)\ f_\emptyset(x) = 0 \\ (\forall x \in B)\ f_{P\cup Q}(x) = f_P(x) \cup f_Q(x) \end{cases}$$

$$\Delta \in SN \quad \text{iff} \quad \begin{cases} f_P \text{ is normal and additive} \\ (\forall x \in B)\ x \neq 0 \Rightarrow f_\emptyset(x) = 1 \\ (\forall x \in At_B)\ f_{P\cup Q}(x) = f_P(x) \cap f_Q(x) \end{cases}$$

$$\Delta \in WCN \quad \text{iff} \quad \begin{cases} f_P \text{ is co-integral and co-multiplicative} \\ (\forall x \in B)\ x \neq 1 \Rightarrow f_\emptyset(x) = 1 \\ (\forall x \in At_B)\ f_{P\cup Q}(\neg x) = f_P(\neg x) \cap f_Q(\neg x) \end{cases}$$

Information Frames. An Ob-frame K is called **strong** if $R_\emptyset = Ob^2$ and if for any $P, Q \subseteq Att$ we have $R_{P\cup Q} = R_P \cap R_Q$. An Ob-frame K is called **weak** if $R_\emptyset = \emptyset$ and if for any $P, Q \subseteq Att$ we have $R_{P\cup Q} = R_P \cup R_Q$. We will denote by **FS** the class of *strong frames* and by **FW** the class of *weak frames*. By Information Frame (**IF**) we mean any strong or weak frame.

Let Δ be an Ob-Algebra. We derive the following IFs:

$$|\Delta| = (Ob, \{|f_P| : P \subseteq Att\}) \quad \text{and} \quad \|\Delta\| = (Ob, \{\|f_P\| : P \subseteq Att\})$$

where the binary relations denoted by $|f_P|$ and $\|f_P\|$ respectively, are defined for any $x, y \in Ob$ by

$$x|f_P|y \iff x \in f_p(\{y\}) \quad \text{and} \quad x\|f_P\|y \iff x \notin f_p(\neg\{y\}) \tag{1}$$

Concrete IAs from frames. Let K be an IF. We will denote by $\langle K \rangle$ the Ob-Algebra $(\wp(Ob), \{\langle R_P \rangle : P \subseteq \text{Att}\})$ and by $\langle\!\langle K \rangle\!\rangle$ the Ob-Algebra $(\wp(Ob), \{\langle\!\langle R_P \rangle\!\rangle : P \subseteq \text{Att}\})$ where the operators $\langle R_P \rangle$ and $\langle\!\langle R_P \rangle\!\rangle$ on $\wp(Ob)$ are defined for any $y \in Ob$ and $X \subseteq Ob$ by

$$y \in \langle R_P \rangle(X) \iff (\exists x \in X)\, y R_P x \tag{2}$$
$$y \in \langle\!\langle R_P \rangle\!\rangle(X) \iff (\exists z \notin X)\, y(\neg R_P)z \iff y \in \langle \neg R_P \rangle(\neg X) \tag{3}$$

Proposition 1. *Let R be a binary relation on a nonempty set Ob. Then*

1. $R = |\langle R \rangle| = \|\langle\!\langle R \rangle\!\rangle\|$,
2. $\langle R \rangle$ *is normal and completely additive,*
3. $\langle\!\langle R \rangle\!\rangle$ *is co-integral and completely co-multiplicative.*

Proof. By way of example we prove $\|\langle\!\langle R \rangle\!\rangle\| = R$ and Item 3.

For any $(x, y) \in Ob^2$, we obtain the following equivalent conditions:

$$
\begin{aligned}
(x, y) \notin \|\langle\!\langle R \rangle\!\rangle\| &\iff x \in \langle\!\langle R \rangle\!\rangle(\neg\{y\}) \\
&\iff (\exists z \notin \neg\{y\})\, x(\neg R)z \\
&\iff (\exists z \in \{y\})\, x(\neg R)z \\
&\iff (x, y) \notin R
\end{aligned}
$$

Observe that an operator f on $\wp(Ob)$ is completely co-multiplicative iff for any $X \subseteq Ob$, $f(X) = \bigcup_{x \notin X} f(\neg\{x\})$, since $X = \bigcap_{x \notin X} \neg\{x\}$.

Thus to show Item 3, let $X \subseteq Ob$ and $R \subseteq Ob^2$. If $X = Ob$ then by definition $\langle\!\langle R \rangle\!\rangle(Ob) = \emptyset$, otherwise $\langle\!\langle R \rangle\!\rangle(X) = \bigcup_{x \notin X}\{y \in Ob : (y, x) \notin R\} = \bigcup_{x \notin X} \langle\!\langle R \rangle\!\rangle(\neg\{x\})$. So $\langle\!\langle R \rangle\!\rangle$ is co-integral and completely co-multiplicative. $\square$

Proposition 2. *Let $\Delta = (\wp(Ob), \{f_P : P \subseteq \text{Att}\})$ be an Ob-Algebra such that for any $P \subseteq \text{Att}$, f_P is a **complete** operator. Then*

1. f_P *is normal and additive iff $\langle|f_P|\rangle = f_P$,*
2. f_P *is co-integral and co-multiplicative iff $\langle\!\langle \|f_P\| \rangle\!\rangle = f_P$,*
3. $\Delta \in SN \iff |\Delta| \in FS$ *and* $\Delta \in WN \iff |\Delta| \in FW$,
4. $\Delta \in SCN \iff \|\Delta\| \in FS$ *and* $\Delta \in WCN \iff \|\Delta\| \in FW$.

Proof. By way of example we prove Item 2 and Item 4 for $\Delta \in WCN$. Let f_P, f_Q and $f_{P \cup Q}$ be three co-integral and complete co-multiplicative operators on $\wp(Ob)$.

For any $X \subseteq Ob$, we infer the following equivalent conditions:

$$
\begin{aligned}
x \in \langle\!\langle \|f_P\| \rangle\!\rangle (X) &\Longleftrightarrow (\exists z \notin X)\,(x, z) \notin \|f_P\| \\
&\Longleftrightarrow (\exists z \notin X)\, x \in f_P(\neg\{z\}) \\
&\Longleftrightarrow x \in \bigcup_{z \notin X} f_P(\neg\{z\}) \\
&\Longleftrightarrow x \in f_P(\bigcap_{z \notin X} \neg\{z\}) \\
&\qquad \text{by complete co-multiplicativity of } f_P \\
&\Longleftrightarrow x \in f_P(X)
\end{aligned}
$$

So $\langle\!\langle \|f_P\| \rangle\!\rangle = f_P$.

To prove the equivalence $\Delta \in WCN \Longleftrightarrow \|\Delta\| \in FW$, first observe that by definition, $\|f_\emptyset\| = \emptyset$ iff $(\forall x \in Ob)\, f_\emptyset(\neg\{x\}) = Ob$ iff $(\forall X \subseteq Ob)\, f_\emptyset(X) = Ob$ by complete co-multiplicativity.

We also have to prove that: (a) $(\forall x \in Ob)\, f_{P \cup Q}(\neg\{x\}) = f_P(\neg\{x\}) \cap f_Q(\neg\{x\})$ holds iff (b) $\|f_{P \cup Q}\| = \|f_P\| \cup \|f_Q\|$ holds.

By way of example we show that if (a) holds then (b) holds.

For any $(y, x) \in Ob^2$, the following equivalent conditions hold:

$$
\begin{aligned}
(y, x) \in \|f_{P \cup Q}\| &\Longleftrightarrow y \notin f_{P \cup Q}(\neg\{x\}) \\
&\Longleftrightarrow y \notin f_P(\neg\{x\}) \cap f_Q(\neg\{x\}) \text{ by hypothesis} \\
&\Longleftrightarrow y \notin f_P(\neg\{x\}) \text{ or } y \notin f_Q(\neg\{x\}) \\
&\Longleftrightarrow (y, x) \in \|f_P\| \text{ or } (y, x) \in \|f_Q\| \\
&\Longleftrightarrow (y, x) \in \|f_P\| \cup \|f_Q\|
\end{aligned}
$$

$\square$

In [12], and using [6], we have noted that IAs derived from Information Frames, as well as those where operators verify $f(x) \wedge y = 0 \Longleftrightarrow x \wedge f(y) = 0$, are complete. But we will see in next section that abstract IAs are not in general complete.

3   Canonical extensions of information algebras

Proposition 2 in Section 2 requires operators to be **complete**. In the general case, there is a construction given by Bjarni Jónsson and Alfred Tarski [6], to embed any standard BAO into a complete and atomic one with complete operators, called the "perfect extension" in [6] and the "canonical extension" in [4]. The authors of [6] restrict their study to additive operators, but part of their study can be easily extended to co-multiplicative operators, as we will see hereafter.

We introduce some usual notations.

Let $(P, \leq)$ be a poset. We will denote by $\uparrow p$ the subset $\{q \in P : p \leq q\}$. In particular if the poset is $(2^{Ob}, \subseteq)$, where Ob is a nonempty set, then for any $x \in Ob$, $\uparrow \{x\} = \{X \subseteq Ob : x \in X\}$ (i.e. the collection of subsets of Ob containing x) is an ultrafilter of $\wp(Ob)$.

Let $B = (B, \wedge, \vee, \neg, 0, 1)$ be a Boolean algebra. We will denote by At_B the set of the atoms of B, by U_B the set of the ultrafilters, by s the Stone isomorphism, by $\mathcal{T}_B$ the Stone topology on U_B, by C_B the closed sets and by $B^s = \{s(x)\}_{x \in B}$ the clopen sets of U_B according to $\mathcal{T}_B$. By definition, the *canonical extension* of B is $\widehat{B} = \wp(U_B)$. Recall that for any $x \in B$, $s(x)$ is the set of all ultrafilters of B containing x and $s(1) = U_B$. Note that for each atom a of B, $s(a) = \{\uparrow a\}$ and then $s(a)$ is also an atom of $\widehat{B}$. We also have that each atom of $\widehat{B}$ is the meet of elements of B^s. As B^s is a base of $(U_B, \mathcal{T}_B)$, the open sets are the join of elements of B^s, and the closed sets, the meets. If B is a complete and atomic Boolean algebra, as will be the case here, then $s(At_B)$ is a dense subset of $(U_B, \mathcal{T}_B)$.

If f is an operator on B, then we will denote f^s the operator on B^s defined by $f^s = s \cdot f \cdot s^{-1}$ and f^+, $f^\times$ the extensions of f that will be defined below following B. Jónsson and A. Tarski. If f is isotone then f^s is also isotone.

In [6], f^s is denoted f because the authors identify B and $s(B)$.

The operators defined on a complete and atomic Boolean algebra (such as $\widehat{B}$) are not necessarily complete as it is shown by the following example.

Example 1. Let $(\widehat{B}, f)$ be the canonical extension of a complete and atomic Boolean algebra B and f defined on $\widehat{B} = \wp(U_B)$ in the following way:

$$X \subseteq U_B \xmapsto{f} s(\Sigma\{a \in At_B : s(a) \subseteq X\})$$

If B is infinite, then f is not complete since $f(\bigcup_{a \in At_B} s(a)) = U_B \neq \bigcup_{a \in At_B} f(s(a))$.

Another example is the following. Let B be any infinite complete and atomic Boolean algebra and $f : B \to B$ any Boolean homomorphism that has a kernel which is nonprincipal.

Definition 1 (Canonical extensions). Let $\Delta = (B, \{f_P : P \subseteq Att\})$ be an *Ob*-Algebra. We will denote by Δ^+ and $\Delta^\times$ the *Ob*-Algebras :

$$(\widehat{B}, \{f_P^+ : P \subseteq Att\}) \quad \text{and} \quad (\widehat{B}, \{f_P^\times : P \subseteq Att\})$$

respectively, where for any $P \subseteq Att$ and $X \subseteq U_B$,

$$f_P^+(X) = \bigcup_{u \in X} \bigcap_{x \in u} s \cdot f_P(x) \tag{4}$$

$$f_P^\times(X) = \bigcup_{u \notin X} \bigcap_{x \notin u} s \cdot f_P(x) = (f_{P\neg})^+(\neg X) \tag{5}$$

As a union of any empty family of sets is empty, we have that for any operator f_P, f_P^+ is normal and $f_P^\times$ is co-integral. In [6], f_P^+ is defined in an abstract and more general way. The following lemma links both definitions when f_P is normal and additive.

Lemma 1. *For any BAO $\Delta = (B, f)$, where f is a unary normal additive operator we have, for any $X \subseteq U_B$ the following equality:*

$$f^+(X) = \bigcup_{Y \subseteq X, Y \in C_B} \bigcap_{Z \supseteq Y, Z \in B^s} f^s(Z)$$

Proof. We have to prove

$$\bigcup_{u \in X} \bigcap_{x \in u} s \cdot f(x) = \bigcup_{Y \subseteq X, Y \in C_B} \bigcap_{Z \supseteq Y, Z \in B^s} f^s(Z)$$

This equality follows directly from equation (1) in the proof of Theorem 2.4 in [6]. However, as f is unary, the proof can be simplified as follows.

If $X = \emptyset$ then the result is true. If u is an ultrafilter and $s(x)$ is the set of all the ultrafilters containing x, we have that :

$$\begin{aligned}
\{s \cdot f(x) : x \in u\} &= \{s \cdot f(x) : u \in s(x)\} \\
&= \{f^s(s(x)) : u \in s(x)\} \\
&= \{f^s(Z) : u \in Z, Z \in B^s\} \\
&= \{f^s(Z) : Z \supseteq \{u\}, Z \in B^s\}
\end{aligned}$$

So we only need to prove

$$\bigcup_{u \in X} \bigcap_{Z \supseteq \{u\}, Z \in B^s} f^s(Z) = \bigcup_{Y \subseteq X, Y \in C_B} \bigcap_{Z \supseteq Y, Z \in B^s} f^s(Z) \tag{6}$$

If $X \neq \emptyset$ and $u \in X$ then

$$\bigcap_{Z \supseteq \{u\}, Z \in B^s} f^s(Z) \subseteq \bigcup_{Y \subseteq X, Y \in C_B} \bigcap_{Z \supseteq Y, Z \in B^s} f^s(Z)$$

because $\{u\}$ is closed, so

$$\bigcup_{u \in X} \bigcap_{Z \supseteq \{u\}, Z \in B^s} f^s(Z) \subseteq \bigcup_{Y \subseteq X, Y \in C_B} \bigcap_{Z \supseteq Y, Z \in B^s} f^s(Z)$$

To prove the converse, let us remark that for any a in U_B, a is not in the first member of (6) iff for any $u \in X$ there exists $Z_u \in B^s$ such that $u \in Z_u$ and $a \notin f^s(Z_u)$. For any closed set $Y \subseteq X$, since $Y \subseteq \bigcup_{v \in Y} Z_v$, we can deduce by compactness that there is a finite set $S \subseteq Y$ such that $Y \subseteq \bigcup_{v \in S} Z_v$. Since $\bigcup_{v \in S} Z_v \in B^s$ and f is additive, we have that $u \notin \bigcup_{v \in S} f^s(Z_v)$ iff $u \notin f^s\left(\bigcup_{v \in S} Z_v\right)$. Thus taking $Z_a = \bigcup_{v \in S} Z_v$, we have found for any closed set $Y \subseteq X$, a clopen set Z_a such that $Y \subseteq Z_a$ and $a \notin f^s(Z_a)$, which proves that a is not in the second member of (6). $\square$

The following proposition, which can also be deduced from Lemma 1 and [6] (Theorems 2.3 and 2.4), shows that the canonical extensions introduced in Definition 1 satisfy the property of being complete as required by Proposition 2.

Proposition 3. *Assume that $\Delta = (B, \{f_P : P \subseteq Att\})$ is an IA, $P \subseteq Att$ and $x \in B$. Then*

1. *if $\Delta \in WN \cup SN$ then f_P^+ is completely additive and $f_P^+ \cdot s(x) = s \cdot f_P(x)$.*
2. *if $\Delta \in SCN \cup WCN$ then $f_P^\times$ is completely co-multiplicative and $f_P^\times \cdot s(x) = s \cdot f_P(x)$.*

Proof. By way of example we show Item 1. f_P^+ is completely additive since we have, for any $X \subseteq U_B$,

$$f_P^+(X) = \bigcup_{u \in X} \bigcap_{x \in u} s \cdot f_P(x) = \bigcup_{u \in X} \bigcup_{u \in \{u\}} \bigcap_{x \in u} s \cdot f_P(x) = \bigcup_{u \in X} f_P^+(\{u\})$$

We show now the equality $f_P^+ \cdot s(x) = s \cdot f_P(x)$ for any $x \in B$. Since $s(x) \in C_B$ and f_P is isotone we have, by Lemma 1,

$$f_P^+(s(x)) = \bigcap_{Z \supseteq s(x), Z \in B^s} f_P^s(Z)$$

But

$$\bigcap_{Z \supseteq s(x), Z \in B^s} f_P^s(Z) = f_P^s(s(x)) = s \cdot f_P(x)$$

since $s(x) \in B^s$ and f_P^s is isotone.   □

The following result will be used later.

Corollary 1. *Let $\Delta = (B, \{f_P : P \subseteq Att\})$ be an IA, $P \subseteq Att$ and $X \subseteq U_B$. If $\Delta \in WN$ then $f_\emptyset^+(X) = \emptyset$ and if $\Delta \in SCN$ then $f_\emptyset^\times(X) = \emptyset$.*

Proof. By way of example we prove the first assertion.

If $\Delta \in WN$ then for any $x \in B$, $f_\emptyset(x) = 0$ and by Definition 1 we have, for any $u \in U_B$, $f_\emptyset^+(\{u\}) = \bigcap_{x \in u} s \cdot f_\emptyset(x) = \bigcap_{x \in u} s(0) = \emptyset$. As $f_\emptyset^+$ is completely additive (Proposition 3) we obtain $f_\emptyset^+(X) = \bigcup_{u \in X} f_\emptyset^+(\{u\}) = \emptyset$.   □

Proposition 3 allows us to derive, from any IA Δ, in two steps, an Information Frame K such that Δ can be embedded into $\langle K \rangle$ or $\langle\!\langle K \rangle\!\rangle$. We will say that K is a **frame representation** of Δ. The first step consists in extending Δ into a complete algebra and the second in applying Proposition 2. In the case of a standard BAO $\Delta = (B, f)$, the frame representation is $|\Delta^+| = (U_B, |f^+|)$.

Note that least upper bounds and greatest lower bounds of infinite sets in B differ from the corresponding set theoretic unions and intersections in $\widehat{B}$ by a nowhere dense set (for more details see Sect. 21 in [3]).

Proposition 4. *Assume that $\Delta = (B, \{f_P : P \subseteq Att\})$ is an Ob-Algebra and $u, v \in U_B$. Then*

$$u|f_P^+|v \iff (\forall x \in v)(f_P(x) \in u) \quad and \quad u\|f_P^\times\|v \iff (\exists x \notin v)(f_P(x) \notin u)$$

Proof. By way of example we prove $u\|f_P^\times\|v \iff (\exists x \notin v)(f_P(x) \notin u)$.
For any $u, v \in U_B$, the following equivalent conditions hold:

$$(u, v) \in \|f_P^\times\| \iff u \notin f_P^\times(\neg\{v\}) \text{ by (1)}$$
$$\iff u \notin \bigcap_{x \notin v} s(f_P(x)) \text{ by Definition 1}$$
$$\iff (\exists x \notin v) \, f_P(x) \notin u$$

$\square$

Proposition 5 (Links to Kripke semantics). *For any IA $\Delta = (B, \{f_P : P \subseteq Att\})$, $P \subseteq Att$ and $x \in B$, then*

1. *if Δ is in $WN \cup SN$ then $f_P(x) = 1$ iff for any ultrafilter (i.e. a possible world) u of B there is an ultrafilter v of B containing x (i.e. a possible world where x is true) such that $u\|f_P^+\|v$.*
2. *if Δ is in $SCN \cup WCN$ then $f_P(x) = 1$ iff for any ultrafilter u of B there is an ultrafilter v of B not containing x such that not $u\|f_P^\times\|v$.*

Proof. By way of example we prove that if f is a co-integral and co-multiplicative operator on B (this is verified if $\Delta \in SCN \cup WCN$), then we ought to have for any $x \in B$, $f_P(x) = 1$ iff $(\forall u \in U_B)(\exists v \notin s(x)) \, (u, v) \notin \|f^\times\|$.
In fact, for any $x \in B$, we have $f(x) = 1$ iff $s(f(x)) = U_B$ iff $f^\times(s(x)) = U_B$ by Proposition 3, and as :

$$f^\times(s(x)) = f^\times(\bigcap_{v \notin s(x)} \neg\{v\}) = \bigcup_{v \notin s(x)} f^\times(\neg\{v\})$$

by complete co-multiplicativity of $f^\times$, it follows that $f(x) = 1$ iff $(\forall u \in U_B)$ $u \in f^\times(s(x))$ iff $(\forall u \in U_B) \, (\exists v \notin s(x)) \, u \in f^\times(\neg\{v\})$. This completes the proof.
$\square$

Canonical extensions of Information Frames could also be considered. The extension of an IF $K = (Ob, \{R_P : P \subseteq Att\})$ is $|\langle K \rangle^+| = (U_{\wp(Ob)}, \{|\langle R_P \rangle^+| : P \subseteq Att\})$ and verifies:

$$x R_P y \iff \uparrow\{x\}|\langle R_P \rangle^+|\uparrow\{y\}$$

So there is a one-to-one embedding from K into $|\langle K \rangle^+|$.

For any $P \subseteq Ob$, let R_P^s be the binary relation on $\{\uparrow\{x\} : x \in Ob\}$ defined by $\uparrow\{x\} \, (R_P^s) \, \uparrow\{y\}$ iff $x R_P y$. As R_P^s is a subset of $U_{\wp(Ob)} \times U_{\wp(Ob)}$, we can define the topological closure $\overline{R_P^s}$ of R_P^s in the $\mathcal{T}_{\wp(Ob)} \times \mathcal{T}_{\wp(Ob)}$ topology.
We recall from [5] the following result.

Theorem 1. *Let R be a binary relation on a set Ob, we have:*

$$|\langle R \rangle^+| = \overline{R^s}$$

4   Identities preserved by canonical extensions

The work presented in [6] should not be reduced to the above constructions. We introduce the main result proved by B. Jónsson and A. Tarski concerning the identities preserved by canonical extensions. Such identities are called **canonical**. Theorem 2 below follows from Theorem 2.18 in [6] proved by B. Jónsson and A. Tarski.

Theorem 2. *Let Δ be an IA in $WN \cup SN$. Then every identity that holds in Δ and does not involve complementation, holds in Δ^+.*

The proof of the powerful Theorem 2.18 of [6] requires that the canonical extension of any additive function with a finite number of arguments is also completely additive on each of its arguments. This generalization was proved in [6] for standard BAOs and used by Hugo Ribeiro [11] to show that: if f is an additive function on each of its n arguments (n being an integer), and if $h_1 \cdots h_n$ are n isotone functions, then the canonical extension of $f(h_1 \cdots h_n)$ is $f^+(h_1^+ \cdots h_n^+)$ [1]

Corollary 2. *Let Δ be an Ob-Algebra, then Δ is in WN iff $|\Delta^+|$ is in FW and Δ is in SCN iff $\|\Delta^\times\|$ is in FS.*

Proof. Let $\Delta = (B, \{f_A : A \subseteq Att\})$ be in WN such that $B = \wp(Ob)$, for some Ob.

Since Δ^+ is a complete BAO, Proposition 2 implies that $|\Delta^+|$ is in FW iff Δ^+ is in WN.

By Proposition 3 and Corollary 1 we just need to show that operators in Δ^+ verify for any $X \subseteq U_B$, $f_{P \cup Q}^+(X) = f_P^+(X) \cup f_Q^+(X)$ as required by definitions in Section 2. Since this equality does not involve complementation it follows from Theorem 2.

Concerning the second assertion, we remark that $f_P^\times(X) = (f_P \neg)^+(\neg X)$. We show by way of example that Δ is in SCN iff $\|\Delta^\times\|$ is in FS.

First we obtain $\|f_\emptyset^\times\| = U_B^2$, as a consequence of the following equivalences: $(u, v) \in \|f_\emptyset^\times\|$ iff $u \notin f_\emptyset^\times(\neg\{v\})$ iff $u \notin \emptyset$ by Corollary 1.

To prove $\|f_{P \cup Q}^\times\| = \|f_P^\times\| \cap \|f_Q^\times\|$, for any $P, Q \subseteq Att$, let us remark that $\forall X \subseteq Ob$,

$$f_{P \cup Q}(X) = f_P(X) \cup f_Q(X) \iff f_{P \cup Q}(\neg X) = f_P(\neg X) \cup f_Q(\neg X) \quad (7)$$

Since for any $P \subseteq Att$, $f_P \neg$ is a normal additive operator we deduce by Theorem 2:

---

[1] A direct proof of Ribeiro's lemma in the general context of bounded distributive lattices with operators can be found in [2].

$(7) \iff (\forall X \subseteq U_B)\,(f_{P \cup Q}\neg)^+(X) = (f_P\neg)^+(X) \cup (f_Q\neg)^+(X)$
$\qquad \iff (\forall X \subseteq U_B)\,(f_{P \cup Q}\neg)^+(\neg X) = (f_P\neg)^+(\neg X) \cup (f_Q\neg)^+(\neg X)$
$\qquad \iff (\forall X \subseteq U_B)\, f_{P \cup Q}^{\times}(X) = f_P^{\times}(X) \cup f_Q^{\times}(X)$
$\qquad \iff \|f_{P \cup Q}^{\times}\| = \|f_P^{\times}\| \cap \|f_Q^{\times}\|$

$\square$

We cannot deduce a similar result for IAs in SN or WCN because identities true for any atom in At_B, are not necessarily true for any atom in $At_{\widetilde{B}}$.

Indeed, let Ob be a countable set of objects and consider the following operator φ on $\wp(Ob)$ defined by: $\varphi(X) = \emptyset$ if X is a *finite* subset of Ob and $\varphi(X) = Ob$ otherwise. φ is normal and additive. Let Ω be an ultrafilter of $\wp(Ob)$ containing all the co-finite subsets of Ob (for the existence of such ultrafilter see for example Exercice 9.9 in [1]). The atoms of $s(\wp(Ob))$ are the images of the singletons $\{x\}$. For any $\{x\} \in At_{\wp(Ob)}$, we have $\varphi(\{x\}) = \emptyset$, but for $\{\Omega\} \in At_{\widetilde{\wp(Ob)}}$, $\varphi^+(\{\Omega\}) = U_{\wp(Ob)}$ by Definition 1.

A consequence of Theorem 2 is that identities $x \le f(x)$, $f^2(x) \le f(x)$, and $f(x) \wedge y = 0 \iff x \wedge f(y) = 0$ are canonical, for any additive operator f [6].

This is because $x \le y$ is equivalent to $x = x \wedge y$, and $f(x) \wedge y = 0 \Rightarrow x \wedge f(y) = 0$ is equivalent to $\chi(f(x) \wedge y) \vee (x \wedge f(y)) = \chi(f(x) \wedge y)$, where for any $x \in B$, $\chi(x) = 0$ if $x = 0$ and $\chi(x) = 1$ otherwise (observe that χ is a normal and additive operator).

Since $f^{\times} = (f\neg)^+\neg$, we deduce that identities $\neg x \le f(x)$, $f\neg f(x) \le f(x)$, and $f(x) \le y \iff f(y) \le x$ are also canonical, for any co-integral and co-multiplicative operator f.

Indeed, observe that $f\neg$ is an additive operator and that we have the following equivalences:

1. $(\forall x \in B)\neg x \le f(x)$ iff $(\forall x \in B)x \le (f\neg)(x)$
2. $(\forall x \in B)f\neg f(x) \le f(x)$ iff $(\forall x \in B)(f\neg)^2(x) \le (f\neg)(x)$
3. $(\forall x, y \in B)f(x) \le y \iff f(y) \le x$
   iff $(\forall x, y \in B)f(x) \wedge \neg y = 0 \iff f(y) \wedge \neg x = 0$
   iff $(\forall x, y \in B)(f\neg)(x) \wedge y = 0 \iff (f\neg)(y) \wedge x = 0$

In [12], we proposed an algebraic characterization of specific Information Frames defined in [8], based on these identities.

Following [7], we will exhibit a simple example where an identity involving only one complementation and some unary operators is not preserved by canonical extension. The complementation is a particular co-integral and co-multiplicative unary operator, so a general result similar to Theorem 2 cannot be expected for BAOs where operators are co-integral and co-multiplicative, like in algebras from classes SCN and WCN.

Example 2. Let us consider the following Boolean algebra with two normal and additive operators $\wp(Z) = (2^Z, \cap, \cup, \neg, \emptyset, Z, \chi, \tau_2)$ and the inequality

$$\chi(\neg X) \cap X \subseteq \chi(\tau_2(X) \triangle X) \tag{8}$$

where Z is the set of integers $\{\cdots, -i, \cdots, -1, 0, 1, 2, \cdots, j, j+1, \cdots\}$ and for any $X \subseteq Z$: $\chi(X) = \emptyset$ if $X = \emptyset$ and $\chi(X) = Z$ otherwise; $\tau_2(X) = \{i + 2 : i \in X\}$; $X \triangle Y = (X \cap \neg Y) \cup (\neg X \cap Y)$.

Let $FC(Z)$ be the subalgebra of $\wp(Z)$ of finite or co-finite subsets of Z (Note that $FC(Z)$ is atomic but incomplete). The canonical extension $\widehat{FC(Z)}$ of $FC(Z)$ is $\wp(\{\uparrow\{i\} : i \in Z\} \cup \{\omega\})$ where ω is the ultrafilter of all co-finite subsets of Z (see for example [10, p. 66]). Then (8) is an identity of $FC(Z)$ but not an identity of $\wp(Z)$ (take $\{2i : i \in Z\}$ as X). Also identity (8) is satisfied on $s(FC(Z))$ but fails for the element $\bigcup_{i \in Z} s(\{2i\}) \in \widehat{FC(Z)}$.

5   General conclusion

The BAO theory developed by B. Jónsson and A. Tarski gives us the right framework to work within the paradigms of duality and representation. The reasons are both in the algebraic and logical fields. Indeed, this theory provides us with a way to embed any IA into a complete, atomic, compact and separated Boolean algebra with complete operators. We also suggested in Proposition 5 how standard completeness theorem on Kripke semantics for Modal Logics could have been deduced from standard BAO theory. Finally, we would like to recall that Theorem 2.18 in [6] on canonical identities also allows a simple proof of the canonicity of Sahlqvist identities as well as other non-Sahlqvist identities, as shown in [5].

Acknowledgment
We would like to thank the referees for helpful remarks and suggestions.

References

1. Davey B.A., Priestley H.A. (1990) Introduction to Lattices and Order. Cambridge University Press
2. Gehrke M., Jónsson B. (1994) Bounded Distributive Lattices with Operators. Mathematica Japonica 40:207-215
3. Halmos P.R. (1963) Lectures on Boolean algebras. D. Van Nostrand Company
4. Jónsson B. (1991) A Survey of Boolean Algebras with Operators. In: Rosenberg I.G. and Sabidussi G. (Eds.) Algebras and Orders, Kluwer Academic Publishers, Dordrecht, 239-284
5. Jónsson B. (1994) On the Canonicity of Sahlqvist Identities. Studia Logica 53:473-491
6. Jónsson B., Tarski A. (1951-1952) Boolean algebras with operators I and II. American Journal of Mathematics 73:891-939, 74:127-162

7. Kramer R., Maddux R. (1982) Equations not preserved by complete extensions. Algebra Universalis 15:86-89
8. Orlowska E. (1995) Information Algebras, LNCS 936:50-65
9. Pawlak Z. (1991) Rough Sets. Kluwer Academic Publishers, Dordrecht
10. Ponasse D., Carrega J-C. (1979) Algèbre et topologie Booléennes. Masson, Paris
11. Ribeiro H. (1952) A remark on Boolean Algebras with operators, American Journal of Mathematics 74:163-167
12. SanJuan E., Iturrioz L. (1998) Duality and Informational Representability of some Information Algebras. In: Polkowski L. and Skowron A. (Eds.) Rough Sets in Knowledge Discovery, Methodology and Applications, Physica-Verlag, Heidelberg, 233-247

Part V

Theories of Relations

Chapter 13
Proof Systems in Relation Algebra

Lev Gordeev

Tübingen University
WSI für Informatik, Logik und Sprachtheorie
Köstlinstr. 6, D-72074 Tübingen, Germany
gordeev@informatik.uni-tuebingen.de

Abstract. We expose two different notions of validity in relation algebras: one is based on Tarski's equational calculus (say, 'T-validity'), and the other arises by the canonical 1-order translation from the ordinary semantic validity (say, 't-validity'). In the first section we characterize both validities via provability in finite-variable logics and the corresponding cutfree derivability in formula-rewriting 1-order systems. In the second section we characterize T-validity via derivability in a suitable cutfree term-rewriting system in the basic algebraic language, which is equivalent to the algebraic display calculus of Gore. In the third section we address 1-order 2-variable decidability and validity using both methods.
Keywords: relational algebra, proof theory, term rewriting systems

1 Relation algebra and finite-variable logic

1.1 Background

Following [20], consider the language $\mathcal{L}$ of relation algebras that contains basic (binary) relations $X_1, ..., X_n$ and basic algebraic operations $+, ^-, ^\cup, \odot, 1$, $\overset{\circ}{1}$ (*boolean sum, negation, conversion, relative product, boolean unity, relative identity*). Below, for purely typographical reasons, we rename $\overset{\circ}{1}$ by !. In $\mathcal{L}$, *terms* (abbr.: A, B, C, D, S, W) are built up as usual in algebra, and equations are expressions $A = B$ where A, B are arbitrary terms. There are two basic concepts of validity of $A = B$ in $\mathcal{L}$:

(a) $A = B$ is valid iff it is derivable in Tarski's equational calculus for relation algebras, **RA**,

(b) $A = B$ is valid iff its canonical 1-order translation yields a valid formula, i.e., in other words, iff $A = B$ is true of all representable relation algebras.

For the sake of brevity, we'll refer to (a) and (b) as *Tarski's validity* (abbr.: *T-validity*) and *true validity* (abbr.: *t-validity*), respectively. Clearly, *T-validity* implies *t-validity*, and it is known that the converse fails, i.e. there are equations which are true of all representable algebras, but not all relation algebras (cf. e.g. [20] for precise references). That is to say, *T-validity* is stronger that *t-validity*. For obvious reasons, *t-validity* seems more important for applications, although *T-validity* is also remarkably strong. In particular,

RA is *relative complete*, i.e. complete modulo interpretation, and *4-variable complete*, on the other hand. This is expressed more precisely below.

1.2   Basic results

Theorem 1. *Let $\mathcal{L}^*$ extend $\mathcal{L}$ by adding two new basic relations P and Q. There is an algorithm μ^* correlating with any formula F of the 1-order language of $X_1, ..., X_n$ with equality a $\mathcal{L}^*$-term $\mu^*(F)$ such that F is valid iff $\mu^*(F) = 1$ is T-valid (in $\mathcal{L}^*$).*

Different variants of this theorem are (differently) proved in [20], [13], [6,7]. It should be noted that μ^* has exponential growth, since this holds true for the underlying translation from the 1-order into the algebraic language (cf. [20]). On the other hand, the reverse translations from the algebraic into the 1-order language have polynomial growth (cf. [20], [13], [6]).

In order to address the latter completeness, we'll briefly recall two basic 1-order finite-variable formalisms. Call *Tarski m-variable logic* the m-variable modus-ponens formalism used in [20]. Note that the equality is crucial in this formalism, e.g. in order to handle variable substitutions $[x/y]$. Moreover, the *general Leibniz law* $x = y \rightarrow (F \rightarrow F[x/y])$, for every formula F, is a crucial axiom (schema) of Tarski m-variable logic. Call *Hilbert-Bernays m-variable logic* a weaker modus-ponens formalism used e.g. in [6,8], in which the Leibniz law is postulated only for literals F, and whose equality-free reduct coincides with the corresponding m-variable restriction of the familiar Hilbert-Bernays 1-order formalism. By definition, both Tarski and Hilbert-Bernays m-variable logics include only m distinct inividual variables (whether free or bound). Now the 4-variable completeness in question is expressed by

Theorem 2. *A given $\mathcal{L}$-equation is T-valid iff its canonical 1-order 3-variable translation is provable in Tarski 4-variable logic of the 1-order language of $X_1, ..., X_n$ with equality.*

Theorem 2 is proved in [14]. According to [1], this result can be refined as follows.

Theorem 3. *A given !-free $\mathcal{L}$-equation is T-valid iff its canonical 1-order 3-variable translation is provable in Hilbert-Bernays 4-variable logic of the 1-order language of $X_1, ..., X_n$ without equality.*

Indeed, the !-free reduct of **RA** can be axiomatized by rewriting the identity axiom (VI) to

$$A \leqslant A \odot ((B^{\cup} \odot B^-) + (B^{-\cup} \odot B))^-$$

(cf. [1]) which along with the rest of **RA** axioms (see e.g. Definition 4 below) is easily provable in Hilbert-Bernays 4-variable logic without equality. In fact, this refinement holds true for the whole **RA**:

Theorem 4. *A given $\mathcal{L}$-equation is T-valid iff its canonical 1-order 3-variable translation is provable in Hilbert-Bernays 4-variable logic of the 1-order language of $X_1, ..., X_n$.*

This result follows by an observation that the general Leibniz law for 3-variable F is provable in Hilbert-Bernays 4-variable logic (see [7] and the proof of Theorem 12 below).

On the other hand, *t-validity* can be analogously characterized via *5-variable quasi-compactness* with respect to Tarski's *conjugated quasi-projections* (see [20] for the latter notion). This is a particular case $n = 3$ of the variable quasi-compactness theorem stating that $f(n) = n+2$ is the affirmative quasi-solution of the Open problem (a) posed in [11] (see [7]). The corresponding specification is as follows.

Theorem 5. *A given !-free $\mathcal{L}$-equation is t-valid iff its canonical 1-order 3-variable translation is provable in Hilbert-Bernays 5-variable logic of the 1-order language of $P, Q, X_1, ..., X_n$ without equality extended by the axiom expressing that P and Q are Tarski's conjugated quasi-projections.*

Theorem 6. *A given $\mathcal{L}$-equation is t-valid iff its canonical 1-order 3-variable translation is provable in Hilbert-Bernays 5-variable logic of the 1-order language of P, Q, $X_1, ..., X_n$ extended by the axiom expressing that P and Q are Tarski's conjugated quasi-projections.*

Remark 1. Unlike Theorem 1, the canonical translations of Theorems 2-6 do not essentially change the shape of a given equation. On the other hand, the shape of $\mu^*(F)$ from Theorem 1 differs essentially from the one of F, provided that F has more than 3 variables. In the latter case, a relevant improvement reads that a given n-variable formula F (with/without equality) is valid iff it is provable in Hilbert-Bernays $(n+2)$-variable logic of the corresponding $(n+2)$-variable language of P, Q, $X_1, ..., X_n$ (with/without equality) extended by the axiom expressing that P and Q are Tarski's conjugated quasi-projections. This is a Hilbert-Bernays-style variable quasi-compactness theorem stating that $f(n) = n + 2$ is the affirmative quasi-solution of the Open problem (a) posed in [11] (see [7])[1].

Theorems 2-6 yield proof theoretical characterizations of both T- and t-validity via provability in 1-order finite-variable logic. Besides, there is an obvious straightforward way to characterize *t-validity* via 1-order provability with the infinite supply of individual variables (see e.g. [4,5], [15,16]).

1.3 Cutfree derivability

Still, modus-ponens calculi do not admit natural proof search. However, we can use instead 4-variable cutfree *nested sequent calculi* (also called *reduction*

---

[1] I was unable to confirm [20] Theorem 4.8 (xvi) whose intended proof's unpublished clause (2) was irreparably defective.

calculi, see [6]-[8]) which admit quite reasonable proof search techniques (see [18,19]). These nested sequent calculi are Herbrand-style formula-rewriting proof systems. Note that the nested, non-deterministic character is essential for any cutfree formalization of finite variable logic, since Gentzen-style cut-free finite-variable sequent calculi are decidable (see [6]). In what follows we sketch basic definitions and results which (in slightly different notations) are established in [7,8].

Definition 1. For any $s, m > 0$, let $Y_1, ..., Y_m$ be a given list of predicate symbols whose arity does not exceed m. We fix the restricted *'positive'* 1-order language $\mathcal{L}_m^0$ with equality $=$, basic predicates $Y_1, ..., Y_m$, truth values $\top, \bot$, propositional connectives $\wedge, \vee, \neg$, quantifiers $\forall, \exists$ and individual variables $v_0, ..., v_{m-1}$ (abbr.: x, y, z). The formulas of $\mathcal{L}_m^0$ (abbr.: D, F, G, H) are now built up as usual in 1-order logic, except applying $\neg$ only to proper atoms, i.e. $Y_i(y_1, ..., y_j)$. As usual, we call literals (abbr.: L) both atoms and negated atoms. By $\mathcal{L}_m$ we'll denote the correlated full 1-order m-variable language with equality. It is well-known that $\mathcal{L}_m$ is embeddable into $\mathcal{L}_m^0$ (we omit the details); by F^0 we'll denote the resulting $\mathcal{L}_m^0$-counterpart of a given $\mathcal{L}_m$-formula F.

Definition 2. Working in the language $\mathcal{L}_m^0$, consider the formula-rewrite rules (1)-(15), below, where $x \neq y$ exposed in (13) stands for $\neg x = y$, while $[x/y]$ and (x/y) exposed in (10), (11), (13)-(15) are two different variable-substitutions. Namely, $F[x/y]$ denotes the result of substituting y for all free occurrences of x in F (while renaming by x all bound occurrences of y), whereas $L(x/y)$ denotes an arbitrary replacement of one or more occurrences of x by y in L.

(1) $F \vee G \hookrightarrow G \vee F$
(2) $F \vee (G \vee H) \hookrightarrow (F \vee G) \vee H$
(3) $F \vee (G \wedge H) \hookrightarrow (F \vee G) \wedge (F \vee H)$
(4) $F \hookrightarrow F \vee F$
(5) $\top \vee F \hookrightarrow \top$
(6) $\top \wedge F \hookrightarrow F$
(7) $L \vee \neg L \hookrightarrow \top$
(8) $\forall x D \hookrightarrow D$ [x not free in D]
(9) $\forall x F \vee \forall x G \hookrightarrow \forall x (F \vee \forall x G)$
(10) $F[x/y] \hookrightarrow \forall x F$
(11) $\exists x F \hookrightarrow F[x/y]$
(12) $x = x \hookrightarrow \top$
(13) $x \neq y \vee L \hookrightarrow L(x/y) \vee L(y/x)$
(14) $\neg P(z, x) \vee \neg P(z, y) \vee L \hookrightarrow L(x/y)$
(15) $\neg Q(z, x) \vee \neg Q(z, y) \vee L \hookrightarrow L(x/y)$

Definition 3. The nested sequent calculi in question are defined as follows. Denote by NL_m (m-variable nested logic) the system of formula-rewrite rules

(1)-(11). Let NLE_m (m-variable nested logic with equality) denote NL_m extended by (12), (13), let NLU_m (m-variable nested logic with uniformity) be NL_m extended by (14), (15), and let NLEU_m (m-variable nested logic with equality and uniformity) denote the whole system of formula-rewrite rules (1)-(15). The derivability in any system NX_m under consideration in defined as follows. Call a reduction in NX_m the relation $G \rightsquigarrow G'$ such that for some rewrite rule (i) $H \hookrightarrow H'$ from $\mathsf{NX}_m (1 \leqq i \leqq 15)$ it holds $G' = G[H := H']$, i.e. G' arises by rewriting to H' (=the contractum of (i)) a chosen positive (i.e. non-negated) occurrence of H (=the redex of (i)) in G. A formula F is called derivable in NX_m if $F \rightsquigarrow^* \top$ holds in NX_m, where as usual $\rightsquigarrow^*$ denotes the transitive closure of $\rightsquigarrow$. That is, F is derivable in NX_m if $F = \top$ or else there exists a finite 'reduction chain' $F = F_0 \rightsquigarrow F_1 \rightsquigarrow ... \rightsquigarrow F_k = \top$ of subsequent reductions in NX_m. Note that both $\hookrightarrow$ and $\rightsquigarrow$ informally express the reverse 1-order implication.

Theorem 7. *([8]) A given $\mathcal{L}_m$-formula F is provable in Hilbert-Bernays logic (without equality) of $\mathcal{L}_m$ iff F^0 is derivable in the corresponding calculus NLE_m (NL_m). Moreover, F is provable in Hilbert-Bernays logic (without equality) expressing the uniformity of P and Q iff F^0 is derivable in NLEU_m (NLU_m).*

Having this, Theorems 3-6 provide us with the following refinements, where by $\mathcal{L}_3^0$ ($\mathcal{L}_3^{*0}$) we denote the canonical 1-order positive 3-variable analogue of our basic algebraic language $\mathcal{L}$ ($\mathcal{L}^*$).

Theorem 8. *A given (!-free) $\mathcal{L}$-equation $A = B$ is $\top$-valid iff the canonical translation of the $\mathcal{L}$-term $((A + B^-)^- + (A^- + B)^-)^-$ into $\mathcal{L}_3^0$ is derivable in NLE_4 (NL_4).*

Theorem 9. *A given (!-free) $\mathcal{L}$-equation $A = B$ is t-valid iff the canonical translation of the $\mathcal{L}^*$-term $1 \odot (P^{\cup} \odot Q^- \odot 1) + ((A + B^-)^- + (A^- + B)^-)^-$ into $\mathcal{L}_3^{*0}$ is derivable in NLEU_4 (NLU_4).*

Indeed, $((A + B^-)^- + (A^- + B)^-)^-$ is the canonical term-analogue of $A = B$. Furthermore, $1 \odot (P^{\cup} \odot Q)^- \odot 1$ is semantically equivalent to *there exist x and y such that for all z, $\neg P(z,x) \vee \neg Q(z,y)$*, while the negation of the latter expression together with the uniformity of P and Q just says that P and Q are Tarski's conjugated quasi-projections (cf. e.g. [20]).

Remark 2. The contraction formula-rewrite rule (4) is not good for the nested proof search, since it may produce too many copies of the same formula F. However, it is possible to to get rid of (4), while simultaneously adding the principal left-hand (sub)formulas on the right-hand side of the proper logic rues (see [8]). Although nested sequent calculi are completely inderterministic, they admit natural proof strategies which, loosely speaking, assert that all rules should be applied to all subformulas, in any order and as long as possible.

2   Algebraic cutfree formalisms

Another, quite different idea was involved in the 'display calculus' $\delta\mathbf{RA}$ of Gore (see [9], [3]), being a Belnap-style cutfree calculus in the algebraic display-extension of the original language $\mathcal{L}$. The main result of [9] reads:

Theorem 10. *A given $\mathcal{L}$-equation is T-valid iff it is derivable in the cutfree fragment of $\delta\mathbf{RA}$.*

This theorem yields another proof theoretical characterization of *T-validity*. Note that the display translation of $\mathcal{L}$ requires new operations which increase the calculus' complexity and complicate the underlying proof search. In this section we show that it is possible to get rid of all these display operations thus pushing the solution back to the original language $\mathcal{L}$ – however, the resulting modified proof system will be nested. We'll designate this modification NRA (*nested relation algebra*) and prove that it has the same derivable $\mathcal{L}$-equations as $\delta\mathbf{RA}$. Hence by the previous theorem we'll arrive at the desired

Theorem 11. *A given $\mathcal{L}$-equation is T-valid iff it is derivable in NRA.*

Notably, a direct, i.e. omitting $\delta\mathbf{RA}$, proof that NRA is $\mathbf{RA}$-complete would be much more involved.

2.1   Descriptions

Definition 4. Recall that the axioms of $\mathbf{RA}$ are the following equations (I)-(X) (cf. e.g. [20]), while 1 is regarded as an abbreviation (say, of $!+!^-$).

$$
\begin{array}{ll}
\text{(I)} & A + B = B + A \\
\text{(II)} & A + (B + C) = (A + B) + C \\
\text{(III)} & (A^- + B)^- + (A^- + B^-)^- = A \\
\text{(IV)} & A \odot (B \odot C) = (A \odot B) \odot C \\
\text{(V)} & (A + B) \odot C = (A \odot C) + (B \odot C) \\
\text{(VI)} & A \odot ! = A \\
\text{(VII)} & A^{\cup\cup} = A \\
\text{(VIII)} & (A + B)^{\cup} = A^{\cup} + B^{\cup} \\
\text{(IX)} & (A \odot B)^{\cup} = B^{\cup} \odot A^{\cup} \\
\text{(X)} & A^{\cup} \odot (A \odot B)^- + B^- = B^-
\end{array}
$$

Definition 5. The definition of NRA consists of two parts. In the first part, we fix the restricted 'positive' variant $\mathcal{L}^0$ of $\mathcal{L}$, which has operations $+, \cdot, ^-, ^{\cup}, \odot, \oplus, 0, 1, ?, !$ ($\cdot, \oplus, 0, ?$ being dual to $+, \odot, 1, !$, respectively[2]), whose terms are built up as usual except applying $^{\cup}$ and $^-$ to X_i and to X_i or $X_i^{\cup}$, respectively

---

[2] Note that ? and ! designate $\mathring{0}$ and $\mathring{1}$ of [20]. Other familiar names for ? and ! are 0' and 1', respectively.

$(1 \leq i \leq n)$. The terms X_i or $X_i^{\cup}$ we'll abbreviate by L. The duality is understood as usual in algebra, i.e. the interpretation of $\cdot$ (boolean product), $\oplus$ (relative sum) and ? (relative difference) in $\mathcal{L}$ is $A \cdot B = (A^- + B^-)$, $A \oplus B = (A^- \odot B^-)^-$ and ? = !$^-$. Let $\mathcal{L}^1$ denote the language extending both $\mathcal{L}$ and $\mathcal{L}^0$ and being closed under all operations involved. The notions of T- and t-validity are specified accordingly.

Lemma 1. *Every $\mathcal{L}^1$-term A reduces to the uniquely determined positive normal form A^0 in $\mathcal{L}^0$ by applying the following De Morgan-Schroeder reductions as long as possible.*

- $0^{\cup} \hookrightarrow 0$, $1^{\cup} \hookrightarrow 1$, $?^{\cup} \hookrightarrow ?$, $!^{\cup} \hookrightarrow !$
- $0^- \hookrightarrow 1$, $1^- \hookrightarrow 0$, $?^- \hookrightarrow !$, $!^- \hookrightarrow ?$
- $A^{-\cup} \hookrightarrow A^{\cup -}$, $A^{\cup\cup} \hookrightarrow A$, $A^{--} \hookrightarrow A$
- $(A + B)^{\cup} \hookrightarrow A^{\cup} + B^{\cup}$, $(A \cdot B)^{\cup} \hookrightarrow A^{\cup} \cdot B^{\cup}$
- $(A + B)^- \hookrightarrow A^- \cdot B^-$, $(A \cdot B)^- \hookrightarrow A^- + B^-$
- $(A \odot B)^{\cup} \hookrightarrow B^{\cup} \odot A^{\cup}$, $(A \oplus B)^{\cup} \hookrightarrow B^{\cup} \oplus A^{\cup}$
- $(A \odot B)^- \hookrightarrow A^- \oplus B^-$, $(A \oplus B)^- \hookrightarrow A^- \odot B^-$

Proof. As usual, a term is called *normal* (in *normal form*) if it is irreducible. That normal terms are positive, i.e. $\mathcal{L}^0$-terms, is readily seen. That every input A determines the unique normal form A^0 (if it exists) follows by standard arguments from the confluence, i.e. 'diamond', or Church-Rosser property of the reductions exposed. This, in turn, easily follows e.g. from [12]. Finally, in order to establish the existence of A^0 we observe that every chain of these reductions terminates. This is easily verified, since each reduction decreases the depth of the occurrence of $^-$ or $^{\cup}$. □

Definition 6. NRA has the following term-rewrite rules {1}-{12}, in $\mathcal{L}^0$.

{1} $A + B \hookrightarrow B + A$
{2} $A + (B + C) \hookrightarrow (A + B) + C$
{3} $A + (B \cdot C) \hookrightarrow (A + B) \cdot (A + C)$
{4} $A \hookrightarrow A + A$
{5} $A + B \hookrightarrow A$
{6} $A \hookrightarrow 0$
{7} $1 \cdot A \hookrightarrow A$
{8} $? + ! \hookrightarrow 1$, $L + L^- \hookrightarrow 1$
{9} $A \oplus (B \oplus C) \hookrightarrow (A \oplus B) \oplus C$, $(A \oplus B) \oplus C \hookrightarrow A \oplus (B \oplus C)$
{10} $(A \oplus B) + (C \odot D) \hookrightarrow (A + C) \cdot (B + D)$
{11} $(A \oplus B) + C \hookrightarrow (A^{\cup 0} \oplus C) + B$, $(A \oplus B) + C \hookrightarrow (C \oplus B^{\cup 0}) + A$
{12} $A \hookrightarrow ? \oplus A$, $? \oplus A \hookrightarrow A$, $A \hookrightarrow A \oplus ?$, $A \oplus ? \hookrightarrow A$

Definition 7. The derivability NRA is specified a follows. For any $\mathcal{L}^0$-term W, let S be any positive subterm occurrence in W. Let $S \hookrightarrow S'$ be any rewrite rule {k}$(1 \leq k \leq 12)$, and let $W' = W[S := S']$ denote the result of rewriting S to S' in W. The corresponding relation $W \rightsquigarrow W'$ is called a reduction if one of the two conditions holds (see below). W is called derivable in NRA if there exists a reduction chain $W \rightsquigarrow^* 1$, i.e., a finite 'reduction chain' $W = W_0 \rightsquigarrow W_1 \rightsquigarrow \ldots \rightsquigarrow W_k = 1$, in NRA (cf. the analogous passage in Definition 10. For any $\mathcal{L}$-terms A and B, an equation $A = B$ is called derivable in NRA if so is the correlated $\mathcal{L}^0$-term $(A^0 + B^{-0}) \cdot (A^{-0} + B^0)$. Now the two conditions in question are as follows.

- $k \leqq 9$ or $k = 12$
- $11 \leqq k \leqq 12$ and $W = S_1 \cdot \ldots \cdot S_j$ (in any associative order) such that $S = S_i$ for some $1 \leqq i \leqq j$.[3]

Hence, by Theorem 11 and quasiprojection results of [20] we get

Corollary 1. *A given $\mathcal{L}$-equation $A = B$ is T-valid iff $(A^0 + B^{-0}) \cdot (A^{-0} + B^0)$ can be rewritten to 1 by a reduction chain in* NRA. *Furthermore, $A = B$ is t-valid iff $1 \odot ((P^{\cup -} \oplus Q^-) + (P^\cup \odot P) \cdot ? + (Q^\cup \odot Q) \cdot ?) \odot 1 + (A^0 + B^{-0}) \cdot (A^{-0} + B^0)$ can be rewritten to 1 by a reduction chain in* NRA *(in the language $\mathcal{L}^{*0}$).*

2.2   Proofs

Soundness

Lemma 2. *The following equations (1)-(5) and equivalence (6) are T-valid.*

(1) $0^\cup = 0$, $1^\cup = 1$
(2) $?^\cup = ?$, $!^\cup = !$
(3) $A^{\cup -} = A^{-\cup}$
(4) $C \odot (A + B) = (C \odot A) + (C \odot B)$, $C \oplus (A \cdot B) = (C \oplus A) \cdot (C \oplus B)$
(5) $(A \cdot B)^\cup = A^\cup \cdot B^\cup$
(6) $(A \odot B) \cdot C = 0 \Leftrightarrow B \cdot (A^\cup \odot C) = 0 \Leftrightarrow A \cdot (C \odot B^\cup) = 0$

Proof. This is well-known (see e.g. [20]).   □

Lemma 3. *For any $\mathcal{L}^1$-term A, the equation $A^0 = A$ is T-valid.*

Proof. This follows easily from Definition 4 and Lemmata 1, 2 by induction on the length of the normalization.   □

Lemma 4. *Let $S \hookrightarrow S'$ be any term-rewrite rule exposed in Lemma 1 and/or Definition 6, except for $\{k\}$ for k=5, 6, 10, 11. Then $S = S'$ is T-valid.*

Proof. This can be easily checked using provable equations (I)-(X) of Definition 4 and (1)-(5) of Lemma 2.   □

---

[3] This restriction is essential. For example, by an easy unrestricted combination of $\{1\}$, $\{4\}$, $\{5\}$, $\{11\}$ one can reduce $(A \oplus B) + 0$ to $A + B$, whose reverse implication is obviously invalid.

Lemma 5. *As usual, let $A \leqslant B$ denote $A + B = B$. Let A be any positive subterm occurrence in a $\mathcal{L}^0$-term W. Suppose $A \leqslant B$ is T-valid, then so is $W \leqslant W[A := B]$. In particular, if $A = B$ is T-valid then so is $W = W[A := B]$.*

Proof. We argue by induction on the complexity of W. The basis of induction is clear. Boolean induction steps are obvious, since the boolean part of **RA** is complete. For example, let $W = W_1 + W_2$ where A occurs in W_2. Then by the induction hypothesis we have $W_2 \leqslant W_2[A := B]$, i.e. $W_2 + W_2[A := B] = W_2[A := B]$, provable in **RA**. Hence $W_1 + W_2 + W_1 + W_2[A := B] = W_1 + W_2[A := B]$, i.e. $W \leqslant W[A := B]$, is provable in **RA**. The remaining non-boolean cases of $\odot$ and $\oplus$ are in fact analogous. For let $W = W_1 \odot W_2$ where A occurs in W_2. By the induction hypothesis, $W_2 + W_2[A := B] = W_2[A := B]$ is provable in **RA**. Hence, by Lemma 2 (4), $W_1 \odot W_2 + W_1 \odot W_2[A := B] = W_1 \odot (W_2 + W_2[A := B]) = W_1 \odot W_2[A := B]$, i.e. $W \leqslant W[A := B]$, is provable in **RA**. If $W = W_1 \odot W_2$ then we replace the assumption $A \leqslant B$ by its boolean, and hence **RA**-provable, equivalent $A \cdot B = A$, and argue analogously via the second equality of Lemma 2 (4). $\qquad\square$

Lemma 6. *Suppose $S \hookrightarrow S'$ via $\{10\}$ or $\{11\}$. If $S' = 1$ is T-valid then so is $S = 1$.*

Proof. $\{10\}$: Suppose $(A + B) \cdot (B + D)$ is provable in **RA**. Since the boolean part of **RA** is complete, both $A + C = 1$ and $B + D = 1$, and hence also $A^- \leqslant C$ and $B^- \leqslant C$ are provable in **RA**. This passage is readily verified: $X + Y = 1$ implies $X^- + Y = 1 \cdot (X^- + Y) = (X + Y) \cdot (X^- + Y) = (X + X^-) \cdot Y = 1 \cdot Y = Y$. Now, by the last lemma, we have $A^- \odot B^- \leqslant A^- \odot D \leqslant C \odot D$, and hence, by the boolean completeness, $(A \oplus B)^- \leqslant A^- \odot B^- \leqslant C \odot D$. Hence $A \oplus B + C \odot D = 1$ is provable in **RA**.

$\{11\}$: Suppose $(A^{\cup 0} \oplus C) + B = 1$ is provable in **RA**. Hence, by the duality and Lemma 2 (3), so is $((A^\cup \oplus C) + B)^- = (A^{\cup-} \odot C^-) \cdot B^- = (A^{-\cup} \odot C) \cdot B^- = 0$. Hence, by Lemma 2 (6), $(A^- \odot B^-) \cdot C^- = 0$ is provable in **RA**, and hence, by the duality, so is $(A \oplus B) + C = 1$. $\qquad\square$

Lemma 7. *For any L-terms A, B, suppose $A = B$ is derivable in NRA. Then $A^0 = B^0$ is T-valid.*

Proof. Suppose $(A^0 + B^{-0}) \cdot (A^{-0} + B^0)$ is reducible to 1 by a reduction chain Δ in NRA. By Lemma 3 and the boolean completeness of **RA**, it will suffice to prove that Δ preserves the value 1 while moving in the left-hand side direction. That is, for any reduction $W \rightsquigarrow W' = W[S := S']$ correlated with a term-rewrite rule $\{k\}$: $S \hookrightarrow S'$, if $W' = 1$ is provable in **RA** then so is $W = 1$. By Lemmata 3-5, this holds for all k except for 5, 6, 10, 11. Moreover, if k is 5 or 6 then we are done by Lemma 5 via $W' \leqslant W'[S' := S]$, since $0 \leqslant A \leqslant A + B$ is provable in **RA**. In the remaining cases $k = 10, 11$, we argue by Lemma 6. Namely, let $W = S_1 \cdot \ldots \cdot S_j$ and $W' = W[S_i := S'_i]$

such that $S_i \hookrightarrow S_i'$ is $\{10\}$ or $\{11\}$, $1 \leq i \leq j$. Suppose $W' = 1$ is provable in **RA**, then so is $S_i' = 1$, as well as $S_l = 1$ for all $l \neq i$. Then, by Lemma 26, $S_i' = 1$ is provable in **RA**, and hence so is $W = 1$.   □

Obviously, this lemma together with Lemma 3 completes the soundness proof for NRA.

Completeness

Lemma 8. $A^0 = A$ *holds for any* $\mathcal{L}^0$-*term* A. *Moreover, the following are identities for all* $\mathcal{L}^1$-*terms* A, B.

1. $0^{\cup 0} = 0$, $1^{\cup 0} = 1$, $?^{\cup 0} = ?$, $!^{\cup 0} = !$
2. $(A + B)^0 = A^0 + B^0$, $(A \cdot B)^0 = A^0 \cdot B^0$
3. $(A \odot B)^0 = A^0 \odot B^0$, $(A \oplus B)^0 = A^0 \oplus B^0$
4. $A^{\cup\cup 0} = A^0$, $A^{0\cup 0} = A^{\cup 0}$
5. $(A + B)^{\cup 0} = A^{\cup 0} + B^{\cup 0}$, $(A \cdot B)^{\cup 0} = A^{\cup 0} \cdot B^{\cup 0}$
6. $(A \odot B)^{\cup 0} = B^{\cup 0} \odot A^{\cup 0}$, $(A \oplus B)^{\cup 0} = B^{\cup 0} \oplus A^{\cup 0}$
7. $0^{-0} = 1$, $1^{-0} = 0$, $?^{-0} = !$, $!^{-0} = ?$
8. $(A + B)^{-0} = A^{-0} \cdot B^{-0}$, $(A \cdot B)^{-0} = A^{-0} + B^{-0}$
9. $(A \odot B)^{-0} = A^{-0} \oplus B^{-0}$, $(A \oplus B)^{-0} = A^{-0} \odot B^{-0}$
10. $A^{--0} = A^0$, $A^{0-0} = A^{-0}$, $A^{-\cup 0} = A^{\cup-0}$

Proof. This is readily verified by induction in term complexity and Lemma 1.   □

Lemma 9. *If* W *is derivable in* NRA *then so is* $W^{\cup 0}$.

Proof. This is readily verified by induction on the length of the reduction chain from W to 1, in that we show that all rewrite rules preserve $^{\cup 0}$. For example, consider the first rule in $\{11\}$. Applying $^{\cup}$ to both the redex and contractum results in $((A \oplus B) + C)^{\cup 0} \hookrightarrow ((A^{\cup 0} \oplus C) + B)^{\cup 0}$ which, by Lemma 8, is identical with $(B^{\cup 0} \oplus A^{\cup 0}) + C^{\cup 0} \hookrightarrow (C^{\cup 0} \oplus A^{\cup 0 \cup 0}) + B^{\cup 0}$ which, in turn, is an instance of the second rule in $\{11\}$ (being in fact, by Lemma 8, identical with $(B^{\cup 0} \oplus A^{\cup 0}) + C^{\cup 0} \hookrightarrow (C^{\cup 0} \oplus A^0) + B^{\cup 0}$).   □

Sketch of the completeness proof

In order to complete the proof of Theorem 11, it will suffice to show that NRA is complete for δ**RA**, i.e. every equation provable in δ**RA** is in fact derivable in NRA. To this end, we'll embed δ**RA** derivations into the NRA reduction chains. Recall that δ**RA**-sequents have the form $X \vdash Y$ where X, Y are arbitrary terms of the appropriate display extension $\delta\mathcal{L}$ of the language $\mathcal{L}^1$ (see [9]; note that the names of some algebraic operations used in [9] differ from our's). Moreover, there are two canonical translations t_1 and t_2 from $\delta\mathcal{L}^1$-terms into $\mathcal{L}^1$-terms such that a $\delta\mathcal{L}^1$-sequent $X \vdash Y$ is being viewed as a $\mathcal{L}^1$-expression $t_1(X) \leqslant t_2(Y)$ (see [9]: Ch.4). We wish to pursue this translation in a natural way in order to arrive at an appropriate $\mathcal{L}^0$-equation $t_3(X, Y) = 1$. To this end, we put

$$t_3(X,Y) = t_1(X)^{-0} + t_2(Y)^0$$

(cf. the analogous passage in the proof of Lemma 6). Furthermore, recall that $t_1(X) = t_2(X) = X$ holds for all $\mathcal{L}^1$-terms X (cf. [9]: Ch.4). Hence, by Theorem 10 (see [9]: Theorems 2, 4, for the details and proofs [4]) and boolean completeness of **RA**, we arrive at the following

Lemma 10. *(a) For any $\mathcal{L}^1$-terms A, B, if $A = B$ is T-valid then so are both $A \leqslant B$ and $B \leqslant A$. (b) For any $\mathcal{L}^1$-terms A, B, if $A \leqslant B$ is T-valid then $A \vdash B$ is cutfree derivable in δ**RA**.*

Thus, in order to complete the proof of Theorem 11, it will suffice to prove the crucial

Lemma 11. *For any $\delta\mathcal{L}^1$-terms X, Y, if $X \vdash Y$ is cutfree derivable in δ**RA** then $t_3(X, Y)$ is derivable in* NRA.

Indeed, it will suffice to reverse Lemma 7. So suppose that $A = B$ is T-valid. By Lemma 10 (a), $A \leqslant B$ and $B \leqslant A$ are both T-valid. By Lemma 10 (b), $A \vdash B$ and $B \vdash A$ are both cutfree derivable in δ**RA**. Then, by Lemma 11, $t_3(A, B)$ and $t_3(B, A)$ are both derivable in NRA, and hence so are both $A^{-0} + B^0$ and $B^{-0} + A^0$. Hence there exist two NRA-derivations, i.e. reduction chains, Δ_1 and Δ_2 which reduce $A^{-0} + B^{-0}$ and $B^{-0} + A^0$, respectively, to 1. By adding to Δ_2 one instance of $\{1\}$ we arrive at a derivation Δ_3 of $A^0 + B^{-0}$. But, then, we obtain a desired reduction chain from $(A^0 + B^{-0}) \cdot (A^{-0} + B^0)$ to 1 by first using Δ_3, while keeping the second coefficient $A^{-0} + B^0$ unchanged, until we arrive at $1 \cdot (A^{-0} + B^0)$, and then by $\{7\}$ followed by Δ_1.

Proof of Lemma 11

We argue by induction on the length of a given δ**RA**-derivation of $X \vdash Y$. Since δ**RA**-derivations preserve basic operations, we do not need rules dealing with 'relative' and 'material' implications and 'self dual De Morgan negation' (see [9]). As for the rest of δ**RA** rules, we'll briefly specify them as *boolean*, *relational* and *display* rules, as follows. *Boolean* rules are those 'structural' (see [9]: Fig.1) and 'logical' rules (see [9]: Fig.2) whose principal algebraic operations are boolean. *Relational* are the remaining rules exposed in [9]: Fig.1-2. Now *display* rules include the axiom (id) $X_i \vdash X_i$ and the rules called 'display postulates' in [9]. Turning to the proof proper, first consider *boolean* 'structural' rules. By Lemma 8, the algorithm $t_3(-,-)$, transforms these rules into the following $\mathcal{L}^0$-inferences and equivalences, where $\vdash W$ stands for 'W *is derivable in* NRA' (below, for the sake of brevity, we'll often drop associative parentheses in iterated sums, which is justified in NRA by the rule $\{2\}$).

---

[4] The reader is strongly encouraged to gain an insight into basic definitions and techniques invented in [9]. Unfortunately, a more exhaustive presentation would exceed the scope of this paper.

- $\vdash A + B$ *iff* $\vdash A + 0 + B$ *iff* $\vdash 0 + A + B$ *iff* $\vdash A + B + 0$
- *if* $\vdash 0 + B$ *or* $\vdash B + 0$, *then* $\vdash A + B$
- *if* $\vdash A + C$ *then* $\vdash A + B + C$
- *if* $\vdash A + A + B$ *or* $\vdash A + B + B$, *then* $\vdash A + B$
- $\vdash A + (B + C) + D$ *iff* $\vdash (A + B) + C + D$
- $\vdash D + A + (B + C)$ *iff* $\vdash D + (A + B) + C$
- *if* $\vdash A + B + C$ *then* $\vdash B + A + C$
- *if* $\vdash C + A + B$ *then* $\vdash C + B + A$

These rules of inference are readily derivable using $\{10\}$, $\{2\}$, $\{4\}$-$\{6\}$. For example, the inference exposed in the third line is verified as follows. Let Δ be a reduction chain from $A + C$ to 1, then $\Gamma = \{1\}\{5\} : A + B + C \rightsquigarrow A + C + B \rightsquigarrow A + C$ followed by Δ is the required reduction chain from $A + B + C$ to 1. Consider *boolean* 'logical' rules. By the same token, $t_3(-, -)$ transforms them into the following NRA-inferences.

- $\vdash 1 + 0$ *and* $\vdash 0 + 1$
- *if* $\vdash A$ *then* $\vdash A$
- *if* $\vdash A + C$ *and* $\vdash B + D$, *then* $\vdash A \cdot B + C + D$
- *if* $\vdash C + A$ *and* $\vdash D + B$, *then* $\vdash C + D + A \cdot B$

Except for the second (trivial) line, these rules are derivable by $\{1\}$, $\{3\}$, $\{5\}$. We show only the last inference. Let Δ_1 and Δ_2 be given reduction chains respectively from $C + A$ and $D + B$ to 1. Then $\Delta_3 = \{3\}\{1\}\{5\}\{1\}\{5\} : C + D + A \cdot B \rightsquigarrow (C + D + A) \cdot (C + D + B) \rightsquigarrow (C + A + D) \cdot (C + D + B) \rightsquigarrow (C + A) \cdot (C + D + B) \rightsquigarrow (C + A) \cdot (D + B + C) \rightsquigarrow (C + A) \cdot (D + B)$ followed by Δ_1 reduces $C + D + A \cdot B$ to $1 \cdot (D + B)$, while $\Delta_4 = \{7\} : 1 \cdot (D + B) \rightsquigarrow D + B$ followed by Δ_2 completes the required reduction chain from $C + D + A \cdot B$ to 1. Consider *relational* 'structural' rules. These rules are being transformed by $t_3(-, -)$ into the following NRA-inferences and equivalences.

- *if* $\vdash (A \oplus B) + C$ *then* $\vdash (B^{\cup 0} \oplus A^{\cup 0}) + C^{\cup 0}$
- $\vdash (A \oplus (B \oplus C)) + D$ *iff* $\vdash ((A \oplus B) \oplus C) + D$
- $\vdash D + (A \oplus (B \oplus C))$ *iff* $\vdash D + ((A \oplus B) \oplus C)$
- $\vdash A + B$ *iff* $\vdash (A \oplus ?) + B$ *iff* $\vdash (? \oplus A) + B$ *iff* $\vdash A + (? \oplus B)$ *iff* $\vdash A + (B \oplus ?)$
- $\vdash A$ *iff* $\vdash A$

Arguing as above, the last four lines are readily derivable by $\{1\}$, $\{9\}$ and $\{12\}$. The first inference is a consequence of Lemma 9, since $((A \oplus B) \oplus C)^{\cup 0} = (B^{\cup 0} \oplus A^{\cup 0}) \oplus C^{\cup 0}$. Now consider *relational* 'logical' rules. These rules are being transformed into the following NRA-inferences..

- $\vdash ! + ?$ *and* $\vdash ? + !$
- *if* $\vdash A$ *then* $\vdash A$
- *if* $\vdash C + A$ *and* $\vdash D + B$, *then* $\vdash (C \oplus D) + (A \odot B)$

- *if* $\vdash A + C$ *and* $\vdash B + D$, *then* $\vdash (A \odot B) + (C \oplus D)$

The first line (axioms) are readily derivable by $\{1\}$ and $\{8\}$, the second line is trivial, and the last two inferences are readily derivable by $\{1\}$ and $\{10\}$. The remaining cases deal with *display* rules. The translation of the axiom (id) is derivable by $\{8\}$. The rules proper are being transformed into the following NRA-inferences and equivalences.

- *if* $\vdash A^{\cup-0} + B^0$ *then* $\vdash A^{-0} + B^{\cup 0}$
- *if* $\vdash A^\cup + B$ *then* $\vdash A + B^\cup$
- $\vdash (A \oplus B) + C$ *iff* $\vdash A + (C \oplus B^\cup)$ *iff* $\vdash B + (A^\cup \oplus C)$
- $\vdash C + (A \oplus B)$ *iff* $\vdash (C \oplus B^\cup) + A$ *iff* $\vdash (A^\cup \oplus C) + B$
- $\vdash (A + B) + C$ *iff* $\vdash A + (C \oplus B)$ *iff* $\vdash B + (A \oplus C)$
- $\vdash C + (A + B) + C$ *iff* $\vdash (C \oplus B) + A$ *iff* $\vdash (A \oplus C) + B$

The first and the last two lines are readily derivable by $\{1\}$ and $\{2\}$. The second inference follows by Lemma 9. Indeed, applying $^{\cup 0}$ to the premise we obtain $(A^{\cup-0} + B^0)^{\cup 0}$ which is in fact identical with $A^{\cup-0\cup 0} + B^{0\cup 0}$, i.e. $A^{\cup-\cup 0} + B^{\cup 0}$, i.e. $A^{\cup\cup-0} + B^{\cup 0}$, i.e. $A^{-0} + B^{\cup 0}$ (see Lemma 8). The third and the fourth lines are readily derivable by $\{1\}$ and $\{11\}$. This completes the proof of Lemma 11 and thereby establishes **RA**-completeness of NRA. Q.E.D.

Example 1. We wish to confirm [2]: Theorem 2.9, stating that $A \leqslant (A \odot A^\cup) \odot A$ holds in **RA**. For the sake of brevity (but without loss of generality) we put $A = X_i$. By Theorem 11, it will suffice to construct a reduction chain in NRA reducing $(A \odot A^\cup) \odot A$ to 1. This is done as follows, where the tags $\{k\}$ to the left of $\leadsto$ are the names of the underlying rewrite-rules:

$$t_3(A, (A \odot A^\cup) \odot A) = A^- + ((A \odot A^\cup) \odot A)$$
$$\{4\} \leadsto A^- + A^- + ((A \odot A^\cup) \odot A)$$
$$\{12\} \leadsto (A^- \oplus ?) + A^- + ((A \odot A^\cup) \odot A)$$
$$\{11\} \leadsto (A^{\cup-} \oplus (A^- + ((A \odot A^\cup) \odot A))) + ?$$
$$\{5\} \leadsto A^{\cup-} \oplus (A^- + ((A \odot A^\cup) \odot A))$$
$$\{4\} \leadsto (A^{\cup-} \oplus (A^- + ((A \odot A^\cup) \odot A))) + (A^{\cup-} \oplus (A^- + ((A \odot A^\cup) \odot A)))$$
$$\{11\} \leadsto (A^{\cup-\cup 0} \oplus (A^{\cup-} \oplus (A^- + ((A \odot A^\cup)) \odot A))) + A^- + ((A \odot A^\cup) \odot A)$$
$$= (A^- \oplus (A^{\cup-} \oplus (A^- + ((A \odot A^\cup) \odot A)))) + A^- + ((A \odot A^\cup) \odot A)$$
$$\{1\} \leadsto (A^- \oplus (A^{\cup-} \oplus (A^- + ((A \odot A^\cup) \odot A)))) + ((A \odot A^\cup) \odot A) + A^-$$
$$\{5\} \leadsto (A^- \oplus (A^{\cup-} \oplus A^-)) + ((A \odot A^\cup) \odot A) + A^-$$
$$\{5\} \leadsto (A^- \oplus (A^{\cup-} \oplus A^-)) + ((A \odot A^\cup) \odot A)$$
$$\{9\} \leadsto ((A^- \oplus A^{\cup-}) \oplus A^-) + ((A \odot A^\cup) \odot A)$$
$$\{10\} \leadsto ((A^- \oplus A^{\cup-}) + (A \odot A^\cup)) \cdot (A^- + A)$$
$$\{10\} \leadsto ((A^- + A) \cdot (A^{\cup-} + A^\cup)) \cdot (A^- + A)$$
$$\{8\} \leadsto (1 \cdot (A^{\cup-} + A^\cup)) \cdot (A^- + A)$$
$$\{7\} \leadsto (A^{\cup-} + A^\cup) \cdot (A^- + A)$$
$$\{8\} \leadsto 1 \cdot (A^- + A)$$
$$\{7\} \leadsto A^- + A$$
$$\{8\} \leadsto 1$$

Remark 3. As compared to $\delta\mathbf{RA}$, derivations in NRA are shorter. The one reason is that we "spare" subsequent introductions and eliminations of the display operations. The other – NRA nested rewritings simulate Schütte-Rasiowa-Sikorski one-sided (sequents and) rules which allow to get rid of Gentzen-Belnap dual repetitions in antecedents in succedents. Finally, nested rewritings can essentially accelerate proof search. On the other hand, the freedom of nested rewritings makes NRA derivations completely indeterministic, whereas $\delta\mathbf{RA}$ admits natural deterministic proof search. In fact, $\delta\mathbf{RA}$ provides at least one natural deterministic proof search strategy in NRA, for the display operations roughly correspond to markers showing principal redex subterms in the correlated NRA reduction chains.

Remark 4. As compared to the nested sequnt calculi (see Section 1), NRA requires more efforts in order to get rid of the contraction {4} and weakening {5}which are troublesome for a good proof search. The corresponding refinement of NRA is yet to be done.

Remark 5. The very idea that $\mathbf{RA}$ admits a cutfree algebraic formalization is highly untrivial. Loosely speaking, this is due to the provability in $\mathbf{RA}$ of the Schroeder equivalence (see Lemma 2 (6)) which allows to 'display' as boolean components arbitrary subterms occurring in relative products and/or sums. This feature is crucial for the underlying display cut elimination (see [9]).

3   2-variable satisfaction/validity

3.1   Background

Consider SAT-problem in 2-variable logic. Although 2-variable logic (both with and without equality) has Finite Model Property (see e.g. [10]), the known straightforward decision algorithms still have "irrational" complexity. Note that the ordinary restricted (with respect to the number of computation steps) implementations of the correlated model checking actually do not approximate the solution, since partial negative results can only simulate *negation-as-failure*. That is to say, only positive solution stating that a given 2-variable formula F is satisfied in a chosen finite model of the cardinality $\leq n$ can serve as the (positive) answer, whereas knowing that F is not satisfied in any finite model of the cardinality $\leq n$ can't really contribute to the solution, unless n is sufficiently big. In the case of 2-variable satisfaction, known estimates on such "big" n are just too big to be of any practical importance. However, searching for a proof of $\neg F$ in a suitable complete proof system enables to avoid this trouble, since every partial solution stating that $\neg F$ is valid, i.e. derivable using $\leq n$ steps of computation, yields the desired negative answer. Therefore, in order to avoid verifications in all finite models, it seems reasonable to address the corresponding validity and search simultaneously for a model of F and a proof of $\neg F$. Thus also addressing 2-variable VAL-problem can contribute to "practical" implementation of the corresponding "theoretical" decidability, which, in turn, can serve as an argument in favor of cutfree proof theory of 2-variable logic. The approach presented in previous sections allows us to replace 2-variable validity by the derivability in a suitable finite-variable nested sequent calculus on the one hand and a nested algebraic calculus on the other hand. (Besides, any 1-order theorem prover can also do the job, provided that we do not care about the number of variables used). In what follows we use previous m-variable notations $\mathcal{L}_m$, $\mathcal{L}_m^0$, $\mathcal{L}^1$ etc.; moreover, writing in the same context both $\mathcal{L}_m$ and $\mathcal{L}_{m+n}$ we mean that the language $\mathcal{L}_{m+n}$ extends $\mathcal{L}_m$ by adding n new individual variables.

3.2   Finite-variable approach

Theorem 12. *A given $\mathcal{L}_2$-formula is valid iff it is provable in Hilbert-Bernays 3-variable logic (and hence also in Tarski 3-variable logic) in the language $\mathcal{L}_3$.*

Proof. Consider Henkin's 2-variable completeness proof (see [11]). Recall that this proof was originally formalized in the logic with two individual variables x and y that actually extends the corresponding Hilbert-Bernays 2-variable logic by the following 'special axioms' (SE1)-(SE3).

(SE1) $\exists x(x = y \wedge F) \rightarrow \forall x(x = y \rightarrow F)$

(SE2) $\exists y \forall x(D \longleftrightarrow x = y) \rightarrow (\exists x(D \wedge F) \longleftrightarrow \forall x(D \rightarrow F))$
         [y not free in D]

(SE3) $\forall x F \longleftrightarrow \forall x(x = y \rightarrow \forall y F^r)$

where F^r is defined recursively as follows in basic syntax $\{\neg, \rightarrow \forall\}$:

(i)   If F is atomic then F^r is obtained by interchanging x an y,

(ii) $(\forall x G)^r = \forall y(x = y \rightarrow \forall x G^r)$, $(\forall y G)^r = \forall x(x = y \rightarrow \forall y G^r)$,

(iii) $(\neg G)^r = \neg G^r$, $(G \rightarrow H)^r = G^r \rightarrow H^r$.

Denote by **HBL₂** basic Hilbert-Bernays 2-variable formalism of $\mathcal{L}_2$, and consider the following variants (λ), $(\lambda 1)$, $(\lambda 2)$ of the general Leibniz law, in $\mathcal{L}_3$, for F ranging over arbitrary $\mathcal{L}_2$-formulas.

(λ) $x = y \rightarrow (F \rightarrow F[x/y])$

$(\lambda 1)$ $x = z \rightarrow (F \rightarrow F[x/z])$

$(\lambda 2)$ $y = z \rightarrow (F \rightarrow F[y/z])$

We notice (see [7]) that (SE1) and (SE3) are derivable in **HBL₂** extended by (λ). Furthermore, we claim that (SE2) is derivable in **HBL₃** extended by $(\lambda 1)$. To check this, first note that (SE2) (in positive form) is easily derivable in **HBL₂** from the conjunction of the following (j) and (jj) where y is not free in D.

(j) $\forall y \exists x(D \wedge x \neq y) \vee \forall x(\neg D \vee \neg F) \vee \forall x(\neg D \vee F)$

(jj) $\forall y \exists x(\neg D \wedge x = y) \vee \exists x(D \wedge F) \vee \exists x(D \wedge \neg F)$

Now (j) is derivable by easily completing the following sequence of formulas to a reduction chain in NLE₃ extended by a new rewrite rule $x \neq z \vee F \hookrightarrow F[x/z]$ corresponding to $(\lambda 1)$, and hence provable in **HBL₃** extended by $(\lambda 1)$ (see above Subsection 1.3; note that the rewrite-rule (7) is admissible in NL$_m$ for an arbitrary formula B instead of L).

$\forall y \exists x (D \land x \neq y) \lor \forall x (\neg D \lor \neg F) \lor \forall x (\neg D \lor F),$

$\forall z \exists x (D \land x \neq z) \lor \forall x (\neg D \lor \neg F) \lor \forall x (\neg D \lor F),$

$\forall z (\forall x (\exists x (D \land x \neq z) \lor \neg D \lor \neg F) \lor \forall x (\exists x (D \land x \neq z) \lor \neg D \lor F)),$

$\forall z (\forall x ((D \land x \neq z) \lor \neg D \lor \neg F) \lor \forall x ((D \land x \neq z) \lor \neg D \lor F)),$

$\forall z (\forall x (x \neq z \lor \neg D \lor \neg F) \lor \forall x (x \neq z \lor \neg D \lor F)),$

$\forall z (\forall x (x \neq z \lor \neg D \lor \neg F[x/z]) \lor \forall x (x \neq z \lor \neg D \lor F[x/z])),$

$\forall z (\forall x (x \neq z \lor \neg D) \lor \neg F[x/z] \lor \forall x (x \neq z \lor \neg D) \lor F[x/z]),$

$\top.$

By the token, the second conjunct (jj) is easily derivable already in NLE_2:

$\forall y \exists x (\neg D \land x = y) \lor \exists x (D \land F) \lor \exists x (D \land \neg F),$

$\forall x \exists y (\neg D[x/y] \land y = x) \lor \exists x (D \land F) \lor \exists x (D \land \neg F),$

$\forall x (\exists y (\neg D[x/y] \land y = x) \lor \exists x (D \land F) \lor \exists x (D \land \neg F)),$

$\forall y ((\neg D \land x = x) \lor (D \land F) \lor (D \land \neg F)),$

$\forall y (\neg D \lor (D \land F) \lor (D \land \neg F)),$

$\forall y (\neg D \lor F \lor \neg F),$

$\top.$

To complete the proof of the theorem, we show that (λ), $(\lambda 1)$ and $(\lambda 2)$ are all admissible in $\mathbf{HBL}_3$. This proof runs by simultaneous induction on the complexity of A, where for the sake of brevity we work in basic syntax $\{\neg, \lor, \exists\}$. The basis of induction is clear, since Hilbert-Bernays formalism postulates the atomic Leibniz law. Consider the induction step. Case $\lor$ is trivial. Case $\neg$ is easy for (λ), since Hilbert-Bernays formalism postulates the symmetry of $=$. Case $\neg$ for $(\lambda 1)$ is provable via easy variable renaming by the induction hypothesis of $(\lambda 2)$, and vice versa. Case $\exists$ for both $(\lambda 1)$ and $(\lambda 2)$ is trivial, since in the only relevant subcase $F = \exists y G(x, y)$ (resp. $F = \exists x G(x, y)$) the bound variable y (resp. x) does not occur in the premise $x = z$ (resp. $y = z$). In the remaining case $\exists$ for (λ), the crucial subcase $x = y \rightarrow (\exists y G(x, y) \rightarrow \exists x G(y, x))$ is, by variable renaming, equivalent to $x = z \rightarrow (\exists y G(x, y) \rightarrow \exists x G(z, x))$, thus being provable by the induction hypothesis of $(\lambda 1)$. □

Together with Theorem 11, this yields the desired proof theoretical characterization:

Corollary 2. *A given $\mathcal{L}_2$-formula F is valid iff F^0 is derivable in NLE_3.*

Algebraic characterization

Definition 8. Without loss of generality we consider the 2-variable language $\mathcal{L}_2$ that includes binary relations $X_1, ..., X_n$, propositional connectives $\neg, \land$, truth value $\top$, quantifier $\exists$ and two variables x, y. Formulas $F \lor G$, $F \rightarrow G$, $F \longleftrightarrow G$, $\forall x F$, $\forall y F$ are regarded as standard abbreviations $\neg(\neg F \land \neg G)$, $\neg(F \land \neg G)$, $(F \rightarrow G) \land (G \rightarrow F)$, $\neg \exists x F$, $\neg \exists y F$, respectively. We assign to every $\mathcal{L}_2$-formula F a $\mathcal{L}^1$-term F^* (whose length is linear in the length of F) by the following recursive clauses.

- $\mathsf{T}^* = 1$
- $(X_i(x,y))^* = X_i$, $(X_i(y,x))^* = X_i^{\cup}$
- $(X_i(x,x))^* = (X_i\cdot!) \odot 1$, $(X_i(y,x))^* = 1 \odot (X_i\cdot!)$
- $(x=y)^* = (y=x)^* = !$, $(x=x)^* = (y=y)^* = 1$
- $(\neg G)^* = G^{*-}$, $(G \wedge H)^* = G^* \cdot H^*$
- $(\exists x D)^* = (\exists y D)^* = D^*$ [x, resp. y, not free in D]
- $(\exists x G)^* = 1 \odot G^*$, $(\exists y G)^* = G^* \odot 1$ [x, resp. y, free in G]

Lemma 12. *For any basic relation symbol X and any formula G, the following are provable in Tarski 3-variable logic with individual variables x, y, z.*

(a) $\exists z(X(x,z) \wedge x = z) \longleftrightarrow X(x,x)$, $\exists z(X(x,z) \wedge x = z) \longleftrightarrow X(x,x)$
(b) $\forall z G \to G[z/x]$, $\forall z G \to G[z/y]$
(c) $\exists z D \longleftrightarrow \exists z D[x/z]$, $\exists y(D \longleftrightarrow \exists z D[y/z]$ [z not free in D]

Proof. Straightforward. We refer to [20] for Tarski's non-boolean axioms (AIV)-(AIX), (AIX') in basic syntax $\{\neg, \to, \forall\}$. We show only the clause (b) and the first equivalence in (c).

(b):
1 $z = x \to (G \to G[z/x])$ [(AIX')],
2 $\forall z(z = x \to (G \to G[z/x]))$ [generalization],
3 $\forall z(G \to (\neg G[z/x] \to z \neq x))$ [propositional inference],
4 $\forall z G \to (\forall z \neg G[z/x] \to \forall z(z \neq x))$ [by (AV)],
5 $\forall z \neg G[z/x] \to (\forall z G \to \forall z(z \neq x))$ [propositional inference],
6 $\neg G[z/x] \to (\forall z G \to \forall z(z \neq x))$ [by (AVII)],
7 $\exists z(z = x) \to (\forall z G \to G[z/x])$ [propositional inference],
8 $\forall z G \to G[z/x]$ [by (AVIII)].

(c$\to$): It will suffice to deduce dual implication $\forall z D[x/z] \to \forall x D$:
1 $\forall z D[x/z] \to D[x/z][z/x] = D$ [(b)],
2 $\forall x(\forall z D[x/z] \to D)$ [generalization],
3 $\forall x \forall z D[x/z] \to \forall x D$ [by (AV)],
4 $\forall z D[x/z] \to \forall x D$ [by (AVII)].

(c$\leftarrow$): It will suffice to deduce dual implication $\forall z D \to \forall z D[x/z]$:
1 $\forall z D \to D[x/z]$ [(b)],
2 $\forall z(\forall x D \to D[x/z])$ [generalization],
3 $\forall z \forall x D \to \forall x D[x/z]$ [by (AV)],
4 $\forall z D \to \forall x D[x/z]$ [by (AVII)]. □

Lemma 13. *The algorithm $(-)^*$ of Definition 8 preserves the ordinary "true" validity. Moreover, the equivalence between any given $\mathcal{L}_2$-formula F and the canonical 1-order translation of $F^* = 1$ is provable in Tarski 3-variable logic.*

Proof. For any $\mathcal{L}_2$-formula F, denote by $t(F^* = 1)$ the canonical 1-order translation of the $\mathcal{L}^1$-equation $F^* = 1$. By the boolean completeness of Tarski 3-variable logic, $t(F^* = 1)$ is provably equivalent to the $\mathcal{L}_3$-formula $t(F^*)$ which is defined by the following recursive clauses.

1    $t(1) = \top$, $t(!) = (x = y)$
2    $t(X_i) = X_i(x, y)$, $t(X_i^{\cup}) = X_i(y, x)$
3    $t(A^-) = \neg t(A)$, $t(A \cdot B) = t(A) \wedge t(B)$
4    $t(A \odot B) = \exists z(t(A)[y/z] \wedge t(B)[x/z])$

Note that z is not free in $t(F^*)$. It will suffice to show that the equivalence $F \longleftrightarrow t(F^*)$ is provable in Tarski 3-variable logic. The proof runs by induction on the complexity of F. Propositional induction steps and the basic cases $F = \top, X_i(x, y), X_i(y, x)$ are trivial. Suppose $F = X_i(x, x)$. Then $t(F^*) = t((X_i \cdot !) \odot 1) = \exists z(t(X_i)[y/z] \wedge t(!)[x/z] \wedge t(1)[x/z]) = \exists z(X_i(x, z) \wedge x = z \wedge \top)$, and hence $t(F^*) \longleftrightarrow \exists z(X_i(x, z) \wedge x = z)$ is provable, which yields the result by the induction hypothesis and Lemma 12 (a). Case $F = X_i(y, y)$ is analogous. Suppose $F = \exists x D$ where x is not free in D. Then $t(F^*) = t(D^*)$, while $\exists x D \longleftrightarrow D$ is deducible by (AVI), (AVII), which yields the result by the induction hypothesis. Case $F = \exists y D$ where y is not free in D is analogous. Now suppose $F = \exists x G$ where x is free in G. We have $t(F^*) = t(1 \odot G^*) = \exists z(t(1)[y/z] \wedge t(G^*)[x/z]) = \exists z(\top \wedge t(G^*)[x/z])$, and hence $t(F^*) \longleftrightarrow \exists z(t(G^*)[x/z])$ is provable, which yields the result by the induction hypothesis and Lemma 12 (c). Case $F = \exists y G$ where y is free in G is analogous. This completes the proof of the lemma.   □

Theorem 13. *For any $\mathcal{L}_2$-formula F, F is valid iff $F^* = 1$ is provable in Tarski 3-variable formalism of $\mathcal{L}_3$.*

Proof. See Theorem 12 and Lemma 12.   □

While embedding Tarski 3-variable logic into the 4-variable one, by Theorem 2 we arrive at a weaker

Corollary 3. *For any $\mathcal{L}_2$-formula F, F is valid iff $F^* = 1$ is T-valid.*

Together with Theorem 12, this yields

Corollary 4. *For any $\mathcal{L}_2$-formula F, F is valid iff F^{*0} is derivable in NRA.*

Remark 6. By a result of Maddux, Tarski 3-variable logic is characteristic to the semi-associative relation algebras, **SA**, which can be axiomatized like **RA** (see e.g. Definition 4), except weakening (V) to $(A \odot 1) \odot 1 = A \odot (1 \odot 1)$ (see references e.g. in [20], [14]). In order to characterize **SA** in the spirit of Section 2, we let NSA be an algebraic term-rewriting system that arises from NRA by, say, asserting that in the rule {9} at most one of A, B, C differs from 0. It is very likely that the proof of Theorem 12 also holds for **SA** and such NSA instead of **RA** and NRA, respectively (however, this has not yet been verified in full detail). If true, this conjecture together with the last theorem would enable us to strengthen the last corollary by rewriting NRA to NSA.

References

1. Andreka H. and Nemeti I. (1996) Axiomatization of identity-free equations valid in relation algebras. Algebra Universalis 35:256-264
2. Chin L. and Tarski A. (1951) Distributive and modular laws in the arithmetic of relation algebras. Univ. of Calif. Publ. in Math 9:341-384
3. Dawson J.E. and Gore R. (1998) A mechanised proof system for relation algebra using display logic. **JELIA'98**, LNAI 1489:264-278
4. Frias M. and Orłowska E. (1995) A proof system for fork algebras and its applications to reasoning in logics based on intuitionism. Logique et Analyse 150-151-152:239-284
5. Frias M. and Orlowska E. (1998) Equational reasoning in non-classical logics. Journ. of Applied Non-Class. Logics 8 (1-2):27-66
6. Gordeev L. (1995) Cut free formalization of logic with finitely many variables. **CSL'94**, LNCS 933:136-150
7. Gordeev L. (1999) Variable compactness in 1-order logic. Journ. of IGPL 7:327-357
8. Gordeev L. (2000) Finite proof theory: basic result. To appear in Archive for Math. Logic
9. Gore R. (1997) Cut-free display calculi for relation algebras. **CSL'96**, LNCS 1249:198-210
10. Grädel E., Kolaitis P. and Vardi M. (1997) On the decision problem for two-variable first-order logic. Bull. of Symb. Logic 3:53-69
11. Henkin L. (1967) Logical systems containing only a finite number of symbols. Les Presses de l'Universite Montreal
12. Hindley J.R. (1969) An abstract form of Church-Rosser theorem I. Journ. of Symb. Logic 34:545-560
13. Maddux R. (1989) Finitary algebraic logic. Zeit. f. math. Log. Grundl. d. Math. 35:321-332
14. Maddux R. (1989) Nonfinite axiomatizability results for cylindric and relation algebras. Journ. of Symb. Logic 54:951-974
15. Orłowska E. (1988) Relational interpretation of modal logics. In: Andreka H., Monk D. and Nemeti I. (eds) Algebraic Logic, North-Holland, 443-471
16. Orłowska E. (1992) Relational proof system for relevant logic. Journ. of Symb. Logic 57:1425-1440
17. Orłowska E. (1995) Relational proof systems for modal logics. In: Wansing H. (ed) Proof theory of modal logics, Kluwer, 55-57
18. Sinz C. (1998) Untersuchung und Implementation der RPC_n Reduktions-skalküle. Studienarbeit Universität Tübingen
19. Sinz C. (2000) System description: ARA - an automatic theorem prover for relation algebras. CADE-17 (to appear)
20. Tarski A. and Givant S. (1987) A formalization of set theory without variables. AMS Coll. Publ. 41

Chapter 14
Connections Between Cylindric Algebras and Relation Algebras

Robin Hirsch[1],* and Ian Hodkinson[2],**

[1] Department of Computer Science
University College, London
hirsch@cs.ucl.ac.uk
[2] Department of Computing
Imperial College, London
imh@doc.ic.ac.uk

Abstract. We investigate the class $\mathbf{S}RaCA_n$ for $4 \leq n < \omega$ and survey some recent results. We see that RA_n — the subalgebras of relation algebras with relational bases — is too weak, and that the class of relation algebras whose canonical extension has an n-dimensional cylindric basis is too strong to define the class. We introduce the notion of an n-dimensional hyperbasis and show that for any relation algebra $\mathcal{A}$ the canonical extension $\mathcal{A}^+$ has such a hyperbasis if and only if $\mathcal{A} \in \mathbf{S}RaCA_n$.

We introduce techniques that can be used to show that the hierarchies $RA_4 \supset RA_5 \supset \ldots$ and $\mathbf{S}RaCA_4 \supset \mathbf{S}RaCA_5 \supset \ldots$ are strict and each step is not finitely axiomatisable.

We outline a relativized semantics that characterises RA_n and another one for the class of subalgebras of relation algebras with n-dimensional cylindric bases.
Keywords: relation algebra, cylindric algebra, relativization.

1 Relation algebra reducts by bases

This paper summarises our investigations into the connections between relation algebras and cylindric algebras. The detailed proofs have been omitted, but fuller accounts of the material can be found in [3,6,4,5]. Our intention here is to provide a concise overview of a number of different but related results.

Algebraic logic is the study of algebraic counterparts to logical systems and historically an important part of algebraic logic concerns the algebraic treatment of relations. The simplest algebraic logic, *boolean algebra*, can be thought of as the algebra of unary relations. The correspondence between boolean algebras and fields of unary relations (or just fields of sets) is precise: every field of sets is a boolean algebra and every boolean algebra is isomorphic to a field of sets [14].

* Research of first author partially supported by UK EPSRC grant GR/L85961.
** Research of second author partially supported by UK EPSRC grants GR/K54946 and GR/L85978.

There are a number of algebras that are intended to correspond to relations of higher ranks, though the correspondence is less accurate. For binary relations, the most important kind of algebra is a *relation algebra*, based on the work of De Morgan, Peirce and Schröder and formalised by Tarski. But not every relation algebra is isomorphic to a field of binary relations (not every relation algebra is *representable*) and it requires infinitely many axioms to characterise the isomorphism class of the representable relation algebras [9,13].

For higher-order relations there are alternative algebraizations: cylindric algebra, diagonal-free cylindric algebra, polyadic algebra and so on. The one which has received most attention is cylindric algebra. As with binary relations, not every n-dimensional cylindric algebra is representable as an n-dimensional generalised cylindric set algebra (which is a generalisation of a field of n-ary relations) and it requires infinitely many axioms to characterise this representation class.

There is a well-known technique for obtaining a relation algebra $Ra(\mathcal{C})$ (for $n \geq 4$) from an n-dimensional cylindric algebra $\mathcal{C}$. $Ra(\mathcal{C})$ is constructed by taking the two-dimensional elements of $\mathcal{C}$ (i.e. the elements $a \in \mathcal{C}$ such that $c_i a = a$ for $2 \leq i < n$) and using the spare dimensions to define converse and composition [8, definition 5.3.7]. $Ra(\mathcal{C})$ is called the relation algebra reduct of $\mathcal{C}$. The fact that $n \geq 4$ is enough to ensure that $Ra(\mathcal{C})$ is associative and hence a relation algebra [8, theorem 5.3.8]. For $m < n$ there is a similar (and rather easier) method of constructing an m-dimensional cylindric algebra $Nr_m(\mathcal{C})$ from an n-dimensional one $\mathcal{C}$.

The focus of this paper is to investigate the connections between cylindric algebras of dimension $n \geq 4$ and relation algebras. In particular we will address the question: for which relation algebras $\mathcal{A}$ is there an n-dimensional cylindric algebra $\mathcal{C}$ such that $\mathcal{A} \subseteq Ra(\mathcal{C})$? Thus we wish to characterise the class $\mathbf{S}Ra\mathbf{CA}_n \subseteq \mathbf{RA}$ of subalgebras of relation algebra reducts of n-dimensional cylindric algebras.

A number (two) of candidates present themselves as characterisations of $\mathbf{S}Ra\mathbf{CA}_n$. Maddux defines n-dimensional cylindric bases and n-dimensional relational bases. Part of his motivation in defining these bases is the connection with reducts of relation algebras though, particularly for relational bases, Maddux was also interested in the connections with first-order proof theory using only n variables. Before we define these bases we need to define a *n-network* (sometimes referred to as a basic matrix or as an atomic network).

Definition 1. An n-network N for an atomic relation algebra $\mathcal{A}$ is a function $N : n \times n \to At(\mathcal{A})$ such that for all $i, j, k < n$ we have $N(i, i) \leq 1'$ and $N(i, j); N(j, k) \geq N(i, k)$. From this we can also deduce that $N(i, j) = N(j, i)^{\smile}$.

For two n-networks M, N and for $k < n$ we write $M \equiv_k N$ if M and N *agree off k*, i.e. for $i, j \in n \setminus \{k\}$ we have $N(i, j) = M(i, j)$. Similarly, for $k, l < n$ we write $M \equiv_{kl} N$ if for all $i, j \in n \setminus \{k, l\}$ we have $N(i, j) = M(i, j)$.

Definition 2. [12, section 4] An n-dimensional relational basis for an atomic relation algebra $\mathcal{A}$ is a set $\mathcal{R}$ of n-networks such that

- for all $a \in At(\mathcal{A})$ there is some $N \in \mathcal{R}$ with $N(0,1) = a$
- if $N \in \mathcal{R}$, $i, j < n$ and $a, b \in At(\mathcal{A})$ satisfy $N(i,j) \leq a; b$ and if $k \in n \setminus \{i, j\}$ then there is $M \in \mathcal{R}$ with $M \equiv_k N$ and $M(i,k) = a$, $M(k,j) = b$.

Definition 3. [11, definition 11, page 138] An n-dimensional cylindric basis S for $\mathcal{A}$ is an n-dimensional relational basis such that if $M, N \in S$, $i \neq j < n$ and $M \equiv_{ij} N$ then there is $L \in S$ with $M \equiv_i L \equiv_j N$. We may refer to this condition as the *amalgamation condition*. CB_n denotes the class of all atomic relation algebras with n-dimensional cylindric bases.

From a relational basis $\mathcal{R}$ for a relation algebra $\mathcal{A}$, you might hope to embed $\mathcal{A}$ in a cylindric algebra $\mathcal{C}$ whose domain is $\wp(\mathcal{R})$ (so that atoms are of the form $\{N\}$, which we identify with N, for $N \in \mathcal{R}$) where the diagonals and cylindrifications of $\mathcal{C}$ are defined by

- $N \leq d_{ij}$ if and only if $N(i,j) \leq 1'$ for $N \in \mathcal{R}$ and $i, j < n$.
- $c_i(N) = \{M \in \mathcal{R} : M \equiv_i N\}$.

This nearly gives a cylindric algebra but it may fail to satisfy the commutativity axiom

$$c_i c_j x = c_j c_i x$$

which holds in cylindric algebras. So the condition that $\mathcal{A}$ should extend to a relation algebra with an n-dimensional relational basis seems too weak to characterise the class $\mathbf{SRaCA}_n$. Indeed, for $n \geq 5$, the algebra $\mathcal{A}_{n-1}$, defined below, has an n-dimensional relational basis but does not belong to $\mathbf{SRaCA}_n$.

So we consider atomic relation algebras with n-dimensional cylindric bases. From such a relation algebra we can use the elements of a cylindric basis as atoms in a cylindric algebra with the definitions given just above. This time, because of the amalgamation condition on cylindric bases, the commutativity axiom is satisfied. Thus, $\mathbf{SCB}_n \subseteq \mathbf{SRaCA}_n$ [11, theorem 13, page 140]. Indeed, Maddux shows elsewhere that for any relation algebra $\mathcal{A}$, if its canonical embedding algebra $\mathcal{A}^+ \in \mathbf{CB}_n$ then $\mathcal{A} \subseteq \mathcal{A}^+ \in RaCA_n$.

One might hope for a converse to this. Starting from an arbitrary n-dimensional cylindric algebra $\mathcal{C}$, consider a relation algebra $\mathcal{A} \subseteq Ra(\mathcal{C})$. Note first that $\mathcal{A} \subseteq Ra(\mathcal{C}) \subseteq Ra(\mathcal{C}^+)$. Now we might try to show that $\mathcal{A}^+$ has an n-dimensional cylindric basis as follows. For each atom $x \in At(\mathcal{C}^+)$ define an n-network N_x for $\mathcal{A}^+$ by

$$N_x(i,j) = \{a \in \mathcal{A} : x \leq s_{ij}a\}$$

where s_{ij} is a certain string of substitutions mapping the 'free variables' 0 and 1 of a to i and j respectively, e.g. $s_{34} = s_3^0 s_4^1$. Now the set $N_x(i,j)$ is an ultrafilter of $\mathcal{A}$ and hence an atom of $\mathcal{A}^+$ and it can be shown (for

$n \geq 4$), using elementary but technical properties of substitutions, that N_x is indeed an n-network. But the set $\{N_x : x \in At(\mathcal{C}^+)\}$ may fail to satisfy the amalgamation condition and hence it may fail to be a cylindric basis. The reason for this failure, roughly, is that from $N_x \equiv_{ij} N_y$ we cannot deduce that $x \leq c_i c_j y$. (If we could deduce that then of course we could find an atom z with $x \leq c_i z$ and $z \leq c_j y$. The amalgam would then be N_z.) So the condition that $\mathcal{A}^+$ has an n-dimensional cylindric basis is too strong a condition to characterise $\mathbf{S}Ra\mathbf{CA}_n$.

Indeed we can find a counter example: a finite relation algebra $\mathcal{A}$ in $\mathbf{S}Ra\mathbf{CA}_n$ but such that $\mathcal{A}^+ \cong \mathcal{A}$ has no n-dimensional cylindric basis. The required example is a *Lyndon algebra* as in [10]. Lyndon showed that some of these algebras are representable and that a representation must be isomorphic to a certain affine geometry. It has also been shown that these representations are never *homogeneous*: there is a local isomorphism σ (i.e. a partial map on the representation X such that if $x, y \in dom(\sigma)$ then $X, x, y \models a \Leftrightarrow X, \sigma(x), \sigma(y) \models a$ for all $a \in \mathcal{A}$) such that σ does not extend to a full automorphism of X [2, section 6.2]. From the fact that $\mathcal{A}$ is representable, [8, theorem 5.3.16] proves that $\mathcal{A} \in \mathbf{S}Ra\mathbf{CA}_n$ for all $n < \omega$ but from the fact that it has no homogeneous representation it can be proved that there is an $n < \omega$ such that $\mathcal{A}$ has no n-dimensional cylindric basis, in fact it can be shown that $\mathcal{A}$ has no 5-dimensional cylindric basis.

Thus we seek a condition stronger than the existence of a relational basis but weaker than the existence of a cylindric basis. Let $\mathcal{A}$ be an atomic relation algebra, $n \geq 4$ and let Λ be any set (of 'labels').

Definition 4. An *n-dimensional Λ-hypernetwork over $\mathcal{A}$*, $N = (N^-, N^+)$, is an n-network N^- extended with a labelling function $N^+ : {}^{<n-1}n \to \Lambda$ such that for every $\bar{a}, \bar{b} \in {}^{<n-1}n$ of equal length, if $N^-(a_i, b_i) \leq 1'$ for each $i < |\bar{a}|$, then $N^+(\bar{a}) = N^+(\bar{b})$.

For two such hypernetworks N, M we write $N \equiv_i M$ to mean $N^-|_{n \setminus \{i\}} = M^-|_{n \setminus \{i\}}$ and $N^+|_{n \setminus \{i\}} = M^+|_{n \setminus \{i\}}$. $N \equiv_{ij} M$ is defined similarly.

Definition 5. An *n-dimensional Λ-hyperbasis for $\mathcal{A}$* is a set $\mathcal{H}$ of Λ-hypernetworks over $\mathcal{A}$ satisfying

1. If $a \in At(\mathcal{A})$ then there is $N \in \mathcal{H}$ with $N^-(0, 1) = a$
2. If $N \in \mathcal{H}$, $i, j < n$, $k \in n \setminus \{i, j\}$, and $a, b \in At(\mathcal{A})$ satisfy $N^-(i, j) \leq a; b$, then there is $M \in \mathcal{H}$ with $M \equiv_k N$, $M^-(i, k) = a$ and $M^-(k, j) = b$.
3. If $N, M \in \mathcal{H}$, $i, j < n$ are distinct, and $N \equiv_{ij} M$, then there is $P \in \mathcal{H}$ with $N \equiv_i P \equiv_j M$.

This is the same as the definition of a cylindric basis, except the elements are hypernetworks instead of networks. This definition gives us the characterisation we require.

Theorem 1. *Let $\mathcal{A}$ be a relation algebra and $4 \leq n < \omega$. Then $\mathcal{A} \in \mathbf{S}Ra\mathbf{CA}_n$ if and only if $\mathcal{A}^+$ has an n-dimensional Λ-hyperbasis, for some set Λ.*

The proof from right to left closely follows Maddux's proof for algebras with cylindric bases. The other direction involves technical arguments based on some results of Thompson on substitutions in cylindric algebras [16].

2 A strict hierarchy

Now it is quite easy to see that $SRaCA_n \supseteq SRaCA_{n+1}$, because if $A \subseteq Ra(C)$ for some $C \in CA_{n+1}$, then it can be seen that $Ra(C) = Ra(Nr_n(C))$ and since $Nr_n(C) \in CA_n$, it follows that $A \in SRaCA_n$. A question raised in [1, problem 17] is to show that each of these inclusions is strict, i.e. $SRaCA_n \neq SRaCA_{n+1}$ for $3 \leq n < \omega$. For this, we define a finite relation algebra A_n and show that $A_n \in SRaCA_n \setminus SRaCA_{n+1}$. An alternative construction is in [6]. The atoms of A_n are $1'$ and $a^r(p) : p < n-1$, $r < m_0$ where m_0 is some large integer, say $m_0 = n^n$. All atoms are self-converse. To define composition we let the set of *inconsistent triples of atoms* consist of permutations of $(1', x, y)$ $(x \neq y)$ and

$$(a^r(p), a^s(p), a^t(p)) \quad \text{any } p < n-1, \ r, s, t < m_0$$

so, if p is the 'colour' of $a^r(p)$ then monochromatic triples are not allowed. Composition is defined by this: for any $a, b \in A_n$,

$$a; b = \sum \{\gamma \in At(A_n) : \exists \alpha \leq a, \beta \leq b, \ (\alpha, \beta, \gamma) \text{ is not an inconsistent triple}\}$$

It is not too hard to show that the set of all n-networks forms an n-dimensional cylindric basis for A_n (exercise) so $A_n \in SRaCA_n$, and a more complex argument proves that A_n does not have an $n + 1$ dimensional hyperbasis and so cannot be in $SRaCA_{n+1}$. Maddux points out that this solves [7, problem 2.12] negatively: $SNr_nCA_{n+i} \neq SNr_nCA_{n+i+1}$ for $2 < n < \omega$, $i < \omega$. A corollary (see [6]) is that a certain $n + 1$-variable proof system $\vdash_{n+1}$ defined in [15] using only one binary predicate symbol is strictly stronger than its n-variable counterpart $\vdash_n$.

We can go further and construct rather similar relation algebras $A_{n,r} \in SRaCA_n$ for $4 \leq n, r < \omega$ and show that the second player can win the games $G_\omega^n(A_{n,r})$ and $G_r^{n+1}(A_{n,r})$ but not $G_\omega^{n+1}(A_{n,r})$ (the game G_r^n tests membership of $SRaCA_n$ V r times, see section 1.3 below). From this we can deduce that $A_{n,r} \in SRaCA_n \setminus SRaCA_{n+1}$ (all r) but that player two has a winning strategy in $G_\omega^{n+1}(B)$ where B is a certain countable relation algebra, elementarily equivalent to a non-principal ultraproduct of the $A_{n,r}$. From this, using Los' theorem, we deduce that $SRaCA_{n+1}$ is not finitely axiomatisable over $SRaCA_n$. A corollary of this is that for a certain standard n-variable first-order proof system $\vdash_{m,n}$ of m-variable formulas, there is no finite set of m-variable schemata whose m-variable instances, when added to $\vdash_{m,n}$ as axioms, yield $\vdash_{m,n+1}$. (Though our current version of this [5] does not reduce the language to one with just a single binary predicate and equality, still we do not anticipate serious problems with this.)

A different algebraic construction was used in [3] to show that RA_{n+1} is not finitely axiomatisable over RA_n $(4 \leq n < \omega)$.

3   Representation theory

Theorem 1 tells us that for any relation algebra $\mathcal{A}$ we have $\mathcal{A} \in \mathsf{SRaCA}_n$ iff $\mathcal{A}^+$ has an n-dimensional hyperbasis. But we would like to characterise when $\mathcal{A} \in \mathsf{SRaCA}_n$ purely in terms of $\mathcal{A}$, indeed we can obtain a recursive set of equations $\sigma_k : k < \omega$ such that $\mathcal{A} \models \{\sigma_k : k < \omega\} \Leftrightarrow \mathcal{A} \in \mathsf{SRaCA}_n$ and another recursive set of equations that characterise RA_n. We do this by first providing a relativized semantics for algebras in RA_n and SRaCA_n.

Definition 6.

- A *relativized representation* of a relation algebra $\mathcal{A}$ is a map $h : \mathcal{A} \to \wp(X \times X)$ (for some domain X) such that for all $a, b \in \mathcal{A}$,

$$h \text{ is } 1-1, \quad h(a+b) = h(a) \cup h(b), \quad h(-a) = h(1) \setminus h(a)$$
$$h(1') = \{(x,x) \in h(1) : x \in X\}, \quad h(\breve{a}) = \{(y,x) \in h(1) : (x,y) \in h(a)\}$$
$$h(a;b) = \{(x,y) \in h(1) : \exists z \in X, (x,z) \in h(a) \wedge (z,y) \in h(b)\}$$

  So this is like an ordinary representation except that all operations are relativized to some biggest binary relation $h(1) \subseteq X \times X$.
- A *clique* C in a relativized representation h is a subset of the domain X such that for all $c, c' \in C$ we have $(c, c') \in h(1)$.
- An *n-square relativized representation* h has the property that for any clique C containing fewer than n points, any $c, c' \in C$ and any $r, s \in \mathcal{A}$ such that $(c, c') \in h(r; s)$, there is a point d in the domain of the relativized representation such that $C \cup \{d\}$ is a clique and $(c, d) \in h(r)$ and $(d, c') \in h(s)$.
- An *n-smooth relativized representation* h is an n-square representation with domain X such that if ρ is any local isomorphism on X with $|\rho| \leq n-2$ and if $\{x\} \cup dom(\rho)$ and $\{y\} \cup rng(\rho)$ are cliques $(x, y \in X)$ then there is a point $x' \in X$ such that $\{x', y\} \cup rng(\rho)$ is a clique and $\rho \cup \{(x, x')\}$ is a local isomorphism.
- Let $\mathcal{L}_n(\mathcal{A})$ be the first-order language using only the variables $x_0, \ldots, x_{n-1}$ with atomic predicates $a(x_i, x_j)$ $(i, j < n)$ for each $a \in \mathcal{A}$ and all $i, j < n$. (We use the same symbol a to stand for an element of $\mathcal{A}$ and a binary predicate symbol in this language.) Let h be a relativized representation of $\mathcal{A}$. We can evaluate a formula $\varphi \in \mathcal{L}_n(\mathcal{A})$ over the cliques of h under any variable assignment $v : \{x_0, \ldots, x_{n-1}\} \to X$ such that $rng(v)$ is a clique, by

  $- h, v \models a(x_i, x_j) \Leftrightarrow (v(x_i), v(x_j)) \in h(a)$

- boolean connectives behave as expected
- $h, v \models \exists x_i \varphi \Leftrightarrow h, v' \models \varphi$ for some variable assignment v' (with $rng(v')$ a clique of h) that agrees with v except perhaps on x_i.

We say that h is *n-flat* if $h, v \models (\exists x_i \exists x_j \varphi \leftrightarrow \exists x_j \exists x_i \varphi)$ for any variable assignment v, such that $rng(v)$ is a clique, and any $\varphi \in \mathcal{L}_n(A)$.

These relativized representations exactly characterise the classes under consideration.

Theorem 2. *Let A be any relation algebra (or more generally a non-associative algebra) and $n \geq 4$.*

1. *$A \in \mathsf{RA}_n$ if and only if A has an n-square relativized representation.*
2. *For finite A, $VA \in \mathsf{CB}_n$ if and only if A has an n-smooth relativized representation.*
3. *$A \in \mathsf{SRaCA}_n$ if and only if A has an n-flat relativized representation.*

4   Recursive axiomatisations

These relativized semantics can be used to obtain recursive axiomatisations of the classes under consideration. As an example consider n-flat relativized representations, which correspond to SRaCA_n. We define a game $G_r^n(A)$ played by two players $\forall$ and $\exists$ with r rounds in the game. Roughly, the two players build better and better approximations to an n-flat relativized representation, $\forall$ picks defects in the current approximation and $\exists$ repairs the defect if she can. We show that a winning strategy for $\exists$ in $G_\omega^n(A)$ is equivalent to the existence of an n-flat relativized representation. And using the fact that $\exists$ only has a finite number of choices for each of her moves we show that a winning strategy for her in each game $G_k^n(A)$ for $k < \omega$ is equivalent to a winning strategy for $\exists$ in $G_\omega^n(A)$. Finally we can find a first-order formula σ_k such that $A \models \sigma_k$ iff $\exists$ has a winning strategy in $G_k^n(A)$ (any $k < \omega$). Thus $A \in \mathsf{SRaCA}_n \Leftrightarrow A \models \{\sigma_k^n : k < \omega\}$. We can axiomatise the class RA_n in the same way.

5   Summary of relations between the classes

$$\mathsf{RRA} = \bigcap_{n<\omega} \mathsf{RA}_n = \bigcap_{n<\omega} \mathsf{SRaCA}_n = \bigcap_{n<\omega} \mathsf{SCB}_n$$

$$\mathsf{RA}_4 \supset \mathsf{RA}_5 \supset \ldots, \qquad\qquad \mathsf{SRaCA}_4 \supset \mathsf{SRaCA}_5 \supset \ldots$$

[8,12,3] and each of these inclusions is strict and not finitely axiomatisable.

$$\mathsf{RA}_n \supset \mathsf{SRaCA}_n \supseteq \mathsf{SCB}_n, \quad \text{for each } n \text{ with } 5 \leq n < \omega$$

(whether the second inclusion is strict or not remains open.) For a finite relation algebra A we have

$$A \in \bigcap_{n<\omega} \mathsf{CB}_n \Leftrightarrow A \text{ has a homogeneous representation}$$

References

1. Andréka H., Monk J.D. and Németi I. (1991) Algebraic Logic. Colloq. Math. Soc. J. Bolyai. North-Holland, Amsterdam, 1991. Conference Proceedings, Budapest, 1989
2. Hirsch R. and Hodkinson I. (1997) Step by step — building representations in algebraic logic. Journal of Symbolic Logic, 62(1):225–279, March
3. Hirsch R. and Hodkinson I. (1998) Relation algebras with n-dimensional bases. submitted to Annals of Pure and Applied Logic
4. Hirsch R. and Hodkinson I. (1999) Relation algebras from cylindric algebras, I. Submitted to the Annals of Pure and Applied Logic
5. Hirsch R. and Hodkinson I. (1999) Relation algebras from cylindric algebras, II. Submitted to the Annals of Pure and Applied Logic
6. Hirsch R., Hodkinson I. and Maddux R. (1998) On the number of variables required in proofs. in preparation
7. Henkin L., Monk J.D. and Tarski A. (1971) Cylindric Algebras Part I. North-Holland
8. Henkin L., Monk J.D. and Tarski A. (1985) Cylindric Algebras Part II. North-Holland
9. Lyndon R. (1950) The representation of relational algebras. Annals of Mathematics, 51(3):707–729
10. Lyndon R. (1961) Relation algebras and projective geometries. Michigan Mathematics Journal, 8:207–210
11. Maddux R. (1978) Topics in Relation Algebra. PhD thesis, University of California, Berkeley
12. Maddux R. (1992) Relation algebras of every dimension. Journal of Symbolic Logic, 57(4):1213–1229
13. Monk J.D. (1964) On representable relation algebras. Michigan Mathematics Journal, 11:207–210
14. Stone M. (1936) The theory of representations for boolean algebras. Transactions of the American Mathematical Society, 40:37–111
15. Tarski A. and Givant S.R. (1987) A Formalization of Set Theory Without Variables. Number 41 in Colloquium Publications in Mathematics. American Mathematical Society, Providence, Rhode Island
16. Thompson R. (1993) Complete description of substitutions in cylindric algebras and other algebraic logics. In: Rauszer C. (Ed.) Algebraic methods in logic and in computer science, 28:327–342. Banach Center publications, Institute of mathematics, Polish Academy of Sciences

Chapter 15
Lattices in Dedekind Categories

Yasuo Kawahara

Department of Informatics
Kyushu University 33
Fukuoka 812-8581, Japan
kawahara@i.kyushu-u.ac.jp

Abstract. Lattice structures are fundamental and useful in mathematics and theoretical computer science. It is well-known that lattice structures with meet and join operations satisfying associative, commutative and absorption laws are equivalent to lattice structures defined by ordering relations having joins and meets. This paper defines a notion of lattices in Dedekind categories and studies some basic properties of lattice structures. Following relational calculus, an element-free representation of these properties is discussed.
Keywords: lattice, Dedekind category, allegory, relational calculus

1 Introduction

A lattice is a triple $(X, \vee, \wedge)$ consisting of a set X and two functions $\vee :$ $X \times X \to X$ and $\wedge : X \times X \to X$ satisfying:
Associative Law: (L1$\vee$) $(x \vee y) \vee z = x \vee (y \vee z)$ and (L1$\wedge$) $(x \wedge y) \wedge z = x \wedge (y \wedge z)$
Commutative Law: (L2$\vee$) $x \vee y = y \vee x$ and (L2$\wedge$) $x \wedge y = y \wedge x$
Absorption Law: (L3$\vee$) $x \wedge (x \vee y) = x$ and (L3$\wedge$) $x \vee (x \wedge y) = x$
for all elememts x, y and z of X.

It is well-known that a lattice $(X, \vee, \wedge)$ has a natural ordering $\leq$ defined by $x \leq y$ for $x, y \in X$ iff $x \vee y = y$. The proof consists of checking that the ordering $\leq$ is in fact reflexive, transitive and antsymmetric, and that it has a few alternative definitions such as $x \leq y$ iff $x \wedge y = x$. Conversely, it is also well-known that the concept of lattice is obtained from ordered sets with joins and meets.

The motivation of this paper is to demonstrate these facts in categories [4]. To discuss binary operations such as $\vee : X \times X \to X$ and $\wedge : X \times X \to X$ the involved category needs to have (finite) cartesian products. Furthermore the category has to be equipped with a kind of relational structure, as we treat it with an ordering on it. This is a reason why categorical lattice theory is formalized in Dedekind categories [5]. The modern algebraic theory of binary relations was founded by Tarski [7], and the categorical study of relations was initiated by Mac Lane [3]. Though Dedekind categories in this note are synonyous with allegories due to Freyd and Scedrov [1] and heterogeneous relation algebras by Schmidt and Ströhlein [6], the author adopt Dedekind

categories for the historical reason. The paper is organised as follows:
In section 2 we define Dedekind categories and relational products, and review
some fundamentals of Dedekind categories. In section 3 a notion of lattices
in Dedekind categories is defined, and some basic facts on a natural partial
ordering on a lattice in a Dedekind category are investigated. In section 4 we
construct a lattice from a partial ordering with joins and meets in a Dedekind
category.

2   Dedekind categories

In this section we recall the fundamentals of relation categories, which we
will call elementary Dedekind categories.

Throughout this paper, a morphism α from an object X into an object
Y in a Dedekind category (which will be defined below) will be denoted by a
half arrow $\alpha : X \rightharpoonup Y$, and the composite of a morphism $\alpha : X \rightharpoonup Y$ followed
by a morphism $\beta : Y \rightharpoonup Z$ will be written as $\alpha\beta : X \rightharpoonup Z$. Also we will
denote the identity morphism on X as id_X.

Definition 1. A Dedekind category $\mathcal{D}$ is a category satisfying the following:
D1. [Distributive Lattice] For all pairs of objects X and Y the hom-set
$\mathcal{D}(X,Y)$ consisting of all morphisms of X into Y is a distributive lattice
with the least morphism 0_{XY} and the greatest morphism ∇_{XY}. Its lattice
structure will be denoted by

$$\mathcal{D}(X,Y) = (\mathcal{D}(X,Y), \sqsubseteq, \sqcup, \sqcap, 0_{XY}, \nabla_{XY}).$$

D2. [Converse] There is given a converse operation $^\sharp : \mathcal{D}(X,Y) \to \mathcal{D}(Y,X)$.
That is, for all morphisms $\alpha, \alpha' : X \rightharpoonup Y$, $\beta : Y \rightharpoonup Z$, the following converse
laws hold:
(a) $(\alpha\beta)^\sharp = \beta^\sharp \alpha^\sharp$, (b) $(\alpha^\sharp)^\sharp = \alpha$, (c) If $\alpha \sqsubseteq \alpha'$, then $\alpha^\sharp \sqsubseteq \alpha'^\sharp$
for all morphisms $\alpha, \alpha' : X \rightharpoonup Y$ and $\beta : Y \rightharpoonup Z$.
D3. [Dedekind Formula] For all morphisms $\alpha : X \rightharpoonup Y$, $\beta : Y \rightharpoonup Z$ and
$\gamma : X \rightharpoonup Z$ the Dedekind formula $\alpha\beta \sqcap \gamma \sqsubseteq \alpha(\beta \sqcap \alpha^\sharp\gamma)$ holds.
D4. [Residues] For all morphisms $\beta : Y \rightharpoonup Z$ and $\gamma : X \rightharpoonup Z$ the residue
(or division) $\gamma \div \beta : X \rightharpoonup Y$ is a morphism such that $\alpha\beta \sqsubseteq \gamma$ if and only if
$\alpha \sqsubseteq \gamma \div \beta$ for all morphisms $\alpha : X \rightharpoonup Y$. $\square$

The following is a basic property of Dedekind categories, which will be
repeatedly used in this paper.

Proposition 1. *Let $\alpha, \alpha' : X \rightharpoonup Y$ and $\beta, \beta' : Y \rightharpoonup Z$ be morphisms in a
Dedekind category. If $\alpha \sqsubseteq \alpha'$ and $\beta \sqsubseteq \beta'$, then $\alpha\beta \sqsubseteq \alpha'\beta'$.*

Proof. Assume $\alpha \sqsubseteq \alpha'$ and $\beta \sqsubseteq \beta'$. First we will see $\alpha\beta \sqsubseteq \alpha'\beta$. The characteristic property of residues leads $\alpha' \sqsubseteq \alpha'\beta \div \beta$ from the reflexivity $\alpha'\beta \sqsubseteq \alpha'\beta$.
Hence we have $\alpha \sqsubseteq \alpha'\beta \div \beta$ by the assumption $\alpha \sqsubseteq \alpha'$, and so $\alpha\beta \sqsubseteq \alpha'\beta$

again by the characteristic property of residues. Finally we will see $\alpha\beta \sqsubseteq \alpha\beta'$. As $\beta^{\sharp} \sqsubseteq \beta'^{\sharp}$ by D2(c), the former result shows $\beta^{\sharp}\alpha^{\sharp} \sqsubseteq \beta'^{\sharp}\alpha^{\sharp}$ and so we have $\alpha\beta = (\beta^{\sharp}\alpha^{\sharp})^{\sharp} \sqsubseteq (\beta'^{\sharp}\alpha^{\sharp})^{\sharp} = \alpha\beta'$ by D2(a)-(c). $\qquad\square$

More details on fundamental properties of relational categories can be found in [2]. The following is a basic lemma [1] in Dedekind categories.

Lemma 1. *For two relations* $\alpha : X \to Y$ *and* $\beta : Y \to X$ *an equality* $\mathrm{id}_X \sqcap (\alpha \sqcap \beta^{\sharp})(\alpha^{\sharp} \sqcap \beta) = \mathrm{id}_X \sqcap \alpha\beta$ *holds.*

Proof.

$$\begin{aligned}
\mathrm{id}_X \sqcap \alpha\beta &= \mathrm{id}_X \sqcap \mathrm{id}_X \sqcap \alpha\beta \\
&\sqsubseteq \mathrm{id}_X \sqcap (\mathrm{id}_X\beta^{\sharp} \sqcap \alpha)(\alpha^{\sharp}\mathrm{id}_X \sqcap \beta) \; \{ \text{ Dedekind Formula } \} \\
&= \mathrm{id}_X \sqcap (\alpha \sqcap \beta^{\sharp})(\alpha^{\sharp} \sqcap \beta) \\
&\sqsubseteq \mathrm{id}_X \sqcap \alpha\beta.
\end{aligned}$$

$\qquad\square$

A morphism $f : X \to Y$ such that $f^{\sharp}f \sqsubseteq \mathrm{id}_Y$ (*univalent*) and $\mathrm{id}_X \sqsubseteq ff^{\sharp}$ (*total*) is called a *function* and may be introduced as $f : X \to Y$.

Corollary 1. *Let* $\alpha : X \to Y$ *and* $\beta : Y \to X$ *be relations in a Dedekind category* $\mathcal{D}$. *If* $\alpha\beta = \mathrm{id}_X$ *and* $\beta\alpha = \mathrm{id}_Y$, *then* $\alpha = \beta^{\sharp}$.

Proof. As $\alpha\beta = \mathrm{id}_X$ we have $\mathrm{id}_X = \mathrm{id}_X \sqcap \mathrm{id}_X = \mathrm{id}_X \sqcap \alpha\beta = \mathrm{id}_X \sqcap (\alpha \sqcap \beta^{\sharp})(\alpha^{\sharp} \sqcap \beta)$ by Lemma 1. Hence $\mathrm{id}_X \sqsubseteq \alpha\alpha^{\sharp}$ and $\mathrm{id}_X \sqsubseteq \beta^{\sharp}\beta$. Also it follows from $\mathrm{id}_X \sqsubseteq \alpha\alpha^{\sharp}$ and $\beta\alpha = \mathrm{id}_Y$ that $\beta^{\sharp}\beta \sqsubseteq \beta^{\sharp}\beta\alpha\alpha^{\sharp} = \beta^{\sharp}\alpha^{\sharp} = (\alpha\beta)^{\sharp} = \mathrm{id}_X$. Therefore $\beta^{\sharp}\beta = \mathrm{id}_X$ and so $\beta^{\sharp} = \beta^{\sharp}\beta\alpha = \alpha$ from $\beta\alpha = \mathrm{id}_Y$. $\qquad\square$

Definition 2. A Dedekind category $\mathcal{D}$ has *relational products* if for each pair of objects A and B there is a pair of functions $p : A \times B \to A$ and $q : A \times B \to B$ such that $p^{\sharp}q = \nabla_{AB}$ and $pp^{\sharp} \sqcap qq^{\sharp} = \mathrm{id}_{A \times B}$. The functions p and q will be called a *pair of projections* of relational products. $\qquad\square$

Throughout the rest of the paper we assume that $\mathcal{D}$ is a fixed Dedekind category with relational products.

Proposition 2. *Let* $p : A \times B \to A$ *and* $q : A \times B \to B$ *be a pair of projections of* $A \times B$. *For each pair of functions* $f : X \to A$ *and* $g : X \to B$, *a relation* $f\top g = fp^{\sharp} \sqcap gq^{\sharp} : X \to A \times B$ *is a unique function such that* $(f\top g)p = f$ *and* $(f\top g)q = g$.

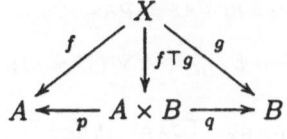

*Proof.*Set $h = f \top g$. The univalency (or, single-valuedness) of h simply follows from

$$
\begin{aligned}
h^\sharp h &= (fp^\sharp \sqcap gq^\sharp)^\sharp (fp^\sharp \sqcap gq^\sharp) \\
&= (pf^\sharp \sqcap qg^\sharp)(fp^\sharp \sqcap gq^\sharp) \\
&\sqsubseteq pf^\sharp fp^\sharp \sqcap qg^\sharp gq^\sharp \\
&\sqsubseteq pp^\sharp \sqcap qq^\sharp \quad \text{(by } f^\sharp f \sqsubseteq \mathrm{id}_A \text{ and } g^\sharp g \sqsubseteq \mathrm{id}_B) \\
&= \mathrm{id}_{A \times B}.
\end{aligned}
$$

Also the totality of h comes from

$$
\begin{aligned}
\mathrm{id}_X \sqcap hh^\sharp &= \mathrm{id}_X \sqcap (fp^\sharp \sqcap gq^\sharp)(fp^\sharp \sqcap gq^\sharp)^\sharp \\
&= \mathrm{id}_X \sqcap (fp^\sharp)(gq^\sharp)^\sharp && \{ \text{ Lemma 1 } \} \\
&= \mathrm{id}_X \sqcap fp^\sharp qg^\sharp \\
&\sqsupseteq \mathrm{id}_X \sqcap ff^\sharp gg^\sharp && \{ f^\sharp g \sqsubseteq \nabla_{AB} = p^\sharp q \} \\
&= \mathrm{id}_X && \{ \mathrm{id}_X \sqsubseteq ff^\sharp \text{ and } \mathrm{id}_X \sqsubseteq gg^\sharp \}
\end{aligned}
$$

The uniqueness of h follows from $h = h\,\mathrm{id}_{A \times B} = h(pp^\sharp \sqcap qq^\sharp) = hpp^\sharp \sqcap hqq^\sharp$. $\square$

Remark. It is trivial that $p \top q = \mathrm{id}_{A \times B}$.

Corollary 2. *For a function $k : X \to A$ an equality $k(f \top g) = kf \top kg$ holds.*
$\square$

Proposition 3. *Let $p_{AB} : A \times B \to A$ and $q_{AB} : A \times B \to B$ be a pair of projections of $A \times B$, and $p_{BA} : B \times A \to B$ and $q_{BA} : B \times B \to A$ a pair of projections of $B \times A$. The twist function $t_{AB} : A \times B \to B \times A$ is defined as the unique function such that $t_{AB}p_{BA} = q_{AB}$ and $t_{AB}q_{BA} = p_{AB}$. (That is, $t_{AB} = q_{AB}p_{BA}^\sharp \sqcap p_{AB}q_{BA}^\sharp = q_{AB} \top p_{AB}$.) Then $t_{AB}t_{BA} = \mathrm{id}_{A \times B}$ and $t_{BA}t_{AB} = \mathrm{id}_{B \times A}$.*

*Proof.*Using Corollary 2 we have

$$
t_{AB}t_{BA} = t_{AB}(q_{BA} \top p_{BA}) = t_{AB}q_{BA} \top t_{AB}p_{BA} = p_{AB} \top q_{AB} = \mathrm{id}_{A \times B}.
$$

$\square$

In general the pair of projections will be denoted by $p_{AB} : A \times B \to A$ and $q_{AB} : A \times B \to B$. The diagonal function $d_A : A \to A \times A$ is defined as a unique function such that $d_A p_{AA} = \mathrm{id}_A$ and $d_A q_{AA} = \mathrm{id}_A$. That is, $d_A = \mathrm{id}_A \top \mathrm{id}_A = p_{AA}^\sharp \sqcap q_{AA}^\sharp$. The associative function $a_{ABC} : (A \times B) \times C \to A \times (B \times C)$ is defined by

$$
a_{ABC} = p_{A \times BC}p_{AB} \top (p_{A \times BC}q_{AB} \top q_{A \times BC})
$$

Another associative function $b_{ABC} : A \times (B \times C) \to (A \times B) \times C$ is defined by

$$
b_{ABC} = (p_{AB \times C} \top q_{AB \times C}q_{BC}) \top q_{AB \times C}q_{BC}.
$$

It is trivial that a_{ABC} and b_{ABC} are mutually inverse, that is, $a_{ABC}b_{ABC} = \mathrm{id}_{(A \times B) \times C}$ and $b_{ABC}a_{ABC} = \mathrm{id}_{A \times (B \times C)}$.

For a pair of functions $f : A \to X$ and $g : B \to Y$ we define a function $f \times g : A \times B \to X \times Y$ by $f \times g = p_{AB}f \top q_{AB}g (= p_{AB}fp_{XY}^{\sharp} \sqcap q_{AB}gq_{XY}^{\sharp})$. That is, $f \times g$ is a unique function such that $(f \times g)p_{XY} = p_{AB}f$ and $(f \times g)q_{XY} = q_{AB}g$.

$$
\begin{array}{ccccc}
A & \xleftarrow{\ p_{AB}\ } & A \times B & \xrightarrow{\ q_{AB}\ } & B \\
{\scriptstyle f}\downarrow & & \downarrow{\scriptstyle f \times g} & & \downarrow{\scriptstyle g} \\
X & \xleftarrow{\ p_{XY}\ } & X \times Y & \xrightarrow{\ q_{XY}\ } & Y
\end{array}
$$

The following lemma indicates a well-known example of pullbacks.

Lemma 2. *An equality $p_{AB}^{\sharp}(f \times \mathrm{id}_B) = fp_{XB}^{\sharp}$ holds for every function $f : A \to B$.*

$$
\begin{array}{ccc}
A \times B & \xrightarrow{\ f \times \mathrm{id}_B\ } & X \times B \\
{\scriptstyle p_{AB}}\downarrow & & \downarrow{\scriptstyle p_{XB}} \\
A & \xrightarrow[\ \ f\ \ ]{} & X
\end{array}
$$

*Proof.*Note that $p_{AB}^{\sharp}q_{AB}q_{XB}^{\sharp} = \nabla_{AB}q_{XB}^{\sharp} = \nabla_{AX \times B}$ by $p_{AB}^{\sharp}q_{AB} = \nabla_{AB}$ and the totality of q_{XB}. ($\nabla_{AX \times B} \sqsubseteq \nabla_{AX \times B}q_{XB}q_{XB}^{\sharp} \sqsubseteq \nabla_{AB}q_{XB}^{\sharp} = p_{AB}^{\sharp}q_{AB}q_{XB}^{\sharp}$.)

$$
\begin{aligned}
p_{AB}^{\sharp}(f \times \mathrm{id}_B) &= p_{AB}^{\sharp}(p_{AB}fp_{XB}^{\sharp} \sqcap q_{AB}q_{XB}^{\sharp}) \\
&\sqsubseteq p_{AB}^{\sharp}p_{AB}fp_{XB}^{\sharp} \\
&\sqsubseteq fp_{XB}^{\sharp} && \{\ p_{AB}^{\sharp}p_{AB} \sqsubseteq \mathrm{id}_A\ \} \\
&= fp_{XB}^{\sharp} \sqcap p_{AB}^{\sharp}q_{AB}q_{XB}^{\sharp} && \{\ p_{AB}^{\sharp}q_{AB}q_{XB}^{\sharp} = \nabla_{AX \times B}\ \} \\
&\sqsubseteq p_{AB}^{\sharp}(p_{AB}fp_{XB}^{\sharp} \sqcap q_{AB}q_{XB}^{\sharp}) && \{\ \text{Dedekind Formula}\ \} \\
&= p_{AB}^{\sharp}(f \times \mathrm{id}_B)
\end{aligned}
$$

$\square$

Lemma 3. *Let $p : A \times B \to A$, $q : A \times B \to B$ and $p_0 : A \times B' \to A$, $q_0 : A \times B' \to B'$ be projections of products $A \times B$ and $A \times B'$, respectively. Then*

(a) $\alpha = p^{\sharp}(p\alpha \sqcap q) = p^{\sharp}p\alpha$ *for every relation $\alpha : A \to B$.*

(b) *If relations $\delta_0, \delta_1 : A \times B \to B$ satisfy $\delta_0 \sqsubseteq q$ and $\delta_1 \sqsubseteq q$, then $p^{\sharp}\delta_0 \sqcap p^{\sharp}\delta_1 = p^{\sharp}(\delta_0 \sqcap \delta_1)$.*

(c) *If relations $\gamma_0, \gamma_1 : A \times B' \to A \times B$ satisfy $\gamma_0 \sqsubseteq p_0 p^{\sharp}$ and $\gamma_1 \sqsubseteq p_0 p^{\sharp}$, then $p_0^{\sharp}\gamma_0 \sqcap p_0^{\sharp}\gamma_1 = p_0^{\sharp}(\gamma_0 \sqcap \gamma_1)$ and $\gamma_0 q \sqcap \gamma_1 q = (\gamma_0 \sqcap \gamma_1)q$.*

Proof.(a) $\alpha = \alpha \sqcap p^{\sharp}q \sqsubseteq p^{\sharp}(p\alpha \sqcap q) \sqsubseteq p^{\sharp}p\alpha \sqsubseteq \alpha$.

(b)

$$
\begin{aligned}
p^{\sharp}\delta_0 \sqcap p^{\sharp}\delta_1 &\sqsubseteq p^{\sharp}(\delta_0 \sqcap pp^{\sharp}\delta_1) && \{\text{Dedekind Formula}\} \\
&= p^{\sharp}(\delta_0 \sqcap pp^{\sharp}\delta_1 \sqcap q) && \{\delta_0 \sqsubseteq q\} \\
&\sqsubseteq p^{\sharp}[\delta_0 \sqcap (pp^{\sharp} \sqcap q\delta_1^{\sharp})\delta_1] && \{\text{Dedekind Formula}\} \\
&\sqsubseteq p^{\sharp}[\delta_0 \sqcap (pp^{\sharp} \sqcap qq^{\sharp})\delta_1] && \{\delta_1 \sqsubseteq q\} \\
&= p^{\sharp}(\delta_0 \sqcap \delta_1). && \{pp^{\sharp} \sqcap qq^{\sharp} = \text{id}_{A\times B}\}
\end{aligned}
$$

(c)

$$
\begin{aligned}
\gamma_0 q \sqcap \gamma_1 q &\sqsubseteq (\gamma_0 \sqcap \gamma_1 qq^{\sharp})q && \{\text{Dedekind Formula}\} \\
&= (\gamma_0 \sqcap p_0 p^{\sharp} \sqcap \gamma_1 qq^{\sharp})q && \{\gamma_0 \sqsubseteq p_0 p^{\sharp}\} \\
&\sqsubseteq [\gamma_0 \sqcap \gamma_1(\gamma_1^{\sharp}p_0 p^{\sharp} \sqcap qq^{\sharp})]q && \{\text{Dedekind Formula}\} \\
&\sqsubseteq [\gamma_0 \sqcap \gamma_1(pp_0^{\sharp}p_0 p^{\sharp} \sqcap qq^{\sharp})]q && \{\gamma_1 \sqsubseteq p_0 p^{\sharp}\} \\
&\sqsubseteq [\gamma_0 \sqcap \gamma_1(pp^{\sharp} \sqcap qq^{\sharp})]q && \{p_0^{\sharp}p_0 \sqsubseteq \text{id}_A\} \\
&= (\gamma_0 \sqcap \gamma_1)q. && \{pp^{\sharp} \sqcap qq^{\sharp} = \text{id}_{A\times B}\}
\end{aligned}
$$

$\square$

3   Lattices

In this section we will see that lattice structures with meet and join operations satisfying associative, commutative and absorption laws induce reflexive, transitive and antisymmetric relations. We will write $p = p_{XX}$, $q = q_{XX}$, $t = t_{XX}$, $d = d_X$, $a = a_{XXX}$ and $b = b_{XXX}$.

Definition 3. A lattice in a Dedekind category $\mathcal{D}$ is a triple $(X, \vee, \wedge)$ of an object X, and two functions (binary operations) $\vee : X \times X \to X$ and $\wedge : X \times X \to X$ satisfying

Associative Law:

(L1$\vee$) $(\vee \times \text{id}_X)\vee = a(\text{id}_X \times \vee)\vee$ $\qquad$ $\{ (x \vee y) \vee z = x \vee (y \vee z) \}$

(L1$\wedge$) $(\wedge \times \text{id}_X)\wedge = a(\text{id}_X \times \wedge)\wedge$ $\qquad$ $\{ (x\wedge y)\wedge z = x\wedge(y\wedge z) \}$

Commutative Law:

(L2$\vee$) $t\vee = \vee$ $\qquad$ $\{ x \vee y = y \vee x \}$

(L2$\wedge$) $t\wedge = \wedge$ $\qquad$ $\{ x\wedge y = y\wedge x \}$

Absorption Law:

(L3$\vee$) $(p\top\vee)\wedge = p$ $\qquad$ $\{ x\wedge(x \vee y) = x \}$

(L3$\wedge$) $(p\top\wedge)\vee = p$ $\qquad$ $\{ x \vee (x\wedge y) = x \}$

$\square$

The above laws for lattices are illustrated by the following commutative diagrams:

(L1∨)

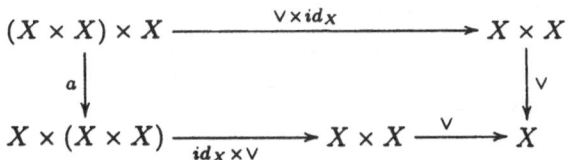

(L2∨)

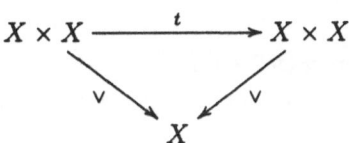

(L3∨)

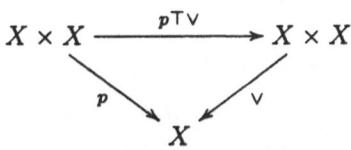

Recall that $(p\top\vee)t = \vee\top p$ by the property of the twist function t and so $(\vee\top p)\wedge = (p\top\vee)t\wedge = (p\top\vee)\wedge = p$ by (L2∧) and (L3∨). Hence (L3∨′) $(\vee\top p)\wedge = p$ and (L3∧′) $(\wedge\top p)\vee = p$ are equivalent to (L3∨) and (L3∧), respectively.

Proposition 4. *An identity* $d\vee = \mathrm{id}_X$ *holds in every lattice* $(X, \vee, \wedge)$ *in a Dedekind category.*

Proof. First note that $d(p\top p) = dp\top dp = \mathrm{id}_X\top\mathrm{id}_X = d$ by Corollary 2. Hence

$$
\begin{aligned}
d\vee &= d(p\top p)\vee & &\{\ d = d(p\top p)\ \} \\
&= d\{(p\top\vee)p\top(p\top\vee)\wedge\}\vee & &\{\ (p\top\vee)p = p \text{ and (L3∨) }\} \\
&= d(p\top\vee)(p\top\wedge)\vee & &\{\ \text{Corollary 2 }\} \\
&= d(p\top\vee)p & &\{\ (L3\wedge)\ \} \\
&= dp & &\{\ (p\top\vee)p = p\ \} \\
&= \mathrm{id}_X
\end{aligned}
$$

□

Define relations $\xi = p^{\sharp}(q \sqcap \vee) : X \rightharpoonup X$ and $\eta = (p \sqcap \wedge)^{\sharp}q : X \rightharpoonup X$. (For concrete relations: $\forall x, y \in X,\ x\xi y \iff y = x \vee y \iff x \le y$, and $x\eta y \iff x = x\wedge y \iff x \le y$.)

Note. It is easy to see the following basic fact on concrete lattices:

$$(x, y) \in \xi = p^\sharp(q \sqcap \vee)$$
$$\iff \exists (x', y') :: (x, (x', y')) \in p^\sharp \text{ and } ((x', y'), y) \in q \sqcap \vee$$
$$\iff \exists (x', y') :: x = x' \text{ and } y' = y \text{ and } x' \vee y' = y$$
$$\iff x \vee y = y.$$

$$(x, y) \in p^\sharp \vee$$
$$\iff \exists (x', y') :: (x, (x', y')) \in p^\sharp \text{ and } ((x', y'), y) \in \vee$$
$$\iff \exists y' :: y = x \vee y'.$$

$$(x, y) \in \eta = (p \sqcap \wedge)^\sharp q$$
$$\iff \exists (x', y') :: (x, (x', y')) \in (p \sqcap \wedge)^\sharp \text{ and } ((x', y'), y) \in q$$
$$\iff \exists (x', y') :: x = x' \text{ and } x' \wedge y' = x \text{ and } y' = y$$
$$\iff x \wedge y = x.$$

$$(x, y) \in \wedge^\sharp q$$
$$\iff \exists (x', y') :: (x, (x', y')) \in \wedge^\sharp \text{ and } ((x', y'), y) \in q$$
$$\iff \exists x' :: x = x' \wedge y.$$

Proposition 5. *Let* $(X, \vee, \wedge)$ *be a lattice in a Dedekind category and set* $\xi = p^\sharp(q \sqcap \vee) : X \to X$. *Then an identity* $\mathrm{id}_X \sqcap d\vee = \mathrm{id}_X \sqcap \xi$ *holds.*

Proof.

$$\begin{aligned}
\mathrm{id}_X \sqcap \xi &= \mathrm{id}_X \sqcap p^\sharp(q \sqcap \vee) \\
&= \mathrm{id}_X \sqcap (p \sqcap q \sqcap \vee)^\sharp(p \sqcap q \sqcap \vee) \quad \{ \text{ Lemma 1 } \} \\
&= \mathrm{id}_X \sqcap (p \sqcap q)^\sharp \vee \qquad\qquad\quad \{ \text{ Lemma 1 } \} \\
&= \mathrm{id}_X \sqcap d\vee. \qquad\qquad\qquad\quad \{ d = p^\sharp \sqcap q^\sharp \}
\end{aligned}$$

$\square$

Combining with Propositions 3.1 and 3.1 we have the following

Corollary 3. *Let* $(X, \vee, \wedge)$ *be a lattice in a Dedekind category. Then* $\xi = p^\sharp(q \sqcap \vee) : X \to X$ *satisfies* $\mathrm{id}_X \sqsubseteq \xi$ *(reflexive).* $\square$

Proposition 6. *Let* $(X, \vee, \wedge)$ *be a lattice in a Dedekind category. Then* $\xi = p^\sharp(q \sqcap \vee) : X \to X$ *satisfies* $\xi \sqcap \xi^\sharp \sqsubseteq \mathrm{id}_X$ *(antisymmetric).*

Proof.

$$\begin{aligned}
\xi \sqcap \xi^\sharp &= p^\sharp(q \sqcap \vee) \sqcap (q \sqcap \vee)^\sharp p \\
&\sqsubseteq (q \sqcap \vee)^\sharp [(q \sqcap \vee)p^\sharp \sqcap p(q \sqcap \vee)^\sharp](q \sqcap \vee) \quad \{ \text{ Dedekind Formula } \} \\
&\sqsubseteq \vee^\sharp(qp^\sharp \sqcap pq^\sharp)\vee \\
&= \vee^\sharp t\vee \qquad\qquad\qquad\qquad\qquad\qquad\quad \{ t = qp^\sharp \sqcap pq^\sharp \} \\
&= \vee^\sharp \vee \qquad\qquad\qquad\qquad\qquad\qquad\quad \{ \text{(L2}\vee\text{)} \} \\
&\sqsubseteq \mathrm{id}_X. \qquad\qquad\qquad\qquad\qquad\qquad\quad \{ \text{ The univalency of } \vee \}
\end{aligned}$$

$\square$

Proposition 7. *Let $(X, \vee, \wedge)$ be a lattice in a Dedekind category, and set $\xi = p^{\sharp}(q \sqcap \vee) : X \to X$ and $\eta = (p \sqcap \wedge)^{\sharp}q : X \to X$. Then an identity $\xi = p^{\sharp}\vee = \wedge^{\sharp}q = \eta$ holds.*

*Proof.*First note $p = p \sqcap p = (p\top\vee)p \sqcap (p\top\vee)\wedge = (p\top\vee)(p \sqcap \wedge)$ by (L3$\vee$) and Corollary 2. Hence

$$\begin{aligned}
\xi &= p^{\sharp}(q \sqcap \vee) \\
&\sqsubseteq p^{\sharp}\vee \\
&= [(p\top\vee)(p \sqcap \wedge)]^{\sharp}(p\top\vee)q \quad \{\ p = (p\top\vee)(p \sqcap \wedge) \text{ and } (p\top\vee)q = \vee\ \} \\
&= (p \sqcap \wedge)^{\sharp}(p\top\vee)^{\sharp}(p\top\vee)q \\
&\sqsubseteq (p \sqcap \wedge)^{\sharp}q \qquad\qquad \{\text{ The univalency of } p\top\vee\ \} \\
&= \eta.
\end{aligned}$$

Similarly it follows from $p = p \sqcap p = (\wedge\top p)q \sqcap (\wedge\top p)\vee = (\wedge\top p)(q \sqcap \vee)$ by (L3$\wedge'$), Proposition 2 and Corollary 2 and so $q = tp = t(\wedge\top p)(q \sqcap \vee) = (t\wedge\top tp)(q \sqcap \vee) = (\wedge\top q)(q \sqcap \vee)$ by by (L2$\wedge$). Hence

$$\begin{aligned}
\eta &= (p \sqcap \wedge)^{\sharp}q \\
&\sqsubseteq \wedge^{\sharp}q \\
&= [(\wedge\top q)p]^{\sharp}(\wedge\top q)(q \sqcap \vee) \quad \{\ q = (\wedge\top q)(q \sqcap \vee) \text{ and } (\wedge\top q)p = \wedge\ \} \\
&= p^{\sharp}(\wedge\top q)^{\sharp}(\wedge\top q)(q \sqcap \vee) \\
&\sqsubseteq p^{\sharp}(q \sqcap \vee) \qquad\qquad \{\text{ The univalency of } \wedge\top q\ \} \\
&= \xi.
\end{aligned}$$

$\square$

Proposition 8. *Let $(X, \vee, \wedge)$ be a lattice in a Dedekind category. Then $\xi = p^{\sharp}(q \sqcap \vee) : X \to X$ satisfies $\xi\xi \sqsubseteq \xi$ (transitive).*

Proof.

$$\begin{aligned}
\xi\xi &= p^{\sharp} \vee p^{\sharp}\vee & \{\text{ Proposition 7 }\} \\
&= p^{\sharp}p_0{}^{\sharp}(\vee \times \mathrm{id}_X)\vee & \{\text{ Lemma 2 }\} \\
&= p^{\sharp}p_0{}^{\sharp}a(\mathrm{id}_X \times \vee)\vee & \{\ (\text{L1}\vee)\ \} \\
&= p^{\sharp}p_0{}^{\sharp}b^{\sharp}(\mathrm{id}_X \times \vee)\vee & \{\ a = b^{\sharp}\ \} \\
&= (bp_0p)^{\sharp}(\mathrm{id}_X \times \vee)\vee \\
&= [(\mathrm{id}_X \times \vee)p]^{\sharp}(\mathrm{id}_X \times \vee)\vee & \{\ bp_0p = p_1 = (\mathrm{id}_X \times \vee)p\ \} \\
&= p^{\sharp}(\mathrm{id}_X \times \vee)^{\sharp}(\mathrm{id}_X \times \vee)\vee \\
&\sqsubseteq p^{\sharp}\vee & \{\text{ The univalency of } \mathrm{id}_X \times \vee\ \} \\
&= \xi. & \{\text{ Proposition 7 }\}
\end{aligned}$$

$\square$

Note. The following three diagrams may help to understand the proof of the last proposition.

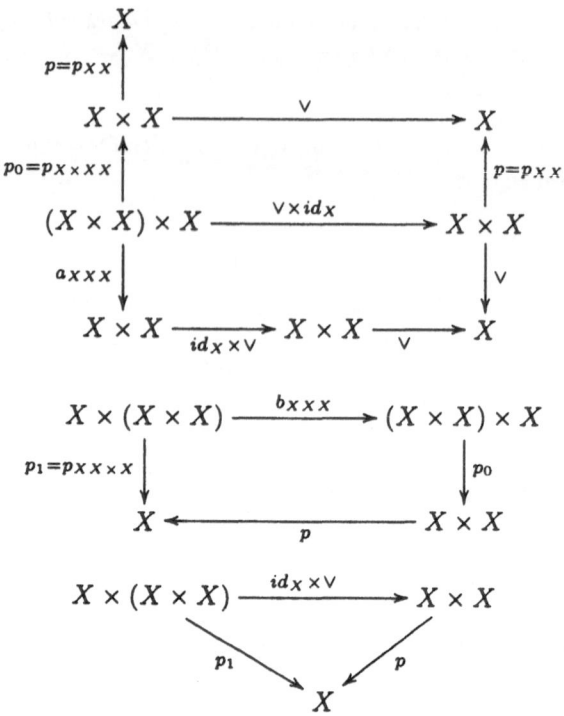

Theorem 1. *Let* $(X, \vee, \wedge)$ *be a lattice in a Dedekind category. Then* $\xi = p^{\sharp}(q \sqcap \vee) : X \rightharpoonup X$ *is reflexive, transitive and antisymmetric. Moreover,* $\xi = p^{\sharp}(q \sqcap \vee) = p^{\sharp}\vee = \wedge^{\sharp}q = (p \sqcap \wedge)^{\sharp}q$ *holds.*   □

4   Orderings

In this section we will see that orderings having joins and meets induce lattice structures also in Dedekind categories. First we show a technical lemma needed later.

Lemma 4. *Let* $\xi : X \rightharpoonup X$ *and* $\gamma : Y \rightharpoonup X$ *be relations, and let* $h : Z \to Y$ *and* $k : Y \to X$ *be functions. Then*

(a) $h\{(\xi \div \gamma)^{\sharp} \sqcap \gamma\} = (\xi \div h\gamma)^{\sharp} \sqcap h\gamma,$
(b) *If* $\mathrm{id}_X \sqsubseteq \xi$ *and* $\gamma\xi = \gamma$, *then* $k \sqsubseteq (\xi \div \gamma)^{\sharp} \sqcap \gamma$ *if and only if* $k\xi = \gamma$.

Proof.
(a)
$$
\begin{aligned}
h\{(\xi \div \gamma)^{\sharp} \sqcap \gamma\} &= h(\xi \div \gamma)^{\sharp} \sqcap h\gamma \\
&= \{(\xi \div \gamma)h^{\sharp}\}^{\sharp} \sqcap h\gamma \\
&= \{(\xi \div \gamma) \div h\}^{\sharp} \sqcap h\gamma \\
&= (\xi \div h\gamma)^{\sharp} \sqcap h\gamma.
\end{aligned}
$$

(b)

$$k \sqsubseteq (\xi \div \gamma)^\sharp \sqcap \gamma \iff k \sqsubseteq (\xi \div \gamma)^\sharp \text{ and } k \sqsubseteq \gamma$$
$$\iff k^\sharp \gamma \sqsubseteq \xi \text{ and } k \sqsubseteq \gamma$$
$$\iff \gamma \sqsubseteq k\xi \wedge k \sqsubseteq \gamma \qquad \{\ k \text{ is a function } \}$$
$$\iff \gamma = k\xi \qquad\qquad \{\ \mathrm{id}_X \sqsubseteq \xi \text{ and } \gamma\xi = \gamma \ \}$$

□

Definition 4. A relation $\xi : X \rightharpoonup X$ is an *ordering* on X if $\mathrm{id}_X \sqsubseteq \xi$ (reflexive), $\xi\xi \sqsubseteq \xi$ (transitive) and $\xi \sqcap \xi^\sharp \sqsubseteq \mathrm{id}_X$ (antisymmetric). □

For two relations $\xi, \xi' : X \rightharpoonup X$ we define relations $\xi|\xi' : X \times X \rightharpoonup X$ and $\vee_0 : X \times X \rightharpoonup X$ by $\xi|\xi' = p\xi \sqcap q\xi' (= (\xi^\sharp \top \xi'^\sharp)^\sharp)$ and $\vee_0 = (\xi \div \xi|\xi)^\sharp \sqcap \xi|\xi$. Note that this definition was suggested by Dr. Wolfram Kahl, Universität der Bundeswehr München, when he visited to Kyushu University in August, 1997.

Note. The following may give concrete meanings of relations $\xi|\xi$ and $\vee_0$.

$$x \le z \text{ and } y \le z$$
$$\iff (x, z) \in \xi \text{ and } (y, z) \in \xi$$
$$\iff ((x, y), z) \in p\xi \text{ and } ((x, y), z) \in q\xi$$
$$\iff ((x, y), z) \in p\xi \sqcap q\xi = \xi|\xi.$$

$$\forall z' :: x \le z' \text{ and } y \le z' \Rightarrow z \le z'$$
$$\iff \forall z' :: ((x, y), z') \in \xi|\xi \Rightarrow (z, z') \in \xi$$
$$\iff (z, (x, y)) \in \xi \div \xi|\xi$$
$$\iff ((x, y), z) \in (\xi \div \xi|\xi)^\sharp.$$

□

It is clear that if ξ is antisymmetric then $\vee_0$ is univalent.

$$\vee_0^\sharp \vee_0 \sqsubseteq (\xi \div \xi|\xi)(\xi|\xi) \sqcap (\xi|\xi)^\sharp (\xi \div \xi|\xi)^\sharp$$
$$\sqsubseteq \xi \sqcap \xi^\sharp$$
$$\sqsubseteq \mathrm{id}_X$$

As usual we say ξ has joins (least upper bounds) if $\vee_0 = (\xi \div \xi|\xi)^\sharp \sqcap \xi|\xi$ is total, and ξ has meets (greatest lower bounds) if $\wedge_0 = (\xi^\sharp \div \xi^\sharp|\xi^\sharp)^\sharp \sqcap \xi^\sharp|\xi^\sharp$ is total.

Theorem 2. *Let* $\xi : X \rightharpoonup X$ *be an ordering on* X, $\vee_0 = (\xi \div \xi|\xi)^\sharp \sqcap \xi|\xi$ *and* $\wedge_0 = (\xi^\sharp \div \xi^\sharp|\xi^\sharp)^\sharp \sqcap \xi^\sharp|\xi^\sharp$. *If* ξ *has least upper bounds and greatest lower bounds, then*

(a) $\vee_0\xi = \xi|\xi,$
(b) $p^\sharp \vee_0 = \xi$ *and* $q^\sharp \vee_0 = \xi,$

(c) $t\vee_0 = \vee_0$ and $t\wedge_0 = \wedge_0$,

(d) $(p\top\vee_0)\wedge_0 = p$ and $(p\top\wedge_0)\vee_0 = p$,

(e) $(\vee_0 \times \mathrm{id}_X)\vee_0 = a(\mathrm{id}_X \times \vee_0)\vee_0$.

Proof.(a) By the transitivity $\xi\xi \sqsubseteq \xi$ of ξ we have $(\xi|\xi)\xi \sqsubseteq \xi|\xi$. Hence an equality $\vee_0\xi = \xi|\xi$ follows from the definition of $\vee_0$ and Lemma 4(b).

(b) It is trivial that $p^{\sharp}\vee_0 \sqsubseteq p^{\sharp}(\xi|\xi) \sqsubseteq p^{\sharp}p\xi \sqsubseteq \xi$. Recall that $\xi = p^{\sharp}(p\xi \sqcap q)$ by Lemma 3(a). So it suffices to show that $p\xi \sqcap q \sqsubseteq \vee_0$. First $p\xi \sqcap q \sqsubseteq \xi|\xi$ follows from $p\xi \sqcap q = p\xi \sqcap q(\xi \sqcap \xi^{\sharp}) \sqsubseteq p\xi \sqcap q\xi$. Now note that $p\xi \sqcap q \sqsubseteq (\xi \div \xi|\xi)^{\sharp}$ if and only if $(p\xi \sqcap q)^{\sharp}(\xi|\xi) \sqsubseteq \xi$. However, the latter condition follows from $(p\xi \sqcap q)^{\sharp}(\xi|\xi) = (p\xi \sqcap q)^{\sharp}(p\xi \sqcap q\xi) \sqsubseteq q^{\sharp}q\xi \sqsubseteq \xi$.

(c) First note that $t(\xi|\xi) = tp\xi \sqcap tq\xi = q\xi \sqcap p\xi = \xi|\xi$. By Lemma 4(a) we have

$$t\vee_0 = \{\xi \div t(\xi|\xi)\}^{\sharp} \sqcap t(\xi|\xi) = (\xi \div \xi|\xi)^{\sharp} \sqcap \xi|\xi = \vee_0.$$

(d) An inequality $p\xi^{\sharp} \sqsubseteq \vee_0\xi^{\sharp}$ follows from $p\xi^{\sharp} \sqsubseteq \vee_0 \vee_0^{\sharp} p\xi^{\sharp} = \vee_0(p^{\sharp}\vee_0)^{\sharp}\xi^{\sharp} = \vee_0\xi^{\sharp}\xi^{\sharp} = \vee_0\xi^{\sharp}$ (since ξ is transitive). Then we have $(p\top\vee_0)(\xi^{\sharp}|\xi^{\sharp}) = (p\top\vee_0)p\xi^{\sharp} \sqcap (p\top\vee_0)q\xi^{\sharp} = p\xi^{\sharp} \sqcap \vee_0\xi^{\sharp} = p\xi^{\sharp}$, and so

$$
\begin{aligned}
(p\top\vee_0)\wedge_0 &= (p\top\vee_0)\{(\xi^{\sharp} \div \xi^{\sharp}|\xi^{\sharp})^{\sharp} \sqcap \xi^{\sharp}|\xi^{\sharp}\} \\
&= \{(\xi^{\sharp} \div (p\top\vee_0)(\xi^{\sharp}|\xi^{\sharp}))\}^{\sharp} \sqcap (p\top\vee_0)\xi^{\sharp}|\xi^{\sharp} \quad \{ \text{ Lemma 4(a) } \} \\
&= (\xi^{\sharp} \div p\xi^{\sharp})^{\sharp} \sqcap p\xi^{\sharp}.
\end{aligned}
$$

Therefore Lemma 4(b) proves $p \sqsubseteq (p\top\vee_0)\wedge_0$, and so $p = (p\top\vee_0)\wedge_0$.

(e) Define two relations $\vee_1 : (X \times X) \times X \rightarrow X$ and $\vee_2 : X \times (X \times X) \rightarrow X$ by

$$\vee_1 = \{\xi \div (\xi|\xi)|\xi\}^{\sharp} \sqcap (\xi|\xi)|\xi \text{ and } \vee_2 = \{\xi \div \xi|(\xi|\xi)\}^{\sharp} \sqcap \xi|(\xi|\xi).$$

First we will prove that $(\vee_0 \times \mathrm{id}_X)\vee_0 = \vee_1$ and $(\mathrm{id}_X \times \vee_0)\vee_0 = \vee_2$, which follows from $(\vee_0 \times \mathrm{id}_X)\vee_0 \sqsubseteq \vee_1$ and $(\mathrm{id}_X \times \vee_0)\vee_0 \sqsubseteq \vee_2$, respectively, since $(\vee_0 \times \mathrm{id}_X)\vee_0$ and $(\mathrm{id}_X \times \vee_0)\vee_0$ are total functions, and $\vee_1$ and $\vee_2$ are partial functions. Hence, by Lemma 4(b) we have to see that $(\vee_0 \times \mathrm{id}_X)\vee_0\xi = (\xi|\xi)|\xi$ and $(\mathrm{id}_X \times \vee_0)\vee_0 \xi = \xi|(\xi|\xi)$. But we have

$$
\begin{aligned}
(\vee_0 \times \mathrm{id}_X)\vee_0\xi &= (\vee_0 \times \mathrm{id}_X)(\xi|\xi) \\
&= (\vee_0 \times \mathrm{id}_X)(p\xi \sqcap q\xi) \\
&= (\vee_0 \times \mathrm{id}_X)p\xi \sqcap (\vee_0 \times \mathrm{id}_X)q\xi \\
&= p_0(\xi|\xi) \sqcap q_0\xi \\
&= p_0 \vee_0 \xi \sqcap q_0\xi \\
&= (\xi|\xi)|\xi,
\end{aligned}
$$

and

$$
\begin{aligned}
(\mathrm{id}_X \times \vee_0)\vee_0 \xi &= (\mathrm{id}_X \times \vee_0)(\xi|\xi) \\
&= (\mathrm{id}_X \times \vee_0)(p\xi \sqcap q\xi) \\
&= (\mathrm{id}_X \times \vee_0)p\xi \sqcap (\mathrm{id}_X \times \vee_0)q\xi \\
&= p_0\xi \sqcap q_0 \vee_0 \xi \\
&= \xi|(\xi|\xi).
\end{aligned}
$$

This proves that $(\vee_0 \times \mathrm{id}_X)\vee_0 = \vee_1$ and $(\mathrm{id}_X \times \vee_0)\vee_0 = \vee_2$. Finally we have $(\vee_0 \times \mathrm{id}_X)\vee_0 = a(\mathrm{id}_X \times \vee_0)\vee_0$ from $a\{\xi|(\xi|\xi)\} = (\xi|\xi)\xi$ and

$$
\begin{aligned}
a(\mathrm{id}_X \times \vee_0)\vee_0 &= a\vee_2 \\
&= a\{\xi \div \xi|(\xi|\xi)\}^\sharp \sqcap a\{\xi|(\xi|\xi)\} \\
&= [\xi \div a\{\xi|(\xi|\xi)\}]^\sharp \sqcap a\{\xi|(\xi|\xi)\} \\
&= \{\xi \div (\xi|\xi)|\xi\}^\sharp \sqcap (\xi|\xi)|\xi \\
&= \vee_1 \\
&= (\vee_0 \times \mathrm{id}_X)\vee_0,
\end{aligned}
$$

which completes the proof.   □

Theorem 3. *Let* $(X, \vee, \wedge)$ *be a lattice in a Dedekind category* $\mathcal{D}$. *If* $\xi = p^\sharp(\vee \sqcap q)$ *and* $\vee_0 = (\xi \div \xi|\xi)^\sharp \sqcap \xi|\xi$, *then* $\vee = \vee_0$.

*Proof.*Since $\vee$ is a function and $\vee_0$ is univalent, it suffices to show that $\vee \sqsubseteq \vee_0$. To see this we have to show that $\vee \sqsubseteq \xi|\xi$ and $\xi|\xi \sqsubseteq \vee\xi$ by Lemma 4(b). (Note that ξ is an ordering on X by the result in Section 2.) First, $\vee = \vee \sqcap \vee \sqsubseteq pp^\sharp \vee \sqcap qq^\sharp\vee = p\xi \sqcap q\xi = \xi|\xi$. Noticing that $(p \times \mathrm{id}_X)q = q_0$ and $(q \times \mathrm{id}_X)q = q_0$ and $\mathrm{id}_X \times f = p_0p^\sharp \sqcap q_0fq^\sharp \sqsubseteq p_0p^\sharp$, it follows that

$$
\begin{aligned}
\xi|\xi &= pp^\sharp(\vee \sqcap q) \sqcap qp^\sharp(\vee \sqcap q) \\
&= p_0^\sharp(p \times \mathrm{id}_X)(\vee \sqcap q) \sqcap p_0^\sharp(q \times \mathrm{id}_X)(\vee \sqcap q) \\
&\quad \{ \text{ Lemma 2 } \} \\
&= p_0^\sharp\{(p \times \mathrm{id}_X)(\vee \sqcap q) \sqcap (q \times \mathrm{id}_X)(\vee \sqcap q)\} \\
&\quad \{ \text{ Lemma 3(b) } \} \\
&= p_0^\sharp\{(p \times \mathrm{id}_X) \vee \sqcap(q \times \mathrm{id}_X) \vee \sqcap q_0\} \\
&= p_0^\sharp\{a(\mathrm{id}_X \times q) \vee \sqcap a(\mathrm{id}_X \times \vee)q \sqcap a(\mathrm{id}_X \times q)q\} \\
&= p_0^\sharp a\{(\mathrm{id}_X \times q) \vee \sqcap(\mathrm{id}_X \times \vee)q \sqcap (\mathrm{id}_X \times q)q\} \\
&= p_0^\sharp a\{(\mathrm{id}_X \times q) \vee \sqcap((\mathrm{id}_X \times \vee) \sqcap (\mathrm{id}_X \times q))q\} \\
&\quad \{ \text{ Lemma 3(c) } \} \\
&\sqsubseteq p_0^\sharp a\{(\mathrm{id}_X \times \vee) \sqcap (\mathrm{id}_X \times q)\}\{((\mathrm{id}_X \times \vee) \sqcap (\mathrm{id}_X \times q))^\sharp(\mathrm{id}_X \times q) \vee \sqcap q\} \\
&\sqsubseteq p_0^\sharp a(\mathrm{id}_X \times \vee)\vee \\
&= p_0^\sharp(\vee \times \mathrm{id}_X)\vee \\
&\quad \{ \text{ (L1}\vee\text{) } \} \\
&= \vee p^\sharp\vee \\
&\quad \{ \text{ Lemma 2 } \} \\
&= \vee\xi.
\end{aligned}
$$

□

Note. The following four diagrams may help to understand the proof of the last theorem.

$$(X \times X) \times X \xrightarrow{f \times id_X} X \times X$$

$$p_0 \downarrow \qquad (PB) \qquad \downarrow p$$

$$X \times X \xrightarrow{\quad f \quad} X$$

$$(X \times X) \times X \xrightarrow{p \times id_X} X \times X$$

$$a \downarrow \qquad\qquad \downarrow id_{X \times X}$$

$$X \times (X \times X) \xrightarrow{id_X \times q} X \times X$$

$$X \times (X \times X) \xrightarrow{id_X \times g} X \times X$$

$$q_1 \downarrow \qquad (PB) \qquad \downarrow q$$

$$X \times X \xrightarrow{\quad g \quad} X$$

$$(X \times X) \times X \xrightarrow{q \times id_X} X \times X$$

$$a \downarrow \qquad\qquad \downarrow id_{X \times X}$$

$$X \times (X \times X) \xrightarrow{\quad q_1 \quad} X \times X$$

□

Acknowledgment

The author is grateful to Wolfram Kahl, Universität der Budeswehr München, and an anonymous referee for reading and commenting on this paper.

References

1. Freyd P. and Scedrov A. (1990) Categories, allegories. North-Holland, Amsterdam
2. Kawahara Y. (1995) Relational set theory. Sprinver-Verlag, Lecture Notes in Computer Science, 953:44–58
3. Mac Lane S. (1961) An algebra of additive relations. Proc. Nat. Acad. Sci. U.S.A. 47:1043–1051
4. Mac Lane S. (1972) Categories for the working mathematician. Sprinver-Verlag
5. Olivier J.P. and Sarrato D. (1980) Catégories de Dedekind. Morphismes dans les categories de Schröder. C. R. Acad. Sci. Paris 290:939–941
6. Schmidt G. and Ströhlein T. (1993) Relations and graphs – Discrete Mathematics for Computer Science. Springer-Verlag
7. Tarski A. (1941) On the calculus of relations. J. Symbolic Logic 6:73–89

Part VI

Generalizations
of Theories of Relations

Chapter 16
Beyond Modalities: Sufficiency and Mixed Algebras

Ivo Düntsch[1] and Ewa Orłowska[2]

[1] School of Information and Software Engineering
University of Ulster at Jordanstown
Newtownabbey, BT 37 0QB, N.Ireland
I.Duentsch@ulst.ac.uk
[2] Institute of Telecommunications
Szachowa 1, 04–894, Warszawa, Poland
orlowska@itl.waw.pl

Abstract. In [24] a generalisation of relation algebras to Boolean algebras with normal and additive operators is introduced. These operators are the counterparts to the modal operators of possibility. In this paper we introduce a class of Boolean algebras with co-normal and co-additive operators referred to as sufficiency operators. They are the algebraic counterpart to the logical sufficiency operators introduced in [17] for an extension of modal logics. Next, we define a class of mixed algebras i.e., Boolean algebras with an additional modal operator and a sufficiency operator. We study representation and duality theory for these new classes of algebras. The motivation for those algebras comes from the problems of reasoning with incomplete information and spatial reasoning.
Keywords: Boolean algebras with operators, modal operator, sufficiency operator, Kripke frame, incomplete information, spatial reasoning

1 Introduction

Relational systems (Kripke frames) are widely used as semantics for traditional modal logics. Vice versa, correspondence theory looks for modal expressions which describe relational properties [41]. Several simple properties of binary relations, however, cannot be expressed by modal sentences, a case in point being co-reflexivity (irreflexivity). Noting that a relation is co-reflexive if and only if its complement is reflexive – and reflexivity is modally expressible – [20] introduced an "inaccessibility " operator, which was determined by the complement of a frame relation; a similar idea was put forward in [17] where a "sufficiency" operator is used. We invite the reader to consult this paper for a discussion on the merits or otherwise of Kripke semantics and its "sufficiency" extension.

Just as Kripke frames are dual to a class of Boolean algebras with modal operators [18,24], one can build a duality for frames and Boolean algebras with sufficiency operators. Mixed structures occur when modal and sufficiency operators arise from the same accessibility relation.

In this paper we introduce the classes of sufficiency algebras and that of mixed algebras which include both a modal and a sufficiency operator, and study representation and duality theory for these classes of algebras. We also give examples for classes of first-order definable frames, where such operators are required for a "modal-style" axiomatisation.

2   Why sufficiency and mixed algebras?

One primary area, where sufficiency and mixed operators are required is the treatment of relations arising from information systems. In its general form, such a system consists of a set OB of objects and a set A of functions $a : OB \to 2^{V_a}$, each of which assigns to an object x a set of attribute values $a(x)$; such a system $\mathcal{I} = \langle OB, A, \{V_a : a \in A\}\rangle$ is called an *information system*.

Suppose that P is a set of attributes, and that R_a is a binary relation on OB for each attribute a. P determines two relations (strong and weak relation) on the object set OB with respect to the family $\langle R_a \rangle_{a \in A}$, namely,

$$x R_P^s y \Leftrightarrow a(x) R_a a(y) \text{ for all } a \in P,$$
$$x R_P^w y \Leftrightarrow a(x) R_a a(y) \text{ for some } a \in P.$$

Let $P, Q \subseteq A$. In an algebraic setting, strong relations are characterised by the condition

$$R_{P \cup Q}^s = R_P^s \cap R_Q^s,$$
$$R_\emptyset^s = OB^2,$$

and weak relations by

$$R_{P \cup Q}^w = R_P^w \cup R_Q^w,$$
$$R_\emptyset^w = \emptyset.$$

These relations are commonly called *information relations*, and an overview can be found in [29,32]. There are two types of information relations: Those which express similarity of objects, and those which describe some form of distinctness. The most prominent example of the first type is that of *indiscernibility*:

$$x \text{ind} y \Leftrightarrow a(x) = a(y) \text{ for all } a \in P.$$

While relations of similarity have been frequently studied and are well understood [31], the situation of the distinctness relations is much less clear.

The relations of complementarity and incomplementarity in an information system are defined as follows:

$$x \ \text{comp}_P^s \ y \Leftrightarrow a(x) = -a(y) \text{ for all } a \in P, \tag{1}$$

$$x \ \text{comp}_P^w \ y \Leftrightarrow a(x) = -a(y) \text{ for some } a \in P, \tag{2}$$

$$x \ \text{icomp}_P^s \ y \Leftrightarrow a(x) \neq -a(y) \text{ for all } a \in P, \tag{3}$$

$$x \ \text{icomp}_P^w \ y \Leftrightarrow a(x) \neq -a(y) \text{ for some } a \in P. \tag{4}$$

Logical aspects of these relations are studied in [8,10,28]; some applications are outlined in [7].

In order to define the frames which these relations generate, we recall some definitions: A binary relation R on U is called

$$3\text{-}transitive \Leftrightarrow R; R; R \subseteq R,$$

$$co\text{-}3\text{-}transitive \Leftrightarrow -R; -R; -R \subseteq -R,$$

$$reflexive \Leftrightarrow I \subseteq R,$$

$$co\text{-}reflexive \Leftrightarrow I \subseteq -R,$$

$$symmetric \Leftrightarrow R^\smile \subseteq R.$$

Here, ; is relational composition, $\smile$ is relational converse, and I is the identity relation.

The relations defined by (1)-(4) give rise to the following classes of frames of the form $\langle U, \{R_P : P \subseteq A\}\rangle$, where U and A are nonempty sets, and A is finite:

COM   Strong complementarity frames; the relations are strong, symmetric, 3-transitive, and for each $a \in A$, $R_{\{a\}}$ is co-reflexive.

WCOM   Weak complementarity frames; the relations are weak, symmetric, and for each $a \in A$, $R_{\{a\}}$ is co-reflexive and 3-transitive.

ICOM   Strong incomplementarity relations are strong, symmetric, and for each $a \in A$, $R_{\{a\}}$ is reflexive and co-3-transitive.

WICOM   Weak incomplementarity frames; the relations are weak, symmetric, co-3-transitive, and for each $a \in A$, $R_{\{a\}}$ is reflexive.

The algebraic study of the operators arising from the parameterised frames defined above requires mixed algebras.

However, in the present paper we consider frames with a single relation, and therefore we do not (need to) distinguish between strong and weak relations.

Our second example for mixed structures are *contact relations*. These arise in the context of qualitative geometry and spatial reasoning, going back to the work of [6,27,42], and, more recently, of [3,4,11,13,34] and others. They are a generalisation of the "part of" relation which for the first time was formalised by [26] in his mereology. We shall show that the class of frames $\langle U, C \rangle$, where C is a contact relation, can be captured by a mixed modal – sufficiency system, but not by equations of either system alone.

In this paper, we investigate sufficiency algebra with a single sufficiency operator, and mixed algebras with a single modal operator and a single sufficiency operator. In the forthcoming [12], we will present sufficiency and mixed algebras with multiple operators, arising from the parametrised frames mentioned above.

Some of the results below have been announced in [9].

3   Definitions and notation

In this Section we will recall the basic relationships between frames and modal algebras. We assume a basic knowledge of the theory of Boolean algebras and modal logic, and invite the reader to consult [25] for the first topic and [2] for the second one.

A *frame* is a pair $\langle U, R \rangle$, where R is a binary relation on U, called an *accessibility relation*. If $x, y \in U$, we usually write xRy for $\langle x, y \rangle \in R$, and set $R(x) = \{y \in U : xRy\}$. The *converse of* R, denoted by $R^{\smile}$, is the relation $\{\langle x, y \rangle : yRx\}$.

Suppose that $\langle B, +, \cdot, , -, 0, 1 \rangle$ is a Boolean algebra (BA). The set of atoms of a BA B will be denoted by $At(B)$. If $f : B \to B$ is a mapping, then its *dual* is the mapping $f^{\partial} : B \to B$ defined by

$$f^{\partial}(x) = -f(-x). \tag{5}$$

The *canonical extension of* B is a complete and atomic BA B^{σ} containing an isomorphic copy of B as a subalgebra with the properties

$$\text{Every atom of } B^{\sigma} \text{ is the meet of elements of } B. \tag{6}$$

If $A \subseteq B$ such that $\sum_{B^{\sigma}} A = 1$, then there is a finite subset A_0 of A

$$\text{whose join is 1.} \tag{7}$$

It is well known, that each BA has a canonical extension which is unique up to isomorphism. One such construction is given by Stone's representation theorem for Boolean algebras: Let B^{σ} be the powerset algebra of the set of ultrafilters X of B, and embed B into B^{σ} by $b \mapsto \{U \in X : b \in U\}$. For more details and discussions we refer the reader to [24] and [21–23].

An operator $f : B \to B$ is called *completely additive*, if

$$\text{If } \sum_{i \in I} b_i \text{ exists, then } \sum_{i \in I} f(b_i) \text{ exists, and is equal to } f\left(\sum_{i \in I} b_i\right). \tag{8}$$

A *modal operator* on B is a mapping $f : B \to B$ for which

$$f(0) = 0, \qquad \text{Normal} \tag{9}$$
$$f(a + b) = f(a) + f(b) \quad \text{Additive} \tag{10}$$

for all $a, b \in B$.

A *modal algebra* is a Boolean algebra with additional modal operators. Modal algebras are normal Boolean algebras with operators in the sense of [24]. The class of all modal algebras will be denoted by MOA. If B is a complete Boolean algebra, and f is a completely additive normal operator, then $\langle B, f \rangle$ is a *complete modal algebra*.

If f is a modal operator on B, then the mapping $f^\sigma : B^\sigma \to B^\sigma$ defined by

$$f^\sigma(x) = \sum \{ \prod \{ f(z) : z \in B, \ p \le z \} : p \in At(B^\sigma), p \le x \} \qquad (11)$$

is called the *canonical extension* of f. $\langle B^\sigma, f^\sigma \rangle$ is complete modal algebra, called the *canonical extension* of $\langle B, f \rangle$.

A *necessity operator* on B is a function $g : B \to B$, for which

$$g(1) = 1, \qquad (12)$$
$$g(a \cdot b) = g(a) \cdot g(b) \qquad \text{Multiplicative} \qquad (13)$$

for all $a, b \in B$.

Modal and necessity operators are dual to each other: If g is a necessity (modal) operator, then, g^∂ defined by (5) is a modal (necessity) operator. Thus, a *dually modal algebra* is a Boolean algebra with an additional necessity operator.

If $\langle U, R \rangle$ is a frame, then we define two mappings on the powerset algebra 2^U by

$$\langle R \rangle(X) = \{ x \in U : R(x) \cap X \ne \emptyset \}, \qquad (14)$$
$$[R](X) = \{ x \in U : R(x) \subseteq X \}. \qquad (15)$$

In other words,

$$\langle R \rangle(X) = \{ x \in U : (\exists y \in X) x R y \}, \qquad (16)$$
$$[R](X) = \{ x \in U : (\forall y \in U)[x R y \Rightarrow y \in X] \}, \qquad (17)$$

and, in particular,

$$\langle R \rangle(\{x\}) = R^\smile(x). \qquad (18)$$

The following result is fundamental:

Proposition 1. *[24, Theorem 3.3.]*

(a) *If $K = \langle U, R \rangle$ is a frame, then $\langle R \rangle$ is a complete modal operator on 2^U, $[R]$ is a necessity operator, and both are dual to each other.*

(b) *If f is a modal operator on 2^U, and f^∂ its dual, then there is exactly one binary relation S_f on U such that $\langle S_f \rangle = f$, and $[S_f] = f^\partial$. This relation is defined by*

$$x S_f y \Leftrightarrow x \in f(\{y\}). \qquad (19)$$

The algebra $\langle 2^U, \langle R \rangle \rangle$ is called the *full complex algebra of* K. There is the following representation theorem:

Proposition 2. *[24, Theorem 3.10]*
If $\langle B, f \rangle$ *is a modal algebra, then there is, up to isomorphism, a unique frame* $\langle U, R \rangle$, *such that* $\langle 2^U, \langle R \rangle \rangle \cong \langle B^\sigma, f^\sigma \rangle$.

$\langle U, R \rangle$ *as above is called the* atomic structure of $\langle B, f \rangle$.

4   Representation theory for sufficiency algebras

In this section we introduce sufficiency algebras and prove representation theorems in analogy to those for modal algebras in the spirit of [24].

An operator $g : B \to B$ is called *completely co-additive*, if

If $\sum_{i \in I} b_i$ exists, then $\prod_{i \in I} g(b_i)$ exists, and is equal to $g\left(\sum_{i \in I} b_i\right)$.   (20)

A *sufficiency operator* on B is a function $g : B \to B$ which satisfies

$$g(0) \quad = 1, \qquad \text{Co-normal} \qquad (21)$$
$$g(a + b) = g(a) \cdot g(b) \quad \text{Co-additive} \qquad (22)$$

for all $a, b \in B$. This is called a "strong permission operator" in [40]. A sufficiency operator which is completely co-additive is a *complete sufficiency operator*.

A *sufficiency algebra* is a Boolean algebra with an additional sufficiency operator; the class of sufficiency algebras will be denoted by SUA. With some abuse of language we will use MOA and SUA also for the respective algebras. A SUA $\langle B, g \rangle$ is atomic, if B is atomic, and complete, if B is complete, and g is completely co-additive.

The next result is recorded for later use:

Lemma 1. *Suppose that* g *is a sufficiency operator on* B. *Then,* g *is antitone.*

Proof. Let $x \leq y$. Then, $g(y) = g(x + -x \cdot y) = g(x) \cdot g(-x \cdot y) \leq g(x)$.   □

If $g : B \to B$ is a mapping, we let $g^c : B \to B$ be defined by $g^c(x) = g(-x)$. We call the mapping g^c the *complementary mapping of* g, and two mappings f, g on B are *complementary*, if $f = g^c$.

Our first result is an algebraic version of the "correspondence theorem" for modal and sufficiency logic of [38], quoted in [17].

Proposition 3. (a) *If* $\langle B, g \rangle$ *is a dually modal algebra, then* $\langle B, g^c \rangle$ *is a sufficiency algebra.*
(b) *If* $\langle B, g \rangle$ *is a sufficiency algebra, then* $\langle B, g^c \rangle$ *is a dually modal algebra.*

Proof. We only show the first part, and leave the second part to the reader. Let $\langle B, g \rangle$ be a dually modal algebra. First,

$$g^c(0) = g(1) = 1.$$

Let $a, b \in B$. Then,

$$g^c(a + b) = g(-a \cdot -b) = g(-a) \cdot g(-b) = g^c(a) \cdot g^c(b),$$

which completes the proof. □

Thus, necessity and sufficiency operators are mutually term definable, and the classes MOA and SUA are equipollent in the sense of [37].

If $\langle B, g \rangle \in$ SUA, we let $g^\sigma : B^\sigma \to B^\sigma$ be defined by

$$g^\sigma(x) = \prod \left\{ \sum \{g(z) : p \le z, \ z \in B\} : \ p \in At(B^\sigma), p \le x \right\}. \tag{23}$$

The pair $\langle B^\sigma, g^\sigma \rangle$ is called the *canonical extension of* $\langle B, g \rangle$. The mapping g^σ does what we would expect it to do:

Proposition 4. g^σ *is a complete sufficiency operator, and* $g^\sigma \restriction B = g$.

Proof. First, $g(0) = \prod \emptyset = 1$. Next, let $\{b_i : i \in I\} \subseteq B^\sigma$. Then,

$$g^\sigma \left(\sum \{b_i : i \in I\} \right) =$$
$$= \prod \left\{ \sum \{g(z) : p \le z, \ z \in B\} : p \le \sum \{b_i : i \in I\}, \ p \in U \right\},$$
$$= \prod \left\{ \sum \{g(z) : p \le z, \ z \in B\} : p \le b_i, \ i \in I, \ p \in U \right\},$$
$$= \prod \left\{ \prod \left\{ \sum \{g(z) : p \le z, \ z \in B\} : p \le b_i, \ p \in U \right\} : i \in I \right\},$$
$$= \prod \{g^\sigma(b_i) : i \in I\}.$$

Finally, we show that $g^\sigma(x) = g(x)$ for $x \in B$:

"$\le$": Let $q \in U$, $q \le g^\sigma(x)$. Then, $q \le g^\sigma(p)$ for each $p \in U$, $p \le x$, and thus, $q \le \sum \{g(z) : z \in B, \ p \le z\}$. Therefore, for each such p, there is some $z_p \in B$, such that $p \le z_p$ and $q \le g(z_p)$. We can choose $z_p \le x$ because of the following: Since $p \le z_p$ and $p \le x$, we have $p \le z_p \cdot x$; furthermore, $q \le g(z_p) \le g(z_p \cdot x)$ by Lemma 1. Now, $x = \sum_{p \le x} z_p$, and we may choose $\{z_p : p \le x\}$ to be finite because of (7). Therefore,

$$q \le \prod g(z_p) = g \left(\sum z_p \right) = g(x).$$

"$\ge$: $g(x) \le \sum \{g(z) : p \le z, z \in B\} = g^\sigma(p)$ for each $p \le x$, $p \in U$, and thus, $g(x) \le \prod \{g^\sigma(p) : p \le x, \ p \in U\} = g^\sigma(x)$. □

In the rest of this Section, we will establish a representation theorem between frames and sufficiency algebras in analogy to Proposition 1.

Proposition 5. *Suppose that $K = \langle U, R \rangle$ is a frame. The mapping $[[R]]$: $2^U \rightarrow 2^U$ with*

$$[[R]](X) = \{x \in U : X \subseteq R(x)\} \tag{24}$$

is a complete sufficiency operator.

Proof. 1. $[[R]](\emptyset) = \{x \in U : \emptyset \subseteq R(x)\} = U$.
  2. Let $X = \bigcup_{i \in I} X_i$. Then,

$$x \in [[R]](X) \Leftrightarrow X \subseteq R(x),$$
$$\Leftrightarrow \bigcup_{i \in I} X_i \subseteq R(x),$$
$$\Leftrightarrow (\forall i \in I) X_i \subseteq R(x),$$
$$\Leftrightarrow (\forall i \in I) x \in [[R]](X_i),$$
$$\Leftrightarrow x \in \bigcap_{i \in I} [[R]](X_i).$$

This completes the proof.   □

Observe that

$$x \in [R](X) \Leftrightarrow (\forall y)[xRy \Rightarrow y \in X] \quad (y \in X \text{ is necessary for } xRy)$$
$$x \in [[R]](X) \Leftrightarrow (\forall y)[y \in X \Rightarrow xRy]. \quad (y \in X \text{ is sufficient for } xRy)$$

which explains the names of the operators. Furthermore,

$$[R](X) = [[-R]](-X), \tag{25}$$
$$[[R]](X) = [-R](-X), \tag{26}$$
$$[[R]](\{x\}) = \langle R \rangle(\{x\}). \tag{27}$$

The last equation reflects the fact that on a one element set, $\exists$ and $\forall$ are the same operation. This is also present in the equality of weak and strong information operators of the same type on one element attribute sets [29].

The *full co-complex algebra* $[[K]]$ *of a frame* $K = \langle U, R \rangle$ is the Boolean powerset algebra of U with the additional sufficiency operator $[[R]]$ defined by (24).

Conversely, suppose that $B = \langle 2^W, g \rangle$ is a complete and atomic SUA, and set

$$R_g = \{\langle x, y \rangle \in W \times W : x \in g(y)\}. \tag{28}$$

Proposition 6. *Let $K = \langle U, R \rangle$ be a frame, and $B = \langle 2^W, g \rangle$ be a complete and atomic SUA. Then,*

$$R_{[[R]]} = R. \tag{29}$$
$$[[R_g]] = g. \tag{30}$$

Furthermore, if S is a binary relation on W with $[[S]] = g$, then $S = R_g$.

Proof. First,

$$xR_{[[R]]}y \Leftrightarrow x \in [[R]](\{y\})$$
$$\Leftrightarrow y \in R(x)$$
$$\Leftrightarrow xRy.$$

Let $X \subseteq U$. Then,

$$x \in [[R_g]](X) \Leftrightarrow x \in [[R_g]]\left(\bigcup_{y \in X}\{y\}\right)$$
$$\Leftrightarrow x \in \bigcap_{y \in X}[[R_g]](\{y\})$$
$$\Leftrightarrow (\forall y \in X)y \in R_g(x)$$
$$\Leftrightarrow (\forall y \in X)xR_g y$$
$$\Leftrightarrow (\forall y \in X)x \in g(y)$$
$$\Leftrightarrow x \in \bigcap_{y \in X} g(y)$$
$$\Leftrightarrow x \in g\left(\bigcup_{y \in X}\{y\}\right)$$
$$\Leftrightarrow x \in g(X).$$

Finally, let $[[S]] = g$. Then,

$$xSy \Leftrightarrow \{y\} \subseteq S(x),$$
$$\Leftrightarrow x \in [[S]](\{y\}),$$
$$\Leftrightarrow x \in g(\{y\}),$$
$$\Leftrightarrow xR_g y.$$

This completes the proof.   □

We now have the following representation theorem for SUAs, corresponding to Proposition 2:

Proposition 7. *If $\langle B, g \rangle$ is a sufficiency algebra, then there is (up to isomorphism) a unique frame $\langle U, R \rangle$, such that $\langle 2^U, [[R]]\rangle \cong \langle B^\sigma, g^\sigma \rangle$.*

Proof. This follows from Propositions 4 and 6.   □

$\langle U, R \rangle$ as above is called the *atomic structure* of $\langle B, g \rangle$.

Proposition 8. *Let $\langle B, f \rangle \in MOA$, and set $g = (f^\partial)^c$. If $\langle U, R \rangle$ is the atomic structure of $\langle B, f \rangle$, and $\langle U, S \rangle$ is the atomic structure of $\langle B, g \rangle$, then $R = -S$.*

Proof.

$$xRy \Leftrightarrow x \in f^{\sigma}(\{y\})$$
$$\Leftrightarrow x \notin (f^{\sigma})^{\partial}(U \setminus \{y\})$$
$$\Leftrightarrow x \notin g^{\sigma}(\{y\})$$
$$\Leftrightarrow x(-S)y.$$

$\square$

5   Duality between frames and sufficiency algebras

We will now develop the machinery for the duality theory in analogy to the duality for modal algebras [19].

A *co–bounded morphism* from a frame $K = \langle W, S \rangle$ to a frame $L = \langle U, R \rangle$ is a mapping $h : W \to U$ such that for all $x, y \in W$, $t \in U$,

$$x(-S)y \Rightarrow h(x)(-R)h(y) \tag{31}$$
$$t(-R)h(y) \Rightarrow (\exists w \in W)[h(w) = t \text{ and } w(-S)y]. \tag{32}$$

Proposition 9. *Let $K = \langle W, S \rangle$, $L = \langle U, R \rangle$ be frames.*

(a) *If $h : W \to U$ is a co–bounded morphism, then, the mapping $h^+ : [[L]] \to [[K]]$ defined by*
$$h^+(X) = \{y \in W : h(y) \in X\}$$
is a complete SUA homomorphism.

(b) *Let $p : [[L]] \to [[K]]$ be a complete SUA homomorphism, and $B \stackrel{\text{def}}{=} \{p(X) : X \subseteq U\}$. Then, the mapping $p_+ : W \to U$ with*
$$p_+(w) = u, \text{ where } u \in U \text{ and } p(u) \text{ is the atom of } B \text{ above } \{w\}$$
is a co–bounded morphism.

Proof. 1. It is well known that h^+ is a complete Boolean homomorphism, so, all that is left to show is that

$$h^+([[R]](X)) = [[S]](h^+(X)).$$

First, observe that

$$z \in h^+([[R]](X)) \Leftrightarrow (\forall u \in U)[h(z)(-R)u \Rightarrow u \notin X], \tag{33}$$
$$z \in [[S]](h^+(X)) \Leftrightarrow (\forall w \in W)[z(-S)w \Rightarrow h(w) \notin X]. \tag{34}$$

"$\subseteq$": Let $z \in h^+([[R]](X))$ and $z(-S)w$. By (31), we have $h(z)(-R)h(w)$, and (33) implies $h(w) \notin X$.

"$\supseteq$": Let $z \in [[S]](h^+(X))$, and $h(z)(-R)u$. By (32), there is some $w \in W$ such that $z(-S)w$ and $h(w) = u$. Then, $h(z)(-R)h(w)$ by (31), and by (34), we have $u = h(w) \notin X$.

2. Since p is a complete homomorphism, B is complete and atomic. Let $w \in W$, and M_w be the atom of B containing w. If $F_w = \{X \subseteq U : w \in p(X)\}$, the completeness of p implies that $\bigcap F_w = \{u\}$ for some $u \in U$, and $p(u) = M_w$. Thus, p_+ is well defined.

"(31)": Let $x, y \in W$, and M_x, M_y be the atoms of B above them. We will prove the contrapositive:

$$
\begin{aligned}
p_+(x)Rp_+(y) &\Rightarrow p_+(x) \in [[R]](p_+(y)), \text{ by (25)} \\
&\Rightarrow p(p_+(x)) \subseteq p([[R]](p_+(y))), \\
&\Rightarrow M_x \subseteq [[S]](M_y), \text{ by definition of } p \\
&\Rightarrow xSy, \text{ since } x \in M_x, \ y \in M_y, \text{ and (25)}.
\end{aligned}
$$

"(32)": Let $x, y \in W$, and $t \in U$. Then,

$$
\begin{aligned}
p_+(x)(-R)t &\Rightarrow p_+(x) \notin [[R]](t), \text{ by (25)} \\
&\Rightarrow x \notin [[S]]p(t), \text{ by definition of } p \\
&\Rightarrow (\exists w)(w \in p(t) \text{ and } x(-S)w), \text{ by (25)} \\
&\Rightarrow (\exists w)(p_+(w) = t \text{ and } x(-S)w, \text{ by definition of } p.
\end{aligned}
$$

This finishes the proof. $\square$

Corollary 1. *Let $\mathcal{K}_1$ be the category of power set SUAs with complete homomorphisms, and $\mathcal{K}_2$ be the category of frames with co–bounded morphism.*

(a) *The assignments r, s*

$$
\langle 2^W, g \rangle \xmapsto{r} \langle W, R_g \rangle, \ p \xmapsto{r} p_+,
$$
$$
\langle U, R \rangle \xmapsto{s} \langle 2^U, [[R]] \rangle, \ h \xmapsto{s} h^+
$$

are mutually inverse covariant functors.
(b) *If the homomorphism $p : \langle 2^U, f \rangle \to \langle 2^W, g \rangle$ is injective (surjective), then $p_+ : \langle W, R_g \rangle \to \langle U, R_f \rangle$ is surjective (injective).*
(c) *If $K = \langle W, S \rangle$, $L = \langle U, R \rangle$, and the co–bounded morphism $h : K \to L$ is injective (surjective), then $h^+ : [[L]] \to [[K]]$ is surjective (injective).*

Proof. This follows from the Propositions 6 and 9. $\square$

Suppose that $\mathcal{L}$ is a logic for sufficiency structures with formula set Fml. In the usual set formulation of sematics, originating in [16] and commonly used in [1,14], for a frame $K = \langle W, S \rangle$, the meaning function $m : Fml \to 2^W$ for formulas with the sufficiency operator is defined by

$$
m([[S]](\psi)) = \{z \in W : m(\psi) \subseteq S(z)\}. \tag{35}
$$

As usual, a formula φ is true in K, if $m(\varphi) = W$ for all meaning functions $m : Fml \to 2^W$.

Corollary 2. *Let* $K = \langle W, S \rangle$, $L = \langle U, R \rangle$ *be frames,* $h : W \twoheadrightarrow U$ *be an onto co-bounded morphism, and* φ *be a formula of* $\mathcal{L}$, *such that* $K \models \varphi$. *Then,* $L \models \varphi$.

Proof. Suppose that for all meaning functions $m : Fml \to 2^W$ we have $m(\varphi) = W$, and let $v : Fml \to 2^U$ be a meaning function. Using the notation and the result of Proposition 9, the function $m : Fml \to 2^W$ defined by $m(\chi) = h^+(v(\chi))$ is a meaning function. Now,

$$m(\varphi) = W \Rightarrow h^+(v(\varphi)) = W, \tag{36}$$
$$\Rightarrow h(h^+(v(\varphi)) = h(W), \tag{37}$$
$$\Rightarrow v(\varphi) = U, \tag{38}$$

which completes the proof.   □

A *sufficiency substructure* of a frame $\langle U, R \rangle$ is a frame $\langle W, S \rangle$ such that

$$W \subseteq U, \tag{39}$$

$$S = R \upharpoonright (W \times W), \tag{40}$$

$$(-R)(x) \subseteq W \text{ for all } x \in W. \tag{41}$$

If $\langle W, S \rangle$ is a sufficiency substructure of $\langle U, R \rangle$, we simply write $W \Subset U$, assuming that the relations involved are understood from the context.

Observing that

$$S = R \upharpoonright (W \times W) \Leftrightarrow (-S) = (-R) \upharpoonright (W \times W),$$

and in view of Corollary 1, we immediately arrive at

Proposition 10. *Let* $\langle W, S \rangle$ *and* $\langle U, R \rangle$ *be frames, and* $g : W \to U$ *be a mapping. Then,*

$$g(W) \Subset U \Leftrightarrow g \text{ is a co-bounded morphism.}$$

6   An example of a sufficiency algebra

Consider a binary relation R which is co-reflexive, symmetric, and co-3-transitive.

Proposition 11.

$$R \text{ is co-reflexive } \Leftrightarrow [[R]](X) \subseteq -X, \tag{42}$$
$$R \text{ is symmetric } \Leftrightarrow X \subseteq [[R]][[R]](X), \tag{43}$$
$$R \text{ is 3-transitive } \Leftrightarrow \langle R \rangle \langle R \rangle \langle R \rangle (X) \subseteq \langle R \rangle (X), \tag{44}$$
$$R \text{ is co-3-transitive } \Leftrightarrow [[R]](X) \subseteq [[R]](-[[R]](-[[R]](X))) \tag{45}$$

for all $X \subseteq U$.

Proof. "(42)": If $x \in [[R]](X) \cap X$, then xRx by (25).

Conversely, suppose $[[R]](X) \subseteq -X$; then, in particular, $x \notin [[R]](\{x\})$, and it follows that $x(-R)x$.

"(43)": "$\Rightarrow$": Suppose that R is symmetric, and assume there is some $x \in X \setminus [[R]][[R]](X)$. Then, there is some z such that $z \in [[R]](X)$ and $x(-R)z$. The first condition implies that

$$(\forall y)[y \in X \Rightarrow zRy].$$

Since $x \in X$, it follows that $x(-R)z$, contradicting that R is symmetric.

"$\Leftarrow$": Assume that aRb, $b(-R)a$ for some $a, b \in U$. Consider a model $M = \langle U, R, m \rangle$ such that $m(p) = \{x \in U : x(-R)a\}$ for some propositional variable p; then, $b \in m(p)$, and hence, $M, b \models p$. By our assumption we have $m(p) \subseteq [[R]][[R]]m(p)$, and it follows that $M, b \models [[R]][[R]]p$, in other words,

$$(\forall y)(\forall z)[(M, z \models p \Rightarrow yRz) \Rightarrow bRy].$$

If $y = a$, $z = b$, then the hypothesis of the implication is true, while its conclusion is not, since $b(-R)a$.

We leave the proof of (44) and (45) to the reader. $\square$

Thus, an algebra appropriate for an abstract characterization of operator $[[R]]$ with R satisfying (42), (43), (45) is a sufficiency algebra $\langle B, g \rangle$ characterised by

$$g(x) \leq -x,$$

$$x \leq g(g(x)),$$

$$g(x) \leq g(-g(-g(x))).$$

Since it is well known that co-reflexivity cannot be expressed by a modal operator, this class of algebras cannot be captured by modal operators alone.

7   Mixed algebras

In this Section we shall look at algebras $\langle B, f, g \rangle$, where f is a modal operator, g a sufficiency operator, and the corresponding atomic structures $\langle U, R \rangle$ and $\langle U, S \rangle$ satisfy $R = S$.

By Proposition 3, the classes MOA and SUA are mutually term–definable, and Proposition 8 tells us that, in terms of atomic structures, a necessity operator f talks about R, while its complementary sufficiency operator f^c talks about $-R$. It follows that terms built from the necessity operator $[R]$ express properties of the relation R, while terms built with $[[R]]$ express properties of $-R$. We read in [17] (modified for our notation),

"Necessity and sufficiency split the modal realm into two dual branches each of which spreads over less than half the Boolean realm. The complement $-R$ remaining outside the scope of both branches cannot be framed before uniting them: $[-R](X) = [[R]](-X)$ and $[[-R]](X) = [R](-X)$."

The definition of $[R]$ and $[[R]]$ is such that these conditions are fulfilled. Since both R and $-R$ are used, we have to find suitable condition for an algebraic characterisation which involves only the operators without any reference to the accessibility relations. A necessary condition was given in (27), namely,

$$\langle R \rangle(\{x\}) = [[R]](\{x\}).$$

We shall show below that this condition is sufficient to guarantee the desired interplay between a modal and a sufficiency operator. A *mixed modal sufficiency algebra* (MIA) is a BA B with two additional operators f, g such that

$$f \quad \text{is a modal operator.} \tag{46}$$
$$g \quad \text{is a sufficiency operator.} \tag{47}$$
$$f^\sigma(p) = g^\sigma(p) \text{ for each atom } p \text{ of } B^\sigma. \tag{48}$$

Next, we show that a common canonical extension exists:

Proposition 12. *For each MIA $\langle B, f, g \rangle$ there is (up to isomorphism) a unique frame $\langle U, R \rangle$ such that $\langle 2^U, \langle R \rangle, [[R]] \rangle \cong \langle B^\sigma, f^\sigma, g^\sigma \rangle$.*

Proof. The construction of the atomic structures $\langle U, R \rangle$ of $\langle B^\sigma, f^\sigma \rangle$ and $\langle U, S \rangle$ of $\langle B^\sigma, g^\sigma \rangle$ was such that

$$xRy \Leftrightarrow x \in f^\sigma(\{y\}),$$
$$xSy \Leftrightarrow x \in g^\sigma(\{y\}).$$

Condition (48) now assures that $R = S$.   □

Proposition 13. *If $\langle B, f, g \rangle \in MIA$ and $x, y \in B$, then*

$$x \cdot y \neq 0 \text{ implies } g(x) \leq f(y). \tag{49}$$

Proof. Let B^σ be the canonical extension of B, and suppose that p is an atom of B^σ. Then, by (11) and (23), we have

$$f^\sigma(p) = \prod\{f(x) : p \leq x, x \in B\},$$
$$g^\sigma(p) = \sum\{g(x) : p \leq x, x \in B\}.$$

If $p \leq x, y$, then $x \cdot y \neq 0$, and thus, $g(x) \leq f(y)$ for all such $x, y \in B$. It follows that $g^\sigma(p) \leq f^\sigma(p)$.   □

We do not know whether the class MIA is first order axiomatisable, but we doubt very much that it is. The following result may (weakly) point into this direction:

Proposition 14. *Let B be an atomless Boolean algebra, and f be the identity mapping on B. Then, there is no sufficiency operator on B such that $\langle B, f, g \rangle \in$ MIA.*

Proof. Let $p \in At(B^\sigma)$; then, by (11),

$$f^\sigma(p) = \prod \{f(b) : p \leq b, b \in B\},$$
$$= \prod \{b : p \leq b, b \in B\},$$
$$= p,$$

the latter by (6). Assume that g is a sufficiency operator on B such that $\langle B, f, g \rangle \in$ MIA. By (48), we have $g^\sigma(p) = f^\sigma(p) = p$. Since

$$g^\sigma(p) = \sum \{g(b) : p \leq b, b \in B\},$$

and p is an atom, there is some $b \in B$, $p \leq b$, such that $p = g^\sigma(p) = g(b) \in B$. Since p is an atom in B^σ, it is an atom in B. This contradicts that B is atomless.   □

Suppose that $\langle B, f, g \rangle$ is a MIA, and define $e : B \times B \to B$ by

$$e(x, y) = f^\partial(x) \cdot g(y). \tag{50}$$

Then, e is in the clone generated by the operations of $\langle B, f, g \rangle$. Conversely,

$$e(x, 0) = f^\partial(x) \cdot g(0) = f^\partial(x), \tag{51}$$
$$e(1, x) = f^\partial(1) \cdot g(x) = g(x) \tag{52}$$

show that f and g are definable from e and the Boolean operations. Let $m : B \to B$ be defined by

$$m(x) = e(x, -x). \tag{53}$$

Lemma 2.

$$m(x) = \begin{cases} 1, & \text{if } x = 1, \\ 0, & \text{otherwise.} \end{cases}$$

Proof. First, note that

$$m(1) = e(1, 0) = f^\partial(1) \cdot g(0) = -f(0) \cdot g(0) = 1.$$

Next, let $x \lneq 1$. Then, $-x \gneq 0$, and

$$g(-x) \leq f(-x) \text{ by } (49)$$

$$-f(-x) \cdot g(-x) = 0$$
$$f^\partial \cdot g(-x) = 0$$
$$m(x) = 0,$$

which completes the proof.   □

If B is the full co–complex algebra of a frame $\langle U, R \rangle$ and $X, Y \subseteq U$, then

$$z \in e(X, Y) \Leftrightarrow Y \subseteq R^\smile(z) \subseteq X. \tag{54}$$

In particular,

$$z \in e(X, X) \Leftrightarrow R^\smile(z) = X. \tag{55}$$
$$\tag{56}$$

[17] presented a sound and complete system for mixed structures with operators $[R], [[-R]]$ which, translated into our terminology, is as follows:

$$e(a, -b) \cdot e(-a + a', b \cdot -b') \le e(a', -b'), \tag{57}$$

$$m(1) = 1, \tag{58}$$

$$m(a) \le a, \tag{59}$$

$$m(a) \le m(m(a)), \tag{60}$$

$$a \le m(m^\partial(a)). \tag{61}$$

There is one derivation rule:

$$a \le a' \text{ and } b \le b' \text{ imply } e(a, -b) \le e(a', -b'). \tag{62}$$

Proposition 15. (a) *Every MIA satisfies (57) – (62).*
(b) *There is an algebra $\langle B, f, g \rangle$ such that f is a modal operator, g a sufficiency operator, B satisfies (57) – (62), but is not a MIA.*

Proof. 1. (58) – (61) follow immediately from Lemma 2, and because of the monotony of f and the anti-monotonity of g, it is easy to see that the rule holds.

To show (57), we first note that

$$-f(a \cdot -a' + -a) \le -f(-a'), \tag{63}$$

since $-a' = -a \cdot -a' + a \cdot -a' \le a \cdot -a' + -a \cdot -a'$, and f is monotone. Similarly, since g is anti-monotone by Lemma 1,

$$g(b \cdot -b' + -b) \le g(-b'). \tag{64}$$

The following statements are now equivalent:

$$e(a, -b) \cdot e(-a + a', b \cdot -b') \leq e(a', -b')$$

$$f^{\partial}(a) \cdot g(-b) \cdot f^{\partial}(-a + a') \cdot g(b \cdot -b') \leq f^{\partial}(a') \cdot g(-b')$$

$$-f(-a) \cdot g(-b) \cdot -f(a \cdot -a') \cdot g(b \cdot -b') \leq -f(-a') \cdot g(-b')$$

$$-f(a \cdot -a' + -a) \cdot g(b \cdot -b' + -b) \leq -f(-a') \cdot g(-b'),$$

and the last line is true because of (63) and (64).

2. Let $f, g : B \rightarrow B$ be defined as follows:

$$f(a) = \begin{cases} 1, & \text{if } a \neq 0, \\ 0, & \text{otherwise,} \end{cases}$$

$$g(a) = \begin{cases} 1, & \text{if } a = 0, \\ 0, & \text{otherwise.} \end{cases}$$

First, note that

$$g(a) = f^{\partial}(-a),$$

$$e(a, -b) = f^{\partial}(a) \cdot g(-b) = f^{\partial}(a) \cdot f^{\partial}(b) = f^{\partial}(a \cdot b),$$

and thus,

$$e(a, -b) = \begin{cases} 1, & \text{if } a = b = 1, \\ 0, & \text{otherwise,} \end{cases}$$

$$m(a) = f^{\partial}(a).$$

It is now straightforward to show that f and g satisfy the axioms as well as the rule. If f^{σ} and g^{σ} are the canonical extensions of f, resp. g, and if $a \in B^{\sigma}$ such that $0 \lneq a \lneq 1$, then, by (11) and (23), we have

$$f^{\sigma}(a) = 1, \quad g^{\sigma}(a) = 0.$$

Condition (48) now assures that $\langle B, f, g \rangle \notin$ MIA. $\quad\square$

The logic of [17] enables us to explicitly express properties of relations in frames of the form $\langle U, R, S \rangle$ where the relations R and S satisfy $R \cup S = U \times U$. The specific operators in these logics are of the form $[R]$ and $[[-S]]$. The completeness theorem for the standard frames such that the above condition and $R \cap S = \emptyset$ are satisfied, is obtained indirectly by the copying method of [39]. The class MIA of mixed algebras provides a framework for directly expressing and reasoning about the interplay between a modal operator $\langle R \rangle$ and a sufficiency operator $[[R]]$ which are determined by the same frame relation.

8   Examples of mixed algebras

8.1   Complementarity algebras

Recall that a relation R on U is complementarity relation, if it is co-reflexive, symmetric, and 3-transitive. It is shown in [7] that these are the defining properties of the $comp^s_{\{a\}}$ – relation obtained from an attribute a of an information system as defined in (1). We will show that complementarity can be expressed by mixed algebra, but not by purely modal or sufficiency operators.

It is well known, that co-reflexivity is not modally expressible. Furthermore, unlike symmetry and co-3-transitivity, the property of 3-transitivity cannot be defined by the sufficiency operator. To show this, we first quote (part of) a result from [41]:

Proposition 16. *If a first order definable class of frames is modally definable, then it is closed under disjoint unions.*   □

Here, the $\langle L, T \rangle$ is the disjoint union of the frames $\langle U, R \rangle, \langle W, S \rangle$, if $U \cap W = \emptyset$, $L = U \cup W$, and $T = R \cup S$.

Proposition 17. *3–transitivity is not definable by a sufficiency formula.*

Proof. Let $\langle U, R \rangle$ be 3–transitive, $S = -R$, and observe that

$$xSt \text{ implies } xSy \text{ or } ySz \text{ or } zSt. \tag{65}$$

Then,

$$R \text{ is 3–transitive iff } S \text{ satisfies (65).}$$

If we show that (65) is not definable in the modal language with the necessity operator $[S]$, then 3–transitivity is not definable with the sufficiency operator $[[R]]$, since

$$[S]F = [-R]F = [[R]]\neg F.$$

Let $U = \{a, b\}, Q = \{\langle a, b \rangle\}, V = \{c, d\}, T = \{\langle c, d \rangle\}, W = U \cup V, S = Q \cup T$. Then, both frames $\langle U, Q \rangle$ and $\langle V, T \rangle$ satisfy (65), but $\langle W, S \rangle$ does not: Just let $x = a, t = b, y = d, z = c$.   □

We conclude that a complementarity algebra is a mixed modal/sufficiency algebra (B, f, g), characterised by

$$g(x) \leq -x,$$
$$x \leq g(g(x)),$$
$$f(f(f(x))) \leq f(x).$$

Similarly, since reflexivity is not expressible with a suffciciency operator, the algebras of incomplementarity are mixed algebras characterised by

$$x \leq f(x),$$
$$x \leq g(g(x)),$$
$$g(x) \leq -g(-g(-g(x))).$$

Fig. 1. A contact structure

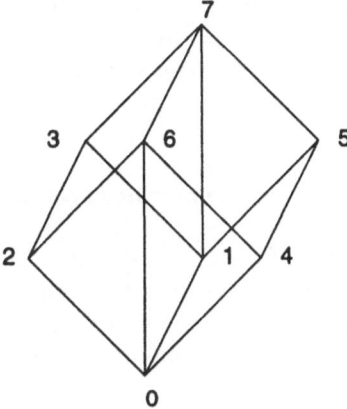

8.2   Contact relations

A *contact relation* C on a set U satisfies the following properties:

$$C \text{ is reflexive.} \tag{66}$$

$$C \text{ is symmetric.} \tag{67}$$

$$C(x) = C(y) \text{ implies } x = y. \tag{68}$$

Contact relations go back to the qualitative geometry of [6,27], and they nowadays play a prominent role in spatial reasoning [3,35,34]. Our next result shows that to describe the class of contact frames we indeed need a "truly" mixed modal – sufficiency logic, where both operators are needed in one equation:

Proposition 18. *The class of contact structures is not closed under onto bounded or co–bounded morphisms.*

Proof. We have shown in [11] that the extensionality condition (68) cannot be expressed by modal operators, and we repeat the construction for the convenience of the reader.

Consider $W = \{0, 1, \ldots, 7\}$, $U = \{1, 3, 5, 7\}$ and $C \in Rel(W)$ as depicted in Figure 1; there aCb iff $a = b$ or a and b are direct neighbours. It is not hard to check that C is a contact relation. Let S be the restriction of C to $U \times U$; then,

$$S(1) = \{1, 3, 5, 7\} = S(7),$$

and thus, S does not satisfy (68). On the other hand, the mapping $f : W \to U$ defined for all $a \le 7$ by

$$f(a) = \begin{cases} a + 1, & \text{if } a \text{ is even}, \\ a, & \text{otherwise}, \end{cases}$$

is a bounded morphism.

For the second part, consider two frames $\langle W, S \rangle$, $\langle U, R \rangle$, where $W = \{x, y\}$, S is the identity on W, $U = \{a\}$, and $R = \emptyset$. Then, S is a contact relation, while R is not. Since $x(-S)y$, it is easy to see that the mapping defined by $h(x) = h(y) = a$ is a co – bounded morphism.   □

Corollary 3. *The class of contact frames cannot be axiomatized by equations which contain only modal or only sufficiency operators.*

Proof. A necessary condition for a first order property to be expressible by a modal formula is invariance under bounded morphisms, see [41]. Furthemore, we have shown in Corollary 2 that co-bounded morphisms preserve truths of formulas of a logic with a sufficiency operator.   □

On the other hand, contact frames can be described by mixed structures:

Proposition 19. *Let $\langle U, C \rangle$ be a frame, and $\langle B, f, g \rangle$ its mixed complex algebra, i.e. $B = 2^U$, $f = \langle C \rangle$, and $g = [[C]]$. Then, C is a contact relation iff*

$$[C](X) \subseteq X, \tag{69}$$

$$X \subseteq [[C]][[C]](X), \tag{70}$$

$$m(-(e(X, X) \cap -Y)) \cup m(-(e(X, X) \cap Y)) = U. \tag{71}$$

Here, the mappings m and e are as defined by (50) and (53).

Proof. It is well known that (69) expresses reflexivity, and we have shown above that (70) expresses symmetry. So, all that is left to show is that C satisfies (71) if and only if it satisfies (68). Suppose that C is reflexive and symmetric, and recall that

$$z \in e(X, X) \Leftrightarrow C(z) = X, \tag{72}$$

and that

$$m(-X) = \begin{cases} U, \text{ if } X = \emptyset, \\ \emptyset, \text{ otherwise.} \end{cases} \tag{73}$$

"$\Rightarrow$": Suppose that $x \in U$, and let $X = C(x)$. (71) tells us that for each $Y \subseteq U$ we have $e(X, X) \cap -Y = \emptyset$ or $e(X, X) \cap Y = \emptyset$, in other words, $e(X, X)$ can have at most one element. By reflexivity of C we have $x \in X$, and thus, if $C(y) = X$, then $x = y$.

"$\Leftarrow$": If $e(X, X) = \emptyset$, there is nothing more to show; thus, suppose that $x \in e(X, X)$. By (68) we know that $e(X, X) = \{x\}$ for some $x \in U$. Thus, (71) is fulfilled for every $Y \subseteq U$.   □

9   Concluding remarks

In this paper we presented the classes SUA and MIA of algebras that emerged from an algebraic analysis of information systems and spatial reasoning. In the algebras derived from information systems the modal and sufficiency operators are determined by the relations that reflect either similarity of objects or their distinctness. The classes of algebras that model similarity have been studied in [5,36]. The need for the algebras for the relations from the second group is one of the motivations for the present paper; some of these algebras have been suggested in [29,36] and in the paper by SanJuan and Iturrioz in this volume. The extensive presentation of a broad class of these algebras will be the subject of a separate paper.

In spatial reasoning the need for considering the class MIA comes from the problem of characterisation of the contact relation between regions. We have shown that the properties of this relation require both the modal and the sufficiency operator in one equation.

The present paper is but a starting point for developing correspondence theories for linking expressibility of relational properties in first order logic and logics based on the classes SUA and MIA, respectively. A correspondence theory for SUA-expressibility could possibly be obtained following the methodology of the standard correspondence theory for modal expressibility. A correspondence theory for mixed logics with both a modal and a sufficiency operator determined by the same relation would probably require its own concepts and methods in order to characterise the properties that need both operators in an essential way. The other direction for further work is a development of Sahlqvist-like results for the SUA and MIA algebras and/or the underlying logics [22,23].

Acknowledgement

We would like to thank Valentin Goranko and Bjarni Jónsson for helpful suggestions.

References

1. Andréka H., Németi I. & Sain I. (1998) Algebraic logic. Mathematical Institute, Hungarian Academy of Sciences
2. Bull R. & Segerberg K. (1984) Basic modal logic. In [15], 1–88
3. Clarke B.L. (1981) A calculus of individuals based on 'connection'. *Notre Dame Journal of Formal Logic*, **22**, 204–218
4. Cohn A.G. (1997) Qualitative spatial representation and reasoning techniques. Research report, School of Computer Studies, University of Leeds
5. Comer, S. (1991) An algebraic approach to the approximation of information. *Fundamenta Informaticae*, **14**, 492–502

6. de Laguna T. (1922) Point, line and surface as sets of solids. *The Journal of Philosophy*, **19**, 449–461
7. Demri S. & Orłowska E. (1998) Complementarity relations: reduction of decision rules and informational representability. In [33], 99–106
8. Demri S., Orłowska E. & Vakarelov D. (1999) Indiscernibility and complementarity relations in information Systems. In J. Gerbrandy, M. Marx, M. de Rijke, Y. Venema (eds.) JFAK. Essays Dedicated to Johan van Benthem on the Occasion of his 50th Birthday. Amsterdam University Press
9. Düntsch I. & Orłowska E. (1999) Mixing modal and sufficiency operators. *Bulletin of the Section of Logic, Polish Academy of Sciences*, **28**, 99–106
10. Düntsch I. & Orłowska, E. (2000a) Logics of complementarity in information systems. *Mathematical Logic Quarterly*, **46**
11. Düntsch I. & Orłowska E. (2000b) A proof system for contact relation algebras. *Journal of Philosophical Logic*, **29**, 241–262
12. Düntsch I. & Orłowska E. (2000c) Boolean algebras with relative operators. Draft paper
13. Düntsch I., Wang H. & McCloskey S. (1999) Relation algebras in qualitative spatial reasoning. *Fundamenta Informaticae*, **39**, 229–248
14. Fitting M. (1993) Basic modal logic. In D. M. Gabbay, C. J. Hogger & J. A. Robinson (Eds.), *Logical foundations*, vol. 1 of *Handbook of Logic in Artificial Intelligence and Logic Programming*, 368–448. Oxford: Clarendon Press
15. Gabbay D.M. & Guenthner F. (Eds.) (1984) Extensions of classical logic, vol. 2 of *Handbook of Philosophical Logic*. Dordrecht: Reidel
16. Gallin D. (1975) Intensional and Higher Order Modal Logic. North-Holland
17. Gargov G., Passy S. & Tinchev T. (1987) Modal environment for Boolean speculations. In D. Skordev (Ed.), *Mathematical Logic and Applications*, 253–263, New York. Plenum Press
18. Goldblatt R. (1989) Varieties of complex algebras. *Annals of Pure and Applied Logic*, **44**, 173–242
19. Goldblatt R. (1991) On closure under canonical embedding algebras. In H. Andréka, J. D. Monk & I. Németi (Eds.), *Algebraic Logic*, vol. 54 of *Colloquia Mathematica Societatis János Bolyai*, 217–229. Amsterdam: North Holland
20. Humberstone I.L. (1983) Inaccessible worlds. *Notre Dame Journal of Formal Logic*, **24**, 346–352
21. Jónsson B. (1993) A survey of Boolean algebras with operators. In *Algebras and Orders*, vol. 389 of *NATO Adv. Sci. Inst. Ser. C, Math. Phys. Sci.*, 239–286
22. Jónsson B. (1994) On the canonicity of Sahlqvist identities. *Studia Logica*, **53**, 473–491
23. Jónsson B. (1995) The preservation theorem for canonical extensions of Boolean algebras with operators. In *Lattice theory and its applications*, 121–130. Lemgo: Heldermann
24. Jónsson B. & Tarski A. (1951) Boolean algebras with operators I. *Amer. J. Math.*, **73**, 891–939
25. Koppelberg S. (1989) General Theory of Boolean Algebras, vol. 1 of *Handbook on Boolean Algebras*. North Holland
26. Leśniewski S. (1927 – 1931) O podstawach matematyki. *Przegłąd Filozoficzny*, **30–34**
27. Nicod J. (1924) Geometry in a sensible world. Doctoral thesis, Sorbonne, Paris. English translation in *Geometry and Induction*, Routledge and Kegan Paul, 1969

28. Orłowska E. (1988) Kripke models with relative accessibility relations and their applications to inference with incomplete information. In G. Mirkowska & H. Rasiowa (Eds.), *Mathematical Problems in Computation Theory*, vol. 21 of *Banach Center Publications*, 327–337. PWN

29. Orłowska E. (1995) Information algebras. In *Proceedings of AMAST 95*, vol. 639 of *Lecture Notes in Computer Science*. Springer–Verlag

30. Orłowska E. (1996) Relational proof systems for modal logics. In H. Wansing (Ed.), *Proof theory of modal logic*, 55–78. Dordrecht: Kluwer

31. Orłowska E. (Ed.) (1997a) Incomplete Information – Rough Set Analysis. Heidelberg: Physica – Verlag

32. Orłowska E. (1997b) Introduction: What you always wanted to know about rough sets. In [31], 1–20

33. Polkowski L. & Skowron A. (Eds.) (1998) Rough sets in knowledge discovery, Vol. 1. Heidelberg: Physica–Verlag

34. Pratt I. & Schoop D. (2000) Expressivity in polygonal, plane mereotopology. *Journal of Symbolic Logic*. To appear

35. Randell D.A., Cohn A. & Cui Z. (1992) Computing transitivity tables: A challenge for automated theorem provers. In *Proc CADE 11*, 786–790. Springer Verlag

36. SanJuan E. & Iturrioz L. (1998) Duality and informational representability of some information algebras. In [33], 233–247

37. Tarski A. & Givant S. (1987) A formalization of set theory without variables, vol. 41 of *Colloquium Publications*. Providence: Amer. Math. Soc

38. Tehlikeli S. (1985) An alternative modal logc, internal semantics and external syntax (A philosophical abstract of a mathematical essay). Manuscript

39. Vakarelov D. (1991) Modal logics for knowledge representation systems. *Theoretical Computer Science*, **90**, 433–456

40. van Benthem J. (1979) Minimal deontic logics (Abstract). *Bulletin of the Section of Logic*, **8**, 36–42

41. van Benthem J. (1984) Correspondence theory. In [15], 167–247

42. Whitehead A.N. (1929) Process and reality. New York: MacMillan

Chapter 17
Cylindric Algebras for Partial Relational Systems. Quasicylindric Algebras

Artur Woliński

Polish-Japanese Institute of Information Technology
ul. Koszykowa 86, 02-008 Warszawa, Poland
awo@pjwstk.waw.pl

Abstract. A fundamental inspiration of this paper is the problem of the construction of the class of algebras which is an algebraic counterpart for partial relational systems. This class, called the class of quasicylindric algebras, arises as an effect of algebraizing the partial elementary logic. The algebraization follows from a general method applicable (among other ways) to the investigation of connections between Boolean algebras and classical propositional calculus or between cylindric algebras and classical elementary logic. For constructing the class of quasicylindric algebras we apply elementary metalogical notions, such as the notion of first-order language or first-order theory. The new class of algebras is discussed with respect to algebraic properties. In particular, an algebraic characterization of quasicylindric algebras and some connections between these algebras and cylindric algebras are briefly described. Moreover, it is shown how the new class may be used in an algebraic proof of Craig's interpolation property and of Beth's definability property for partial elementary logic.

Keywords: first-order language, algebra of formulas, first-order theory, relational system, cylindric algebra

1 Introduction

Algebraic Logic (cf. [1][1],[4]) investigates and describes relationships between two worlds: the world of logic and the world of algebra. Algebraic Logic deals with classes of algebras being - in a sense - algebraic counterparts of logics. The signature of algebras of such a class is closely connected with the structure of the language (the set of formulas) of a logic. There is a bilateral correspondence between some purely algebraic properties of this class and appropriate metalogical properties of the logic, however, in applications both inside and outside mathematics, more natural seems to be the situation, in which logic is supported by algebra. In this way, with the use of the strong and well developed methods of universal algebra, much information about the metatheories of a relatively large class of logics may be obtained. With the growing variety of applications of logic in such diverse areas like: computer science, linguistics, artificial intelligence, law, there is a growing number of

---

[1] Large parts of [1] may be found in the following more easily accessible: [2],[3].

new logics which may be investigated using well known algebraic methods. How can algebraic counterparts of logics be constructed, what kinds of logics are suitable to be algebraized, what are the relationships between concrete algebraic and metalogical properties - these are some of the main questions Algebraic Logic tries to answer.

Alfred Tarski is generally acknowledged as the pioneer of modern algebraic methods in logic. He was one of the leaders of the programme of the algebraization of the classical first-order predicate calculus. As a result of this programme, the class of cylindric algebras emerged and, consequently, better understanding and description of algebraic structures originating in first-order logic have been achieved (cf. [7],[8], see also [3]). Moreover, these investigations led to new tools and results applicable in some areas outside mathematics, like the theory of relational databases (see e.g., [9]).

The small part of Algebraic Logic discussed here is connected with the construction of a new class of algebras called quasicylindric algebras, conceived as an algebraic counterpart of partial elementary logic - first-order logic with models being partial relational systems.

Let us start with a more detailed explanation of the notion of partial elementary logic. What is logic in the traditional sense (see below) ?

$$Logic \equiv \underbrace{(language \rightarrow formulas) + deductive\ system}\ +$$

syntax with a notion of proof
(the key symbol: $\vdash$)

$$\underbrace{(interpretation \equiv meaning\ of\ formulas)}$$

semantics with a notion of a model, falsity
truth, satisfability (the key symbol: $\models$)

There are two ways of algebraizing logics, based on two (different in spirit) aspects of logic: syntactic and semantic, essentially equivalent for the logics with the completeness theorem. In the present approach the semantic option will be used.

2   Partial elementary logic

Partial elementary logic is a new logic, introduced by the author in [12] for the needs of the algebraization of partial relational systems.

Language, formulas. The syntactic part of partial elementary logic is based on the traditional first-order language (with predicate, operation and constant symbols as non-logical constants), understood as an alphabet for constructing expressions of partial elementary logic - classical first-order formulas. The set of all formulas over an arbitrary fixed language Λ will be denoted by Fm^Λ.

Partial models. Concerning the semantic aspect of our partial logic, the cen-

tral role is played by the notion of partial structure (partial model), understood as the following system:

$$\overline{\mathbf{M}} = \langle \overline{M} , (\overline{r}_\xi)_{\xi<\alpha} , (\overline{f}_\xi)_{\xi<\beta} , (\overline{a}_\xi)_{\xi<\gamma} \rangle ,$$

where: $\overline{M}$ - an arbitrary (maybe empty) set, called the universe of the struc-
ture; α, β, γ - fixed ordinal numbers; $\overline{r}_\xi$, $\overline{f}_\xi$, $\overline{a}_\xi$ - interpretations of non-
logical constants [symbols of: predicates P_ξ of some arbitrary fixed finite arity
$m_\xi > 0$, $\xi < \alpha$, operations F_ξ of arbitrary fixed finite arity $n_\xi > 0$, $\xi < \beta$,
and constants c_ξ (operations of arity 0), respectively, of the considered first-
order language, where:

- $\overline{r}_\xi$ is a partial m_ξ-ary relation in $\overline{M}$, i.e. some fixed set of partial sequences
  of length m_ξ, with arguments in the set $\overline{M}$ (partial sequences in the sense
  that the values of arguments of these sequences may be undefined on some
  or all coordinates), in symbols: $\overline{r}_\xi \subseteq {}^{[m_\xi]}\overline{M} = (\overline{M} \cup \{-\})^{m_\xi}$, $\xi < \alpha$ (here
  and in the sequel "$-$" is the "symbol for undefined");
- $\overline{f}_\xi : {}^{[n_\xi]}\overline{M} \longrightarrow \overline{M} \cup \{-\}$, $\xi < \beta$ – n_ξ-ary extrapartial operations i.e.
  operations which may be undefined on some sequences of arguments and
  - moreover - some arguments may be undefined too, under the condition
  that for every $w \in {}^{[n_\xi]}\overline{M}$, if $w(i) = -$ (meaning: $w(i)$ - undefined) for
  some $i < n_\xi$, then $\overline{f}_\xi(w(0),\dots,w(n_\xi - 1))$ is undefined on the sequence
  $\langle w(i) \rangle_{i=0}^{n_\xi - 1}$ [2];
- $\overline{a}_\xi \in \overline{M} \cup \{-\}$ and (as a value of a nullary partial operation) $\overline{a}_\xi \in \overline{M}$ iff
  c_ξ is defined in $\overline{\mathbf{M}}$, $\xi < \gamma$.

Motivations. For a brief motivation for considering a logic with models
being partial structures in the above sense take the following simple problem:
let a model (in the classical sense) of the real numbers $\mathbf{R} = \langle R , > , log \rangle$
with a binary relation of "greaterthan" $>$ and a partial unary operation of
decimal logarithm log, with the standard interpretations in $\mathbf{R}$, be given. Now,
consider the following subset of $R \times R$:

$$\{\langle x, y \rangle \in R \times R \mid y \leq 0 \Rightarrow x > log\ y\}.$$

In the classical approach there are some problems in finding the logical value
(false or true) of the formula defining the above set when $y \leq 0$. The premise
of the implication is true, but the conclusion has no logical value, the right-
hand side argument of the relation $>$ being undefined. The problem is solved
when we assume relational symbols to be interpreted as arbitrary subsets
of the set of all partial valuations. Now on each valuation the conclusion of
the implication has an unambiguously defined logical value - false or true

---

[2] Such a strong condition on the undefinability of operations in partial models
is motivated e.g., by a frequent computational situation, when it is impossible
to obtain any value of a function with incomplete information on values of its
arguments.

- depending on how the interpretation of the relational symbol $>$ has been extended to binary partial sequences of real numbers.

Under common syntactic foundations (the notions of language and formula), the differences between partial and classical first-order logic appear on the semantic level - in the notion of a model, consequently, in the understanding of such notions as false and true.

False and true in partial elementary logic. As in the case of classical first-order logic, partial logic is a two-valued logic with the notions of true and false based on valuations of individual variables in universes of models. However, under the notion of valuation of partial elementary logic, any partial function from the set of individual variables Var to a universe $\overline{M}$: $v \in {}^{[Var]}\overline{M}$ (subsequently called a partial valuation) is understood. This notion is a generalization of the notion of valuation considered in the classical model theory, or the theory of partial algebras, being a total function $u \in {}^{Var}M \subseteq {}^{[Var]}M$. It is well known that each such function may be interpreted as a weak homomorphism from the discrete subalgebra of individual variables Var to the total term algebra and that it may be extended to a closed homomorphism $\backslash u$ on a relative subalgebra of the term algebra generated by Var. We have an analogous situation considering partial valuations: there exists a unique extension of v to a closed homomorphism $\backslash v$ on the relative subalgebra of the total term algebra, generated by dom v. The homomorphism $\backslash v$ in a natural way may be extended to the smallest subalgebra of the term algebra containing all the constant symbols defined in the considered partial model. The latter extension of v will be denoted by $\backslash v \backslash$. Let us define: $< \overline{M}, v > \models \varphi$ - a formula φ is true in a partial model $\overline{M}$ under a partial valuation v - by induction

$< \overline{M}, v > \models P_\xi(t_0 , \ldots, t_{m_\xi - 1})$ iff $\langle \backslash v \backslash (t_i) \rangle_{i < m_\xi} \in \bar{r}_\xi$, for every predicate symbol P_ξ and every term sequence $\langle t_i \rangle_{i=0}^{m_\xi - 1}$,

$< \overline{M}, v > \models t_0 = t_1$ iff $t_0 , t_1 \in$ dom $\backslash v \backslash$ and $\backslash v \backslash (t_0) = \backslash v \backslash (t_1)$, for any terms t_0 , t_1 ,

i.e. the semantics of the equational symbol is the semantics of the existential[3] equation, well known from the theory of partial algebras[4],

$< \overline{M}, v > \models \varphi \wedge \psi, \ \varphi \vee \psi, \ \neg\varphi$ - exactly as in the classical case,

$< \overline{M}, v > \models \exists x_k \ \varphi$ iff $< \overline{M}, v[x_k/m] > \models \varphi$ for some $m \in \overline{M}$, or $< \overline{M}, v[x_k/-] > \models \varphi$, where $v[x_k/m]$, $v[x_k/-]$ are partial valuations formed by assigning the value m or the undefined value to the variable x_k in v, respectively[5].

---

[3] An existential equation is satisfied iff both of its sides are defined and equal.

[4] Among many types of equations considered when partial operations appear, the existential equation plays a fundamental role. The other main types of equations, such as weak or strong equations, are definable by the existential one.

[5] The semantics of the existential quantifier in partial elementary logic is motivated by wide possibilities of interpretating the notion of "undefined", when deciding on the truth of a formula under a partial valuation. The condition $< \overline{M}, v > \models$

Finally, let us define: $\overline{M} \models \varphi$ iff $< \overline{M}, v > \models \varphi$ for every $v \in {}^{[Var]}\overline{M}$, i.e., $\overline{M}$ is a model for a formula φ.

Each set of formulas Γ such that for every formula φ, if $\Gamma \models \varphi$ then $\varphi \in \Gamma$, will be called a *theory* (both in the sense of partial and classical first-order logic), e.g., $\text{Th}\mathcal{M} = \{\varphi \mid \mathcal{M} \models \varphi\}$ - the theory of a model $\mathcal{M}$ (with $\mathcal{M}$ either a partial or a classical model), or $\Gamma = Fm^\Lambda$ (for both: partial and classical case).

In order to obtain a full description of our partial elementary logic, the only thing we need is some deductive system. Generally, deductive systems play an important role in investigating relationships between logics and their algebraic counterparts. It is so in the case of partial and classical first-order logic, however, in the present approach deductive systems are not involved in the process of algebraization, so any detailed discussion of deductive systems for partial logic will be omitted. Let us only note that there exist complete deductive systems for partial elementary logic, with modus ponens, generalization and conjunction as the only inference rules.

More detailed information concerning partial elementary logic (e.g., the proof of the completeness theorem for a given deductive system) may be found in [12].

3 From cylindric algebras to quasicylindric algebras

A direct effect of the algebraization of classical first-order logic is the well known class of the so-called *locally finite-dimensional cylindric algebras* - cf. [7],[8], which will be denoted by $\mathcal{C}$. This class is constructed using few simple algebraic operations on some objects and based on the notion of classical first-order theory. The new class of quasicylindric algebras arises in an analogous way, with first-order theories of partial elementary logic replacing the classical ones. In the considerations concerning cylindric algebras an important role is played by the class $\mathcal{C}s$, consisting of algebras that are algebraic counterparts of models of classical first-order logic. A partial analogon of the class $\mathcal{C}s$ is a new class of algebras corresponding to the class of all models of partial elementary logic. We will call it the class of *quasicylindric set algebras*. All of the four classes of algebras discussed above consist of similar algebras, with all the operations total. Let us go into some more details.

Quasicylindric algebras. Signature of quasicylindric algebras: operation symbols: $\langle +, \cdot, -, 0, 1, c_k, d_{kl}\rangle_{k,l<\omega}$,
of arity: $\langle 2, 2, 1, 0, 0, 1, 0\rangle$ - respectively ,
c_k - k-th cylindrification symbol, $k < \omega$,
d_{kl} - diagonal constant symbol, $k, l < \omega$.

$\exists x_k\,(\psi \wedge \neg x_k = x_k)$ may mean that (e.g.) the logical value of a formula ψ under a valuation v in a model $\overline{M}$ does not depend on the value $v(x_k)$.

An important example of an algebra of the above signature, is an algebra of first-order formulas over some fixed language Λ :

$$\mathbf{Fm}^\Lambda = \langle Fm^\Lambda,\ \vee,\ \wedge,\ \neg,\ \overline{F},\ \overline{T},\ \langle \exists x_k \rangle_{k<\omega},\ \langle x_k = x_l \rangle_{k,l<\omega} \rangle,$$

with some fixed tautology of partial elementary logic $\overline{T}$ and $\overline{F} = \neg\overline{T}$.

For every partial theory $\Gamma \subseteq Fm^\Lambda$, let $\equiv_\Gamma \subseteq Fm^\Lambda \times Fm^\Lambda$ be a relation such that $\varphi \equiv_\Gamma \psi$ iff $\Gamma \models \varphi \Leftrightarrow \psi$ (equivalently, $\varphi \Leftrightarrow \psi \in \Gamma$). It can be easily checked that $\equiv_\Gamma$ is a congruence on the algebra $\mathbf{Fm}^\Lambda$. For every signature σ, let $\overline{C}(\sigma) = \mathbf{I}\{\mathbf{Fm}^\Lambda/\equiv_\Gamma \mid \Gamma \subseteq Fm^\Lambda$ - partial theory, Λ - language of the signature $\sigma\}$, where $\mathbf{I}$ is the operator of isomorphic images.

Definition 1. The class $\overline{C} = \bigcup_\sigma \overline{C}(\sigma)$ will be called the class of *quasicylindric algebras*.

Quasicylindric set algebras. For every partial model $\overline{M}$ over some fixed Λ with the set of individual variables $Var = \{x_k \mid k < \omega\}$, and every partial valuation $v \in {}^{[Var]}\overline{M}$, let us introduce a partial function $\mathbf{v} \in {}^{[\omega]}\overline{M}$, where dom $\mathbf{v} = \{k \in \omega \mid x_k \in \text{dom } v\}$ and $\mathbf{v}(k) = v(x_k)$, $k \in \text{dom } \mathbf{v}$.

Let $\varphi^{\overline{M}} = \{\mathbf{v} \in {}^{[\omega]}\overline{M} \mid\ <\overline{M}, v> \models \varphi\}$, $Cs\overline{M} = \{\varphi^{\overline{M}} \mid \varphi \in Fm^\Lambda\}$, moreover, let us consider the following algebra:

$$\mathbf{Cs\overline{M}} = \langle Cs\overline{M},\ \cup,\ \cap,\ \backslash,\ \emptyset,\ {}^{[\omega]}\overline{M},\ \langle \overline{C}_k \rangle_{k<\omega},\ \langle \overline{D}_{kl} \rangle_{k,l<\omega} \rangle$$

of the signature of the class $\overline{C}$, where:
$\overline{C}_k(\varphi^{\overline{M}}) = (\exists x_k\ \varphi)^{\overline{M}}$, $k < \omega$,
$\overline{D}_{kl} = (x_k = x_l)^{\overline{M}}$, $k, l < \omega$.

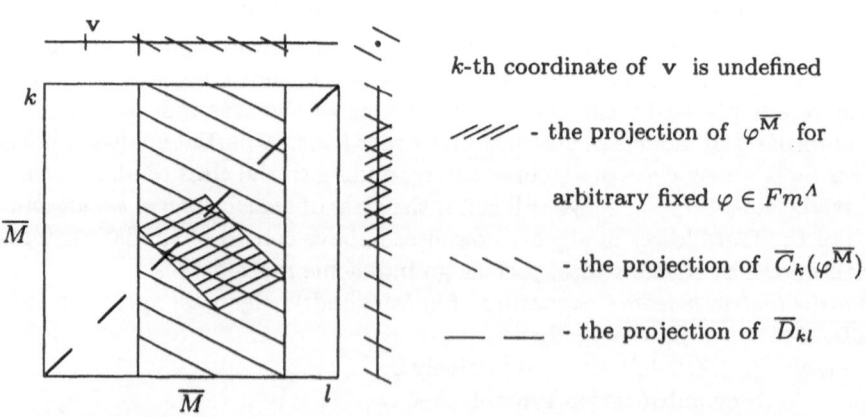

k-th coordinate of $\mathbf{v}$ is undefined

///// - the projection of $\varphi^{\overline{M}}$ for

arbitrary fixed $\varphi \in Fm^\Lambda$

\\\ - the projection of $\overline{C}_k(\varphi^{\overline{M}})$

— — - the projection of $\overline{D}_{kl}$

Fig. 1. The projection of ${}^{[\omega]}\overline{M}$ onto the k-th, l-th plane of coordinates

Let $\overline{C}s(\Lambda) = \{\mathbf{Cs\overline{M}} \mid \mathbf{\overline{M}}$ - partial Λ-model $\}$.

Definition 2. The class $\overline{C}s= \bigcup_{\Lambda}\overline{C}s(\Lambda)$ will be called the class of *quasicylindric set algebras.*

4   Results

The main results have been obtained following a general strategy of using the facts known from the theory of the classes C, Cs and from the metatheory of classical elementary logic. There are two substantial difficulties implied by this strategy. The first is the need of formulating and proving results in the three basic situations: partial, classical and simultaneously for the partial and classical case. The second is the necessity of a strict control over the structure of the set of atomic formulas over any fixed first-order language. In the first case the difficulty may be overcome by introducing a proper (rich enough) language of mathematical description, in the second case - by a subtle application of the known notion of g-algebra, i.e. an algebra with a distinguished (indexed) system of generators (cf. [11]). The algebras in all of the classes introduced so far are considered as g-algebras of some special kind, with the indexed sets of generators corresponding to the sets of all atomic formulas over some fixed first-order language, excluding equations on individual variables.

Some simple relationship holds between the classes $\overline{C}$, C (see Theorem 3 below). Due to this connection, the well known algebraic theory of C allows us to find out something about the algebraic theory of $\overline{C}$, what is more, in consequence - about the metatheory of partial elementary logic.

Auxiliary results. In analogy to the known classical result concerning the classes C, Cs, the following holds (cf. in a more abstract situation [1], Ex.3.1.9)

Theorem 1. *(representation theorem)* $\mathbf{SP\overline{C}} = \mathbf{SP\overline{C}}s$ [6]

Each of the results given below has been proved under the general assumption that there is no operation nor constant symbol in the languages of partial and classical elementary logic. This assumption makes most of the reasonings substantially easier. One of the obtained results states that this assumption has no influence on the generality of the reasonings about the classes $\overline{C}$, C and (due to the representation theorems) the classes $\overline{C}s$, Cs. Some problems (mainly of technical and formal character) connected with the precise proof of this result have been overcome by the use of a new notion of the skeleton of g-algebra.

The main technical tool applied for obtaining the most important results is a new operator **RD** (Renaming Diagonals), acting on every class of

---

[6] Here, the symbols **S**, **P** represent the classical operators of subalgebra and direct product, respectively.

g-algebras similar to algebras of $\overline{C}$ and C. For a given class $\mathcal{K}$ of this kind, $\mathbf{RD}\mathcal{K} = \{_{\mathbf{RD}}\mathbf{A} \mid \mathbf{A} \in \mathcal{K}\}$, where - assuming that $\mathbf{A} \in \overline{C}$ - $_{\mathbf{RD}}\mathbf{A}$ is a g-algebra $\mathbf{A}$ with all of the constants - algebraic counterparts of the existential equations of individual variables (diagonal constants) reinterpreted onto the constants - algebraic counterparts of the strong[7] equations of individual variables (formally: $_{\mathbf{RD}}\mathbf{A}[d_{kl}] = \mathbf{A}[-(d_{kk} + d_{ll}) + d_{kl}]$, k, $l < \omega$) and, moreover, with a modified (extended by all of the diagonal constants) distinguished system of generators. Note the first important result which uses the $\mathbf{RD}$ operator.

Theorem 2. $\mathbf{RD}\overline{C}s \subseteq I\mathcal{C}s$

Main results. Key results are of either algebraic or metalogical character.

The class C is not a variety. It has an "almost-equational" algebraic characterization consisting of a set of equations and a non-equational condition of local finite-dimensionality, which is not preserved by products. With the above characterization at hand, applying Theorem 1 and Theorem 2, it is possible to obtain a similar characterization of our new class $\overline{C}$, as well as the announced connection between the classes $\overline{C}$ and C :

Theorem 3. $\mathbf{RD}\overline{C} \subseteq C$

The Theorems 2, 3, have the following simple metalogical interpretation: the essence of the difference between partial and classical elementary logic lies in the interpretation of the equality symbol "=". More precisely - the logics would be (in a sense) semantically equivalent, if in partial logic the equality symbol were interpreted as the strong equation. The existence of a logic with partial valuations and relations in models, which is semantically close to classical first-order logic, seems to be as much surprising as useful.

The description of the connections between cylindric algebras and classical elementary logic takes an especially easy form under the assumption that the class C is constructed from the logic without operation and constant symbols, with the set of formulas generated exclusively by atomic formulas in reduced form: $P_\xi(x_0, \ldots, x_{m_\xi - 1})$ and by all of the equations on individual variables (cf. [8]). Such a modified classical first-order logic remains - in both semantical and deductive aspect - equivalent to its full version. The algebraic description of the class C, a fundamental element in obtaining the characterization of the class $\overline{C}$ and Theorem 3, refers to such a (reduced) situation. One of the main difficulties in proving these results is the modification of the description of C to the form corresponding to the full (unreduced) situation. Again the notion of g-algebra and its skeleton appear to be the proper tools for solving the problem. It is impossible to use partial logic in the reduced form (which would have notably simplified the situation) because of the general structure of the proof of the theorem on algebraic characterization of $\overline{C}$, requiring the existence of a complete deductive system for partial logic. However, the only

---

[7] A strong equation is satisfied iff both of its sides are defined and equal, or both are undefined.

known systems of this kind correspond to the unreduced version of partial logic (cf. [12]).

As for metalogical results, usually in the research concerning metatheories of logics special attention is given to deciding whether a given logic has Craig's interpolation property or Beth's definability property (cf. [5]). The equivalence between the algebraic property of amalgamation and Craig's interpolation property, or between the surjectiveness of some epimorphisms and Beth's definability property, is well known for a relatively large class of logics (see [1],[6],[10],[11]). These relationships concern classical as well as partial elementary logic. Classical first-order logic has Craig's and Beth's properties ([5],[11]). Both of them may be "transported" to partial logic by an algebraic bridge provided by Theorem 3 (see Figure 2). The main difficulty of the problem lies in the construction of a new apparatus of notions, which would allow to express the metalogical Craig's interpolation property and Beth's definability property in the environment of g-algebras, for partial and classical situations in parallel, giving sufficiently strong technical possibilities for obtaining proofs of the mentioned properties in the case of partial logic.

5   Final remarks

Quasicylindric algebras are new objects, substantially different from cylindric algebras. This may be easily noticed by looking at the different characterizations of these two classes of algebras. The rich positive experience derived from the applications of cylindric algebras, as well as the new results briefly described here, allow us to hope for wide possibilities provided by quasicylindric algebras, in particular by the application of strong algebraic tools in the investigation of the properties of the notion "undefined", both in the aspect of fundamental investigations of logical character and in possible applications outside mathematics, e.g., in reasoning about information systems - relational databases, particularly with incomplete information.

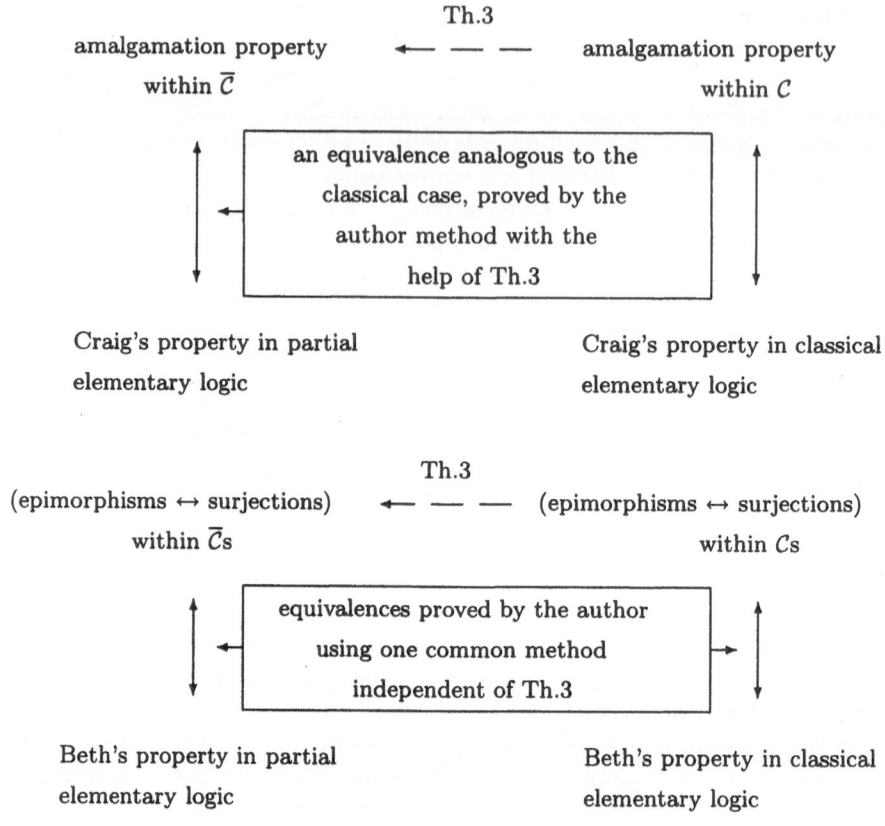

Fig. 2. Craig's and Beth's properties may be "transported" from classical to partial elementary logic, over an algebraic bridge

References

1. Andréka H., Kurucz Á., Németi I., Sain I. (1994) Applying Algebraic Logic; A General Methodology. The papers of the Summer School, Budapest, 11-17 July
2. Andréka H., Kurucz Á., Németi I., Sain I. (1994) Methodology of Applying Algebraic Logic to Logic. In: Nivat M., Rattray C., Rus T., Scollo G. (Eds.) Algebraic Methodology and Software Technology (AMAST'93). Proc. Twente, The Netherlands, June 1993, Springer-Verlag, London, 7-28
3. Andréka H., Németi I., Sain I. (2000) Algebraic logic. In: Gabbay D.M. (Ed.) Handbook of Philosophical Logic, 2-nd ed., Vol. I, Kluwer 1999, 129 (to appear)
4. Blok W.J., Pigozzi D. (1989) Algebraizable logics. Memoirs of the American Math. Soc. 77(396)
5. Chang C.C., Keisler H.J. (1973) Model theory. Studies in Logic and the Foud. of Math. 73, North-Holland
6. Hoogland E. (1998) Algebraic characterizations of various Beth definability properties. ILLC Research Report, University of Amsterdam
7. Henkin L., Monk J.D., Tarski A. (1971) Cylindric Algebras I, Studies in Logic and the Found. of Math. 64, North-Holland
8. Henkin L., Monk J.D., Tarski A. (1985) Cylindric Algebras II, Studies in Logic and the Found. of Math. 115, North-Holland
9. Imieliński T., Lipski W. (1981) The relational model of data and cylindric algebras. ICS PAS Reports 446, Warsaw
10. Madarász J.X. (1998) Interpolation and Amalgamation; Pushing the Limits, Part I. Studia Logica 61(3):311-345. Part II - ibidem (1999) 62(1):1–19
11. Pigozzi D. (1972) Amalgamation, Congruence-Extension, and Interpolation Properties in Algebras. Algebra Universalis 1:269-349
12. Woliński A. (1997) Partial elementary logic. Acta Sci. Math. (Szeged) 63:3-49